Child Care Center Management Guide
A Hands-on Resource

Third Edition

Clare Cherry 1919–1990
Founding Director, Congregation Emanu El Nursery School, Kindergarten, and Elementary School
San Bernardino, California

Barbara Harkness
Professor Emeritus
San Bernardino Valley College
San Bernardino, California

Kay Kuzma
Cleveland, Tennessee

Revised by Barbara Harkness and Deborah Bates

Fearon Teacher Aids
A Division of Frank Schaffer Publications, Inc.

Previously printed as FE4793 *Nursery School & Day Care Center Management Guide,* Second Edition.

Editors: Lisa Schwimmer Marier, Kristin Eclov, Christine Hood, Michael Batty
Cover Design: Riley Wilkinson
Book Design: Good Neighbor Press

© Fearon Teacher Aids
A Division of Frank Schaffer Publications, Inc.
23740 Hawthorne Boulevard
Torrance, CA 90505-5927

Fearon Teacher Aids products were formerly manufactured and distributed by American Teaching Aids, Inc., a subsidiary of Silver Burdett Ginn, and are now manufactured and distributed by Frank Schaffer Publications, Inc. FEARON, FEARON TEACHER AIDS, and the FEARON balloon logo are marks used under license from Simon & Schuster, Inc.

FE211011

Contents

Preface to the Third Edition

The hypothetical Community Child Care Center, which was created when the first edition of this book was written, has undergone a number of changes, necessitating a second, and now third, edition. As the demand for child care has increased nationwide, the entire field of early childhood education has become much more sophisticated and professional. This new edition has retained the essence of the earlier edition—guidelines for the many facets of operating an early childhood center, whether for profit or nonprofit, part-time or full-time, or for nine months a year or year-round.

In this new edition, we have covered the steps to be taken before a center is even opened, including a feasibility study, a survey of community needs, and a guide to preparing plot plans for both zoning and licensing use. We have elaborated on general operating procedures. We have recognized that many centers now offer care for infants, and more centers than in the past are providing facilities for extended day care. We have also recognized the increasing number of working mothers of children under public school age and the number of fathers or mothers who are single parents.

This edition includes essential new guidelines for insurance requirements, important information on hiring practices, a new sample enrollment agreement that offers protection to the director/owner of the program, updated first aid procedures, and a thorough section on disaster preparedness. Legal considerations have been updated, and sample budgets have been expanded to include a wider range of budget possibilities.

The authors have pooled their combined practical experience to provide a guide that is flexible and adaptable for individual needs and geared toward long-term use. It has been put into notebook form to allow the reader to add new material, references, and educational matter as needed. We wish to thank the many individuals who have assisted us in evaluating the previous editions, thus advancing our search for the new material that would be most helpful to the greatest number of people. We hope that this new edition will continue to meet your varying needs—whether assisting you to start your own center, to start a new job as a child care center director, or to evaluate your operating procedures in an already existing center. We also hope that we have presented a practical and useful text for people who are being trained in the field of early childhood education in general, and in administration and staff relationships in particular, with a view to someday being director of a program.

Barbara Harkness
Deborah Bates

Original Preface from Clare Cherry

Directing a nursery school, kindergarten, or child care facility is a stimulating and rewarding job. However, the many and varied responsibilities involved can sometimes seem overwhelming. This handbook is designed to help the director do a better job as a manager by detailing some basic principles and procedures involved in carrying out those responsibilities.

In order to meet the needs of many different types of nursery schools, we have created a hypothetical institution, the Community Child Care Center. Its director faces problems and concerns that are common to most schools. Administrative duties require dealing with students, parents, professional and volunteer staff, trainees, school boards, state and local regulatory agencies, suppliers, and representatives of many other areas of the community. The director manages a private, nonprofit, half-day school sponsored by a nonprofit community service club. The reasons for compiling this material appear in the following letter:

Community Child Care Center

111 THIRD STREET TELEPHONE 123-4579

Dear Reader:

It has always been helpful to me to know how other directors conduct their school programs. Now, after many long years of experience, I would like to be helpful to you by telling you how I manage the Community Child Care Center. I have gathered together my notes, forms, letters, checklists, evaluation forms, procedural records, and other materials that I believe could be of use to you. Naturally, your basic program and mode of operation may differ from mine; however, I hope you'll feel free to adapt my materials to fit your own situation. After all, we all share a common goal—providing wholesome and helpful service to our school families and to our communities.

With best wishes,
Director

This handbook is divided into eleven sections. A detailed table of contents at the beginning of each section and cross-referenced [in brackets] throughout the text, section numbers at the top of each page, and a comprehensive index are all included to make this a systematic, easy-to-use resource. We hope that the loose-leaf format will encourage you to add materials of your own under the appropriate section when you come across anything that applies to your situation.

The authors wish to thank the many friends and colleagues who have made generous contributions of time, reference materials, and ideas. It is impossible to mention each one individually, but we want all of them to know how much we appreciate their help. We especially want to mention Evelyn Acosta, Margery Brown, Edith Goldberg, Drs. Marilyn and Raymond Herber, Anna Johnston, Lois Ledbetter, Marie Lerner, Carolyn Martin, Dr. William Pearson, Janet Peters, Paul Roesel, Sandy Rogers, Alyce Smothers, Barbara Stangl, Robin Valles, Sunny Wallick, and Fannie Weisser. We also gratefully acknowledge the cooperation and assistance given by the members of our families, all of whom helped to make our work easier from the very beginning.

Clare Cherry
Barbara Harkness
Kay Kuzma

A Administration

1 The Director's Responsibilities
2 Problem-Solving Strategies within the Child Care Center
3 Your Role As Troubleshooter for the Center
4 Director Evaluation
5 Starting a New Child Care Program
6 Steps to Take in Opening a Child Care Center
7 How to Make Time Lines
8 Regulatory and Licensing Agencies
9 Regulatory Agencies' Requirements for Your Situation
10 Insurance Needs
11 Board of Directors
12 Reports to the Board or Owner
13 Formation of Center Policy
14 Operating Policies of the Community Child Care Center (Bylaws)
15 Organization of the Child Care Center Program
16 Record Keeping
17 Obtaining Tax-Exempt Status
18 Schedule for Federal Tax and Other Reports
19 Scheduling
20 Staff Management Schedule
21 Administrative Duties in Preparing for a New Program Year
22 Things to Do Before Opening of Program Term
23 Computers and Software
24 Procedures

A1 The Director's Responsibilities

The director is the manager of all the affairs of the child development program. The director acts as a conductor, conducting the various components of child care management. As the director, the first thing that you have to do is become acquainted with your many ongoing responsibilities. Here is a list of those responsibilities.

A. General Responsibilities

1. Contacting state and local regulatory agencies
2. Conforming to health, safety, and licensing regulations
3. Serving as a member of the Child Development Program Board of Directors and attending all meetings of the board and its committees
4. Handling all matters related to the administration of the many aspects of the center
5. Keeping records that pertain to the administration of the center
6. Defining policies of admission, attendance, tuition, and educational goals and special policies for special programs, such as infants, toddlers, school-age, and special needs
7. Evaluating your own work as director
8. Planning and implementing a program for professional growth
9. Preparing periodic reports on the state of the Child Care Center
10. Keeping abreast of research and new developments in the field of early childhood
11. Playing an active role in professional organizations
12. Maintaining a professional library
13. Planning the yearly calendar of program holidays
14. Planning and scheduling administrative responsibilities
15. Supervising the management of program schedules
16. Scheduling the use of shared space and equipment
17. Scheduling the responsibilities of the child care staff
18. Development of a Parent and Caregiver Advisory Council or Board
19. Planning and implementing a site evaluation program

B. Fiscal Responsibilities

1. Preparing the annual budget
2. Operating the center within the budget
3. Purchasing equipment and supplies
4. Arranging for repairs and maintenance
5. Preparing monthly reports on the status of the budget
6. Collecting enrollment fees and tuition
7. Handling petty cash
8. Preparing a year-end budget analysis
9. Maintaining a bookkeeping or an accounting system

C. Space and Equipment

1. Planning for and equipping outdoor areas
2. Planning for and equipping indoor areas
3. Keeping inventory records
4. Arranging for custodial care, maintenance, and repairs
5. Managing supplies
6. Replacing equipment and stocking supplies as needed

D. Staff

1. Preparing job descriptions
2. Recruiting applicants to fill staff vacancies
3. Selecting staff members
4. Recommending staff members for permanent status or separation after their probationary employment period
5. Arranging for substitute help as needed
6. Conducting regularly scheduled staff meetings
7. Planning and implementing an in-service training program for staff
8. Assisting staff in preparing daily, weekly, and yearly plans
9. Assisting staff in developing a workable plan for using indoor and outdoor space
10. Planning and implementing procedures that lead to wholesome interpersonal relationships between staff members
11. Assisting staff in planning individual programs for professional growth and career development
12. Implementing procedures for meeting with individual staff members to solve any problems that may occur
13. Planning and implementing procedures for keeping accurate records
14. Preparing a staff handbook (update as needed)
15. Keeping personnel records
16. Preparing a personnel policy
17. Supervising staff schedules and vacation days
18. Managing staff timecards and payroll issues

E. Enrollment

1. Enrolling children on an established priority basis
2. Interviewing parents and caregivers of prospective children
3. Planning for the gradual orientation of newly enrolled children
4. Familiarizing parents and caregivers of newly enrolled children with program policies
5. Being alert to enrollment needs at all times
6. Maintaining an advertising and public relations program to promote enrollments

F. Parents and Caregivers

1. Maintaining an active system of family-center relationships
2. Planning for the orientation of parents and caregivers to program policies and procedures

3. Planning and administering a parent and caregiver education program
4. Planning and administering a parent and caregiver participation program
5. Supervising a parents' and caregivers' club
6. Communicating with parents and caregivers in various ways
7. Helping parents and caregivers form car pools
8. Maintaining a parents' and caregivers' library
9. Maintaining a parents' and caregivers' bulletin board
10. Organizing a Parent/Caregiver Resource Manual

G. Health

1. Planning and implementing a health program for the center
2. Keeping health history records and physicians' reports for children, participating parents and caregivers, and staff
3. Contacting recognized agencies able to help children with special needs
4. Maintaining a referral system for children with special needs
5. Keeping links with local health agencies

H. Safety

1. Planning and implementing a safety program for the center
2. Keeping informed of the center's legal responsibilities and liabilities
3. Implementing a program of playground safety
4. Planning for and conducting fire drills
5. Preparing activities to teach the children traffic safety
6. Planning for a natural disaster

I. Children's Program

1. Organizing procedures for the management of the children's program
2. Planning procedures for the management of children's routines
3. Planning and implementing field trips
4. Planning the educational program
5. Planning for the evaluation of the children in relation to their progress, abilities, and special needs
6. Arranging a sound nutritional program
7. Arranging for rest and relaxation (including naps, if appropriate)

J. Community Relationships

1. Welcoming visitors to the center and arranging for visits to be pleasant and worthwhile
2. Planning and administering a student teaching program in cooperation with local educational institutions
3. Being available to community groups for public events that pertain to early childhood and family life as a whole
4. Attending and participating in professional conferences, lectures, and other educational events
5. Arranging for events sponsored by your center as a community service
6. Maintaining a liaison with representatives of various branches of local, state, and federal government for the purpose of supporting legislation concerned with child care centers

K. Food Management

1. Planning and implementing a food program based on sound nutritional principles
2. Meeting state and local regulations regarding meal preparation facilities
3. Communicating with parents and caregivers regarding weekly menu plans
4. Including nutritional information in newsletters to parents and caregivers
5. Keeping the food program within the limits of the budget, making adjustments when needed to avoid denying children healthy foods
6. Providing an attractive, relaxed setting for serving food
7. Establishing and implementing a program to prevent food poisoning
8. Planning and implementing some control over food supplies to prevent wastefulness
9. Planning for special diets that may be required for some children
10. Implementing an inventory system of food and supplies
11. Arranging for a pest control service to monitor your facilities
12. Supervising the record keeping of the food service

A2 Problem-Solving Strategies within the Child Care Center

Below is a compilation of materials and ideas to use in solving problems within your child care center. The following list suggests a procedure.

1. Identify the problem. Be specific. State facts, not opinions or assumptions.
2. Confirm the frequency of occurrence.
3. Who or what is affected by the problem? Be specific.
4. What is the cause of the problem?
5. What can you do to help remedy the problem?
   - Read the sections of this manual that relate to the problem area.
   - List every item you find that relates directly or indirectly to the problem.
   - List each item this manual takes into account that you had not previously thought of.
   - Check each item that may lead to improvement of the situation if recommended procedures are followed, either directly or in a modified manner.
   - Determine the length of time necessary to remedy the problem.
6. Establish a timetable for any changes you decide to make. List steps needed and amount of time required for each.
7. Will any money be needed? Specify.
8. What staff will be involved? List each person.
9. What support staff or outside assistance will be needed? List each one.
10. What is the responsibility of the board, if any, in solving this problem [Section A11]?
11. Keep a diary of activities that are related to solving the problem.
12. Reread the diary from time to time and evaluate your progress.

13. Make necessary modifications in your procedures if your evaluation indicates the need for any.
14. Be persistent and consistent.
15. Go to the next problem.

Your Role As Troubleshooter for the Center

In addition to your specific and not-so-specific responsibilities as director of the center, you will find that you must also act as a general troubleshooter. Since you may have only part-time custodial help, there will be many times when you will find yourself cleaning up spilled materials, sweeping up broken glass, hammering a loose nail, or otherwise taking care of immediate maintenance and repair needs. A good director will not be reluctant to delegate responsibility, but also will not be reluctant to assume someone else's responsibility when the need arises.

If your actions show that no job is "beneath you," you will encourage your coworkers to take a similar attitude. As a result of developing such attitudes, staff members at your center will never say, "That isn't what I was hired to do." There will be many occasions when you will want to show your appreciation to a staff member by helping out with the children. Perhaps you'll volunteer to take a small group for a walk, to help a child into dry clothes after a toilet accident, or to tell a special story. Such experiences will help you get better acquainted with the children, which in turn will help you promote good center-child-home relationships.

Director Evaluation

In order to promote growth effectively in staff members, parents, caregivers, and children, you must first know yourself. It isn't enough just to agree with principles of good supervision; they must be practiced. The most effective way to evaluate yourself is on the basis of past performance. The following questions can be used for this evaluation.

1. Have I arrived at work most of the time with an enthusiastic attitude?
   Your attitude is reflected by the center as a whole. If you expect your staff to be enthusiastic about their work, you must set the example.
2. Have I greeted my coworkers most of the time in a way that lets them know that I am really glad to see them?
   Even if you are slow getting started in the morning, it is your responsibility as director to let the staff know that you are genuinely glad they have come to work. If you stop to think about it, you really are.
3. Have I maintained flexibility in my dealings with others?
   Flexibility means growth, friendliness, and understanding. Rigidity can only lead to misunderstandings and stagnation.

4. Have I accepted suggestions and constructive criticisms gracefully?
If you expect self-improvement in others, take every opportunity to improve yourself.
5. Have I maintained an attitude of self-assurance?
It is your responsibility to give others confidence and security by letting them know they can depend on you during trying situations.
6. Have I been patient with people who, though they do not express it, are actually looking to me for help?
To help others is the reason your job exists.
7. Have I helped others feel comfortable by being alert to their feelings and reactions and by being tactful?
Sensitivity enables you to give wholesome support and guidance to others in times of need.
8. Have I tried to draw others into the conversation?
This enables you to soften barriers and help establish a participatory feeling among all members of the school family.
9. Have I been considerate in the requests I make of others?
Consideration for others results in respect toward you.
10. Have I been practical in my expectations of others?
A good administrator will distribute tasks according to abilities of individual staff members, thus being helpful and fair.
11. Have I been mature in considering the problems of staff members [Sections D62–63], parents and caregivers [Sections F23, F32–35], and children [Sections F30, F32–35, I23]?
Every problem of the center is your problem. No matter how minor it may seem to you, each problem should be given serious consideration and handled in such a way as to give support to those who depend on you for such support.
12. Have I continued to expand my knowledge of child development and educational methods, and do I keep up with new research in early childhood [Sections D58–61, J6]?
Education is an ever-changing force. Good education requires the involvement of people who recognize and move with those changes.
13. Have I remained aware of my role as a supervisor and been alert to any changing responsibilities?
With increased skill, knowledge, and experience comes increased responsibility.
    a. Have I maintained fiscal responsibility?
    b. Have I worked toward maintenance and ongoing improvement of the facility?
    c. Have I treated parents and caregivers as integral parts of the center community?
    d. Have I promoted wholesome health practices?
    e. Have I maintained an overall ongoing safety check of the program and facilities?
    f. Have I stayed in touch with each of the children's programs in the center?
    g. Have I promoted a wholesome image of our center to the community?
    h. Have I fostered a quality nutritional program within the center?

14. Have I made a practice of taking an overview of situations rather than getting bogged down with details?
The end results are what should be important to you. Pettiness and trivial details can only detract from primary goals.
15. Have I coordinated short-term and long-term plans for the overall growth of the center [Sections A17–22, D73]?
A successful enterprise does not rest on its laurels. Goals for continual growth should be constantly reevaluated.
16. Have I promoted positive relationships among others and between myself and others [Sections D62–63, E28–29, F33–35]?
Wholesome relationships among adults are important for developing wholesome environments for children.
17. Have I encouraged the professional and personal growth of staff members [Sections D58–63, J6]?
Your skill as an administrator has a direct relationship to your ability to encourage others to increase their own skills.
18. Have I been diplomatic in my dealings with others?
Diplomacy will result in greater cooperation from all involved.
19. Have I accepted others as unique individuals and refrained from comparing one person to another?
In all human relationships, differences will occur. But when persons are appreciated as unique individuals, such differences can be minimized.
20. Have I considered the inner world of children in my dealings with them?
Your evaluation of children should not be based on observable behavior alone, but on them as individuals with moods, feelings, needs, and interests of their own.
21. Have I organized my work for maximum efficiency [Sections A19–24]?
Organization conserves energy.
22. Have I been dependable? Generous? Honest? Cooperative? Loyal? Respectful? Kind? Objective? Empathic?
What kind of a person am I, really?

Evaluation of Director by Staff Members

If you, as a director, are sincere and courageous in seeking professional growth, the staff should periodically be asked to provide an evaluation of your performance. In order to facilitate staff assistance, you may want to use a form and letter similar to those on pages 9 and 10.

DIRECTOR EVALUATION

	Outstanding	Adequate	Poor	Need More Information
1. **Administrative Skills** Demonstrates knowledge, skills, and understanding of the director's job regarding fiscal responsibility, maintaining licensing regulations and standards, and meeting personnel needs. Comments: ________				
2. **Communication Skills** Demonstrates effective communication skills in oral and written reports. Keeps in contact with staff, parents and caregivers, and the community through personal availability and conferences. Comments: ________				
3. **Personal Characteristics** Demonstrates personal characteristics such as poise, calmness, fairness, personal grooming, dependability, voice modulation, and friendliness. Reaches out to others in a warm and caring manner, anticipating what will be needed in a given situation. Comments: ________				
4. **Professionalism** Assumes a fair share of the work load while planning for continual growth of parents and caregivers and self. Maintains professional memberships in related organizations, both in and out of the community, to promote positive standards and practices in the profession. Comments: ________				
5. **Creativity** Approaches the position of director with energy, enthusiasm, and innovation in problem solving. Open to new ideas and suggestions of others. Comments: ________				

The following are some specific suggestions for improvement:

1. ________
2. ________

These are what I consider to be special strengths:

1. ________
2. ________

Community Child Care Center

111 THIRD STREET TELEPHONE 123-4579

Dear Staff Members:

I want to be the best director I can be, but I need your help in evaluating my performance and hope that you will share with me specific ideas on how I can improve.

Be truthful. This evaluation is anonymous; please don't give your name.

If you would like to discuss my performance with me personally, I would welcome the opportunity.

Thank you for your interest, your constructive ideas, and your honesty.

Sincerely,
Director

A5

Starting a New Child Care Program

Before starting any kind of child care facility or program, carefully study the number, location, and types of facilities that already exist in your community. You can obtain a list from the telephone book as well as from your chamber of commerce. Chart each facility according to

- name of facility
- location
- hours
- fees
- type of population
- type of business organization, if able to determine
- special services
- length of time in business

Visit as many existing facilities as possible to assess general appearance and method of greeting visitors to broaden your knowledge of the type of competition that you may be facing.

Based on the information obtained from such a survey, you can then study the many options that can be undertaken. The following checklist will help you focus on key points that will be the basis for the entire process of development. In some of the sections, you may find that more than one checkmark will apply to your proposed center.

Target Population

Decide what your target population will be. Use this checklist to help pinpoint areas of need and specific interests for your center.

General Community:

____ Affluent

____ Middle income

____ Low income

____ Economically disadvantaged/welfare

____ Other

Setting:

____ Urban

____ Suburban

____ Rural

____ Apartment or housing complex

Specify:____________________

____ Business or industrial firm

Specify:____________________

____ Catering to one particular business or industrial firm, but located outside the firm's facility

Specify:____________________

____ Located in an industrial business area

Specify:____________________

Religious Organization:

____ Specific denomination, located at religious facility

Specify: ____________________

____ Nondenominational, located at religious facility

____ Catering to a particular religion or denomination, but not located at the religious facility

Specify: ____________________

Ethnic Group(s):

____ Specify: ____________________

____ Bilingual

Specify language(s): ____________________

Children:

____ Children of working parents and caregivers

____ Children with one parent or caregiver at home during the day

____ Children of students at a college or university

____ Children of parents or caregivers that are incapacitated

Special Needs:
____ Emotional problems
____ Abused or neglected
____ Physical handicaps
____ Learning disabled
____ Gifted
____ Other: ______________________________

Schedule of Services

Hours of Service:
____ Half day, A.M. only
____ Half day, P.M. only
____ Not more than five hours daily
____ Full day only
____ Other: ______________________________
____ Extended day care
    ____ Before 9:00 A.M.
    ____ After 12:00 noon
    ____ After 2:00 P.M.
    ____ to 5:00 P.M.
    ____ to 6:00 P.M.
____ Other: ______________________________
    ____ Weekend hours
    ____ Evening hours

Attendance Schedule:
____ two-day attendance accepted
____ three-day attendance accepted
____ four-day attendance accepted
____ Only five-day attendance
____ Other: ______________________________

Yearly Schedule:
____ Open during public school year from September to mid-June
____ Open 11 1/2 months with two weeks closure before start of new year
____ Open 12 months a year
____ Other: ______________________________

Ages of Children to be Served:
____ Infants
____ Infants and toddlers
____ Infants through kindergarten
____ Infants through third grade

____ Toddlers and nursery-school age
____ Toddlers through kindergarten
____ Toddlers through elementary age
____ Nursery school (two years) and up
____ Upper age limit
Specify: ____________________
____ Lower age limit
Specify: ____________________
____ Other: ____________________

Type of Organization (see pages 14–17 for specifics of each type)

____ **Private:**
  ____ Sole proprietorship
  ____ Partnership
  ____ Corporation (for profit)
  ____ Nonprofit corporation
____ Family day care home
____ Parent and caregiver cooperative
____ Day care or child care center for working parents and caregivers
____ Nursery school
____ **Religion-Affiliated School:**
  ____ Parochial
  ____ Nonsectarian
  ____ Community service
____ Community center
____ Franchise
____ Intergenerational day care
____ Laboratory center
____ Chain
____ Employer-related child care center
____ Extended-day center
____ Other

Government Funded Programs

____ Head Start
____ Child care centers funded by state
____ Adult education classes
____ SAPID (School-Age Parent/Infant Development Program)

Source of Funds

____ Personal savings
____ Loans
____ Grants

____ Foundations
____ Private group
____ Public group

Types of Business Organizations

In starting a child care facility, you must decide which type of business organization you will operate.

____ **Sole Proprietorship**

This is a situation in which one person owns and manages the business and is the sole person financially responsible for it. In other words, this person receives all the money from the business but is also legally responsible for all its debts. If you have a sole proprietorship, you are responsible for the income tax of the business.

Aside from the financial responsibilities and licensing regulations, the sole owner of a business has no obligation to an outside authority. This person can make the decisions on curriculum, fees, philosophy, policies, and related matters without having to answer to anyone else.

____ **Partnership**

If two or more persons get together to operate a business, they form a partnership, drawing up an agreement that states each person's share in the business. These persons make decisions and receive monies as would an individual, dividing income according to each person's share. They are also responsible for the debts incurred by the business, again dividing that responsibility according to each person's share in the business. Partnerships do not pay income taxes. Rather, each partner is taxed on his or her proportionate share of the business.

The partnership, like the sole proprietorship, is responsible only to itself, making all decisions related to the operation of the center, as long as it stays within the limits of licensing regulations and financial responsibilities.

____ **Corporation (for profit)**

Usually a corporation is formed when there is more than one person involved in a business, although in some states individuals may also become incorporated. Corporations are organized under state laws and therefore may differ somewhat from state to state. Basically, a corporation operates as though it were an individual. The corporation assumes the responsibility of the business, receives all monies, and assumes all debts. Thus, members of the corporation are not held personally responsible for debts of the business, but only for the share of the business that they own. You will need legal assistance to set up a corporation and may need additional legal assistance for its continuation, should problems arise. Unlike the partnership form of business, a corporation pays income taxes on its profit, while the members of the corporation pay income tax on their share of the profits.

It is conceivable that you could organize a simple corporation and elect members of your family as the Board of Directors and officers. The Board, in turn, hires you as the director, and you draw a salary as your compensation.

____ **Nonprofit Corporation**

If you want to enter the nonprofit field, you must become incorporated. This assures those who contribute to your center that all monies received will go into the project and will not be of benefit to any individual. Nonprofit corporations are not taxed, since they don't profit. All monies earned must be put back into the business.

If the center is operated by a religious organization, a community service organization, or some other type of incorporated group, the center is considered to be nonprofit. It operates under the sponsor's nonprofit incorporation papers. Tuition income may or may not be supplemented by the sponsoring group—either through fund-raising or grants. Often the sponsoring body will just underwrite one or more aspects of the program, such as providing facilities free of charge.

Types of Programs

____ **Family Day Care Home**

A license is obtained for care of six to 12 children in your home.

____ **Parent and Caregiver Cooperative**

A group of parents and caregivers form a corporation to run a child care center. The parents and caregivers operate the center, hiring a director to run the program. The parents and caregivers serve as assistants to the paid director.

____ **Day Care or Child Care Center for Working Parents and Caregivers**

Offers child care for working parents and caregivers.

____ **Nursery School**

Offers an educational component, with or without child care.

____ **Religion-Affiliated School**

May be operated as a parochial school, a nonsectarian school, or as a service to the community. The religious group may or may not be heavily involved in dictating policy.

____ Parochial
Religion is incorporated into the program.

____ Nonsectarian
Some religion is incorporated into the program.

____ Community service
No religion is incorporated into the program, although the religious group operates the school.

____ **Community Center**

Sponsored by a community service organization. Owned by the sponsoring group, which hires a director to run the program. The members may finance the program through various fund-raising efforts, thus being able to serve a low-income population; or they may just establish the center for the general population, charge fees, and establish scholarships for needy families to provide a balance in the enrollment. Many such groups use a sliding scale of fees. The sponsor may be heavily involved in dictating center policy.

____ **Franchise**

Purchased from a franchiser. May include construction of a building, equipment, training, and other components of a good program. Read contracts very carefully to be certain of what the franchise includes, and what you are expected to do in addition to paying for the franchise. Some franchises are very heavy on dictating policies, some conduct training programs, and others only advise, with much encouragement for use of your own creative ideas.

____ **Intergenerational Day Care**

May be tied in with a retirement home, using elderly residents as aides in the center to augment adult/child ratios.

____ **Laboratory Center**

May be operated by a college as a training site for early childhood education students, as a child care facility for students and faculty of the college, and/or as a parent education center. A good college school might be developed into a demonstration school for the community and can reflect strongly on the image of the entire college.

____ **Chain**

Sometimes a group will incorporate and open a series of centers operated by one management group, with individual directors at each center. Advantages are in group purchasing, advertising, and name recognition. Because of the group savings, working for a chain is sometimes very profitable.

____ **Employer-Related Child Care Center**

Provides on-site or nearby child care for the children of employees of a particular business or industrial organization. Many hospitals operate this type of program.

____ **Extended-Day Center**

This may operate in coordination with one of the other types of programs or may be a separate entity. Primarily for school-age children, to provide before-and-after-school care.

____ **Other:** ____

Government Funded Programs

In this group are those child care facilities that receive public funds from either the federal government, the state government, the county, or the city or town in which the facility is located.

____ **Head Start**

City and county agencies, local school districts, and other nonprofit agencies may apply for funds and operate Head Start programs.

____ **Child Care Centers Funded by State**

Different states use various terms such as *child care center*, *child development center*, or *children's center* to designate programs that receive state funding. They may be licensed by state education departments. Such centers may be operated by cities or counties. Funds may be supplemented by city, county, or federal programs.

____ **Adult Education Classes**

Various school districts throughout the nation have a variety of parent/caregiver observation programs. Usually these are run similarly to parent/caregiver cooperatives, except that the teacher-director is paid by the local school district, and the attendance of adults is counted by the school.

____ **SAPID** (School-Age Parent/Infant Development Program)

Various school districts receive funds to offer parenting education and child care for high school students on campus.

Source of Funds

Before you decide on the makeup of your program, the following checklist reminds you of some sources available to proprietary groups and nonprofit groups, whether private or public.

Funding is a major problem when starting a new program. Money needs to be allocated to search for an adequate facility and then to bring that facility up to required standards. Funds are also needed for purchasing furniture, fixtures, equipment, initial materials and supplies, for hiring initial staff, for advertising, and for operating until you have full enrollment. Many licensing agencies require that, as part of your start-up costs, you include sufficient funds to operate for a given period of time (e.g.,three months). This is a wise plan, because you usually do not open a program with full financial potential realized the first week of opening.

Start-up Funds

Many groups depend on more than one source of funding. Consider the following potential funding sources:

____ Personal savings

This is money you already have.

____ Loans

This might include personal loans from banks, a loan against the mortgage on your home, a loan from a private party (who might be considered a silent partner), a loan from an active partner, or loans from other sources.

____ Grants

There are funds available from foundations, private groups, and state and federal allocations.

____ Foundations

Go to your local library and ask for a resource book on foundations.

____ Private group

Hospitals, local businesses, and industries

____ Public group:

____ State education departments

____ State social welfare offices

____ U.S. Government Department of Human Services

Operating Income

Once you have established your center, your source of funds for operation may include the following:

____ Tuition
____ Tuition and public funds
____ Grants:

____ Private businesses/industry/employer
____ Foundations (not generally available for operating costs)
____ Governments/public institutions

city/community
county
school district
recreation department
State Department of Education
state grants
Head Start
other federal grants
private donors

Facilities

Whether to build a totally new structure, purchase and remodel an existing facility, or lease and remodel an existing facility is one of the biggest financial decisions that you will need to make before undertaking your project.

____ **Owning Your Own Facility**

It is ideal to be able to build your own facility and meet your individual wishes from the beginning. The investment in the lot and physical structure would probably be recoverable for at least the full investment price in the future, provided that the structure is fairly conservative. The more unique the structure, the more difficult it may be to resell. Remodeling would be required to meet another's needs. From a tax viewpoint, owning your own facility is advantageous. If you purchase an already existing structure, you can develop very attractive child care centers in remodeled residences, old warehouses, empty store buildings, and similar facilities.

____ **Leasing a Facility**

If funds are more limited, you may have to consider leasing a facility. Unless it is a former school or child care center, quite a bit of remodeling will usually be needed. Frequently, remodeling costs are the responsibility of the owner of the property from whom you are leasing. Sometimes such costs are shared by some mutual agreement reached between the lessor and the lessee. Become familiar with your local building codes and any state regulations regarding facilities. A great deal of money can be saved by planning in advance. Major unanticipated changes can be expensive.

____ **Arrangement with a Religious Organization**

One of the least expensive means of opening a center is to make an arrangement with a religious organization to use its rooms or classrooms on weekdays. Sometimes a religious group will be glad to have you open a center on its premises, only charging a minimal fee for custodial services and utilities. You, in turn, might install playground equipment and other items that can be shared by the children of religious-group members at events and religious school meetings. But care must be taken that each bit of shared space and shared time will be accounted for in a mutually drawn-up agreement. What about the lounge? What about rainy days? What happens when there is a monthly luncheon meeting? What about parking? Who will be responsible for replacing the carpeting? What about custodial care? Yard care? What about parent/caregiver meetings at night? Can bulletin boards be shared with religious schoolteachers? What happens if your classes are full, but a prominent religious-group member suddenly arrives with two children to enroll? These and similar questions need to be asked before an arrangement is made with a religious organization. If you can and do make such arrangements, however, you have the advantage of knowing that the area is already zoned for group use and that the building is already approved for use by children.

If an already existing facility isn't available, consider these possibilities:

____ Residence	____ Unused office space (for industrial child care)
____ Store building	____ Gymnasium
____ Warehouse	____ Recreation center
____ Abandoned school	____ Other: ______________________

Needs Assessment

It's not enough just to assess your own desires. It is important to assess the needs of the community as well. The following two questionnaires can be used for this purpose.

Questionnaire to parents and caregivers:

QUESTIONNAIRE TO ASSESS NEED FOR CHILD CARE

We, (name of organization), are considering the possibility of establishing a new child care center in the community. We would appreciate your help in determining whether the program is needed.

If interested, which of the following programs would you be interested in for the possible enrollment of your child?

Weekly

	Ages of children
___ 2 mornings a week	____________
___ 3 mornings a week	____________
___ 4 mornings a week	____________
___ 5 mornings a week	____________
___ Other (specify):	
____________	____________

Hours of Operation

	Ages of children
___ 6–noon	____________
___ noon–5 P.M.	____________
___ 5–7 P.M.	____________
___ Other (specify):	
____________	____________

If you are currently using a child care facility, how much are you paying?

_____ hourly _____ daily _____ weekly _____ monthly

What would you most like to see in a new facility?

____

____

____

____

Questionnaire to other early childhood facilities:

QUESTIONNAIRE TO ASSESS NEED FOR CHILD CARE

We, (name of organization), are considering the possibility of opening a new child care facility. We would appreciate your help in determining if the demand in this community warrants a new child care facility.

Do you feel that another program is needed in the area?

Yes ___ No ___ Possibly ___

If yes, what type of program do you feel is most urgently needed?

____

Please check the type of program you have:

Private ___ Profit ___ Nonprofit ___ Religion Affiliated ___ State Funded ___

Federally Funded ___ Other (specify) ______________________________

Please describe your program:

____

____

What are your tuition rates? ______________________________
Do you have any openings at this time? Yes ___ No ___
If yes, how many? ______ For what ages? ______________________________
Number of children on waiting list, if any? ______________________________

Director's name ______________________________

Name of program ______________________________

Address ______________________________

Telephone number ______________________________

E-mail address ______________________________

Thank you for responding. I'm looking forward to meeting you. I think it is important that all persons in the field of early childhood services work together to maintain a high quality of service.

Sincerely,

Your name
Address
Telephone number
E-mail address

A6 Steps to Take in Opening a Child Care Center

Once you have decided on the type of center that you want to open, do the following:

1. Familiarize yourself with all licensing regulations. You will save a great deal of time and effort by knowing in advance what legal requirements you will be expected to meet.
2. Search for a property or facility.

Once you have selected a site, the following steps should be taken, some in the order as listed and some simultaneously with others. The entire process may take 9–15 months.

1. Check with local city and county planning ordinances to find out which conditional use permit or other zoning permit will allow you to develop a child care facility at that location [Section A8].
2. If you plan to use space in a religious facility or other already established facility, arrange to have a written agreement drawn up regarding shared use of space, equipment, time, parking, and so on [Section A5].
3. Seek legal advice in drawing up organizational papers for incorporation or partnership [Section A5].
4. Check for names that may be registered in your state. Check for names used by other children's facilities. Then, select a name for your own organization.
5. If required in your community, file for use of a fictitious name and publish it in a newspaper, if necessary. If you are nonprofit, this will probably not be necessary. Check with your city/county/state governments for local regulations.
6. Establish a bank account in the name of the new business. Today there are a wide variety of options for business accounts. Explore the offerings of various institutions.
7. Prepare a budget and open a set of books. It may be advisable to enlist the services of a bookkeeper or accountant.
8. Simultaneously institute licensing procedures through whatever government body performs this function in your community [Section A8].
9. Arrange for insurance prior to having any work done on the premises [Section A10].
10. Clear plans with fire officials.
11. Arrange for building repairs, additions, and/or modifications that may be planned [C].
12. If you are the director, write a job description providing guidelines for yourself. Use Section A1, in a condensed version, for your job description.
13. If you will employ someone else as director, use the job description in helping to select a qualified candidate [Section D2].
14. Draw up a list of personnel policies [Section D27].
15. Prepare job descriptions for other staff members [Sections D2–9].
16. Prepare contracts for employees, including director [Section D26].
17. Prepare an employees' handbook [Section D45].
18. Advertise for and interview potential staff members [Sections D11–22].
19. Prepare forms for children's records according to guidelines of your licensing agency and any other forms that you feel may be useful [E].

20. Prepare a contract to be signed by you and a child's parent or caregiver at time of enrollment [Section E14].
21. Conduct orientation and in-service training for employees [Sections D43–44, D52].
22. Prepare a handbook for parents and caregivers to be distributed at time of enrollment [Section E25].
23. Prepare a brochure about the center [Section E3]. Develop a publicity campaign, advertise for students, and begin the enrollment process [Sections E3–4].
24. Order equipment and supplies [Part C]. Schedule parent and caregiver orientation meetings.

A7 How to Make Time Lines

Conserve energy and accomplish your preset goals efficiently by using time lines. These can take several forms, as illustrated in the following versions:

Style I

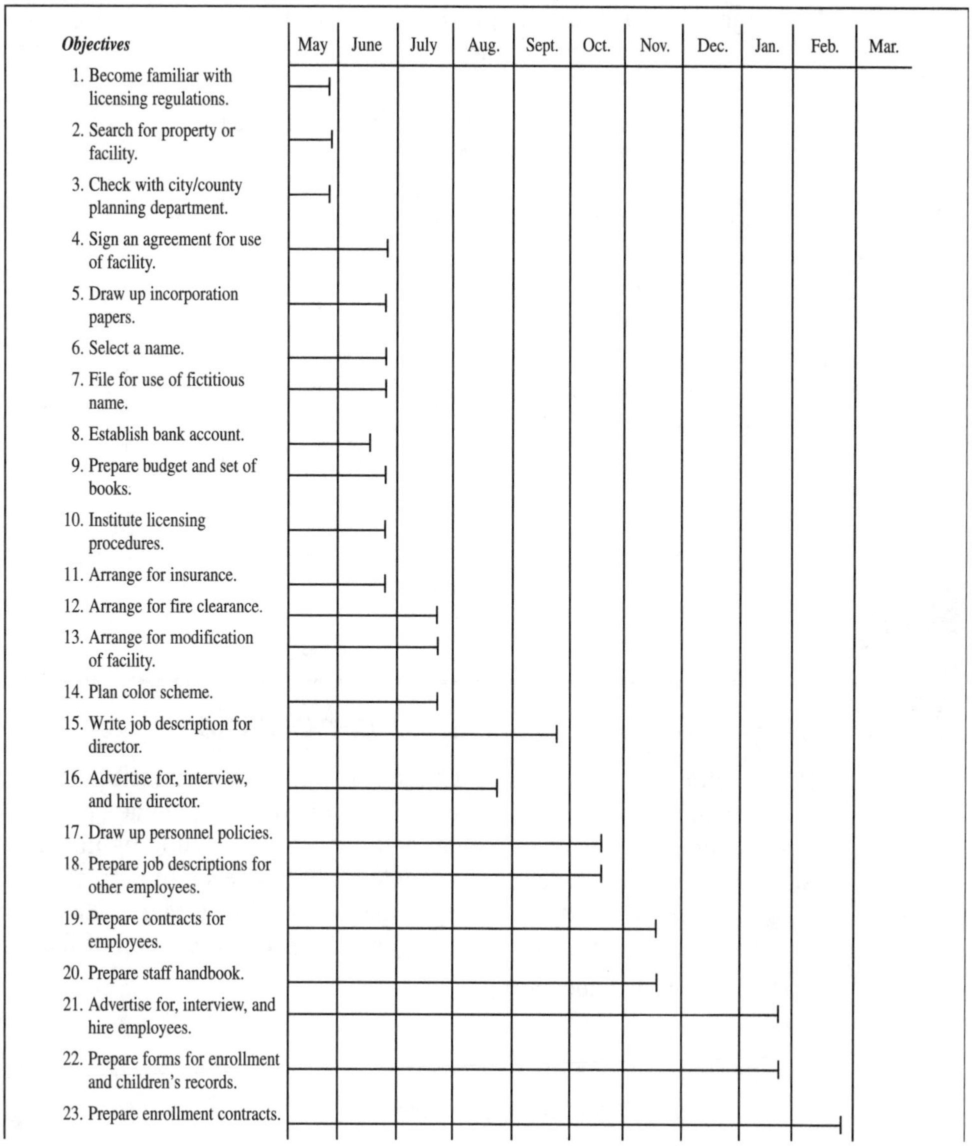

Objectives	May	June	July	Aug.	Sept.	Oct.	Nov.	Dec.	Jan.	Feb.	Mar.
1. Become familiar with licensing regulations.											
2. Search for property or facility.											
3. Check with city/county planning department.											
4. Sign an agreement for use of facility.											
5. Draw up incorporation papers.											
6. Select a name.											
7. File for use of fictitious name.											
8. Establish bank account.											
9. Prepare budget and set of books.											
10. Institute licensing procedures.											
11. Arrange for insurance.											
12. Arrange for fire clearance.											
13. Arrange for modification of facility.											
14. Plan color scheme.											
15. Write job description for director.											
16. Advertise for, interview, and hire director.											
17. Draw up personnel policies.											
18. Prepare job descriptions for other employees.											
19. Prepare contracts for employees.											
20. Prepare staff handbook.											
21. Advertise for, interview, and hire employees.											
22. Prepare forms for enrollment and children's records.											
23. Prepare enrollment contracts.											

Style II (condensed)

Objectives May	June	July	August
Initiate licensing procedures			
Contact zoning; building & safety			
		Renovate bldg.	
		Screen applicants for director	
		Raise additional funds	
		Develop policies & procedures	
			Purchase equip.
			Publicity

Style III (condensed)
List objectives and mark appropriate column as completed.

Objectives	May	June	July	Aug.	Sept.	Oct.
Initiate licensing procedures	X	X				
Contact zoning; bldg. & safety	X	X				
Renovation of building			X	X		
Screen applicants for director				X		
Raise additional funds			X	X		
Develop policies & procedures			X	X		
Screen applicants for staff				X		
Develop publicity campaign				X	X	
Purchase equipment & supplies				X	X	
Develop program						X
Open doors						X

A8 Regulatory and Licensing Agencies

The director of the Community Child Care Center is responsible for establishing and maintaining liaisons with the various government regulatory agencies that must approve the operation of the center and the use of the building in which it is located. Any group or individual who provides child care services to young children must be licensed, but the licensing agency varies from state to state. It may be any one of the following, other similar agencies, or a combination of these:

Department of Education
Department of Public Social Services/Welfare
Department of Health
Department of Children's Services

In some states, the regulations are very lax or almost nonexistent. In others, they are quite detailed, especially regarding children's health and safety. In most cases, any institution that cares for children under two years of age or for children who are sponsored by federal funds must follow federal guidelines in addition to those of their own state. Since these guidelines are more stringent than those of most states, some persons avoid using federal funds or apply for them only as a last resort. In any event, as the field of early childhood education continues to develop, licensing procedures in many states undergo changes.

The licensing and regulatory agencies exist for the purpose of setting and enforcing standards intended to protect the health, safety, and general welfare of each child being served. We must constantly be on guard to be sure that our program meets the legal requirements. Changes do affect the budget, but it is in our own best interests to protect the children with whose care we are entrusted.

Here is a brief guide to the types of concerns that are usually governed by various agencies. Even though they may not all apply to your center, it is important to be aware of them in order to have an overall picture of early childhood education in general and your own specific needs as well.

Regulations Concerning the Space

A. Zoning

Local zoning approval must be the first consideration for operating any center or home for the purpose of group child care. It is therefore important that you find out what the regulations are for your community before doing anything else.

1. Commercially Zoned Areas
   Zoning regulations in most communities do not permit the establishment of child care centers in residential areas without the approval of adjacent neighbors. Frequently, facilities for the care of children are forced to locate in the more expensive commercially zoned areas. This means that the land, building, and taxes will be more expensive; however, with so many working parents and caregivers, this can provide a convenience that pays off in higher tuition rates. More and more centers will be located not only in commercial/industrial areas, but within businesses themselves.
2. Residential Areas
   Locating a center in a residential area usually requires making an application to obtain a zoning variance. The application may be rather costly in terms of time and money. If a variance is granted, it is frequently accompanied by a multitude of restrictions concerning the size of the building, ratio of building to land, height of the building, street frontage, parking facilities, and other factors related to residential requirements.
3. Religious Facilities
   If the center is going to be located in a religious facility that has already been zoned for group child care, additional zoning permission is not usually required. In some communities with strict zoning regulations, it is generally easier to obtain approval for a child care center in areas where apartment buildings, religious facilities, and public schools are located than in residential or highly developed commercial/industrial areas.

B. Application Procedures and the Conditional Use Permit

The Community Child Care Center must obtain a conditional use permit by applying for approval from its local planning commission. The procedure to do so will vary greatly throughout the nation, and even from city to city and county to county. Requirements, however, may include, but not be limited to, steps similar to those listed below:

1. Application
   Obtain an application from the appropriate city or county government office. There are various steps required to fill out this application. You must state your name, address, type of business, and other pertinent information regarding factors that may affect the neighboring community in terms of noise, pollution, appearance, function, traffic, and related areas of concern.
2. Fees
   The application will require a fee, which may be nominal or several hundred dollars. The fee may be good for thirty to ninety days for one application only, or it may be good for as long as a year, with unlimited applications. Be prepared for the possibility of extensive charges for the various steps to be taken through a planning department. Become familiar with your local regulations so you can be well prepared for these costs. Be sure to read all fine print. Talk to others that have been through the process to find out about potential local pitfalls. Be prepared to make a personal appearance, giving both oral and written testimony to justify your application to the planning commission.
3. Preparing a Plot Plan
   The plot plan is for the purpose of helping the regulatory group readily understand and assist you in your application for site approval.
   a. Obtain a sheet of ruled 1⁄8" graph paper, possibly 18" x 24" or larger. Use a scale of 1⁄16" to 1' or any other scale with which you feel comfortable. Note the scale in the lower right-hand corner of the diagram on page 27.
   b. Provide an arrow indicating the north direction.
   c. Diagram the existing structure with a ruler. Show exact distances from the street and from the edges of the lot on all four sides. Show room divisions, with doors. Slant doors slightly in the direction toward which they open. Indicate windows as very narrow rectangles in the spaces where they are located. If you first measure the outside dimensions and are sure that they are correct, the inside ones can be changed if needed, without having to start over. Indicate major built-ins in case there is a question about the amount of available indoor space.
   d. Indicate the following:
      - Fences, driveways, sidewalks
      - Offset parking, including areas for the handicapped
      - Playground locations
      - Landscaping, including trees
      - Drinking fountains
      - Trash areas
      - Frontage street names
      - Property lines
      - Setback distances
      - Square footage of property, buildings, and rooms
   e. In the lower right-hand corner, above the scale, note your name, address, telephone number(s), and e-mail address(es), as well as the location of the property shown on the plot plan.

f. Be sure to indicate any plans for alterations, additions, or deletions of present structures.

g. Under the scale, indicate the existing zoning.

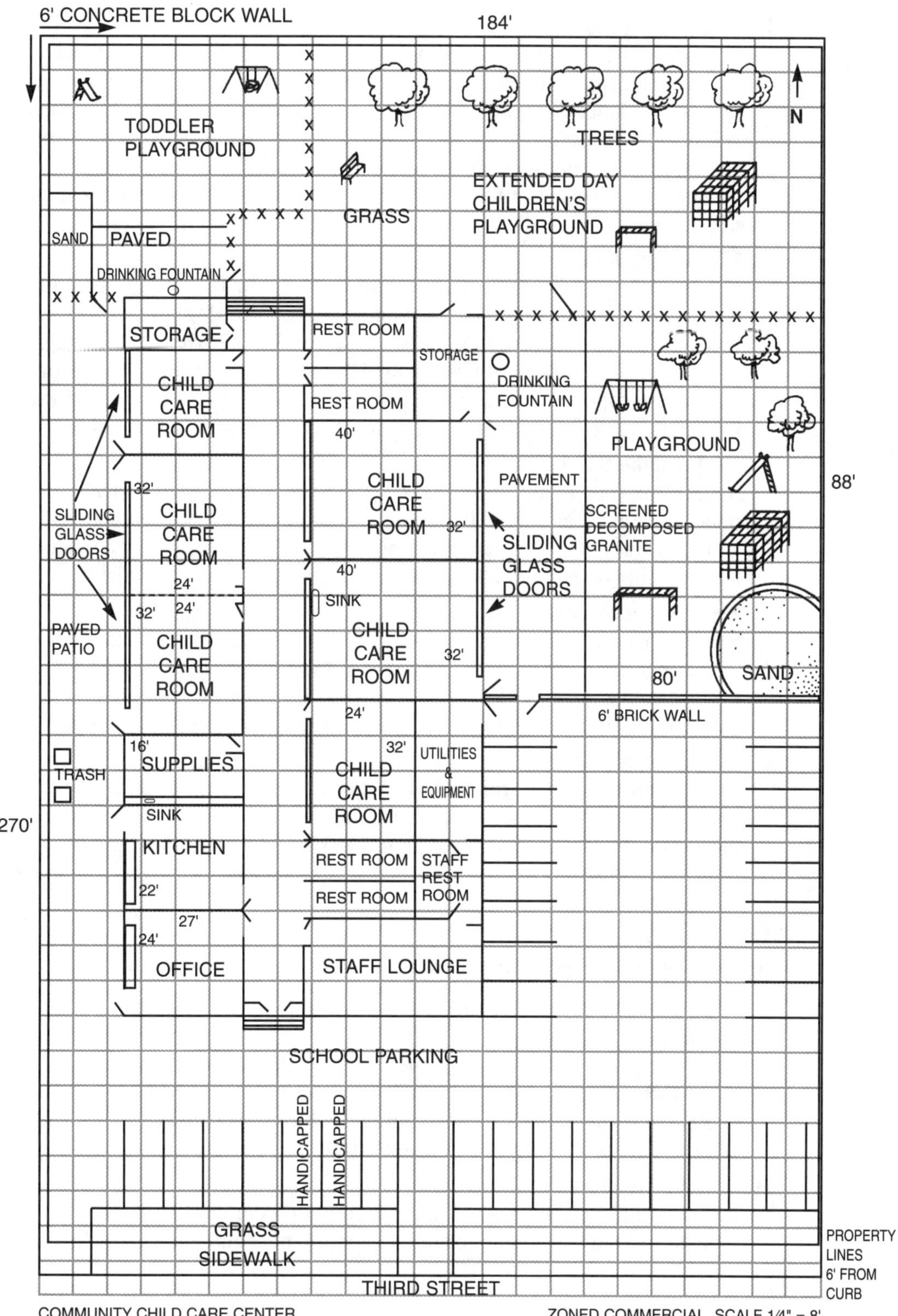

4. Submission of Application
   Once you have submitted your application, be prepared to wait for several weeks before you are notified of acceptance or rejection. You may be required to make a presentation before the planning department to answer any further questions.

C. Building Codes
Most cities have stringent building codes. The local department of building safety, or a comparable department, must give its approval to the type of structure being planned in relation to the functions of that structure. This department will also be concerned with the electrical wiring, the provisions for utilities, ceiling height, plumbing, capacity, and related factors. Usually the zoning agency will be aware of the requirements of the building and safety agency, and these requirements will in some way affect the decision it makes.

D. Fire Regulations
It is necessary to secure the approval of the fire department before a building can be used to house a child care center. This approval might be the responsibility of the state fire marshall's office of a local fire department. Fire regulations will require such things as fire extinguishers, alarms for certain types of buildings, fire escapes, fire walls in certain areas, and plans for evacuating the building in case of fire—as well as provisions for periodic fire drills.

E. Earthquake Safety
Some cities may require approval for earthquake safety standards. A very old building with unreinforced brick walls would probably not be approved today as a facility for young children in earthquake-prone areas. If the site is located in a known geologic fault area, a geologic safety study may be required.

F. Health Regulations
Some cities may require approval by their local health or sanitation department. These regulations will cover facilities for food services, provisions for drinking water, sewage disposal, toilet and hand-washing facilities, ventilation, heating, and lighting. Provisions for isolating a sick child will also be required.

G. Other Regulations
Other regulations concerning the facility may include the ratio of window space to room size, the ratio of toilets and lavatories to the number of children, the location of rooms in relation to ground level, and having screens on windows that open and shades on windows exposed to the sun.

Using the Space

Not only must the facility meet certain standards, but the use of the space is also regulated.

A. Parking
Regulations generally require a specified number of parking spaces in relation to the number of adult employees and other occupants of the building. More than one automobile exit is usually required. Pickup and delivery of the children will be controlled according to its impact on the neighborhood.

B. Furnishings and Equipment
Some regulatory agencies will have minimum requirements and certain restrictions as to kinds, uses, and locations of equipment and other furnishings.

Children

Regulations in regard to children being served will usually include

A. ages of children, usually two through five or six. More increasingly, however, they include birth through age two as well.

B. numbers of children based on available space, indoors and out, generally one child for every 35 to 50 square feet of indoor space and for every 75 to 100 square feet of outdoor space.

C. nondiscriminatory provisions regarding race, religion, or other circumstances [Section A14].

D. a physician's verification of the health of each child enrolled.

Staff

Whatever the facilities, quality care is primarily dependent on the persons providing that care. Regulations concerning staff members may include

A. minimum age for certain categories of employees.

B. Child Abuse Index check, where applicable, in various states.

C. fingerprint clearance of all personnel.

D. FBI clearance, where applicable, amongst licensing requirements.

E. a physician's report of good physical and mental health of employees, including annual tuberculin clearance.

F. minimum educational requirements, as required by licensing regulatory agency.

G. number of staff in relation to number of children enrolled.

Financing and Management

A. In applying for a license for a nonincorporated center, an applicant may be required to prove that he or she is financially able to provide adequate care and supervision until the program starts realizing a profit, which may take at least six months.

B. Records concerning the students and staff must be kept up-to-date by making ongoing notations as conditions change.

C. If incorporated, a Board of Directors must be designated as the responsible body.

Lack of Standards

The regulations of some licensing agencies are quite lax and may take the form of recommendations rather than enforceable rules. Other agencies may be more strict. As the number of centers grow throughout the nation, the enforceable regulations will become more standardized and, hopefully, more relevant to the needs of children, families, and communities. In the meantime, as director, you are charged with the responsibility of meeting the legal standards required by the various regulatory agencies in your area. You also have a moral obligation to provide a safe, healthful, educationally sound, child-oriented program of gentle, loving care. That's what child care is all about.

A9

Regulatory Agencies' Requirements for Your Situation

You will probably want to get in touch with your state, county, and city zoning, health, building safety, fire, and welfare departments, and the department of education, if applicable, to obtain current information on child care center regulations in your community. When you obtain such information, record on these forms specific items relevant to your program.

1. **Zoning Requirements**
   Zoning for your center ______________________
   Street frontage required ______________________
   Building height regulations ______________________
   Parking regulations ______________________
   Square footage required ______________________
   Minimum lot size required ______________________

Number of children enrolled	Size of lot
______________________	______________________
______________________	______________________

   Other zoning regulations ______________________

2. **Business License** ______________________

3. **Building Codes**
   Electrical ______________________
   Utilities ______________________
   Ceiling height ______________________
   Plumbing ______________________
   Capacity ______________________
   Access ______________________
   Other ______________________

4. **Fire Regulations and Earthquake Safety Regulations**
   Extinguishers ______________________
   Sprinklers ______________________
   Alarms ______________________
   Exits and escapes ______________________
   Fire walls ______________________
   Plans for evacuation ______________________
   Drills ______________________
   Emergency supplies ______________________
   Plans for on-site emergencies ______________________
   Other ______________________

5. Health Department Regulations

Food services ______________________________

Environmental health ______________________________

Drinking water ______________________________

Sewage ______________________________

Ventilation ______________________________

Heating ______________________________

Lighting ______________________________

Other ______________________________

6. State Licensing Agency

Name ______________________________

Contact person ______________________________

Address ______________________________

Telephone number ______________________________

E-mail address ______________________________

Requirements not covered by local regulations:

Child/adult ratio ______________________________

Child/space ratio (indoors) ______________________________

Child/space ratio (outdoors) ______________________________

Staff qualifications ______________________________

Director ______________________________

Child care provider ______________________________

Aide or assistant ______________________________

Other ______________________________

Fingerprint requirements ______________________________

Health requirements ______________________________

Isolation facilities ______________________________

Safety requirements ______________________________

Financing requirements ______________________________

Window space ______________________________

Equipment ______________________________

Other ______________________________

Waivers

If you are unable to meet one or more of the requirements of any of the regulatory agencies, you may be able to apply for a waiver, variance, or exemption. Such requests should be in writing, greatly detailed, and justified. Some agencies will supply their own forms for such requests.

A10 Insurance Needs

High Costs

Insurance costs for child care facilities have become exorbitant, and the policies themselves are difficult to obtain. Insurance companies are in the business to make money, and it has not been very profitable for them to insure these facilities. However, if you anticipate this high cost from the outset, you can build it into your total investment.

Urgency

Priority must be given to insurance needs. Without adequate insurance, your total investment is at risk. Insurance is such a highly technical subject, and there is such a wide variety of insurance options, that it is wise to obtain the services of a good agent who can advise you about needs and costs. It is prudent, however, for a director to become familiar with the types of insurance to be considered in order to even select an agent and be adequately insured for the least amount. If you are sponsored by and housed in a building already insured by a nonprofit institution, such as a church, public school, or community service organization, your insurance may be partially covered by what they already have. In any event, it should be obtained in consultation with their insurance representatives.

Types of Insurance

The following types of insurance should be given consideration:

A. **Public liability:** This includes protection against claims that may arise from bodily injury or property damage occurring on the premises. This might be included in a policy for general comprehensive liability, which covers any new hazards that might occur during the life of the policy, unless specifically excluded in the contract. This type of policy will extend its coverage to any center activities that may occur off your own premises, whether for a short walk around the block or while on an extensive field trip out of town.

   Liability policies are legal documents. There must be negligence on the part of the insured in order for coverage to be valid. It will then pay, subject to the limits of liability, all sums that you are legally obligated to pay because of either bodily injury or property damage. To protect yourself, constantly check and recheck against safety hazards [Section H7], staying within the legal limits of your license as to supervision and staffing, and realizing that the health and safety of your clientele is non-negotiable.

B. **Corporations:** Corporations can include in their general liability policy a clause that will relieve the corporate officers of responsibility as individuals in case the corporation is sued for negligence. The laws for corporations vary greatly from state to state; therefore, the provisions of such coverage vary as well. It would be wise to investigate other protections available for corporate officers in your state.

C. **Personal injury:** This type of policy covers any legal obligations that might arise from damages claimed by others due to occurrences such as false arrest, libel or slander, violation of privacy, and similar events. This may occur, for example, if a parent claimed that a child care provider slandered his or her character by telling others that he or she was neglecting a child.

Reporting cases of suspected child abuse or neglect [Section G41–42]: A personal injury policy would cover you if you report such a case to the appropriate authorities and the parents or caregivers decide to sue you for doing so.

D. **Fire and theft:** These are important aspects of any insurance program to protect the contents of your facility as well as the facility itself. In cases in which you are part of a larger organization or if you rent or lease only a portion of a building, care must be taken to be sure you are adequately covered for that portion of the building that you occupy, and all of the contents therein. It is good practice to keep inventory lists and a set of photographs of expensive equipment in a fireproof container for proof of the value of the investment you have in the contents of the building.

E. **Vehicle insurance:**

1. *General:* If the center owns, rents, or leases one or more vehicles, you need to include coverage for them. The usual coverage is for property damage and bodily injury. You should have comprehensive insurance to protect you against loss to the vehicle as a result of vandalism, broken windows, theft, or any other physical damage. Collision insurance will pay for damage to your vehicle as a direct result of a collision.
2. *Medical:* In addition, an important coverage for you is an extensive allowance for medical payments, which will cover both the driver and passengers. Because of the high cost of medical care, this should be given careful consideration and have a high enough limit to cover prolonged hospitalization or related care.
3. *Uninsured motorist:* Another coverage that is important in states that do not require everyone to be insured is uninsured motorist protection. Even in those states that require all vehicles to carry insurance, it is a wise idea to carry protection against those who are "underinsured."
4. *Transportation services:* When using a transportation service, ask to see a copy of their insurance policy. It would be wise to request, in writing, a statement of their coverage in respect to the protection of their passengers, and then to verify it with their insurance agency.

Medical Insurance

There are good medical insurance policies that will pay for costs of any injuries occurring to staff or children while on your premises—up to the limits of the policy. Even if most of your parents and caregivers have medical insurance, it is a tremendous "good will" gesture to say, in case of injury, "Don't worry about that. We will cover the medical expenses. Just send us the bill." This may offset the possibility of someone considering a lawsuit.

Insurance for Employees

A. **Social Security:** Religious institutions were previously exempt from being required to provide this coverage. However, in January 1984, the law was changed to state that only those employees considered to be ministers, and thus technically self-employed, are exempt.

B. **Worker's Compensation:** This is required by law. Worker's compensation covers all employees for injuries sustained during the course of their work—whether on the premises or on a field trip or errand during working hours.

C. **Unemployment insurance:** This is an important coverage for working persons. However, it is optional for religious institutes. If you have a religious-group-operated program and do not take out unemployment insurance, it is incumbent on you to notify persons at the time of employment of this fact.

D. **Medical insurance:** This is a costly employee benefit but is very important to prospective employees. Because medical care is so expensive, medical insurance is becoming an increasingly important benefit to employees in any type of business. It would be wise, if you do not now have such coverage, to set up some long-term plans to include this coverage in the future.

E. **Malpractice insurance:** It has become more and more difficult to obtain protection for child care employees against lawsuits because of the increasing awareness of the possibility of abuse by caregivers, especially sexual abuse. It may be that child care employees, and especially program directors, may have to consider malpractice liability policies. The availability of these is questionable. There is no doubt that the expense will be great.

F. **Salary protection:** Some policies continue a portion of your salary in case of illness or injury.

G. **Cancer coverage:** This is usually very inexpensive in comparison to other policies. It is well worth the money, considering the tremendous costs it might save you should you develop cancer.

H. **Professional liability:** This type of policy can protect a staff member or director against liability that might arise from a suit accusing you of negligence in your performance. Since the malpractice field is changing rapidly at this time, you will have to do some careful research to keep up with what is available. One of the best sources of information is the National Association for the Education of Young Children. Pertinent information can also be obtained from the Child Care Law Center in San Francisco, California.

NAEYC
1509 16th Street, Northwest
Washington, DC 20036
(202) 232-8777
(800) 424-2460

Child Care Law Center in San Francisco
973 Market Street, Suite 550
San Francisco, California 94103
(415) 495-5498

A11 Board of Directors

Incorporated child care centers are governed by a board of one type or another. If the center is sponsored by or affiliated with a religious organization, it might be governed by its Board of Directors, by a Board of Education that answers to the Board of Directors, by a Child Care Committee that answers to the Board of Education or to the Board of Directors of the religious organization, or by a Board of Education that answers only to itself and to the child care center that it governs or advises.

If the program is a cooperative, it is usually governed by a Board of Directors made up of the cooperating parents and caregivers. Other programs may be affiliated with or sponsored by various nonprofit community service organizations or community action agencies. These are usually governed by a board composed of interested members of the sponsoring organization, the community at large, or parents and caregivers of the children. Some child care centers are sponsored by local Boards of Education and administered by school district personnel. Proprietary centers may or may not be incorporated. In the case of franchised centers or centers for which the owner hires a director to administer the school program, the owner frequently serves in the same capacity as a Board of Directors.

In the case of the parent/caregiver cooperative, it is suggested that the board's responsibilities be compiled by drawing from the list at the end of this section as well as from items on the list of the director's responsibilities in Section A1.

Selection of Board Members

Board members are selected by an existing board or an agency of the sponsoring group, or by consultation with educators in the community. Representation on the board should include, if possible, representatives from the sponsoring agency, the parents and caregivers, and the community. They should cover as wide a range of expertise as possible. For example, a good representation might include an educator, an attorney, a pediatrician, a business person, and one or two persons in other fields that may be related to children in some way. Members of the board should be given ample opportunities to be oriented to the program. They should be furnished with the forms you use, copies of various handbooks you give out, and copies of your contracts, operating policies, and other pertinent materials. They should be encouraged to visit the center and, if interested, read some books on child care that you may be using yourself.

If you are responsible to a board or absent owner, your most important task is to acknowledge that responsibility by maintaining a continuous pattern of communication with the board or owner and by adhering to decisions they make.

Relations between the board or owner and the director are sometimes strained because the specific duties and responsibilities of each are not clearly spelled out. A Board of Directors may fall into one of the following categories:

1. **Policy Making**
   This type of board is only concerned with formulation of overall policies of the center and delegates the responsibility for implementation to paid staff.
2. **Advisory**
   This type of board is not only concerned with the overall policies of the center, but also serves in an advisory capacity to professional staff.

3. **Active**
   This type of board helps set policy, serves in an advisory capacity, and actively participates in operating the center with the assistance of paid staff. A parent/caregiver cooperative is often designed in this manner.

Listed below are responsibilities that most boards assume. You may choose to add other items or to delete some.

1. Formulate major center policies for the overall goals of the program.
2. With the director, formulate center policies for the operation of the program, such as admission procedures and personnel policies.
3. Serve as a liaison between the center and the sponsoring body.
4. With the director, formulate a strong program of community relations and services.
5. Interpret the center program to members outside the sponsoring body.
6. Support the program developed by the professional staff.
7. Approve or disapprove all major changes in personnel.
8. With the director, formulate budgetary needs for each year.
9. Authorize purchases and other expenditures over a certain predetermined sum, within the limits of the year's budget.
10. Explore sources of income, other than tuition, to maintain adequate operation of the center.
11. Arrange for an annual auditing of the financial records.
12. With the director, discuss enrollment requirements from time to time.
13. With the director, consider any problem that cannot be handled by staff. The board will have the final say.

Keep a list of members of the Board of Directors. Use the following form for this purpose:

Date Term Expires	Position and Name	Address	E-mail Address	Telephone Home	Telephone Business
	Chairperson				
	Vice-Chairperson				
	Secretary				
	Treasurer				
	Other Members				

A12 Reports to the Board or Owner

The problems of relationships with your ever-changing Board of Directors or with an owner will be negligible if you remember the following guidelines:

1. Make regular, accurate, and complete activity reports to the board or owner. These reports should be sent to each member prior to each board meeting.
2. Mail copies of all newsletters, notices to parents and caregivers, announcements of special events, and similar information to all members of the board or to the owner.
3. Three times yearly (or whatever schedule you prefer), give a "State of the Child Care Center" report, in detail, to each board member or to the owner.

If you keep board members or the owner informed of all functions of the program, they will not have the opportunity to suggest that you are functioning without their guidance. You may also wish to arrange a special visitation day for all board members, conduct an orientation program for new members, and arrange a social event that will enable board members and staff to become acquainted.

Center Activity Report

You may wish to use this form for making your reports to the board or owner.

Community Child Care Center

111 THIRD STREET TELEPHONE 123-4579

PERIOD COVERED: ______________________________

Program highlights: ______________________________

____

____

Program difficulties: ______________________________

____

____

Budget modifications to be considered: ______________________________

____

____

Action proposed: ______________________________

____

____

Submitted by ______________________________

A13 Formation of Center Policy

You may be asked to revise a current center policy plan or to write a complete new policy for the center. In either event, there are certain considerations you should keep in mind.

Be courageous. Stand up for what you believe in. If your ideas are innovative, be prepared to justify them. If you believe that your ideas are valid and important for the welfare of young children, be courageous.

Be sensitive to your own limitations. Do not set a policy that will exceed the limitations of the type of facility you operate. All programs have limitations. You cannot expect your program to meet the needs of all families and all children. You, too, have limitations. Although your duties and responsibilities are many and varied, they are not all-inclusive. Know where to draw the line. For example, are you prepared to handle all children with special needs, or only those with certain types of special needs? Are you geared to serve the working parent and caregiver, or only those whose working hours fit in with the center hours? Can you extend those hours and still maintain the sound financial basis on which the center now operates? Are you able to establish a transportation plan? These are only a few of the questions that you will have to consider from time to time.

Establish and understand priorities. You must decide which program goals are primary and which are secondary. Not only must you set these priorities, but you must also be prepared to justify them to the board, and possibly to the community you serve.

Establish relationships with consultant-referral services. Once you have established priorities, you should also establish significant relationships with various persons or groups whom you can consult from time to time or to whom you can refer others.

The policy statement should include statements of the following:

- Name of organization
- Sponsorship/ownership
- Purpose
- Goals
- Enrollment policy
- Child Care Center Board's responsibility
- Staff requirements
- Parent/caregiver participation
- Health requirements
- Child care procedures
- Financial arrangements
- Personnel policies

A14

Operating Policies of the Community Child Care Center (Bylaws)*

I. Name of Organization
The name of this organization is the Community Child Care Center.

II. Sponsorship/Ownership
This organization is a nonprofit, nonsectarian, interracial, and nonpolitical institution founded by a community interest group. No part of its earnings shall be of benefit to any member or individual. All funds earned by the center shall be reinvested in the program (not applicable to a nonincorporated center).

III. Purpose
The purpose of this program shall be to provide a halfday preschool and child care program that will benefit the children, the parents and caregivers, and the community.

IV. Goals

A. For the Children
1. To provide opportunities for being with other children in a setting conducive to the development of wholesome social relationships.
2. To provide appropriate play experiences that contribute to the developmental needs of the children.
3. To provide opportunities for meaningful play based on children's individual needs, interests, handicaps, and abilities, and that build important foundations for future reading skills and other academic pursuits.

B. For Parents and Caregivers
1. To provide opportunities to meet and work with other parents, caregivers, and child care providers who have as their common concern the interests and needs of the preschool child.
2. To provide care for the child while parents and caregivers pursue their own work or other interests.
3. To provide opportunities to grow in the understanding of child development through a planned educational program and by working, under supervision, as a child care assistant.

C. For the Community
1. To help meet the needs of the community for an early childhood child care facility.
2. To contribute to the wholesome growth and development of the future citizens of the community.
3. To enhance the role of the community interest group as an integral part of the community.
4. To provide a setting where people of various religious and ethnic backgrounds can work together for a common interest.

* For a proprietary center, substitute the word *owner* wherever *board* is mentioned. Although a private owner of a nonincorporated center is not required to have bylaws, written policies contribute to a quality, financially sound center.

V. Enrollment Policy

A. Enrollment shall be open to any child, provided that the center can meet the needs of that child.

B. Enrollment in the center shall be granted without discrimination in regard to sex, race, color, creed, or political belief.

C. The child must meet the age limits of enrollment at the center.

VI. Responsibility of the Child Care Center Board

A. Chairperson

The Board of Directors of the community interest group shall be responsible for appointing a board member to become Chairperson of the Child Care Center Board.

B. Members

The board shall consist of

1. three members appointed by the chairperson of the community interest group.
2. three members chosen from the community at large by the chairperson, with recommendations from the director.
3. three representatives of the parents and caregivers who have children enrolled in the center.

C. Officers

1. Officers shall include a chairperson, vice-chairperson, secretary, and treasurer. These officers are elected by board members from their own group.
2. These officers shall comprise the Executive Committee, which shall formulate all major center policy.
3. The director of the Child Care Center shall sit *ex officio* in all meetings of the Executive Committee.

D. Term of Board Membership

1. Rotation of terms
   a. All members shall be appointed to two-year terms, with the exception of the parent/caregiver representatives, who shall be appointed to one-year terms.
   b. In order to ensure the ongoing nature of the board, these terms should expire at varying times so that the majority of members shall never all be new at the same time.
2. Time of assuming responsibilities

   Each board member shall assume initial responsibilities with the board at the beginning of the new fiscal year, beginning July 1 of each year, except for parent/caregiver representatives whose terms will commence on October 1 of each year. If necessary, a parent/caregiver representative may become an interim member to fill vacancies that may occur between July 1 and October 1 (because a parent or caregiver member may no longer have a child in the center and may not wish to continue to serve after July 1).

E. Responsibilities of Board Members

1. Chairperson
   a. Presides at all board meetings and all Executive Committee meetings.

   b. Acts as liaison between the Child Care Center and community interest group.
   c. Appoints committee chairperson.
   d. Is an *ex officio* member of all committees.
   e. Signs letters and other documents for the board, including checks.
   f. Represents the center in the absence of the director or the assistant director.
   g. Serves as chairperson of the Personnel Committee.
2. Vice-Chairperson
   a. Assumes the duties of the chairperson in his or her absence.
   b. Provides general assistance to the chairperson in all functions.
3. Secretary
   a. Records proceedings of all meetings.
   b. Notifies members of meetings.
   c. Conducts correspondence for the Child Care Center Board.
   d. Maintains files of all board records and correspondence.
   e. May cosign checks.
4. Treasurer
   a. May cosign checks.
   b. Audits Child Care Center books and prepares financial reports.
   c. Handles delinquent Child Care Center accounts.
   d. Makes recommendations to ensure the self-supporting nature of the center.
5. Other Board Members
   a. Support and assist, when necessary, the director in the following areas:
      - Public relations for the center
      - Recruitment and enrollment of new children
      - Problems of building and grounds
      - Problems of purchasing materials, supplies, and equipment
   b. Make recommendations for the growth and development of the center.
6. Personnel Committee
   a. Consists of the chairperson of the board and one member from each of the other two groups represented.
   b. Shall set up an evaluation program for staff members and a plan for hiring new staff members on a trial basis.
   c. Shall be responsible for the continual upgrading of personnel practices, making revisions as necessary to meet changing needs.
   d. Shall supervise the handling of all personnel contracts.
7. Staff problems

   When the center has a problem that cannot be handled by the staff, the director will make a report to the board in writing. If the board cannot agree on a solution, the chairperson of the board shall have the final say.

8. Support of Director
   The board shall at all times recognize that its primary function is to provide support to the director in the overall administration of the center.

VII. Staff Requirements

The salaries and duties of the staff shall be in accordance with a statement of personnel policies drawn up by the Personnel Committee and outlined in a working agreement, which is set forth as Part XII of this document, and copies of which are to be attached to all personnel contracts [Section D27].

VIII. Parent/Caregiver Participation

A. Tuition credit shall be given to the parent or caregiver for each three hours of service to the center, on or off the center premises [Section F12].

B. Each child care provider shall ask two parents or caregivers to serve as room representatives. These parents or caregivers shall select three of their group to represent them on the Board of Directors. They shall further provide such services as assisting with the formation of car pools [Section E34], assisting with parent/caregiver meetings [Section F26], arranging special events, and organizing parent/caregiver groups [Section F28].

IX. Health Requirements

A. A certificate of good health, signed by a physician, is required at the time each child is admitted to the center [Section E18]. Such a certificate may also be required before reentrance by a child after any lengthy or serious communicable disease or illness.

B. Each child is to be carefully inspected every morning upon entering the center [Section G16]. If good health is in doubt, the child should not be admitted. Should a child seem ill during the day, the child shall be isolated immediately and the parents or caregivers contacted.

C. Parents or caregivers are required to notify the center whenever a child has been exposed to a contagious disease [Sections E25, G21, G28].

D. All newly enrolled children are required to have completed immunization for diphtheria, whooping cough, measles, and polio. They must also have a tuberculin test [Section E18].

E. All staff members, volunteers, and participating parents and caregivers shall present certificates of good health and negative tuberculin tests [Sections D23–27, F13–14].

X. Child Care Procedures

A. The premises shall be open for child care from 6:00 A.M. to 6:30 P.M., Monday through Friday, except for school holidays.

B. The preschool program shall be conducted from 9:00 A.M. to noon on all weekdays.

C. Children may attend from two to five days per week, either for the 9:00 A.M. to 12:00 P.M. preschool program or for full-day care.

D. Although children shall be initially assigned to a child care group according to age [Section I25], they may later be transferred to other groups, according to their individual needs.

E. Each child care group shall have a qualified child care provider, with an assistant who may be either a teacher [Section D5], a participating parent or caregiver [Section F12], or a student teacher [Section J2].

F. Schedules shall be in keeping with sound principles of child development [Sections E26, I7].

G. The center may be closed on holidays observed by the public school system and on certain other days for teachers' in-services or other reasons. Written notice of such closings shall be made to parents and caregivers.

XI. Financial Arrangements [Part B, E15]

A. The director or secretary collects all fees and tuition. Banking and bookkeeping procedures are handled by the bookkeeper employed by the Community Child Care Center.

B. Fees and tuitions are set by the Child Care Center Board in accordance with the provisions of the annual budget [Section B14].

C. The proposed budget is formulated by the director for each new fiscal year and is submitted to the board by March 1 of each year [Section B14].

D. Total enrollment is not to exceed that which is allowed by the licensing agency [Section A8].

E. Members shall enroll for not less than one full program term or for the balance of the current program term if enrolled after the start of the term [Sections E14, E25]. A program term is from mid-September to mid-June, although the center continues with a summer term from mid-June to mid-September with a reduced staff. (From community to community, be consistent with your school district's school terms.)

F. The center reserves the right to drop a member for reasons of noncooperation, delinquency in payment of fees, or inability of child or parent/caregiver to adjust to the center program, as determined by the board.

G. Members shall be allowed to withdraw prior to the end of the program year for the following reasons [Section E14]:

1. Serious illness of child
2. Death of child
3. Permanent removal from the community
4. Lack of cooperation by parents or caregivers
5. Mutual agreement between the member and the board if the child's adjustment to the center is unsatisfactory
6. Delinquency in payment of fees
7. The center is unable to meet the needs of the child
8. In all cases of withdrawal, two weeks notice shall be required, except in case of serious illness or accident [Section E25].

H. Scholarships
A scholarship may be granted to a family with permission of the chairperson and director [Section B14]. These scholarships shall be kept confidential between these two, the family involved, and the bookkeeper.

I. Tuition
The tuition and credit for absences shall be recommended by the committee for each year, on the basis of a budget prepared by the director [Section E25].

J. A registration fee shall be paid upon the enrollment of each new child, and upon the reenrollment for each new year, on the basis of the budget [Sections B14, E25].

XII. **Personnel Policy**
The school's personnel policy [Section D27], which sets forth wages and working conditions, shall be a part of each staff member's contract.

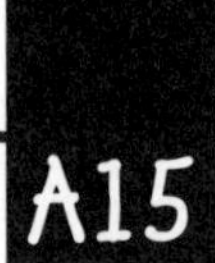

A15 Organization of the Child Care Center Program

Keep a chart that reflects the position of all people and organizations involved in the center. A large program may want to add an administrative assistant position.

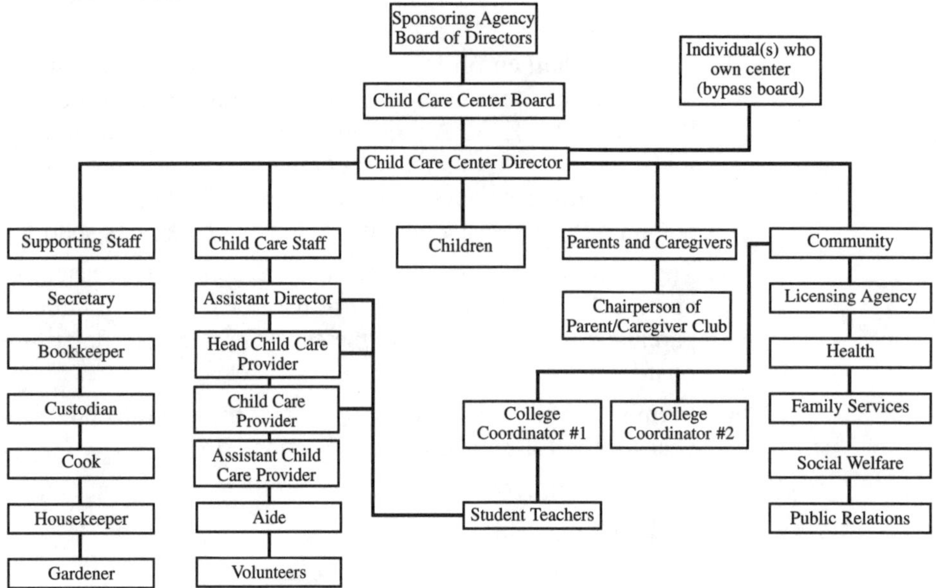

A16 Record Keeping

You will be responsible for seeing that certain records are maintained and that certain information is readily accessible. These records can be a definite asset to the successful operation of your center. Do not keep records that are cumbersome, inaccurate, or irrelevant. They get in the way and detract from more important duties. Evaluate your record-keeping practices and knowledge by using this guide:

- Are your records dated?
- Are your records clear?
- Are they concise?
- Are they kept up-to-date?
- Are they accurately filled out?
- Are they filed systematically?
- Are they properly signed?
- Are they kept confidential?
- Will a successor to your position understand them?
- In case of an extended absence on your part, will another member of your staff be able to maintain the records for you, or will your work accumulate until your return and become a burdensome task to bring up-to-date?
- Are your records about children written in an objective manner?
- Are your records useful to you, other staff members, parents and caregivers, and other members of the center community?

A17 Obtaining Tax-Exempt Status

If you are incorporated as a nonprofit organization, you are eligible for tax-exempt status. This will mean a big savings for your center in not having to pay taxes on its income. Application forms for tax exemption may be obtained from your local U.S. Internal Revenue Service office, or you may write for the form. Ask for Exemption Form 1023. After the form is completed, you will need to show proof that you have incorporated as a nonprofit group.

A word of caution: Tax exemptions are only good for one year. They must be filed each year in order for you to retain your standing. Renewal filings are completed on Form 990-A, which is also available from the Internal Revenue Service.

A18 Schedule for Federal Tax and Other Reports

Following is a summary of the forms and tax reports you may need when filing your taxes. Please check with the IRS as well as your state to make sure you have the correct forms. Contact the U.S. Internal Revenue Service at:

IRS website: http://www.irs.gov

Toll free number: 1-800-829-1040

FILING DATES	FORM NUMBER	FORM TITLE	PURPOSE
When first organized	SS-4	Application for Employer Identification Number	For identification on all tax reports
When first organized	1023	Application for Tax-Exempt Status	For nonprofit institution
	940	Federal Unemployment Tax	Depends on state requirements
Jan. 31, Apr. 30, July 31, Oct. 31	941	Employer's Quarterly Federal Tax Return	To report funds withheld from employees
To employee Jan. 31; filed by Feb. 28	W-2	Federal Wage and Tax Statement	For use in filing tax return for employee
To employee Jan. 31; filed by Feb. 28	W-3	Reconciliation of Income Tax Withheld	Summary for Internal Revenue Service
(When new employee is hired)	W-4	Employee Withholding Allowance Certificate	Employee's statement of exemptions
Jan. 31 and Feb. 28	1099Misc	Information Return	To report payments made to nonemployees for services rendered
Feb. 28	1096	Annual Summary and transmittal of U.S. Information Return	Summary of all Form 1099s

A19 Scheduling

Scheduling your time and the time of your staff will be one of your most important responsibilities as director. Prepare a yearly calendar of program days and holidays. You might want to follow the local public school calendar. Mail your calendar to all parents and caregivers.

- Send the monthly calendar home one week before each new time period.
- Change the color of the paper from month to month so that you can help parents and caregivers by referring (for instance) to the "pink" or "blue" calendar.
- Make the spaces large enough to write whatever you need to say.
- Be precise. This will save unnecessary telephone calls.
- Be child-oriented, even though the calendar is for parents' and caregivers' use.
- Review each new calendar with your staff before putting it in final form.
- Review the calendar with children before sending it home.

We have blocked out a few dates for you to help you get started with your own calendar keeping. Use this basic guide to stimulate brainstorming at staff meetings for changes, additions, and new ideas. We hope you will be innovative and establish some new traditions. But we do suggest not making too many changes the first year. To help maintain the continuity of enrollment and reputation, you would do well to repeat annual events that have been successful.

OCTOBER

Sunday	Monday	Tuesday	Wednesday	Thursday	Friday	Saturday
	1	2	3 Bus trip to lake 9:30–11 All children	4	5	6
7	8 Orientation meeting for parent/caregiver assistants 9:30–11:30	9 Organizational meeting for Parent/Caregiver Club 1:30 p.m.	10 Windy days will soon be here! Be sure to send a sweater with your child.	11	12	13
14	15	16	17	18 Parent/caregiver education meeting - film on childhood development 7:30 p.m.	19 Be sure there are name tags on the inside of your child's clothes.	20
21	22	23 Auto trip to library for groups I & II 10:00–11:15	24	25	26	27
28	29	30	31 Halloween! Funny Hat Parade for all groups 10 a.m. Refreshments			

Staff Management Schedule

Change dates and items to meet your own needs.

Date	Item
June 15	Prepare contracts and fill vacancies for coming year and summer term [Sections D12–29, D38].
June 15	Staff meeting with summer term employees.
Aug. 16	Send out summer newsletters and staff contracts [Sections A21, D26].
Sept. 4	Hold a preterm get-together to introduce new staff members [Section D76].
Sept. 4	Orientation for new staff members [Section D43].
Sept. 5	Preterm staff meeting and planning conference [Section D76].
Sept. 5	Review of W-2 forms, tuberculin test reports, health forms, and so on [Sections A18, D23].
Sept. 5	Make room assignments [Section D46].
Sept. 5	Make class assignments [Section E31].
Sept. 5	Distribute staff members' initial supplies (keys, roll books, forms, and so on) [Sections C15, D45–48].
Sept. 5	Distribute current revision of Employees' Handbook [Section D45].
Sept. 7	Hold individual staff conferences.
Sept. 10	Continue individual staff conferences.
Sept. 10	Have staff finish preparing the room environment, including bulletin boards [Sections I2, I8].
Sept. 10	Staff meeting: Evaluation of plans for opening week events [Section D50].
Sept. 12	Distribute group lists [Section D49].
Sept. 14	Distribute paychecks [Sections B5–6]. Close summer term.
Sept. 17	Staff meeting: General business [Section D50].

A21

Administrative Duties in Preparing for a New Program Year

January

Check for changes in telephone book ad [Section E3].

February

Determine if an increase in tuition or other fees is needed. Notify parents and caregivers of returning children if an increase is planned.

March

- Send letters to parents and caregivers of children eligible to return, requesting advance enrollment information from them and asking who plans to continue

through the summer term. Also send a similar letter to parents and caregivers of children formerly enrolled [Section E1].
- Hold an Open House.

April
- Place newspaper advertising for enrollments [Section E3].
- Plan budget for forthcoming fiscal year [Section B14].

May
- Follow-up on people contacted through Open House, advertising, letters to parents and caregivers of children formerly enrolled, and so on.
- Review enrollment procedures [Part E].
- Plan summer program [Section E37].
- Verify staff employment for following September and summer term. Hire new employees if needed [Sections D21, D29, D38].

June
- Collect all advance enrollment fees [Section B1].
- Inventory your supply needs as of mid-June [Part C].
- Prepare a list of items to be repaired during the summer term [Sections C23, C25, D72].
- Obtain estimates for major repairs [Sections C22, C25].
- Clean and arrange all cupboards and storage cabinets.
- Hold end-of-year staff meeting [Section D74].
- Obtain summer addresses of staff members who will be out of town [Section D73].
- Arrange for building security and yard upkeep if center is closed during summer months.
- Have drapes, curtains, and carpets cleaned. Clean and refinish floors [Section C22].
- Close books for fiscal year ending June 30 [Section B11].

July
- Prepare books for the new fiscal year [Section B11].
- Prepare calendar of holidays for forthcoming program year.
- Revise Parent/Caregivers' Handbook and Assistants' Handbook as needed [Sections E25, F17].
- Take vacation.

August
- Follow-up on inquiries regarding enrollment [Sections E7–8].
- Mail revised Parent/Caregivers' Handbook to all families [Section E25].
- Mail summer newsletters to all families and staff [Section F36].
- Plan orientation and training program for parent and caregiver assistants [Sections F12, F16–17].
- Plan in-service training program for staff [Sections D52–53].
- Plan orientation for new children [Sections E27–28].
- Plan orientation for new families [Sections F4–7].
- Plan agenda for opening staff meetings [Section D50].
- Complete repairs and painting [Sections C22–23, D72].
- Check supply of forms and stationery [Section C18].
- Complete purchase of new equipment and supplies [Section B18].

- Prepare calendar of educational associations' regional and national meetings for which attendance has been budgeted [Section J6].
- Register summer enrollees for new semester if they are going to continue at the center [Section E37].

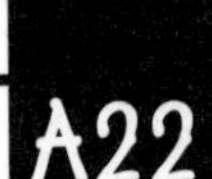

A22 Things to Do Before Opening of Program Term

Verify that all state and local licenses are current and posted. Prepare room assignments for each staff member.

With Custodian

- Check each room to discuss general needs [Section C26].
- Check heating, cooling, ventilation, and lighting systems [Sections C25–26].
- Check fire extinguisher and have it recharged if necessary.
- Check maintenance, repair, and cleaning supplies [Sections C19–21].
- Check lavatory supplies [Section C19].
- Check refrigerator, stove, and other kitchen equipment for cleanliness and function [Sections C25–26].
- Check all outdoor areas, including walls and steps, to see that all repairs have been made [Sections C1–9].
- Check appearance of all parts of the building.

With Staff

- Hold preopening staff meeting [Sections D50, D76].
- Check rooms with each child care provider individually to review
  furnishings and room arrangements [Sections C10–11],
  supplies [Sections C11, C15],
  use of cupboard space [Section C15], and
  bulletin boards and wall space [Section I8].
- Check storeroom with the staff [Sections C16–17].

Staff Records

- Examine health records and dates of tuberculin reports for each employee [Section D36].
- Prepare the W-2 forms needed for new staff members or for changes to be made for returning staff members [Section A18].
- Check employees' files for contents [Section D37].
- Notify each staff member of what deductions will be for each pay period and what actual take-home pay will be [Section B5].
- Distribute child care providers' forms and enrollment lists.

Food Services [Part K]

- Check supplies for kitchenware for both preparation and serving of food.
- Check supplies of food staples.

- Check basic menu plans, adjust where necessary, and make necessary purchases for at least a one-week period.
- Check arrangements for milk and juice delivery, if applicable.
- Review arrangements for bulk purchases in cooperation with other centers.
- Post allergy lists and special food requirements of new children [Section G13].

Refreshment Supplies [Section F11]

Check to see that all items for preparation and serving of refreshments for staff (during relief periods), assistants, parents and caregivers, and other visitors are readily available. Included may be coffee, tea, powdered hot chocolate, sugar, cream substitute, paper goods, coffeemaker (with hot-water provisions), cold-water container, and occasional snacks.

Parent/Caregiver Corner [Section F11]

- Books and sign-out sheets for books
- Bulletin boards
- Table decorations

Enrollments

- Handle any last-minute enrollment interviews [Section E13].
- Complete all enrollment paperwork [Sections E15–22, E30].
- Prepare room assignment cards for all children [Section E27].
- Prepare temporary roll for each child care group [Section D49].
- Prepare files for enrollment records.
- Collect all unpaid registration fees and September tuition [Section B1].

First Day of New Program Term

- Prepare direction signs as needed for first few days of the program. For example:
  Pick up room assignment cards here.
  This way to child care rooms.
  If you need car-pool assistance, sign here.
- Arrange for refreshments for parents and caregivers when they visit their children [Section F11].
- Assign parent/caregiver volunteers as guides during the first days of the program. Remember, even though your parents and caregivers may have visited once or twice, it is still an unfamiliar place to them.
- Greet parents and caregivers on arrival.
- Omit health check other than general appearance of child (on first day only) [Section G16].
- Distribute room assignment cards [Section E27].
- Check attendance against enrollments. Telephone those who enrolled but did not show up. If any indicate that they have changed their plans about sending their child to the center, send an immediate refund of deposits made, except for the enrollment fee. Then review the deferred enrollment list and contact, in order of application, families whose children are eligible to take the places of those who have withdrawn [Section E10].

After New Program Term Has Started

- Hold first fire drill [Section H11].
- Review roll book with each child care provider for corrections, additions, and procedural accuracy [Section E36].
- Review the children's program [Section I2].
- Review room assignments for appropriateness for each child [Part I].
- Present plans to staff for in-service training [Sections D52–53].
- Encourage extension course enrollments [Sections D58–61].
- Plan field trips and other special events for following weeks [Section I11].

A23 Computers and Software

Fairly inexpensive personal or portable laptop computers can be purchased to do the work of larger systems that may cost a great deal more. There are also a number of software programs for specific use by child and day care centers. Before purchasing anything, it is important to determine if the software that you feel is suitable for your center is available for the computer operating system that you wish to use.

You may also consider purchasing software programs that enable you to create your own method of recording data, such as family history information, payment records, attendance records, and related matters. There is also easy-to-use calculation software on which even the novice can perform expert financial record keeping. Other software is available to create letterhead, produce forms specific to your center, and take care of most general written tasks.

Take the time to find the right computer and appropriate software for your center's needs. It will be worth your time to find the right tools. Contact other child care centers and ask them what software they use and if they are satisfied with it.

The use of computers for administrative purposes should not be confused with the use of computers with the children [Section I20].

A24 Procedures

The procedures outlined in this section have been tried and found workable. Perhaps an equal number of procedures were tried over the years and discarded because they were not beneficial to the people involved or were not practical or economical.

If it is observed that a procedure is indeed beneficial but is not receiving full support of staff members, the director needs to arbitrarily state that the new procedure is to be followed by all. This can be done without causing hard feelings if you as the director can admit to being wrong from time to time. Flexibility on your part will serve as an example to your staff.

B Finances

1 Handling Receipts
2 Expenditures
3 Schedule A (Individual Ledger Sheets for Each Child)
4 Schedule B (Cash Journal)
5 Schedule C (Salaried Employee's Time Card and Pay Request)
6 Schedule C-1 (Time Card for Hourly Employees)
7 Schedule D (Expenditures)
8 Schedule E (Request for Reimbursement)
9 Schedule F (Monthly Budget Analysis)
10 Schedule G (Estimated Budget Report and Analysis)
11 Official Financial Statements
12 Financial Management
13 Start-Up and Operating Budgets
14 Analyzing and Preparing the Annual Budget
15 Approval of the Budget
16 Break-Even Analysis
17 Fee Increase Letter
18 Purchase Order Forms
19 Equipment Records
20 Fund-Raising
21 Director's Income Tax

B1 Handling Receipts

It is the director's responsibility to maintain a sound understanding and ongoing control of the budget, seeking assistance and advice from the Child Care Center Board, if one exists. At the Community Child Care Center, all bookkeeping records for child care are kept by the center. The actual cash receipts and expenditures (writing of checks), however, are handled by the bookkeeper for the community center. This alleviates the need for double banking and check writing, since the community center is the sponsoring body that operates the child care through its director and the board.

Some programs maintain a separate checking account, reporting income and expenditures in writing to the sponsoring body. Your own Board of Directors must decide which procedure is best for your organization. If you are a private owner, then handle the following procedures as director. If you are a director hired by a private owner rather than by a board, you may be asked to handle the following procedures, or the owner might share them with you.

1. Tuition (and other fees) statements are mailed or sent home with children on the twenty-fifth day of each month.
2. Tuition payments are received between the first and the fifth day of each month.
3. Checks may be accumulated for two or three days, alphabetized, and posted to individual ledger cards, ledger sheets, or ledger programs on file in your computer. Set up a records file for each child at the time of enrollment [Section B3].
4. Cash payments are posted from the cash receipts book.
5. Receipts are posted in a cash receipts journal [Section B4].
6. Receipts are stored in a safe, which is kept locked at all times, except when in actual use.
7. Deposits are made to the bank, usually once or twice a week.
8. On the fifth day of each month, individual ledgers are checked and informal past-due notices are sent to those who have not yet paid their tuition or any other fees. (See top of page 55 for sample notice.)
9. If the past-due amount has not been paid by the tenth day of the month, personal contact is made with the delinquent party, either when he or she brings a child to the center, or by telephone. Extenuating circumstances are given careful consideration. Follow these guidelines:
    a. If there has been a family or employment emergency, consider extending the due date by one or two weeks.
    b. Do not allow tuition to run more than one full month past due. It will be very difficult for the average family to catch up, no matter what the amount.
    c. Sometimes it may be wiser to waive the fee for one month than to lose an otherwise good client. Such allowances are considered "temporary scholarships." The center will benefit in the long run by such a policy. A well-planned budget will anticipate and allow a percentage of income that can be used for such emergencies.

Community Child Care Center

111 THIRD STREET TELEPHONE 123-4579

Date: ____________

To the parents or caregivers of ____________________________

Your account is now delinquent in the sum of $ _________.
This includes $ __________ that was due on the ______ day of __________.
This also includes a previous past-due balance of $ _________.
When will you pay this account? Please advise, either in person or by telephone.

Very truly yours,

____

Director (or Bookkeeper)

P.S. You may pay your account with MasterCard or Visa.

d. All such special arrangements are confidential.

e. If the party is consistently delinquent and has not honored scholarship assistance arrangements, the following options are then given:

(1) Ask the parents or caregivers to withdraw child from the center.

(2) Ask the parents or caregivers to deposit three months' tuition with the center. Make all future payments, in cash, on the first school day of each month.

Perhaps a tuition and child care bill is $200 a month. A partial scholarship may be given of $50 or $100 a month, with the understanding that the balance will be waived for the current month and that, thereafter, it will be paid by the fifth day of the month. Often, in such cases, you can charge the tuition but waive all child care costs. Since you know the family needs child care, it is difficult to dismiss them from your program. However, the assistance that you offer must be equitably distributed among a growing number of families.

Small Claims Court: Collecting Unpaid Tuition and Other Debts

From time to time, you may find yourself with two or three months' unpaid tuition by a client who has no intention of paying you. The best method for collecting such a debt is to go to Small Claims Court. The amount of money that can be collected through such a court differs from state to state, ranging from a few hundred dollars to a few thousand. The procedure for filing is simple. Go to the court, ask for the forms to be filed, and follow the instructions given. Frequently, when people are notified that they are being taken to Small Claims Court, they will either pay the full amount owed or make arrangements to pay the amount, rather than go to court in a case that they know they will lose. If the party is willing to pay, but is not financially able to do so, it may be better to work out some compromise to receive at least part of the money. Even if the court awards you judgment for the claim, it is up to you to collect.

B2 Expenditures

This is how you can handle the money required to be paid out.

I. Salaries

A. Five days before each pay period, time cards are picked up. Employees' time cards are similar to those shown in B5, Schedule C (page 58) for salaried employees and B6, Schedule C-1 (page 58) for hourly employees. They can easily be modified to meet your own organization's needs. Use these cards for both hourly employees and for those on salary. Keeping such time records for salaried employees avoids problems that may arise as to whether or not a salaried employee is putting in the appropriate hours.

B. The director draws up a Payroll Request form similar to that shown in B5, Schedule C.

C. The bookkeeper figures the appropriate deductions and total salary, and maintains individual payroll records for each employee, showing withholding tax, Social Security deductions, and any other deductions from the total amount due each pay period.

D. The bookkeeper then issues checks immediately and is expected to obtain the required two signatures in time to distribute the checks on the closest work day to the fifteenth and the last day of each month.

E. The bookkeeper also maintains payroll records for the various state and federal government reports that must be filed periodically [Section A18].

II. Fixed Expenditures

A. Fixed expenditures, such as housing, may be paid by the bookkeeper without a special directive from the director.

B. Such transactions are posted to a cash-paid journal.

III. All Other Expenditures (Except Petty Cash)

A. All other expenditures are paid by the bookkeeper at the request of the director. Such requests are made on a form similar to that shown in B8, Schedule E (page 59).

B. Requests are transmitted to the bookkeeper, with invoice or receipt for purchase or service attached. Payments are posted in the cash-paid journal.

IV. Petty Cash

A. The director keeps a petty-cash fund on hand at all times. (If food services are part of the program, keep a separate checking account for food items only. Checks may be signed by either the director or the head of food service.)

B. A Request for Reimbursement (B8, Schedule E) is used by individuals wishing reimbursement for each purchase. A receipt must be attached to the slip.

C. When the petty cash fund begins to run low, the director fills out a Request for Reimbursement form (B8, Schedule E), tallying individual request forms that have been paid.

V. Ledgers

A. After all checks for any one month have been issued, the bookkeeper posts all items to a general ledger, in line with the accounts specified by the director when the Request for Reimbursement (B8, Schedule E) was turned in.

B. A summary of the monthly totals is transferred by the bookkeeper to the Monthly Budget Analysis B9, Schedule F (page 60). These sheets are given to the director as early in each month as possible so that he or she can analyze the state of the budget and make any necessary adjustments.

C. Any adjustments to the budget must be approved by the Executive Committee of the Board (or the owner).

B3

Schedule A

INDIVIDUAL LEDGER SHEETS FOR EACH CHILD

Name: ______________________ Basic tuition: ______________________

Address: ______________________ No. of days per week: ______________________

______________________ Hours: ________ A.M. ______ P.M. ______

Telephone: ______________________ Participation: Yes ________ No ________

Date	Tuition Total	Accommodation Total	Amount Due	Amount Paid	Credit	Balance

B4

Schedule B

CASH JOURNAL

DATE	ITEM	ACCT.	CASH	CHECK	AMOUNT

Schedule C

SALARIED EMPLOYEES' TIME CARD AND PAY REQUEST

Name of employee: ____________________ Salary: ______________________

Date	Period Covered	Salary Deductions	Salary Amount	Federal Tax	State Tax	Unemployment Insurance	Amt. of Check
	(To be completed			(To be completed			
	by director)			by bookkeeper)			

_______________ _____________________

B6

Schedule C-1

TIME CARD FOR HOURLY EMPLOYEES

Name of employee: ___________________________
Social Security No.: ___________________________
Hourly rate: ____________

Date	Arrived	Time Off	Left	Total Regular Hours	Overtime	Total Hours	Amt. Due

Signed: _________________________ (Employee)

Approved: _______________________ (Director)

B7 Schedule D

EXPENDITURES

Date	Item	Check Number	Amount	Account

B8 Schedule E

REQUEST FOR REIMBURSEMENT

(Reimbursements will be made only for receipted items.)

Date	Item	Amount	Check here if receipt is attached.

Requested by ______________________

Paid by ______________________ Date: ____________

Schedule F

MONTHLY BUDGET ANALYSIS

Item	Budgeted Last Year	Budgeted This Year	Year to Date (1st of month)	This Month	Year to Date (end of month)	Balance

B10

Schedule G

ESTIMATED BUDGET REPORT AND ANALYSIS
(Usually prepared in April)

Item (1)	Year (2)	% (3)	Budget (4)	% (5)	Actual to Date (6)	Est. to June 30 (7)	% (8)	Next Year Proposed (9)	% (10)

If this analysis shows that actual costs were over the budgeted amount, reevaluate each item according to the given criteria in the procedural guide and make adjustments for the proposed budget accordingly.

B11 Official Financial Statements

If the Child Care Center records are accurate and complete, then you, the bookkeeper, the treasurer, or an outside accountant can easily prepare monthly financial statements which in turn, will be used to prepare quarterly and annual reports. The principal statements follow:

Profit and Loss

The figures for this statement are taken from the monthly budget analysis (B9, Schedule F).

Profit and Loss Statement for Period __________ to ___________

Income:	Registration fees	$00	
	Tuition	$00	
	Gross income		$00
Expenses:	Expense items	$00	
	Total expenses		$00
	Net income		$00

Balance Sheet

This will summarize assets, liabilities, and net worth for any given period.

Balance Sheet for Period Ending ______________

Current Assets			
Cash on hand	$00		(Cash you have at the center)
Cash in bank	00		(Bank balance)
Accounts receivable	00		(Money owed to the center)
Materials/supplies	00		(Cash value)
(A) Total current assets		$00	
Fixed Assets			
Equipment	$00		(Cash value of investment)
Furniture/fixtures	00		(Cash value of investment)
Less reserve for depreciation	00		(To be taken off for income tax reporting)
(B) Total fixed assets		$00	
(C) Total assets		$00	**(A + B)**
Current Liabilities			
Accounts payable	–$00		(Money center owes)
Long-Term Liabilities			
(if purchasing a building, etc.)	–$00		(Mortgage)
(D) Total liabilities	–$00		
Net worth	$00		**(C – D)**

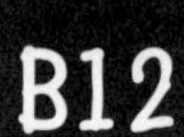

B12 Financial Management

When developing your Community Child Care Center's program budget, you need to ask yourself two key questions. First, who will be responsible for the budget management systems? And second, what will affect the budget?

The Director of the Child Care Center is responsible for budget management. The staff, board members, administration, staff, and parents and caregivers are also responsible. The system must be well-organized and sufficiently understood by all.

Aspects that can affect the budget include staff-child ratios, needs of the children, number of children and their ages, equipment, space, staff training, administrative overhead, salaries, benefits, advertising, and facility maintenance and repair, to name a few. The budget management systems and program design guide the budget-making process.

B13 Start-Up and Operating Budgets

When starting a new center or child care program, or expanding an existing one, you will need to develop two budgets. The first budget is a start-up budget, which will include one-time-only expenses. These types of one-time-only expenses may include permits, licenses, attorney fees, building renovations and repairs, staff recruitment and training, consultant and accountant fees, and any major equipment purchases.

The second budget is your operating budget. This budget covers ongoing income and expenses, such as staff development training, field trips, equipment replacement, capital improvements, marketing and advertising, program supplies, printing, telephone, utilities, and so on. The income for this budget may include parent/caregiver fees, government funding, fund-raising, and special events.

As the director, you must understand the types of expenses and/or costs in your start-up or operating budgets. The following terms are critical to your budget preparation:

1. **Fixed expenses:** These are expenses that remain the same every month. The number of children enrolled does not influence these expenses. Examples of fixed expenses are rent, the director's salary, utilities, and insurance.
2. **Variable expenses**: These expenses vary each month and may depend on the number of children enrolled. Examples of variable expenses are food, program supplies, and staff salaries.
3. **Semi-variable expenses:** These expenses may occur periodically. They are hard to predict because they may be determined by need, such as a van repair, roof replacement, or furniture replacement.
4. **Mixed expenses:** These expenses may have fixed and variable aspects. An example of these expenses may be the telephone, where there is a fixed cost plus an additional cost per call.

B14 Analyzing and Preparing the Annual Budget

Preparing the annual budget is a difficult but important task. Even though you may have excellent advice and professional help from an accountant, you are the one who knows the day-to-day needs of your program and whether or not the previous year's budget was realistic. It will be your task to pinpoint areas in which costs have been rising, areas in which savings might be affected, and areas in which previous allowances have not been adequate.

In the United States, expenses, and thus tuition, seem to be higher in the coastal areas and large urban centers. They run much lower in smaller communities and rural areas. With continuously rising costs, many small proprietary centers find it difficult to maintain high standards. In order to be profitable, pay equitable salaries, and meet the demand for increased services, many such centers have expanded their facilities where space, funds, and licensing regulations permit. Many half-day centers have expanded to full-day operation in order to meet the demand for such services. The additional costs are more than offset by the additional revenue.

Make a very careful analysis of your center's budget each year (B10, Schedule G). In April, have the bookkeeper tally all income and expenses to March 31 (columns 1–6). Then supply the information needed to estimate the amount through June 30 (column 7). The percentages (column 8) are computed on the basis of total income and then compared with the previous two years. Each item is carefully considered, and the amounts needed for next year's budget are then estimated (columns 9 and 10).

Income

The budget of the Community Child Care Center depends on the annual income from tuition and registration fees. Small fund-raising affairs can be held occasionally, but the money raised is used to pay for non-budgeted items or events planned by the parents and caregivers and therefore does not affect the annual budget.

Registration Fees

Charge a yearly registration fee. This fee will encourage parents and caregivers to notify you in advance if they change their plans about sending their child to your center. If they notify you before a specified date, you can refund 75 percent of the fee. In determining how much this fee should be, consider community standards, your reputation, the demand for your services, overall increased costs, and the average turnover of children during the year.

Tuition

The budget analysis [Section B10] for the previous two years may show, as an example, that your costs have been increasing on an average of 5 1/2 to 7 percent per year. There is no reason to expect the coming year to be any different. Therefore, a 7 percent tuition increase is estimated as being in order. Contact other child care centers in the community to learn how many of them are anticipating increases similar to yours. You may find some centers charging as much as 25 percent less than you do and some charging as much as 10 percent more. Upon that basis, consider the following:

1. Community standards
2. Your center's reputation and the demand for your services
3. Expansion of your child care program
4. Overall costs, including salary increases
5. Anticipated total enrollment
6. Number and ages of children enrolled
7. Possible changes in the licensing laws and other regulations that would affect the number of children allowed per child care group or staff member [Section E31]
8. Possible changes in the facilities that would affect the number of children per group or per staff member [Section A9] or that would affect the number of rooms available
9. Special services that you might offer in comparison to those offered by other child care centers

After considering these items, set the new tuition fee. Most child care centers have only two rates, one for half-day and one for full-day care. Give yourself flexibility by charging everyone the same rate for the 9:00 A.M.-to-noon period, and then adding charges according to the times when child care services are needed for each individual. Options are 6:00 to 9:00 A.M., 6:00 A.M. to noon, noon to 5:00 P.M. or 6:00 P.M, evening hours from 5:00 P.M. to 7:00 P.M., or other hourly times appropriate for your center. The more hours used, the lower the hourly rate. You can estimate that your anticipated income from tuition is 97 1/2 percent of your total. This amount, when added to the registration fees, gives you 100 percent of your income.

To calculate tuition income, multiply the number of children in your various categories of enrollment by the tuition for those categories. Add these totals and multiply by the number of program months or weeks you are open. Allow for seasonal losses, if applicable, during the summer.

Allowances Against Income

The figure at which you arrive is not the amount of money that will actually be available for operating expenses. Certain allowances must be planned for to give a true figure of the estimated cash flow that will be available for running the center.

Scholarships

The bylaws of the center [Section A14] may allow you to offer scholarship assistance to low-income families. In determining what allowances to make for scholarships this year, consider

- your projected operating costs
- the economic status of your clients
- the allowance for group participation

With these points in mind, decide to allow 5 percent of the total budget for scholarship assistance.

Sliding Fees

Instead of offering scholarship assistance, which is a direct reduced fee, some programs offer sliding fees. These are based on income. This would involve asking each family who enrolls to fill out a form from which you can determine their financial standing and monthly income. In some states, there are subsidies available to make up the difference in income lost due to low-income persons enrolling their children at a reduced fee. However, these subsidies may be available one year but not another.

If you decide to use a sliding fee schedule, check with the Department of Social Services in your area for income levels to determine your sliding fees schedule proportionately.

Whatever you decide to do with your fees, make a statement to that effect in your center handbook. Make sure that the plan you present is considered equitable to all persons involved.

Less-Than-Capacity Enrollment

Although you may have families waiting for an opening, there can be a lapse between enrollments. Therefore, allow for a 1/2 percent contingency against less-than-capacity enrollment. If you don't have a good plan for summer enrollments [Section E37], you may have to increase this amount, as most centers have big decreases in enrollment during the summer months.

Uncollected Tuition

This is kept to a minimum, because all tuition is payable in advance. However, the possibility must be allowed for. Therefore, set up a reserve of 1/2 percent in the budget to protect yourself from being underbudgeted. Subtracting the total allowances against income from the total estimated income gives you the actual amount of money you have to work with.

Expenses

Salaries and Employee Benefits

By far the most important items in any program budget are salaries and employee benefits. No matter what kind of program you conduct or what philosophy you expound, a center can only be as good as its staff. Salaries should therefore be given as high a place in the total budget as possible. Unfortunately, salaries paid to staff members in many child care centers and preschools are ridiculously low—often minimum wage. Also, some institutions purposely replace staff members each year or two in order to avoid the necessity of giving annual wage increases. Small nonprofit child care centers have the problem of not being able to compete with the high salaries paid by public schools or government-funded programs. Try to compensate for this disadvantage by making working conditions and personnel policies as agreeable as possible [Sections D27, D32, D42]. In preparing the salary schedule for the new budget, review your total salary structure to make sure it takes into account the increase in cost of living. Depending on inflationary factors, the scale can be adjusted for higher or lower increases.

SALARY SCALE

	TRAINEE	ASSIST. CHILD CARE PROVIDER	CHILD CARE PROVIDER	HEAD CHILD CARE PROVIDER	ASSIST. DIRECTOR	DIRECTOR
Step 1	Base Pay	Add 10%	Add 9%	Add 8 1/2%	Add 8%	Add 60%–75%
2	+5%	+5%	+5%	+5%	+5%	+5%
3	+5%	+5%	+5%	+5%	+5%	+5%
4	+6%	+6%	+6%	+6%	+6%	+6%
5	+5%	+5%	+5%	+5%	+5%	+5%
6	+5%	+5%	+5%	+5%	+5%	+5%
7	+5%	+5%	+5%	+5%	+5%	+5%
8	+6%	+6%	+6%	+6%	+6%	+6%

Note that an extra one percent increase is allowed every fourth year, as a bonus for increased skills. These percentages are based on the current rate of cost-of-living increases. They can be adjusted from time to time to keep pace with changes that may occur in cost-of-living percentages. Annual increases may be greater if warranted, but they may not be lowered.

This salary schedule enables you to write into the budget the minimum and maximum salaries for your center, within which range considerable flexibility can be allowed. As a nonprofit child care center, you can allow 60 percent of your gross income for salaries. A proprietary child care center in similar circumstances would probably be able to allow only between 30 and 45 percent of its gross income. Programs funded with public money usually budget between 70 to 80 percent of their yearly income for salaries. If funded by private and foundation grants, it may vary from 40 to 70 percent.

Nonprofit private programs can rarely allow more than 60 percent for salaries unless they have free housing for their child care center. Those with free housing sometimes allow as much as 75 percent. However, the tuition in such centers is generally much lower than in centers that have to pay for housing, so the total amount available for salaries is not necessarily greater.

If you have more than two or three employees, pay scales will become complicated unless appropriately charted. The form on page 67 can help you in working out your own charts. Even if your employees are paid on a monthly, rather than an hourly basis, it is a good idea to note approximately what the salary breaks down to per hour, using as a base the number of hours that a child care provider is required to be on the job, not including voluntary early or late hours, staff meetings, training sessions, and other center-related activities. The director's salary can usually not be broken into an hourly estimate, since administrative duties may frequently carry far over the minimum estimate.

STEP		AIDE	ASSISTANT CHILD CARE PROVIDER	CHILD CARE PROVIDER	ASSISTANT DIRECTOR OR HEAD CHILD CARE PROVIDER	DIRECTOR
1 Minimum Starting Salary	MONTH					
	HOUR					
2	MONTH					
	HOUR					
3	MONTH					
	HOUR					
4	MONTH					
	HOUR					
5	MONTH					
	HOUR					
6	MONTH					
	HOUR					
7	MONTH					
	HOUR					

Salaries are based on a nine- or twelve-month program year, depending on whether the employee works during the summer. The staff may receive full pay for center holidays or vacations. In determining your final figures for the estimated budget, take the following factors into consideration:

1. Have there been changes in the regulatory laws that would require us to change our current staffing pattern [Section A9]?
2. For what salary increases are the child care providers eligible, according to the established salary scale and personnel policy of the center [Section D27]?
3. Are those increases a predetermined annual amount [Section D27], or do they take into consideration the total budget, rising costs of living and center operation, and the professional growth of the staff member involved?
4. Has the salary scale been revised to allow for cost-of-living and minimum wage increases since the scale was established?
5. Have any fringe benefits been added to the program that will increase the amount to be budgeted for personnel costs?
6. Have you estimated the maximum number of days that you may need a substitute, rather than the minimum number of days [Section D32]?
7. Have you compared your salary scale with those prevalent in your community?
8. Have you remained flexible, realizing that new personnel can be started above the first step if exceptionally qualified and that special circumstances may warrant a child care provider a two-step raise during any particular year, because of special contributions by that person to the total staffing pattern?

Child Care Assistants

In considering the salaries for your staff, parents and caregivers who serve as child care assistants are a very important factor [Section F12]. Utilizing parent or caregiver assistants (whom you can call "Participating Parents and Caregivers") in some rooms can help you from having to hire additional employees. Two child care assistants per day receive tuition credit totaling only a little more than what it would cost to hire one assistant child care provider.

Inflation

Inflation can bring your tuition rates close to the maximum for your area. Yet, the same inflation makes it necessary to continue raising salaries. In order to raise money for operating expenses, some centers have to increase their enrollments if they have the space. Small centers may have increasingly larger problems, and many will have to close. This is unfortunate, because small centers are good for children.

This Year's Salary Budget

In view of all of these considerations, figure the salaries that you need to pay this coming year to the following staff:

Director
Assistant Director (8th year)
Head Child Care Provider (7th year)
Child Care Provider 2 (10th year)
Child Care Provider 3 (4th year)
Child Care Provider 6 (1st year)
Child Care Provider 4 (9th year)
Child Care Provider 5 (2nd year)
Assistant 1 (2nd year)
Assistant 2 (1/2 year)
Secretary (3rd year)
Bookkeeper (6th year)
Allowance for substitutes, additional child care staff

Total salaries..	$00	56%
Allowance for Social Security (7.09%) of total salaries	00	4%
Allowance for participating parents and caregivers	00	4%
This is a total of	$00	65%

This amounts to approximately 65 percent of your estimated cash income. See the sample form on page 69 for how to record salaries for a given year.

SALARIES FOR THE __________ PROGRAM YEAR

	STEP THIS YEAR	MONTHLY	YEARLY	PERCENT INCREASE
Director		$	$	
Administrative Assistant				
Assistant Director				
Head Child Care Provider 1				
Head Child Care Provider 2				
Child Care Provider				
Child Care Provider				
Associate Child Care Provider				
Assistant Child Care Provider 1				
Assistant Child Care Provider 2				
Secretary				
Bookkeeper				
Other				
Totals				

Housing

The next major item on a budget is the cost of housing, which includes utilities and janitorial services. If your center is located in a building owned by a local nonprofit organization, you may want to take these questions into consideration:

- Have there been any changes in city, county, or state regulations in regard to the building that may cost money to comply with [Section A8]?
- Have there been any increases in enrollment that will require the use of additional space [Section C10]?
- Have there been any changes in the services provided by the center that will require the use of additional space or a change in the length of time each week that the space will be used?
- Will any major renovations be necessary [Section C23]?

Utilities

Utilities, which are included in overall housing costs, include gas, electricity, and water. Approximately 3 to 5 percent of the total budget is generally needed to take care of these items. Because heating and cooling equipment is expensive to operate, you may have high electric bills, which require you to budget 4 percent of your income for utilities. In estimating the 4 percent utility cost for your center, consider two very important points:

1. Whether or not any rate increase can be anticipated
2. Whether or not changes in hours or other factors will cause the amount of electricity needed to change

Custodial Services

Maintenance, too, is included in your overall housing costs. This covers janitors' salaries, cleaning supplies and equipment, and related costs. In determining what share of the maintenance expense should be allocated to the center, consider the following:

- Have there been any changes in the amount of space used that will affect the amount of time it takes the custodian to do the work [Sections C26]?
- Have there been any changes in the type of floor coverings, painted surfaces, and other materials in the furnishings and equipment that may affect the type and frequency of work to be performed [Section C10]?
- Have there been any changes in the center's services (hours, types of activities, parent/caregiver meetings, food services, and so on) that may affect the amount of custodial work required and the hours when that work will be done?
- Has there been any increase in the number of people using the center or the building that may affect these costs?
- Have there been any changes in licensing regulations that may affect the types and amounts of custodial services required?

After considering these items, the amount allowed for housing costs breaks down as follows:

Use of space ....10% of income

Utilities ....4% of income

Custodial services (four hours daily) ....1% of income

One final factor must be considered in budgeting this amount: You must have a clear, written understanding with the sponsoring organization as to what services are and are not included in the housing fees [Section A8].

Telephone Service

This once was a fairly stable item. However, deregulation has caused costs to rise sharply. Consider the following possibilities when making up each year's budget:

- Have there been any changes in the number of outlets, anticipated usage, or location of telephones that may affect the new budget?
- Have you checked with the Public Utilities Commission or the telephone company to find out what rate increases are anticipated during the coming year?
- Have you considered how many long-distance calls you may need to make throughout the year? If that amount is considerable, you may want to check out the different long-distance carriers available.
- Have you discussed the possibility of additional listings in the telephone book?
- Have you considered the possibility of supplementing newspaper ads with an ad in the telephone book [Section E3]?

Supplies

Divide your supplies into three separate categories:

- Administrative
- Food services
- Child care rooms

Administrative Supplies. These supplies include letter-writing materials, typing supplies, computer supplies and paper, paper for record keeping and general office use, copy machine supplies, envelopes, postage, and any items that are needed for maintenance of office equipment. In estimating the amount needed for your new budget, consider postal rates, the rising cost of paper products, computer program updates, and the fact that you may do a lot in the way of communicating with parents and caregivers, which means more letters and news bulletins [Sections F2, F36].

Food Service Supplies. In addition to lunches and breakfasts for some children, the center provides a mid-morning snack each day for all children. It usually consists of fruit juice and crackers or some kind of fruit or vegetable. This item also includes refreshments for the parent/caregiver room, the staff's breaks, and various center functions and public-relations events. To save money, you may want to arrange with two other centers to buy some items in bulk, which enables you to buy them at a lower rate. Groceries are budgeted at 7 1/2 percent of the total [Part K]. Child care centers and preschools utilize the U.S. Government Child Care Food Program for a substantial saving of money [Section K20].

Child Care Room Supplies. Careful planning in this area can result in substantial savings. Nationwide figures seem to indicate that budgets for early childhood supplies range from 4 to 8 percent. In an effort to save in this area, many child care centers skimp on the materials available for use by the children. By using many free and inexpensive materials to supplement traditional commercial materials, a considerable savings can be effected without skimping. Before setting a figure for room supplies, consider these questions:

- Have you carefully inventoried current supplies in order to evaluate future needs?
- Have you done comparison shopping by studying catalogs, reviewing displays at commercial exhibits, and making personal visits to supply houses to evaluate your purchasing patterns and consider possible changes?
- Have you compared local resources with other child care center directors in your area?
- Do you cooperate with other child care centers in making bulk purchases?
- Have you checked your old supplies to find out why they haven't been used and to encourage their use if there was no valid reason for not using them?

After making allowances for all estimated needs for the coming year, you should have a total of 3 1/2 percent of your estimated income to be used for child care room and administrative supplies, and 7 1/2 percent for groceries, making a total of 11 percent.

Equipment

Allow 3 percent of your income for equipment needs. This covers the cost of new equipment as well as the cost of maintaining and repairing what you already have. In figuring these needs, take the following steps:

1. List all the probable repairs you are aware of as well as the cost of replacing items that are either beyond repair or would be less expensive to replace than to repair [Section C23].
2. Check with your favorite repair workers [Section C22] to find out if their services are still available and if their rates have changed.
3. Consider the quality of an item as being more important than quantity.

4. Check with supply houses that handle used equipment before budgeting for a piece of new equipment.
5. Compare the prices of various suppliers.
6. Include possible shipping costs.
7. Consider having your own equipment made rather than buying it from a retailer.
8. List those items that you plan to purchase to add to what you already have rather than replacing old items [Section C23].

All items budgeted thus far use up 94 percent of the total cash available. This leaves 6 percent to be divided among the remaining five items in your budget: bus trips, public relations, professional activities, insurance, and miscellaneous. In allocating funds for these amounts, compare the figures in the budget analysis [Section B10] and consider the following points:

Public Relations, Advertising, and Family-Center Relationships

- Have you carefully considered the "hidden costs" of parent/caregiver education programs and public-relations events that you sponsor [Sections F10, F27, F36; Part J]? Of family involvement plans [Section F28]?
- Have you considered paper costs and advertising rates in considering amounts needed for advertising [Section E3]?
- Have you considered the costs related to community services provided by you, your staff, and your center [Part J]?

Professional Growth, Conferences, Publications, Conventions, Dues, Courses, and Related Activities

- Have you considered the costs of college and university courses in planning for paying a portion of these costs for staff members [Sections D27, D58–61]?
- Have you made up a master calendar so that you know which national or regional events you plan to attend and make budgetary allowances for [Section A21]?
- Have you included funds for staff members to attend some of these events, too?

Bus Trips [Section I15]

- Have you checked with the bus companies to see if a rate increase is anticipated?
- Have you evaluated with your staff which trips you have taken in the past that you may want to repeat and those which you will probably replace with others [Section I14]?
- Have you considered saving by reducing the number of planned bus trips and replacing them in some instances with trips in which the parents and caregivers provide automobile transportation [Section I17]?

Insurance

Rely on your insurance agent to supply you with the figures you need each year. The cost of insurance premiums used to come to about 1 1/2 percent of your total income. If you anticipate big increases in your premiums, especially for liability insurance [Section A10], you may want to consider adding a monthly "insurance fee" to each child's tuition bill.

Miscellaneous

Budget some money for unanticipated expenses. This allows more flexibility in the total budget and sometimes prevents having to transfer funds from one item to another. Careful management also avoids the necessity of using the tuition loss and enrollment loss items allowed against income, thereby adding to the total income over expenditures. This money can be used for minimizing future tuition increases and capital improvements. Budget 1/2 percent of your total income for miscellaneous items.

SAMPLE BUDGETS

PROPOSED BUDGET FOR ____________ FISCAL YEAR

Income				***Approximate %***
Registration fees	$ 3,000			2 1/2
Tuition, program term	99,700			75
**Tuition, summer term	27,300	$130,000		22 1/2
Less allowances:				
Enrollment loss	$ 450			
Uncollected tuition	450			
*Scholarships	4,100	5,000		
Total		$125,000		100%
Expenses				
*Personnel:				
Salaries and hourly pay	$ 70,500			
Social Security	5,600			
Credit for parent/caregiver participation	5,150	81,250		65
Housing (including custodial services and utilities)		18,750		15
Supplies:				
Food and other grocery items	$ 9,375		7 1/2 %	
Administrative and child care room supplies	4,375	13,750	3 1/2 %	11
Equipment:				
Repairs	$ 1,250		1 %	
Replacements	2,500	3,750	2 %	3
Telephone		1,250		1
Insurance		2,500		2
Public relations and advertising		1,250		1
Bus trips		625		1/2
*Professional advancement: conferences, courses, dues, books, journals, and so on		1,250		1
Miscellaneous		625		1/2
		$125,000		100%

** A proprietary center could build up its summer program through a day camp service or a big advertising campaign if it needs the same income during the summer term as during the rest of the year. The Community Child Care Center runs its summer term to accommodate its clientele, not to increase its income.

* A proprietary center would draw its profits for the owner from lower percentages for these items. Scholarships would probably be eliminated.

The following is an actual start-up budget for a nonprofit child care center for deprived and abused children in a low-income area.

Building & Grounds			
Renovation of building	$100,000		
Playground, inc. block wall	10,000		
Interior furnishing & equipment	10,000	$120,000	40%
Operating Expenses			
Staff Salaries & Costs			
Administration & supervision (2)	30,000		
Supervising child care providers (4)	36,720		
Aides & assistant child care providers (7)	33,280		
Support staff (3)	10,000		
	110,000		
Payroll taxes & fringe benefits	15,000	125,000	42%
Facilities & Administration			
Rent & utilities	24,000		
Telephones	1,600		
Office expenses	800	26,400	9%
Supplies			
Child care room supplies, initial outlay	3,000		
Consumable supplies	2,000		
Nutrition	1,000	6,000	2%
Consultant Services			
** Fund-raising consultant	5,000		
Program consultant (inc. staff training)	2,000	7,000	2%
Other			
Professional growth	600		
Travel	400		
Liability & fire insurance	5,600		
Medical insurance (accidents, staff, children)	400	7,000	2%
Contingency		8,600	3%
TOTAL		$300,000*	100%

* Funds needed from grants, state, and other sources in order to open and operate program for first six months.
** This task will later be taken over by executive director, following a training period.

The following is an actual budget for a child care center licensed for 32 children. This is for a private, for-profit center.

Gross income	$65,000	
Less allowances	1,800	
Net income	63,200	100% cash flow
Annual expenses		
Payroll	14,172	25 %
Housing (mortgage)	16,000	25 %
Supplies	632	1 %
Food	4,500	7 %
Maintenance & repair	2,000	3 %
Telephone	300	1/2%
Utilities	1,000	1 1/2%
Advertising	650	1 %
Accounting & legal	300	1/2%
Insurance	2,000	3 %
	41,554	67 1/2%
Net Profit	$21,646	32 1/2%

Note that 25% of the expenses is actually a capital outlay. It goes toward paying off mortgage.

Note also that only 25% is used for salaries. The owners do much of the work. The net profit becomes their pay.

This is an actual budget of a privately owned child care center licensed for 70 children.

Income	$114,000	
Expenses		
Payroll & payroll taxes	45,000	39.0%
Housing (mortgage payments)	24,000	21.0%
Supplies, child care room	1,500	1.0%
Supplies, food	4,500	4.0%
Office expense	1,000	1.0%
Maintenance & repairs	3,420	3.0%
Telephone	300	0.2%
Insurance	4,500	4.0%
Advertising	2,300	2.0%
Property taxes	1,000	0.8%
Accounting & legal	1,800	1.5%
Professional growth	150	0.1%
	$ 89,470	77.6%
Net Profit	$ 24,530	22.4%

This center allows a higher percentage for payroll than the one with just 32 children. The carefully worked-out budget allows the owners to have a net profit of almost 23%.

B15 Approval of the Budget

After you have made up the budget, your next step is to present it to the Board of Directors for approval. If you have prepared a sound proposal, you will probably be able to get immediate approval from the board. You must be prepared to justify every request and explain why no item should be reduced.

If you raise the tuition, you must make appropriate changes in the Parent/Caregiver Handbook and any other materials in which the fees are stated. Because of the high costs of printing, do not print fees in your brochure; but rather, write in the current tuition rates by hand when you give it to parents and caregivers or add a one-page tuition fact sheet to the brochure. You must also notify parents and caregivers of tuition increases.

B16 Break-Even Analysis

The break-even analysis allows you to identify how you should price your program and how many children you must have in order to break even before your income and expenditures balance. To determine the break-even point, you must first calculate all your expenditures into the three categories of *fixed, variable,* and *semi-variable expenses.* You can determine the break-even point by using the following formulas:

C = number of children

E = enrollment fee per child

FE = fixed expense

VE = variable expense

SV = semi-variable expense

Example 1: Your child care fee at the Community Child Care Center is $90 a week for full-time care. You would like to determine how many children you will need to break even. You have calculated that over a year's time, the fee for one child would be $4,680. Follow the break-even analysis budget example, using $308,100 for fixed, variable and semi-variable expenses.

The calculation formula for this example is

C x $4,680 = $308,100

C = $308,100 ÷ $4,680

C = 66 children needed to break even

Example 2: Your licensed capacity is 75 children. You want to know your break-even point for maximum enrollment. Use the example $308,100 for fixed, variable, and semi-variable expenses. You have determined that your fixed expense is $97,000, your variable expense $206,100, and your semi-variable $5,000.

You would use the following formula:

$$CE = FE + VE + SV$$

(This example assumes that your income is strictly from enrollment fees. When you have additional types of income, subtract that income from the total expenses.) The calculation formula for this example is

$$75E = 97{,}000 + 206{,}100 + 5{,}000$$
$$75E = \$308{,}100$$
$$E = \$308{,}100 \div 75$$
$$E = \$4{,}108 \text{ per year, per child to break even}$$

Sample Community Child Care Center Break-Even Analysis

EXPENSES	Total Expense	Fixed Expense	Variable Expense	Semi-variable Expense
Staffing				
Salaries: managers/director	$ 30,000	$ 30,000	$ 0	$ 0
Staff, child care providers, aides	120,000	10,000	110,000	0
Payroll taxes and insurance	15,000	3,000	12,000	0
Training and education	5,000	0	5,000	0
Program				
Activities expenses	4,000	0	4,000	0
Child care provider supplies	3,000	0	3,000	0
Program supplies	12,000	0	12,000	0
Food Service				
Snacks and lunches	24,000	0	24,000	0
Kitchen supplies	3,000	0	3,000	0
Facility				
Rent	36,000	36,000	0	0
Utilities	4,000	2,000	2,000	0
Custodial, maintenance, and repair	12,000	2,000	5,000	5,000
Property taxes and insurance	3,000	3,000	0	0
Depreciation	5,000	5,000	0	0
Administration				
Accounting/legal fees	5,000	2,000	3,000	0
Office supplies	6,000	0	6,000	0
Telephone	2,000	1,000	1,000	0
Equipment rental/lease	1,000	0	1,000	0
Contributions	500	0	500	0
Insurance-liability	7,000	1,000	6,000	0
Dues/subscriptions	500	0	500	0
Licenses/taxes	1,000	0	1,000	0
Travel	900	0	900	0
Bad debt	1,200	0	1,200	0
Miscellaneous	3,000	0	3,000	0
Public Relations/Advertising	4,000	2,000	2,000	0
TOTAL EXPENSES	$308,100	97,000	206,100	5,000

Licensed capacity: 75	Actual revenue:	$310,000
Weekly fee: $90	Revenue capacity:	$351,000
	Operating expense:	$308,100

B17 Fee Increase Letter

Community Child Care Center

111 THIRD STREET TELEPHONE 123-4579

Dear Parents and Caregivers,

It has always been our goal to keep our tuition rate as low as possible. In order to keep pace with the continuously rising costs of maintaining the excellence of the program to which we are committed, we have spent many weeks analyzing our expenditures in relation to income and enrollment. We have determined that the following increased rates will enable us to continue our program without lessening our services to you and your child. Please note that we have built in flexibility to meet the varying needs of our clientele. If you have different needs, please talk with me about special arrangements. These rates will be in effect for the forthcoming program year:

Registration fee, new children: $00 Registration fee, returning children: $00

Days per Week	Child Care [Full Day]	6–9 A.M.	9–12 P.M.	12–5/6 P.M.	Evening Hours (5–7 P.M.)	Your Total
	Tuition					
2	$00	$00	$00	$00	$00	________
3	$00	$00	$00	$00	$00	________
4	$00	$00	$00	$00	$00	________
5	$00	$00	$00	$00	$00	________

Credit for child care assistance: $00 for each three hours of service. Please check with me for a reduction in tuition and fees when there is more than one child enrolled at the same time.

We do not want these increases to discourage your continued support of our program. If the new rates present a hardship to you, please discuss the matter with me so that we can give consideration to your participation in available scholarship programs.

Sincerely,

Director
Community Child Care Center

B18 Purchase Order Forms

It is the director's responsibility to purchase, or plan for the purchase of items needed for the successful and practical operation of the center. You can use the following form for this purpose. Prepare it in duplicate, sending one copy to the supplier and keeping one copy in your files. Use a purchase order number to help you check on shipments and payments.

PURCHASE ORDER

To: ______________________________

____

____

____________ State ______ Zip ______

From: Community Child Care Center
111 Third Street
Any Town, USA
Telephone 123-4579

Date of order: ______________________

Purchase order #: ____________________

Ordered by: _________________________

____

(signature)

Ship via:

____

When needed:

____

Please ship the following items:

Quantity	Catalog No.	Item (Description)	Each Unit Total

B19 Equipment Records

Part of your control of the budget will be related to the records you keep of equipment purchases, the upkeep of that equipment, and the repair and maintenance costs involved. Use an Equipment Inventory Record Form [Section C24] for this purpose. As soon as the item is received, all pertinent data are entered on the card and additional entries made when appropriate.

B20 Fund-Raising

Grants from Private Foundations and Corporations

Some nonprofit organizations have done extremely well in fund-raising activities by writing for and receiving grants from private foundations and corporations. Your public library can provide you with books that list the names of such organizations that award grants and the types of grants they give. Some are very specific; others are broader in nature. There are also books available that give suggestions on grant writing.

In applying for a grant, remember these important points:

1. Do careful research.
   a. Find out the usual amounts granted by the organization to which you are applying. Keep your own requests within these amounts.
   b. Find out the types of institutions for which each organization seems to show preference. Limit your request to those in whose category you seem to fall.
2. It may pay, in the long run, to hire an experienced grant writer to complete your applications.
3. Meet all deadlines. Do not ask for extensions.

There are some grants available to for-profit organizations through awards to individuals for an explicit research or study project within the center. These may be found listed in various grant publications.

Regardless of whether you are applying for a $500 grant or for $5000 or more, there are some basic guidelines to follow:

Purpose of organization: Be sure you state in very specific terms the purpose of your organization and the population it serves.

Need: Include a statement as to why an organization such as yours is needed, and whether or not there are other organizations that meet these same needs.

Goals: Be very specific in outlining your goals, highlighting the most important ones by listing them first, and following these up with subsidiary goals. These goals should be very explicit.

Methods: This entails a complete description of your program, specifically noting how each listed goal is being met.

Evaluation: Outline the method you will use to provide an ongoing evaluation of meeting your goals.

Budget: Include a very specific, but abbreviated budget. Think in terms of "at-a-glance" understanding.

Supplemental information: Include any other information that you think may stimulate the interest of the reader, and that will supplement the needs and goals you have stated.

You will probably be competing with many other proposals requesting similar grants. Be sure your presentation is neat, attractive, and in some way eye-catching.

School Events and Projects

It is common practice for many centers, especially nonprofit organizations, to put on an event or conduct a special project in order to raise funds for the center. When doing this, be sure that you earmark the funds to be raised for a specific cause, such as new playground equipment, scholarship assistance, new books, and so on. Some types of events that you may be interested in sponsoring include

- spaghetti dinner
- pancake breakfast
- wine and cheese party
- bingo party
- white elephant sale
- art auction (get a print gallery to sponsor)
- cake sale (a different child care group can conduct this each month)
- coffee and doughnut sale (weekly, semi-monthly, or monthly) for parents and caregivers on their way to work
- children's fashion show (get a local clothing store to help)
- gift wrap sale (tissue paper, designs stamped on by children; can be made in seasonal designs, sold year-round)
- sale of holiday decorations and ornaments
- children's art show
- children's magic show
- children's puppet show
- costume jewelry auction (families can donate costume jewelry)

Raffles

Raffles are always a good source of fund-raising. If you have an electronic item donated (television, VCR, stereo), you can have tickets printed at a nominal cost and realize a good profit on the activity. You can purchase the item(s) to be raffled, deducting the cost from the first tickets sold, and still realize a good profit, providing you get the cooperation of all of your center families in selling tickets for you.

Art or Play Kits

Paint shoeboxes and assemble children's kits, which parents, caregivers, and the general public can buy for gifts. An art kit might consist of small scissors, a bottle of white glue or a glue stick, assorted items for making collages, a box of semi-moist watercolors with a good brush, a few sheets of quality watercolor paper, and an instruction sheet for use of the materials. These kits can be made smaller or larger, according to prices being asked.

Art kits can also include crayons, colored pencils and chalk, a paper punch, a stapler, and a variety of paper.

Play kits can include cars, dolls, sewing materials, carpentry tools, or similar items.

Ad Book

For any event you have at the center, you can publish an ad book to give to everyone who attends. If you expect 300 people at an event, you might solicit ads from local merchants to include on the program, thus adding to the income for that event.

You can also make the ad book the "event." Put together a book of recipes, perhaps "Ideas for Children's Lunches." Solicit ads from local merchants to include in the booklet, thus covering the cost of printing the booklet, with additional profit as well.

If you have a parent/caregiver group in connection with your center, that group will often take over your fund-raising projects and give you many new ideas as well.

B21 Director's Income Tax

As director of a Child Care Center, you may be justified in taking certain business deductions when you pay federal and state income taxes. If you are also the owner of the center, you may also take the deductions allowed for any operator of a private business. However, if the center is a nonprofit institution, and thus not taxable, the director must determine allowable deductions on a personal basis. This is done in accordance to the amount and type of responsibilities connected with the job. Some deductions that might be allowed, depending on your particular circumstances, are listed below.

Automobile Expenses

If you use your own automobile for Child Care Center business such as shopping, attending conferences, visiting homes, and related activities, you can deduct the applicable portion of your car expenses. The best way to calculate this is to keep a record of business mileage—every mile adds up.

Conferences

Record all expenses related to attending educational conferences. You may deduct your travel costs, lodging, food, and any other related expenses, provided that you are not reimbursed by your center. Keep all of your receipts in case you are ever asked to provide proof of the expenditures involved.

Education

You may deduct all expenses connected with attending classes at a college or university, provided the classes are directly related to professional growth within the field of early childhood education and child care and not preparing you for a new profession. Allowable expenses include tuition, books and other supplies, and any related travel costs. As in other activities, keep receipts and mileage records.

Entertainment

Do you ever take your staff or visitors to the center out to lunch or breakfast? Do you sometimes pay for the refreshments for a staff meeting or center event? Any such unreimbursed expenses may be deducted as a job expense. Be sure to check with the current tax law, as given in the IRS guide sent to you each year, for the percentage of a business meal that can be deducted. Keep track of where you went, with whom, on what date, and how much you spent.

Gifts

Any money that you spend on gifts for your staff or anyone else in connection with your job is deductible.

Professional Organizations

You may deduct membership fees and other expenses incurred in belonging to a professional organization, provided that such expenses are not paid by the center.

Publications

You may deduct the money that you spend for books, magazines, and professional journals if they are related to your work. Publications for which the center pays are not deductible.

Supplies

Keep track of any supplies that you furnish to the center for which you are not reimbursed. This expense may be deducted.

Telephone

Many directors of half-day programs must depend on their home telephone for much of their family-center communication. If that is your situation, deduct a percentage of your telephone bill as a business expense. It is unlikely, however, that you will be able to justify such an expense for an all-day program.

Your accountant will advise you on other deductions. Some directors of half-day programs may also deduct home office expenses, if they maintain an office at home or hold conferences, staff meetings, or board meetings in their homes.

Keep records and save all receipts. Keep a record of all Child Care Center business done outside of center hours and away from the center's property. These are legal deductions—but the burden of proof of the actual expense is on you. The first time you take these deductions, you might ask the advice of an accountant, even if you customarily prepare your tax return yourself. In subsequent years, you can follow the format that your accountant advised.

When you file your income tax forms, you must provide a justification similar to the letter on page 85.

Community Child Care Center

111 THIRD STREET TELEPHONE 123-4579

To Whom It May Concern:

I am the director of a child care center that enrolls 110 children and meets five days a week, twelve months a year, from 7:00 A.M. until 6:00 P.M. The staff includes nine professional child care providers and four daily volunteer assistants, plus a secretary. Students from nearby colleges also participate in the program. My responsibilities include

- all purchasing. This frequently involves traveling to nearby communities.
- arranging for all repairs and replacements of furnishings and equipment, indoors and out; maintaining the building and grounds area and the storage facilities.
- entertaining and guiding visitors at the center, sometimes taking them to lunch.
- planning and conducting weekly staff meetings and conducting biweekly in-service training programs, sometimes in my home.
- maintaining center records and reports, usually using home office space and personal computer for this purpose.
- planning and conducting family education programs.
- planning and conducting public relations activities.
- meeting with various supervisorial and community groups.
- maintaining an active role in professional organizations.

Sincerely,

Director
Community Child Care Center

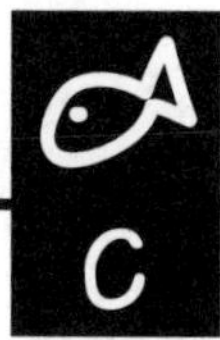

C

Space and Equipment

1 Playground Facilities
2 Outdoor Play Centers
3 Purchasing Outdoor Equipment
4 Wheel Toys
5 Evaluation of Playground Equipment
6 Plants and Shrubs
7 Trees
8 Playground Surfaces and Safety Tips
9 Sandboxes
10 Indoor Child Care Space
11 Interest Centers
12 Lunchroom and Napping Space
13 Director's Office
14 Isolation Center
15 Child Care Providers' Supply Cupboards
16 Storage or Supply Room
17 Paper Supply
18 Inventory List for Office Supplies
19 General Maintenance Supply List
20 Repair Workshop List
21 Garden Tool List
22 Finding Maintenance and Repair Help
23 Replacement and Repair Recommendations List
24 Equipment Inventory and Maintenance Records
25 Extermination Service
26 Housekeeping Schedule

When creating outdoor space for your Community Child Care Center, you must adhere to guidelines based on the state licensing requirements [Section A9]. You must also consider the following criteria:

> *To create a setting in which children will find warmth, comfort, and gentleness: an abundance of opportunities for movement, exploration, and self-discovery according to needs, interests, and abilities; and an overall atmosphere of helpfulness. To create, further, a setting in which the adults are involved and in which they can find support for their involvement.*

Your responsibility as director is that of a stage manager to see that the sets are in order, that the space is well utilized, that the materials and equipment are on hand and appropriately located, and that health, safety, and aesthetic factors are given consideration. I think you will find the evaluations in Sections C1 and C10 to be of use in the successful management of both indoor and outdoor space.

C1 Playground Facilities

1. Space and Location

   Usually, you will not have much choice in determining the size and location of your playground. However, by considering the following items, you should be able to make the most effective use of your facilities.

   a. Is the playground adjacent to and level with the indoor space?

   This is important for ease in supervision, independence of the child, and attractiveness of the center.

   Not adjacent ______ Fairly close ______ Close ______ Adjacent ______

   b. If the playground is not adjacent, can your staff supervise children effectively on their way to and from the playground and still allow the children to have a certain amount of independent movement?

   Moving between the child care room and the playground can give children an opportunity to learn more about space, distance, timing, and independence.

   No _____ Difficult ______ Adequate ______ Excellent ______

   c. Is the playground located on the south or southwest side of the building?

   In placing materials and equipment, consider the changing pattern of shade. The south will have both morning and afternoon sun. Some of the equipment should be movable. Metal play equipment, especially slides, can get too hot to use in warm weather unless they are located in partial shade.

   No sun _______ A little sun _______ Half-sunny _______

   Morning and afternoon sun with a few shady areas _______
   Sun with many shade areas _______

   d. Do you have at least 75 square feet of play area per child (maximum daily attendance) after deducting the space taken up by equipment?

   The law in most states requires a minimum of 75 square feet of playground area for each child.

   Less than legal minimum _______ Have been granted a variance _______

   Legal minimum _______ More than legal minimum _______

2. Surface

   Is there a variety of ground surfaces for different types of activities [Section C8]?

   It is imperative that you have soft surfaces under the fixed climbing and swinging equipment. There should be smoother flat surfaces for running and building. There should also be a small area with plants for either playing on or looking at.

   All the same _______ Two varieties _______ Three varieties _______ Four or more _______

3. Use of Available Space

   a. Is the equipment arranged in a way that leaves open spaces for running, building, and playing with wheel toys?

   Equipment can be placed around the borders of those parts of the yard that do not have fences that children can climb over. Or, equipment can be grouped in "activity areas" to allow for more efficient use of space and safe supervision. For example, all climbing equipment can be placed in one general area.

   Randomly placed _______ Adequate _______ Carefully located _______

   b. Is the equipment arranged in a way that ensures maximum safety?

   No _______ Yes _______

   Are the swings isolated?

   No _______ Somewhat _______ Yes _______

   Is equipment located where it can be supervised easily?

   No _______ Somewhat _______ Yes _______

   c. Is there a special area for wheel toys?

   If you have a special place for children to use wheel toys, those who are not using them can play safely without fear of getting knocked down or injured. Consider roping off a part of the parking lot or having an occasional bike parade around the block. If space is too limited, do not have wheel toys, or have only two or three pieces.

   No designated area ______ Designated area ______ Separate area ______

   d. Do you have traffic lanes (with curves) for wheel toys?

   These help children add some purpose to their use of the wheel toys, to make plans, and to keep from going off in all directions. Traffic lanes keep children from being a possible danger to themselves and others and prevent them from annoying other people.

   No ______ Yes ______

   e. Is there a box for sand play that takes into consideration the recommendations in Section C9?

   None ______ Poor ______ Adequate ______ Excellent ______

   f. Do you have facilities for water play?

   These can include faucets, hoses, washtubs, water-play toys, and mudholes. Small plastic wading pools or large plastic washtubs, which can be emptied when not in use, can be used for floating objects.

   None ______ Fair ______ Good ______ Excellent ______

g. Is there an area for digging in the dirt, for making holes and hills?

It should be near to but not adjacent to the areas for playing with sand and water. Digging in dirt presents different kinds of problems to solve than ones encountered while playing in sand. The dirt-digging area should be away from foot traffic and running places so that holes do not create a hazard. It might be fenced off by a border or markers. A rope strung between two posts would also help keep children from running into holes. Sometimes the digging area can be completely separate from the rest of the playground to allow it to expand into as much space as needed. If it is in the playground proper, it might be best to locate it fairly close to the sandbox. The sand overflow makes the dirt a little easier to work. Tools can be shared for use in both the sand and dirt. But conversely, the dirt area should not be right next to the sand area because you do not want the sand to be mixed with dirt.

None ______ Fair ______ Good ______ Excellent ______

h. Do you have a place to plant flowers and vegetables?

It should be in an area that is protected from wheel toys and running feet, but accessible to water. If water is not easily accessible, watering cans are excellent equipment for any playground.

None ______ Fair ______ Good ______ Excellent ______

i. Is there an outdoor area for keeping small animals?

Cages should be sturdy, roomy, and easy to keep clean. Sawdust on the bottom of the cage is easy to change. (You can get sawdust free or inexpensively from a lumber company.) It is desirable to have cages of at least two different sizes, and preferably three, to accommodate various sizes of animals. They should be located in a place where they can be protected from inclement weather.

None ______ One ______ Two ______ Three ______

j. Do you have adequate, accessible, and functional storage space for keeping movable equipment when it is not being used?

A separate storage shed can serve as a windbreak and provide shade. Such structures are less expensive to build if they are attached to an existing building. An ideal storage area would be a long closet accessible from both indoors and out-, with roll-up fronts to permit easy access, good lighting, and good ventilation. Children can play in the storage areas when equipment has been taken out. Such an area can be used as a workshop with pipes, pulleys, and other equipment attached to one wall. It could also be a separate little area with a non-working stove and sink for quiet "cooking" activities. Storage sheds can be built to look like playhouses from the outside, which will make the playground look more attractive.

Yes ______ No ______

k. Is there a play shelter, such as a climbing platform, small overhang, or garden corner, that can provide a child or two with semi-privacy, if desired?

Yes ______ No ______

4. Are the fence and gate childproof and vandalism-proof?

   If the playground is located near a busy street, it is essential to have hard-to-reach, hard-to-manipulate fasteners on the gates. Climbing equipment and boxes should never be placed near fences that border the street. If the fence is made of wood, it should be kept free of splinters.

   Inadequate ______ Adequate, poor condition ______
   Adequate, good condition ______ Excellent ______

5. Does all your equipment enhance the developmental and educational goals of the center, or does it just occupy space because it looks good to adults?

   For example, merry-go-rounds and teeter-totters require very close supervision and can be dangerous to very young children. Standard swing sets are not necessarily required for a good program of outdoor activities. They require individual supervision and are frequently misused or abused. A horizontal tire swing that more than one child at a time can use is more highly recommended than individual swings. Gliders are also good, because more than one child at a time can use them, and it is easier to determine their exact path of movement. For the comparison of how equipment should be used and for what reasons, see Section C5.

   Poorly selected ______ Fair ______ Useful and safe ______ Excellent ______

6. Are the playground and equipment as natural as possible? Here are some things you may want to add to your playground:

   a. A limb for climbing
   b. A hill for rolling down
   c. A tunnel under the hill
   d. A nature walk trail
   e. An obstacle course made of cut logs of various lengths implanted upright in the ground
   f. A birdbath or bird feeder (children can make these)

   None of these kinds of things ______ Some ______ Many ______

7. Does your playground have adequate drainage?

   A playground that is not usable during rainy weather because of poor drainage or is dangerous because of deep puddles does not serve the needs of the center. Children need opportunities for vigorous playground activities in cold winter months.

   Poor drainage ______ Fair ______ Good ______ Excellent ______

8. Do you have a covered area that can allow children use of outdoor play space during inclement weather?

   Such a cover can extend the use of outdoor space. It can also provide shade on hot summer days and may give some added protection from strong winds.

   No coverage ______ Some coverage ______ Good coverage ______

9. Do you have steps, a ramp, sloping ground, curved pathways, and other surfaces in the playground to promote variations in body movement and control?

   If the entire play area is very flat, you can provide wooden ramps made from large pieces of plywood and portable wooden steps as a part of the playground equipment.

   No variations _____ Some variations _____ Many variations_____

10. Is a drinking fountain readily available?

    Yes ______ Nearby ______ No ______

C2 Outdoor Play Centers

When setting up a play center, take into consideration the health, safety, and educational aspects of the center and the number of children who will be using it. Outdoor play centers are set up so that as few as one or two children can use them at one time, and as many as 10 or 12 can comfortably use others without crowding.

Cooperation between various staff members [Section D54], training programs given to parent/caregiver child care assistants [Sections F15–16], and freedom of choice given to children [Section E26] all result in an easy flow of movement from one activity to another. The supervisory staff should gently encourage children to move away from areas that are too crowded. If no one is riding bicycles, for example, and no one seems interested, the bike area remains an unsupervised, "no-play" area for the time being. However, if many children want to ride bikes at once, one of the adults will take charge of the area and limit children to the appropriate number.

The equipment in the playground should be arranged such that one person can observe two different elements at once. This will ensure that all portions of the playground are supervised comfortably and safely. Use two adult supervisors for the first 15 children, three adults for 15 to 25 children, four adults for 25 to 35 children, and five adults for 35 to 40 children.

A chart similar to that on page 93 can be used to evaluate the number of areas and the amount of playground equipment you have or will need. This list does not include gardening, carpentry, or other activities done by separate groups under the supervision of one or more persons in areas away from regular outdoor play areas.

When there are 12 to 15 children on the playground, there should be approximately two places for each child to play, even if everyone is playing alone. Even on days when there are as many as 30 children playing at one time, there should be enough play areas for everyone to play alone if they like. As a director, plan annually to upgrade the quality of your playground and its supervision.

ITEM	ESTIMATED NUMBER OF CHILDREN PER ITEM: THREE- TO SIX-YEAR-OLDS LOW	THREE- TO SIX-YEAR-OLDS HIGH		TWO-YEAR-OLDS LOW	TWO-YEAR-OLDS HIGH	
Jungle gym	2	4		2	4	
Parallel bars	2	3		1	2	
Slide	2	6		1	6	
Climbing chimney with ladder	1	2	(limit)	0	0	(not allowed)
Acrobat bars	1	1		1	1	
Sandbox	2	10	(limit)	2	10	(limit)
Cooking area (stove, sink, water)	1	4		1	3	
Hole-digging area	1	4		1	3	
Tires (for rolling, jumping, building)	1	6		1	3	
Big tire (for sitting, hiding)	1	6		1	3	
Horizontal tire swing	2	4		2	3	
Punching bag (stuffed canvas sack)	1	2		1	2	
Playhouse (or playstore) (storage shed)	2	6		2	4	
Climbing rail all around fence	2	8		2	2	(limit)
Rocking boat (separated area)	1	8	(capacity)	1	8	
Boxes, planks, sawhorses (26 pieces)	1	10		1	4	
Rocking horses (2)	1	2		1	2	
Water play area (in warm weather)	2	4		2	3	
Bike area, painted roadways	4	12		6	10	
Bike area, unmarked, open, roped off	2	4	(limit)	0	0	(not allowed)
Balls (3)	1	6		1	4	
Bike storage area (jail bars)	2	4		2	4	
Miscellaneous small equipment (4)	1	4		1	4	
"Alone" places (4)	1	4		1	4	
Totals	37*	124		34*	89	

*Recommended maximum total = 40

C3 Purchasing Outdoor Equipment

Before purchasing any piece of equipment, study carefully the safety considerations listed in Part H. Consider the quality and value of any equipment you plan to purchase. It is sometimes more economical to have something made by a good craftsman than to buy ready-made equipment that does not come up to quality standards. For example, you can have climbing equipment built to your own specifications by someone who is skilled in working with specific materials. By building your own, you can make the spacing small enough for even your youngest two- and three-year-olds. Any equipment, whether commercially purchased or handmade, should be durable enough to withstand the heavy usage it will get.

Wooden equipment should be made from hardwood, which is stronger and less apt to splinter than soft woods. All connecting devices should be countersunk. Good wood will feel warm to the touch. Flexible plastic will become faded and somewhat scratched or mottled if it is used outdoors. However, though it can't be repainted, its cost is low enough for occasional replacement.

Metal equipment should be rustproof and free of any sharp edges or rough sections. The metal should be heavy-duty galvanized steel that is cold to the touch, or nonflexible cast aluminum tubing. If painted, it should be with baked-on enamel. Pieces should be arc-welded to prevent sharp connections.

C4 Wheel Toys

What should you look for in wheel toys? Look for good solid construction, for toys that have front and back ball bearings (vehicles that have them will last twice as long as those that don't), and for toys that will not tip over on sharp curves. The number of wheel toys you need depends to some extent on the amount of storage space and available area for using them. For each group of 30 children, we recommend approximately

- three tricycles
- one wagon
- one Big Wheel
- two miniature Big Wheels
- four scooters

Whatever wheel toys you choose, expect to make repairs. Wheels, handles, and even seats need to be replaced from time to time. Plastic wheel toys, such as Big Wheels, are not expensive but usually need to be replaced every year or two.

C5 Evaluation of Playground Equipment

ITEM	PLAY EXPERIENCE	LEARNING EXPERIENCE	COURTESY AND SAFETY RULES
Swings	Swinging while seated or standing; rhythmic movement to pump swing	Waiting for turns; judging safe distances; kinesthetic awareness; motor coordination	Keep clear of moving swings. Empty swings must be left alone.
Horizontal tire swing	Swinging; tricks; sitting; twirling	Sharing; cooperative play; rhythmic movement; kinesthetic awareness	Sit only. No more than four at one time. May be spun round and round only if all occupants want to go that way. Allow time to sit a few moments after spinning until dizziness is gone.
Jungle gym, climbing rope gym	Dramatic play; climbing; stunts; daring	Courage; ego strength; awareness of others; judgment of space, size; self-assurance	Be especially careful of others using the equipment. Hands must be free of objects. Limited to eight children at a time.
Parallel bars	Hanging from; using hands to get from one side to other	Large muscle coordination; eye-hand coordination; visual perception; physical strength; sharing; waiting; courage	Only one person may use bars at one time. One person may wait on steps. Others must wait on the ground. Bars are only for hanging from and not for climbing on. It is dangerous to walk under the bars when they are in use.
Acrobatic bar	Hanging by hands or knees; doing tricks; playing circus	Muscular coordination; courage; imagination	Only one person at a time may use.
Climbing platform (tree house)	Dramatic play; climbing; sliding down pipe (fire station)	Cooperative planning; feelings of importance; independence; self-assurance	Keep a safe spacing behind others on steps and sliding pole. Share materials. Toys or small objects may not be taken up. The top rail is not for climbing.
Slides	Sliding down feet first only, sitting or lying back; performing only safe, simple stunts	Waiting for turns; motor coordination; kinesthetic awareness; understanding of gravity; judging space and time between one child's turn and another's	Keep well spaced behind person ahead of you. Three persons on steps at one time. Only one person on the slide at a time. People may only use the slide (no toys, debris, animals).
Rocking boat	Rocking; dramatic play; singing to movement	Waiting; sharing; cooperative movement; kinesthetic awareness	Only two in each seat. Those waiting for a turn must do so in designated area.

ITEM	PLAY EXPERIENCE	LEARNING EXPERIENCE	COURTESY AND SAFETY RULES
Rocking horses	Rocking	Rhythmic movement; kinesthetic awareness	Preference must be given to younger children by older ones. Only one child at a time on a horse.
Wheel toys	Riding; towing; pulling; hauling; having parades; performing simple, safe stunts	Taking turns; following traffic patterns; cooperating with others; motor coordination; visual perception; depth perception; rhythmic movement; independence; responsibility	Ride in designated areas only. Wheel toys are for riding, not bumping into people or things. Speed must be kept at a reasonable pace.
Bicycles	Dramatizing; exploring; cooperative planning	Making choices; building ego; self-awareness; awareness of others; emotional release; perceptual-motor skills; laterality	Stay within designated areas. May ride in open area only with permission and when supervised. Use of open area limited to four at one time.
Scooters	Riding scooter with one leg; coasting with both legs on	Using each side of the body unequally, but at the same time; moving through space; time and speed; watching for traffic patterns; depth perception; rhythmic patterns; visual decisions; hemispheric integration	Ride in designated areas. Give others the right-of-way. Ride only as fast as you are able to handle the scooter in an upright and stable manner. When replacing scooter, do so with care. Not to be thrown to ground, but rather put down gently or left in upside-down position.
Punching bag	Socking; hitting; punching; pushing; dramatizing	Eye-hand coordination; muscular skills; emotional release	Hit the bag only. Do not hit another person. Only two children at a time.
Balls	Throwing; rolling; sitting; bouncing; playing games	Visual-motor coordination; perceptual development	Must be shared. If ball goes out of yard or over fence, tell an adult. Throw balls *to* others, not *at* them.
Sandbox	Building; dramatic play; digging; pouring; mixing; measuring; "cooking"; straining; sifting; road building; water play; molding; piling	Tactile stimulation; judgment of proportions, amounts, sizes, textures; planning; gravity; effect of moisture; use of various implements; utensils	Sand is not to be thrown, eaten, or taken out of sandbox. Removal of shoes limited to special occasions or for emptying sand after play. No more than 12 children in box at one time. Utensils and implements must be shared.
Hole digging	Digging; piling; road building; dramatic play	Sharing; planning; awareness of sizes, length, width, diameter, depth; sensory and tactile awareness	Only one digging tool per child. Share space. Use only limited amounts of water.
Boxes, planks, ladders, sawhorses	Building; making trains, structures, bridges, tunnels, hideouts; dramatic play; tricks; climbing; jumping; hiding	Cooperative planning; comparative sizes; balancing; counterbalancing; comparing; muscular coordination; manipulative skills; sharing; interdependence	Building may not be higher than child's head. Share materials. Buildings may only be taken apart when they are abandoned. Care must be taken that no one gets pushed off or that no one is kept off unless it is too crowded.
Playhouse	Hiding; dramatic play; arranging; being alone	Division and arrangement of three-dimensional space; cooperative play; keeping order; cleanliness	Occupants limited to six at one time. Doors must remain open when someone is playing in house. A child must be let out upon request. House must be cleaned up when play is finished.

ITEM	PLAY EXPERIENCE	LEARNING EXPERIENCE	COURTESY AND SAFETY RULES
Tires	Jumping; bouncing; leaping; walking around; sitting in middle or around edge; holding hands across middle; rolling; dramatizing; building	Sensory-motor perception; physical strength in legs; balancing; imagination and inventiveness; cooperation	Rolling of tires may be done only away from others.
Oversized tire	Bouncing; walking around; sitting in the middle or on sides; hiding; dramatizing	Sharing; rhythmic movement; cooperative planning; kinesthetic awareness; socialization; interdependence.	Share the space with others; only adults may move tire.
Woodworking equipment	Hammering; sawing; drilling; sanding; fastening; building; dramatic play; gluing; painting	Use and care of tools; sharing and taking turns; carrying out plans; small muscle coordination; visual-motor perception; ego strength	Handle tools properly and with care. Replace them carefully after each use. Saw (with adult supervision) only wood that is in a vise or hammered to tabletop or box. No more than four children at a time.

C6 Plants and Shrubs

Select plants and shrubs carefully, avoiding those whose flowers might draw bees or whose pollens could be potentially dangerous to children with allergies. The local Agricultural Extension Service and the County Health Department will give you advice on the various plants for child care areas. Every plant should be considered absolutely nonedible and possibly dangerous unless it is known for certain to be edible.

First-Aid Precautions

In most instances of plant poisoning, vomiting should be induced as soon as possible by one person, while another person calls an ambulance and notifies the child's parents or caregivers. If you suspect that the child has eaten foxglove, do not induce vomiting unless you do it immediately after the child swallows it. Also do not induce vomiting if the child has lost consciousness. If that is the case, call an ambulance at once, and then notify the child's parents or caregivers. To induce vomiting in a child, first try tickling the back of the throat, preferably with your finger. If that doesn't work, try a solution of warm water with salt, baking soda, dry mustard, or even soapsuds. Use about one tablespoon of one of these items to a glass of water [Section G6].

C7 Trees

In planning new play areas, be sure to include trees. A good shade tree should be fast growing, provide plenty of shade in the summer, not be messy, and have strong, resilient branches for climbing. Shop around before making your selection. Once planted, the tree is usually there to stay for a long time, so be sure that it's the tree you want. You might want to use it for climbing. Be sure to tell the nursery worker where you want to plant it.

If you don't want to wait for a tree to grow and your budget will not allow you to buy a large tree from a nursery, contact the state highway department or a large construction company and ask if they can give you a large tree that has to be moved because of a building project.

C8 Playground Surfaces and Safety Tips

TYPE	ADVANTAGES	DISADVANTAGES	WHERE OBTAINED
Dirt	Cheap and fun.	Hills melt down in a few years without planting or terracing.	New construction sites
Sand	Good to walk in. Good to fall in. Good for building with water. Good for home use.	Tracks into room. Gets in shoes and socks. Not firm—shifts and blows. Has to be replaced. 12" deep.	Near rivers and beaches or see under *Sand-Gravel & Rock Co.* in telephone book yellow pages
Decomposed granite	High sand equivalent—70%. Better than sand. Packs down. Doesn't blow. Drains well. Doesn't get muddy.	More abrasive. Not good for sandpiles. Has to be replaced.	See under *Sand-Gravel & Rock Co.* in telephone book yellow pages
Gravel		Too coarse to play on. Encourages rock throwing.	See under *Sand-Gravel & Rock Co.* in telephone book yellow pages
Asphalt	Good for wheel toys, ball playing, etc. Inexpensive.	Dangerous under climbing equipment. Heats up in summer. May crack and shift. Paving in sand may break off.	See under *Sand-Gravel & Rock Co.* in telephone book yellow pages
Concrete	Anchor for structures. Good for walkways.	Unacceptable under climbing equipment. Heats up in summer. May crack and shift.	See under *Sand-Gravel & Rock Co.* in telephone book yellow pages
Grass	Alive and green. Pollution prevention. Good for physical activities.	Slippery when wet. Wears out quickly if area is heavily used.	Nursery
Tanbark	Porous. Resilient. Good under swings.	Expensive. Washes off slopes. Breaks down into an annoying dust. Has to be replaced yearly. 12" deep.	Nursery
Chopped tree limbs	Free, except for hauling.	May be 100% splinters. Have to be replaced yearly. 12" deep.	Nursery

TYPE	ADVANTAGES	DISADVANTAGES	WHERE OBTAINED
Peat and cinders, mixed and packed	Resilient brown surface.	Must be replaced yearly. 12" deep.	Nursery
Brick	Beautiful. Can be laid on a 4" to 6" base of sand and tapped into place.	Costly, all right for small areas. Unacceptable under climbing areas.	Brick company
Rubber sheets	Soft. Covers hard surfaces.	Very expensive and monotonous. Colored mats are even more expensive. Drainage is required for the surface to dry and to prevent erosion and puddling. Slope ground to the street or to dry walls. Use trenches 3' or 4' deep and 18" across filled with gravel. On hard surfaces these are covered with a grill; on soft surfaces with the material itself.	Carpet company
Indoor-outdoor carpeting	Better than concrete if no choice is available; can soften effect of concrete, especially if padded.	Not resilient; not natural; a little problem in maintenance. Unacceptable under play equipment.	Paint stores, carpet company

Safety Tips

Approximately 200,000 children have been treated in hospital emergency rooms from playground-related injuries. Most of the injuries result from falls. Approximately 15 children die each year from playground accidents resulting from strangulation or falls. According to the United States Consumer Product Safety Commission, the following tips can help you monitor playground safety.

1. Protective surfacing under and around all playground equipment is critical. Asphalt, concrete, grass, and turf are unacceptable; they have no shock-absorbent properties. Loose-fill surfacing materials, such as double-shredded bark mulch, wood chips, fine sand, and fine gravel are acceptable. The recommended depth of these materials is twelve inches. There are also certain types of manufactured synthetic surfaces that are acceptable. When installing these synthetic surfaces, ask for test data from the manufacturer for its shock-absorbing performance.
2. Your play equipment must have a fall zone that is covered with protective surfacing materials. This area must be free from other equipment. Climbing equipment and slides should have a fall zone of six feet minimum in all directions. Swings should have a fall zone of six feet extending from their outer edges on each side of their support structures. The swing's fall zone in front and back should extend out to twice the height of the swing as measured from the ground to the top support.
3. Swings should not be too close together or too close to any support structures. There should be a least 24 inches between adjacent swing seats and at least 30 inches between swing seats and adjacent structural components. Swings must not be attached to playground equipment for multiple activities. Only one tire swing can be suspended in the same section of a support structure. The tire swing must be 30 inches away from the closest support structure when swung.
4. Any elevated surfaces or platforms that are more than 30 inches above the ground must have guardrails to prevent falls.

5. Openings between 3 1/2 and 9 inches can present a head entrapment danger to children. This range is large enough to allow a child's body to go through, feet first, but too small for his or her head to go through. Make sure that openings measure less than 3 1/2 inches or more than 9 inches.
6. Close any S hooks, especially on swings. These hooks, or hardware that acts as hooks, can catch onto children's clothing and may cause strangulation.
7. Moving parts should not be exposed. If exposed, they may present pinching hazards.
8. Your playground should be inspected daily. Note any of the following conditions: Loose or worn hardware, exposed footings, litter, rocks, tree roots, broken glass, rust, chipped paint on metal components, large cracks, splinters, decayed wood, corrosion on structural components that connect to the ground, and any missing equipment such as handrails, swing seats, or guardrails. To prevent injuries, any of these conditions must be repaired or removed immediately.

C9 Sandboxes

The sandbox should be located in a side area of the yard. It should be large enough for children to build things without destroying each other's work. You should have enough room in the sandbox to accommodate four to five children. The sand in the box should be 12" to 18" deep. Some states' laws require that sandboxes be covered when not in use. Heavy plastic tarps can be used for this purpose.

Types of Sandboxes

1. *Sunken box:* Cement border level with playground, with sand in middle. Easy to sweep sand back into box.
2. *Bench-type sides:* A box style constructed of wood or aluminum, with sides that can be used for a seat or table to sit above ground.

TYPES OF SAND	DISADVANTAGES	ADVANTAGES
Plaster	Clean, no rocks. Grains are smaller than concrete sand. No dust.	More expensive than concrete sand.
Silicate #30	Rounded edges. Good for home use.	Expensive.
Concrete	Inexpensive.	Coarser—gets in shoes and socks.
White beach sand	Clean. Fine grade. Fine pebbles.	More expensive than concrete or plaster sands.
Creek sand	Clean. Collecting can be part of a field trip.	Haul it yourself; use small buckets half-full so as not to make any too heavy. (Make sure creek is not contaminated.)

C10 Indoor Child Care Space

The following considerations are desirable when deciding about the arrangement of indoor child care space:

1. Is there at least 35 square feet (preferably 50) of unencumbered room space per child?

   ______ feet

   The larger the group, the more space per child is required for safety. It is possible to conduct a safe program for small groups with even less space than recommended. However, state and community licensing regulations have very rigid space requirements, so you must be sure that you are able to meet legal requirements for the number of children that you serve daily.

2. Is there easy access to toilet facilities?

   Poor ______ Fair ______ Adequate ______ Good ______

   Ideally, the toilets should be adjacent to the child care space. However, unless a facility has been built specifically to house a child care center, this is not usually the case. In arranging for space, then, you must take into account the route that the child will have to take to get to the toilets, what type of supervision will be required, and what type of safety precautions are needed.

3. Is there easy access to the outdoor play area?

   Poor ______ Fair ______ Adequate ______ Good ______

   Again, the ideal situation would be to have the outdoor play area immediately adjacent to the child care room. Since this is not always possible, you must again consider how the child will get to the play area, what type of supervision will be required, and what type of safety precautions are needed. Sometimes it may be possible to spend extra money to move an existing or proposed playground location to a place closer to the room. This will save future expenses brought about by the need for extra personnel to supervise playgrounds that are less conveniently located.

4. Are there two exits from every child care room?

   Number of exits ______

   This is an extremely important factor. Not only should there be two exits, but they should also always be kept clear for easy access.

5. Is the space adequately lighted, both naturally and artificially?

   Poor ______ Fair ______ Adequate ______ Excellent ______

   a. Are the windows low enough for children to see out of them?

      No ______ Yes ______ By standing on a platform ______

   b. Are the windows either of glare-proof glass or sufficiently curtained to prevent glare?

      No ______ Fair ______ Good ______

   c. Can you darken the room during rest periods?

      No ______ Yes ______

d. Is the artificial lighting on two switches, so that the room can be brightened midmorning and midafternoon when moods and feelings usually need an uplift?

No ______ Yes ______

6. Can the room be ventilated without creating floor drafts?

No ______ Yes ______

a. Will the cooling and heating system maintain the room temperature at 60° to 70° in warmer months and at 70° to 72° in winter months?

No ______ Fair ______ Good ______

b. Does each room have an indoor thermometer or thermostat that will enable a staff member to check the temperature?

No ______ Yes ______

c. Are you able to provide supplementary heating if the main heating system fails?

No ______ Yes ______

If your heating system fails, you could use a thermostat-controlled electric heater—placed out of reach of children—to warm up a room temporarily while the defective system is being repaired. It may be necessary at such times to bring all children in the center into one room that is warmed by a supplementary heating system. Children can put on their outdoor clothing if the heating fails.

d. Do you have a plan for changing play areas in very hot weather if the air conditioning fails?

No ______ Yes ______

During such periods, play should be as quiet as possible. Move activities, if you can, to areas that are cooler, shadier, or farther away from outside walls than others.

7. Are the rooms acoustically well planned so that there is a minimum of noise?

Poor ______ Adequate _____ Excellent ______

Carpeting large areas, hanging drapes, and using acoustical ceiling tile are three ways to minimize the noise levels in a child care space. Every effort should be made to employ at least one, if not all, of these methods in order to help create a calm and relaxing atmosphere.

8. Can you use your furniture, equipment, and storage space in many different ways?

No ______ Yes ______

The well-planned child care area and creative curriculum call for furniture and equipment that can be used in different areas and in different ways according to the ever-changing needs of the children and requirements of the curriculum.

9. Do you have separate storage shelves for supplies, children's materials, and cleaning materials?

No ______ Yes ______

10. Does your furniture and equipment stand less than four feet high?

    No ______ Yes ______

    Furniture should be low to accommodate children's range of vision and to enable the child care providers to see all of the room at the same time. Shelves and countertops should remain uncluttered.

11. In regard to furniture and equipment, does the child care space have

    a. a sufficient number of small tables and chairs to enable each child to sit comfortably?

       No ______ Yes ______

    b. a storage shelf for blocks that can be moved from place to place?

       No ______ Yes ______

    c. housekeeping furniture for dramatic play activities?

       No ______ Yes ______

    d. low shelves for children's books?

       No ______ Yes ______

    e. rugs or pieces of carpet for marking off special areas, such as a reading corner or block play area?

       No ______ Yes ______

    f. supplementary tables, shelves, and stands for setting up learning centers?

       No ______ Yes ______

    g. individual cubicles or baskets for personal belongings?

       No ______ Yes ______

    h. individual coat hooks placed low so that children can take care of their own clothing needs and have spaces that they can identify as their own?

       No ______ Yes ______

    i. adult-sized chairs for visiting parents, caregivers, observers and staff?

       No ______ Yes ______

    j. at least one rocking chair to soothe a child, or to use for rhythmic experience?

       No ______ Yes ______

    k. a piano that children can use?

       No ______ Yes ______

    l. easels or tables on which artwork can be created?

       No ______ Yes ______

    m. at least one workbench or sturdy table to use for carpentry and woodworking?

       No ______ Yes ______

    n. cots for children who nap?

       No ______ Yes ______

    o. adequate storage for these cots?

       No ______ Yes ______

    p. a substitute that can be used if cots are not provided?

       No ______ Yes ______

q. furniture proportionately sized to accommodate toddlers and infants where appropriate?

No ______ Yes ______

r. drinking water available at a location where children can obtain it easily?

No ______ Yes ______

C11 Interest Centers

It is always possible that inclement weather might keep you from using your outdoor space. Therefore, plan your indoor areas as though you do not have a playground at all. Each morning before children arrive, prepare enough interest centers to equal two-thirds of the number of children. That is, if you are expecting 15 children, have ten interest centers. If you are expecting 45 children, have 30 interest centers. You might cut that down to 25, but not to fewer.

An interest center can be set up on a tray, a table, a corner of the room, or any other place where a child can spend time pursuing an activity. That activity can range from sitting alone doing "nothing" to joining with others in building a large block structure, exploring manipulative objects, or creating art projects. Most centers have room for one to three children. Some centers have a choice of several activities—others have only one. Sometimes a particular place will have the same interest center for several days in a row. Other times it will be changed day after day.

In setting up an interest center, select materials that will lead to a particular learning experience. Of course, much of the time the child may use the materials in some way other than the way you anticipated. The child's learning experience, in that case, will be something other than what was intended. If you feel that the child still needs the learning experience that was originally intended, another interest center can be prepared another time—perhaps using a different approach to motivate the child in the desired direction.

1. Are there places where children can be alone, sit quietly, or play by themselves [Sections C1, C10]?

   Children need to be alone sometimes, just like adults. Some "alone" places that you can provide in the room are

   - *a large cardboard carton with a door and possibly a window cut in.*
   - *a child's rocking chair in a quiet corner next to a shelf or small table with a few select books.*
   - *small mats in various parts of the room, with or without pillows, with one or two books, a cuddly doll or stuffed animal, or perhaps a book of drapery or fur samples—just to feel.*
   - *a small table with a simple "surprise" box, with room for one child at a time (see #2).*
   - *a corner behind a desk, behind a piano, or behind a bookcase.*
   - *a small table draped with a cloth to make it dark underneath. Put a pillow underneath the table.*

2. Are there places where children can invent their own creations?

   Traditional materials, when given to children, can become the tools for inventing nontraditional creations. The secret of this center is to put out four or five different kinds of things in a "surprise" box or tray. Just be sure that the materials can be used together. Some ideas for materials that can be used with one another are listed in this section. Always put together different combinations of materials to stimulate children's inventive abilities. A surprise box should be prepared so that only one child at a time can use it. It is an "alone" activity.

3. Are there places where children can use their imaginations to create works of art with the painting and drawing materials you supply?

   Provide many different kinds of paper, combinations of colors, and assortments of drawing and painting materials to stimulate the imagination. Select enough items from the following lists to make up at least two different centers (one for paints, one for drawing materials) each day. Provide space for two or three children at each center.

Paper

White, 36-inch wide, 50- to 100-foot rolls (can be cut into 12", 18", or 24" widths) of butcher, banner, Kraft, or wrapping papers
White drawing paper (can be used for painting, too), 80# only
Construction paper of assorted colors, 18" x 24" (can be cut to 18" x 12" or 9" x 12")
Mill screening paper, 18" x 36" (oatmeal, Roughtex, and so on)
Fingerpaint paper, coated, 18" x 36" (or use butcher paper)
Tagboard, assorted sizes
Watercolor paper, 9" x 12", for occasional use, inexpensive
Wallpaper sample books and end rolls, usually no charge
Wrapping paper, brown, 24" x 50' or 35" x 100' (for murals)
Old newspapers, no charge
Newsprint, free (may be a small cutting charge)
Computer paper, used
Japanese rice paper (for occasional use)

Paints, Colors, and Other Ingredients

Powdered tempera, assorted colors
Liquid tempera, assorted colors
Finger paint, commercial
Liquid starch (to extend paints, make finger paint, or use with chalk)
Liquid soap (to extend finger paint)
Shaving cream (to finger-paint with)
Oil pastels, assorted colors
Lecturer's chalk, assorted (to use with liquid starch or buttermilk)
Pastel chalk, assorted
Kindergarten-sized crayons, assorted
Tempera blocks, assorted, boxed sets
Transparent watercolor pans, boxed sets
Marking pens, watercolor, assorted

Brushes and Other Tools

Easel brushes, 1/2" to 3/4", flat and round
Painter's brush, 1 1/2" and 2"
Feather dusters, colored
Tongue depressors (for mixing paint)
Ice-cream sticks (for mixing paint)

Small juice or fruit cans, free (for holding paint)
Plastic containers (for holding paints)
Aluminum foil (for covering paint cans)

4. Do you sometimes let children mix their own powdered tempera by providing them with ingredients, small pitchers of water, and tongue depressors or ice-cream sticks to stir with?
5. Do you vary the size and shape of the paper that you give children for artwork in order to further stimulate their imagination? Some variations are listed below:

9" x 12"	9" x 18"	9" x 24"	9" x 36"	12" x 18"
12" x 24"	12" x 36"	18" x 18"	18" x 24"	18" x 36"
24" x 24"	24" x 36"	36" x 36"		
torn edges	diamond shapes	triangular	round	scalloped
leaf shapes	heart shapes	free-form	trapezoid	

6. Do you provide different kinds of surfaces on which the child can paint?

   Use easels, tabletops, and the floor. Each different position gives the child a different type of experience in eye-hand coordination and sensory-motor exercises.

7. Do you have a collage and construction center where the child can have experience in arranging materials and dividing space each day?

   Provide materials for two- and three-dimensional arrangements. Place them on a lazy Susan or on a tray at a table where there is room for no more than three children at a time. Place more materials on the table than children will use, but not so many that they will "grab" rather than "select."

Collage Materials

Aluminum foil scraps
Ballpoint pens
Beads
Beans
Bottle tops
Buttons
Carbon paper
Cardboard scraps
Cellophane scraps
Charcoal sticks
Cloth scraps
Colored inks
Colored pencils
Cotton balls
Crayons
Fadeless art paper
Felt squares, 6" x 9"
File cards, 3" x 5"
Glitter
Glue
Gravel
Gummed paper scraps
Gummed stars
Hair curlers
Hairpins
Jewelry
Kleenex
Leaves
Lengths of string
Lined notebook paper
Macaroni, assorted shapes
Masonite scraps
Nails
Paper clips
Paper fasteners
Paper punches
Paper scraps
Paper straws
Parts from broken toys
Paste
Pinecones
Pinking shears
Pipe cleaners
Plastic triangle
Plywood scraps
Poster paper
Precut geometric gummed paper shapes
Ribbons
Rickrack
Rock salt
Rulers
Safety pins
Scissors, blunt, 4"
Scotch tape
Screws
Seashells
Sequins
Sewing thread scraps
Small rocks
Small watercolor brushes
Spools
Stapler
Straight pins
Styrofoam cups
Tools
Toothpicks
Tracing paper
Twigs
Washers
Wire screening
Yarn lengths

8. Do you provide materials for your interest centers that are primarily geared toward encouraging children to make choices that will help them learn certain concepts?

   Underlying all preschool experiences are the learning of concepts and the development of cognition in accordance with children's ever-increasing perceptual abilities. This natural growth should be constantly challenged by materials that are goal-directed toward specific concepts. Some examples of these materials are listed below:

   Color games
   Comparative size games
   Matching games and puzzles
   Nesting toys
   Seriation games and puzzles
   Shape games
   Sorting games and puzzles
   Stacking shapes
   Things that are alike
   Things that are different
   Things that are soft, hard, big, little, littlest, biggest, smooth, rough, bumpy, sticky, stretchy, shiny, cold, warm, thick, thin
   Things to compare

9. Do you provide many manipulative materials that will foster children's small muscle development as well as their eye-hand coordination? You may want to provide the following:

   Assorted balancing or connecting blocks, forms, and shapes
   Beads with strings or laces
   Buttoning materials
   Form puzzles
   Hammer and nail set
   Insert puzzles
   Interlocking blocks and shapes
   Jigsaw puzzle
   Jumbo beads
   Lacing beads
   Lego® bricks
   Lock boxes
   Locks with keys
   Magnetic shapes
   Nested boxes
   Nuts and bolts
   Paper and crayons
   Pegboards with pegs (two sizes)
   Pipe fittings
   Purses
   Radio to dismantle, with appropriate tools
   Rubber puzzles such as Fit-a-Size and shape
   Scissors
   Snap blocks
   Snap boards
   Suitcases
   Threading block
   Tinker Toys®
   Turn-a-Gears
   Wire
   Wire cutters

10. Do you provide manipulative materials primarily geared to the development of tactile and sensory awareness as part of both the creative art program and the overall developmental growth of children? These kinds of materials include the following:

    Additives to paints and finger paints to increase textural awareness (such as sand, Karo® syrup, soap, and so on)
    Clay, gray modeling
    Clay, terra-cotta modeling
    Ingredients for making play dough
    Mud
    Papier-mâché (for five-year-olds and older)
    Plasticine
    Play dough
    Wet sand

11. Do you have a special place for unit blocks, and do you change it from time to time in order to motivate imaginative thinking and new ideas? Changing the place where you keep materials leads to new ways of using those materials. Unit blocks and some accessories that you can use with blocks include the following:

    Airplanes
    Automobiles
    Boats
    Bird miniatures
    People
    Planks
    Rockets
    Signs
    Trains
    Trucks, buses, and other vehicles

12. Do you provide a variety of scientific tools children can use to investigate the exciting world and preschool environment?

    Children are naturally curious. If you provide the necessary materials, they will figure out for themselves how to use them. Include any of the following in this interest center:

Dry cells, batteries, wires, buzzers	Magnifying glass	Stethoscope
Flashlight	Opera glasses	Telescope
Kaleidoscope	Outdoor thermometer	Toy compass
Magnets	Prisms	

13. Do you provide a variety of materials from the natural sciences to motivate children to ask questions and explore? You may include the following:

Bark	Grains	Rocks
Bird's nest	Insects	Seed pods
Bugs	Leaves	Shells
Cactus garden	Live fish	Skeletons
Dry flowers	Nuts	Snails
Feathers	Pebbles	Weeds
Flowers	Pets	
Foods	Plants	

14. Do you set up a center where children can perform simple experiments with materials?

    So many things for children come prepackaged and ready-mixed that it is important for children to have opportunities to find out about ingredients, how they react when treated certain ways, and what they can be used for.

Baking soda and vinegar (to make foam)	Liquid bleach with cotton swabs and dark paper	Things to float in water (corks, wood, soap, plastic foam)
Bubble blowers	Red clay, water (to dissolve the clay)	
Cornmeal and sifter	Silver polish and old silver	
Flour, salt, water, oil (for play dough)		

15. Do you provide opportunities to build with wood and carpentry tools?

    The use of woodworking tools increases children's visual-motor abilities and overall coordination. In this world of plastic, wood is a living material. Give children many different experiences with it. Sometimes the wood can be used with hammers, nails, and other tools. Sometimes it can be glued together to make castles, airplanes, and other objects. You can set up two centers on some days—one for gluing, and one for using tools. Sometimes they can be combined. You may choose to ask an adult volunteer to help in this area. Supply your carpentry and wood-gluing centers with the following items:

Hammer	Screwdriver	White glue
Hand drill	Screws	Wood scraps
Nuts and bolts	Soft wood	Wooden box (to saw around the edges)
Pliers	Vise	

16. Do you provide at least one interest center each day where the child can explore music and other sounds?

    We sometimes get so engrossed in helping children develop eye-hand coordination that we neglect auditory perception. Auditory acuity helps children enlarge the scope of their ability to communicate. Experience with musical sounds helps children increase their auditory acuity, especially when they are involved in the creation of those sounds. Select one or more of the following to use each period:

    Bells
    Cassette players with tapes
    Compact disc player and CDs
    Drums
    Homemade instruments
    Maracas
    Rhythm sticks
    Sand blocks
    Tambourines
    Tone blocks
    Triangles
    Wind chimes
    Xylophone

17. Do you provide places for children to use housekeeping equipment and tools in order to role-play family and life experiences, important aids to building self-esteem?

    Dolls
    Doll bed
    Dress-up clothes
    Housecleaning tools
    Play cupboard
    Play refrigerator
    Play sink
    Play stove
    Table and chairs
    Tableware
    Telephone

18. In addition to opportunities for playhouse activities, do you provide opportunities for other types of role-play experiences to help children's understanding and acceptance of the adult world?

    The use of role-playing kits enables children to learn to participate in the choice of games played. These kits should be in similar types of containers, clearly labeled by printed word and illustration as to their contents. They can be kept where children can actually get a kit out and set up their own interest center. Hollow blocks or cardboard cartons can be used as a basis for creating an area for playing such games as the following:

    Bank
    Barber shop
    Beauty shop
    Boat
    Delivery van
    Fish pond
    Garbage truck
    Grocery store
    Library
    Office
    Pet store
    Plane
    Post office
    Puppet show
    Restaurant
    Shoe store
    Train
    TV set

    Accessories can be simple. Children's imaginations will do the rest. For example, for the restaurant, simply stock a kit with a few paper plates, pictures of (or plastic) food, plastic silverware, and a couple of aprons for waiters and waitresses. A cash register should, of course, always be available for most of these activities.

19. Are there places each day where children are challenged to participate in motor activities geared to the overall development of their perceptual skills?

    Although the outdoor play area provides many such opportunities, movement is so important to children's wholesome development as well-integrated people who can use body and mind in harmony, that movement opportunities should be part of the indoor environment as well. On the next page is a list of equipment you can use:

Balloons to throw and catch
Large balls to balance on
Long boards to walk along
Raised sticks to jump over
Sloping boards to walk up and down
Small boxes to jump over or off
Square boards to balance on
Tunnels to crawl through

20. Do you provide special places where children who are interested in numbers can explore their use? Do you set up such centers in a way that will motivate children who are not interested in numbers to use it?

In all interest centers, there are many opportunities for children to learn about the use of numbers and other mathematical concepts. They have a chance to measure, compare, and judge weights, sizes, amounts, and so on. Use numerical references whenever appropriate, such as, how many chairs? how many crackers? what time is it? and so forth. Children can also be motivated to do special tasks to enhance their mathematical understanding. Such a center can be a "double center," divided so that one to three children can work in one part, and one to three in another. Stock it with any of the following materials:

Abacus
Adding machine
Alarm clock
Balance scale
Calculators
Calipers
Cash register
Clock faces
Clock puzzles
Counting cubes
Counting sets
Cuisenaire rods
Dominoes
Egg timer
Fractional shape puzzles
Geometric lotto games
Geometric shapes
Inset number blocks
Magnetic numerals and board
Measuring cups
Number games
Number scale
Numbered stepping stones
Numerical jigsaw puzzles
Numerical lotto games
Play cards
Play money
Rulers
Stopwatch
Tactile number cards
Tape measures
Thermometer

21. Do you have a double center for exploring letters, alphabets, words, and so on for those children who are ready for preliminary reading activities?

As with mathematics, there are numerous ways to motivate children to play with letters and words in such a way that they become a natural part of play and learning experiences, without coercion or pressure. Each day you can set out some of the following materials:

Alphabet lotto
Beaded alphabet cards
Beginning readers
Cutout plastic letters
Cutout wooden letters
Gummed letters
Inset letter blocks
Letters to cut out
Lined paper and kindergarten pencils
Magnetic letters
Rubber alphabet stamps
Rubber word stamps
Sandpaper letters
Tape recorder and cassettes
Three-foot-tall cardboard cutout letters
Typewriter
Word puzzles

Use both upper- and lowercase letters, sometimes together and sometimes separately.

22. Do you have one or two areas where a child can look at books alone, and one area where two or three at a time can share?

Learn to select a book by what's inside—not by its title or outward appearance. Children like books about the following topics:

Animals	Fantasy	Seasons
Business	Growing things	Simple science
Children	Humor	Space
Cities	Make-believe	Vehicles
Families	Photographs	Working

23. Do you have open spaces where children can create their own learning centers according to their own interests and imaginations?

    Even when your room is excitingly prepared with many interest centers, too much can be just as inhibiting as too little. Try to put out enough things at one time to encourage children to make choices, but not so many things that they choose randomly without thought. If you leave plenty of in-between "empty" spaces, children are encouraged to think in terms of not "having" to do any particular thing, and even of being able to just sit and watch others if they feel the need. The well-planned environment should meet children's ever-changing needs, moods, interests, and feelings—just as it does for adults involved.

24. Do you consider your child care provider's needs, too, in setting up the learning centers?

    Think in terms of how much assistance they have each day, and of whether they have private places where they can keep their own materials (things that children do not touch or use) and places where they can store children's work.

25. Do you help your staff maintain an ever-changing array of interest centers by establishing a system for sharing, rotating, and exchanging materials?

    Such a system minimizes duplication of expensive items, thus affecting budgetary savings. It's advisable to make use of a central storage area from which each child care provider may draw materials for a specific activity for a day, a week, or any other period of time. Periodically, perhaps once a month, your staff can take a half-hour period to exchange puzzles, manipulative games, dramatic play kits, books, and other items. Never change all materials of a particular kind at once. Children are comfortable with familiar things. But by changing some things on an ongoing basis, children are constantly provided with new challenges that stimulate growth. In addition, encourage parents and caregivers to bring in "found" materials and homemade games to supplement the commercial materials and expand various interest centers. An item brought from home should be shared by all staff members, rather than used exclusively in the room of the child whose parent or caregiver brought it. Twice yearly, staff meetings can be devoted to making simple learning games.

C12 Lunchroom and Napping Space

Limited space frequently requires the child care rooms to also serve as lunchrooms and napping spaces. The creation of a wholesome, relaxed setting should be your primary consideration in such instances. Play materials, interest centers, and other distractions should be put away, if possible. Before lunch is served, tabletops should be thoroughly cleaned. Plastic covers can be used, if necessary. Tables and seating should be arranged to create pleasant social settings.

Following lunchtime and cleanup [Part K], children can be taken for a walk or to another play area while the furniture is moved out of the way and cots are set up. (Some programs let children help set up cots.) Cots should be placed far enough apart to ensure safe evacuation in case of emergency. The room should be darkened. A record player should be available for soft music to encourage relaxation. Attitudes should be pleasant, and movements of adults should be slow and gentle. A setting that is conducive to rest and relaxation will minimize the number of adults needed to supervise sleeping children, thus allowing time for lunch and staff planning sessions.

In planning a nap program, consider storage areas for cots and bedding. Folding cots take up less storage space, but take a little longer to set up each day. Stacking cots can be stored in stacks of six, with the bottom cot on wheels. Cots can be stored vertically in storage racks. If space is a real problem, consider the low plastic-form cots. Fifty cots make a stack only 30 inches high. Thick mats, too, can be used.

Most health departments have such stringent requirements for kitchens that the cost of equipping the space is almost prohibitive. For this reason, many programs that convert to child care start out by having children bring lunches from home. If a kitchen is available and brought up to building and safety standards, it should be a light, airy, efficient food-preparation center, with utmost thought given to the safety of any child who may wander in [Part K].

C13 Director's Office

The director's office is not an isolated section of the center, but rather an integral part of the total indoor area. Keep the door open except during private conferences or meetings. Include the following equipment in the office:

- Adding machine
- Bookcase, with professional library
- Child's table and two chairs
- Copy machine
- Desk
- Desk for secretary and/or bookkeeper
- Fax machine
- File cabinet
- Parent/caregiver corner, with books for families
- Personal computer
- Posture chair for each desk
- Printer
- Storage shelves for office supplies
- Telephone
- Two armchairs for conferences
- Typewriter
- Worktable

C14 Isolation Center

Set up an area where a child can be isolated and cared for in case of illness or injury. Keep the following items in a screened-off corner of the director's office:

- Child-sized cot with sheets, bedspread, pillow, and blanket
- Low chair for supervising adult
- Several attractive picture books and some storybooks for an adult to read to an isolated child
- Storage shelf nearby for extra bedding
- Two or three appealing pictures for child to look at while lying on cot
- Roll of paper sheeting for individual use

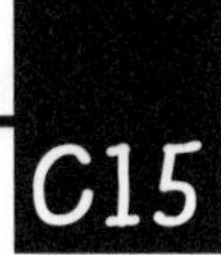

C15 Child Care Providers' Supply Cupboards

In addition to materials and supplies for interest centers, each child care provider needs a basic supply of materials. Keep these materials in a separate cupboard. Use the following checklist for child care room supplies:

Room Supplies

Accident reports
Brads
Calendar
Felt-tip markers
File folders
Glue and rubber cement
Keys
Masking tape
Memo forms
Paper
Paper clips
Pencils
Pens
Record and lesson plan books and forms
Scissors (for adult use)
Scotch® tape
Stapler
Staples

Shared Materials Cupboard

The following materials should be in cupboards accessible to children:

Crayons
Construction paper
Drawing paper
Favorite books
Favorite records
Glue sticks
Library paste
Liquid paste
Magazines and catalogs for cutting
Miscellaneous art paper
Newspapers
Paint aprons
Painting paper
Plastic
Scissors for children
Vegetable glue
White glue

Housekeeping Cupboard

Keep these materials out of the reach of children:

Bottle brush	Liquid soap
Cleaning rags	Pail
Cleanser	Paper towels
Dustpan	Sponges
Liquid cleaner	Steel wool

C16 Storage or Supply Room

A storage room is only useful if it is maintained in an orderly manner. All sections, containers, and shelves should be clearly labeled. Record all items taken on an inventory list. Either once a week or monthly, the director or designated staff member should check the list and restock the supply room before any items run out.

C17 Paper Supply

Purchase good quality paper, avoiding the cheaper kinds. Though this takes a bite out of the budget, you can make up for it by using many kinds of free paper to supplement your supply. Creativity plays an important role in your program. Though creativity does not depend on quality materials, it is discouraging to young children when their art projects fall apart, fade, disintegrate, or deteriorate—sometimes even before they take them home.

In looking for good quality paper, don't go by price alone. Check for high rag content. Most papers today are made primarily of wood pulp and thus have inferior quality.

Check also for weight. Most paper you use should be of at least 60 lb. weight. This is a good weight for cutting. For painting, finger-painting, and general all-around use, 80 lb. weight is excellent.

Purchase your paper goods from any of four sources—school supply companies, wholesale paper supply companies, local stationery stores that will give you a child care or school discount, and wholesale food distributors. By comparison shopping among these sources, you can find quality materials at the lowest available prices.

Always take shipping costs into account. Supplies that you buy locally or pick up in nearby communities may sometimes cost a little more, but the savings in shipping costs offset the extra charges. Good paper scraps can be scrounged from print shops and can be used for many special projects.

C18 Inventory List for Office Supplies

Filing Supplies

Filing cards
Filing folders
Filing labels
Tab guides

Fastening Supplies

Paper clips
Paper fasteners
Paper punch
Pushpins
Staplers
Staples
Straight pins

Adhesives

Library paste
Liquid paste
Magic tape
Mystic tape
Rubber cement
Scotch® tape
Tape dispensers
White glue

Duplicating Supplies

Computer paper
Correction fluid
Correspondence
Envelopes
Ink cartridges for copy machine
Ink cartridges for printer
Letterhead stationery
Other stationery
Second sheets
Type-correction paper
Typewriter erasers
Typewriter ribbons

Appointments

Appointment book and calendar
Month-at-a-glance calendar
Wall calendar

Accounting

Adding-machine paper
Adding-machine ribbon
Billing envelopes
Bookkeeping record forms
Expense books
Payroll record forms
Receipt book
Record books
Withholding exemption forms

Miscellaneous

Ballpoint pens
Clipboards
Felt markers
Fiber-tip pens
Gummed labels
Memo holders
Memo pads
Pencils
Rulers
Scissors
X-acto® knives
ZIP code directory

C19 General Maintenance Supply List

Bleach
Bowl cleaner
Brooms
Cleanser
Disinfectant (liquid)
Dustpan
Mop pail
Mops
Pail (kitchen only)
Pail (toilets only)
Soap powder
Sponge mop (bathroom only)
Sponge mop (kitchen only)
Squeegee
Toilet brush
Wastebasket
Window cleaner

C20 Repair Workshop List

Auger
Awl
Caulking gun
Common nails
Double-headed nails
Electric saw and blades
Files
Finishing nails
Hacksaw (for metal)
Hammer, claw
Hand drill
Hooks and eyes
Hot glue gun and glue sticks
Level
Machine oil
Machine screws, #4 to #12
Masking tape
Masonry nails
Oil can
Paintbrushes
Plane
Plaster screws
Pliers
Plunger
Putty knife
Rasps
Sandpaper
Saw, crosscut
Saw, dovetail
Scraper
Screwdriver, offset
Screwdriver, Phillips
Screwdriver, standard
Screws, flathead and roundhead, #4 to #18
Staple gun
Straightedge or steel ruler
Tape measure
Valve kits
Vise
Washers
Wrench

C21 Garden Tool List

Adjustable hand sprinkler for small forceful spray
Hedge clipper
Hoe
Hose, 50', 75'
Lawn sprinkler
Pruning shears
Rake, grass
Rake, metal
Shovel
Soaker hose, 75'
Trowels

C22 Finding Maintenance and Repair Help

Where can you find someone to help you with maintenance and repair work?

1. Call an employment agency that finds work for the disabled. Many times you can find a disabled worker who is a skilled craftsperson and will appreciate an opportunity to use those skills.
2. Drug and Alcohol Rehabilitation Centers. Many of these organizations provide housing for individuals trying to rebuild their lives. They usually have many skilled workers who are interested in doing repair jobs, gardening, painting, and other types of maintenance work in return for a reasonable salary.
3. The Situations Wanted ads in the classified sections of the paper.
4. Colleges, universities, and trade schools. Many students are in need of work and will appreciate an opportunity to acquire both money and experience.
5. Ask parents and caregivers. Many of them have probably had contact with neighborhood or professional repair workers that they know to be skilled, honest in their work, and fair in their prices.
6. Your own records. Keeping a record of everyone who does repair and maintenance work for you will provide your best resource for future needs.
7. Neighborhood and citywide youth programs. Many communities have programs for students in their early teens to be on call for such jobs as yard work, simple painting, window cleaning, and similar tasks to be performed at nominal fees. In addition to providing a service to the community by hiring these young persons, you can frequently save some of your budgeted funds for the skilled help you will require for more complicated services.
8. Other child care centers. By maintaining contact with other centers in the community, you can exchange information about people available for various types of jobs that come up.
9. Advertise in the classified section of the local newspaper for retired people who would welcome an opportunity to work on an "on call" basis.
10. Help from parents and caregivers. Don't overlook the fact that many children's family members may have the skills needed for certain repair and maintenance jobs at the center. Offer tuition credit or ask for out-and-out volunteers. Organize work parties. This is a good way to get all your playground equipment refinished.

- Ask people to bring their own brushes, hammers, saws, and so on.
- Provide all of the needed materials, such as nails, paints, thinner, paint rags, drop cloths, screws, and nuts and bolts.
- Make up a list in advance of all that you wish to have taken care of on that day.
- Assign crew "managers."
- Provide refreshments—for example, coffee and doughnuts, a spaghetti dinner, or a sandwich lunch or supper.

When you are planning to have work done, be sure to do a little comparative shopping before you hire anyone. Obtain three or four estimates. You will find that they may vary by as much as several hundred dollars, depending on the size of the job. In getting estimates, ask for more than a price. Find out exactly what is to be included—what kinds of materials will be used, what kind of preparation will be made, what guarantee of the work there is, and related items. Don't assume anything. Have all specifications put in writing. Obtain references if possible.

If you hire someone by the hour, specify in advance about time off for lunch and breaks, how many hours a day will be worked, and so on. Put in writing as many details as you can think of about the way you want the work done. Provide all materials in advance, so you don't have to pay someone to do buying that you can do yourself. If you do not have the time to do the shopping yourself, ask another staff member or a parent or caregiver to do it for you. Save your money for actual work done, not for preparatory jobs. If the work to be done is painting, a painter can usually provide the materials at a lower cost than you can. Arrange to pick up materials from the painter's supplier at the trade discount.

Before undertaking any major repairs at your center, consider carefully whether it might be cheaper in the long run to replace the item rather than repair it. If a repair job will only extend the use of the item for a short time, it obviously does not pay to spend the money on it.

Use the forms on the following two pages to list the names of dependable maintenance and repair workers and reliable suppliers.

MAINTENANCE AND REPAIR HELP

Name	Address	Telephone	Hourly Rate	Comments
Carpentry				
Electrical				
Fencing				
General				
Hauling				
Paving				
Pest Control				
Plumbing				
Roofing				
Weed Control				
Window Washing				
Yard Work				
Other				

C22

SUPPLIERS (MAINTENANCE AND REPAIR)

Item	Company Name and Address	Telephone	Comments
Decomposed Granite			
Electrical			
Garden Supplies			
Hardware			
Lumber			
Paint			
Plumbing			
Sand			
Asphalt			
Concrete			
Tanbark			
Adobe and Brick			
Rubber			
Other			

C23 Replacement and Repair Recommendations List

ITEM	REPAIR	REPAINT	REPLACE	ITEM	REPAIR	REPAINT	REPLACE
Child Care Space				***Playground***			
Bookcase				Sandbox			
Chairs				Sand			
Compact disk player				Swings			
Computers				Slide			
Shelves				Jungle gym			
Storage cabinets				Monkey bars			
Tables				Steps			
Tape recorder				Platform			
________				House			
________				Storage			
________				________			
				________			
Office				________			
Bookcase							
Calculator							
Chairs				***Kitchen***			
Copy machine				Stove			
Desk				Microwave oven			
Fax machine				Refrigerator			
Paper cutter				Dishwasher			
Personal computer				Washer			
Printer				Dryer			
Shelf				________			
Table				________			
Typewriter				________			
________							
________							
________				***Other***			
				________			
Grounds				________			
Lawn				________			
Plants				________			
Walks				________			
Driveways				________			
Parking areas							
________							
________							
________							

C24 Equipment Inventory and Maintenance Records

Keep all information about a single piece of equipment in one place for ready reference. Use a 5" x 7" card for this purpose or keep maintenance records in a specific file folder in your computer. You may want to make periodic copies of updates. Carefully kept records of this kind help pinpoint the relative value of various items that you have purchased, the strengths and weaknesses in your budget, and what your future needs might be. They also provide ready information for tax purposes.

Side 1

Item: ______________________ Date acquired: ____________ Cost: ____________

Purchased from ________________________________ Warranty: No _____ Yes _____

Manufacturer: ________________________________ Expiration date: ____________

Dates Inventoried	Accumulated Depreciation	Depreciation This Year	Book Value	Cost of Repairs	Insurance Value

Side 2

Maintenance Record

Item: ______________________

Service Date	Service Rendered	By Whom	Cost

C25 Extermination Service

Subscribe to an extermination service to minimize the danger of insect infestation. The exterminator comes to your center once a month at hours when the program is not in session—most children, as well as many adults, are very sensitive to insecticide. Keep abreast of new research on insecticides and deal with a reliable company that discusses new findings with you so that you may periodically review your pest control options.

Name of exterminator: ______________________________

Address: ______________________________

Phone: ______________________________

C26 Housekeeping Schedule

Item	Monthly	Weekly	Twice Weekly	Daily	Comments
Floors					
Swept and dry-mopped				X	
Wet-mopped			X		
Polished and buffed	X				
Chalkboards		X			Use blackboard cleaner—no water
Woodwork, doors, cupboards					
Finger marks and smudges removed		X			
Doorknobs, polished and washed		X			
Tabletops, wiped and washed				X	
Countertops, washed and wiped clean				X	
Lavatories					
Toilets sanitized				X	
Washbasins cleaned				X	
Floors mopped				X	
Cubicles washed	X				
Cubicle doors washed		X			
Paper supplies checked and replaced as needed				X	
Mirror cleaned		X			

Item	Monthly	Weekly	Twice Weekly	Daily	Comments
Windows, cleaned	X				
Halls, kept free of litter				X	
Wastebaskets, emptied				X	
Wastebaskets, washed		X			
Refrigerator, cleaned, inside			X		baking soda solution
Refrigerator, cleaned, outside		X			
Refrigerator, defrosted	X				
Light fixtures, checked and changed as needed	X				
Storage rooms, cleaned and mopped		X			
Supply room floor mopped	X				
Rugs, vacuumed		X			
Outdoor walks, swept				X	
Patio, swept as needed				X	
Outdoor walks and patio, washed		X			
Garbage cans					
Set out for pickup			X		
Cleaned, disinfected		X			
Stove, cleaned as needed				X	
Kitchen sink, floors, counter, cleaned as needed				X	
Wash *bedding, dish towels*		X			
Sandbox, raked		X			
Leaves, raked			X		
Stairways, washed		X			
Stairs, dusted and mopped		X			
Minor repairs as needed				X	

D Staff

1 Hiring New Staff Members
2 Job Descriptions
3 Job Description for Head Child Care Provider or Assistant Director
4 Job Description for Child Care Provider
5 Job Description for Assistant Child Care Provider
6 Job Description for Volunteer
7 Job Description for Custodian
8 Job Description for Cook-Housekeeper
9 Job Description: All Staff
10 Individual Responsibilities
11 Labor Laws
12 Resources for Staff Recruitment
13 Transmittal of Application
14 Application for Employment
15 Form for Verification of Applicant Experience
16 Interviewing Applicants
17 Selecting an Applicant
18 References
19 Notifying Applicants That Position Has Been Filled
20 Notifying Applicant Who Was Not Hired
21 Notifying Applicant Confirming Employment
22 Fingerprinting and Criminal History Checks
23 Employee Medical Report
24 Disclaimer
25 Lifting Ability
26 Staff Contract
27 Personnel Policy
28 Staff Leasing or Temporary Service
29 Notifying Parents and Caregivers of Change in Staff
30 Personnel Action Sheet
31 Director's Staff List
32 Substitute Child Care Providers
33 Substitute's Folder
34 List of Available Substitutes
35 Record of Employee Absences
36 Employee's Tuberculin Test Record
37 Checklist for Personnel File
38 Availability for Reemployment Questionnaire

D

39 Notification of Intention Not to Rehire
40 Dismissal of an Employee
41 Letter for Dismissal of Employee
42 Staff Management
43 Orientation for New Staff Members
44 Orientation of New Staff Members Hired Midyear
45 Employee's Handbook
46 Child Care Provider's Room and Group Assignment Sheet
47 Child Care Provider's Notice of Child's Withdrawal from Program
48 Receipt for Keys
49 Temporary Group Roll
50 Staff Meetings
51 Sample Minutes of Staff Meeting
52 In-Service Training
53 Plan for In-Service Training Session
54 Chart for Staff Assignments
55 Shared Responsibilities
56 Professional Conduct
57 Confidentiality and Ethics
58 Professional Growth of Staff Members
59 Record of Professional Growth
60 Career Preparation and Advancement Guide
61 Request for Partial Reimbursement of Educational Fees
62 Constructive Criticism of Staff Members
63 Personal Problems of Staff Members
64 Evaluating Child Care Center Employees
65 Employee Evaluation
66 Procedure for Staff Self-Evaluation Form
67 Staff Self-Evaluation Form
68 Child Care Observation and Evaluation
69 Use of Memo Forms
70 Monday Memo
71 Monday Memo—Sample
72 Room Needs for Next Year
73 Maintaining Contact with Staff
74 End of Year (Nine-Month Schedule)
75 Welcome Letter to New Staff Members
76 Advance Planning Letter to Staff for New Program Year

D1 Hiring New Staff Members

One of your most important tasks as director will be hiring new staff members. The atmosphere and quality of a child care facility is primarily dependent upon the staff. The most functional building, the most elaborate equipment, and the most expensive educational materials will not ensure a good program. Although the presence of a certain number of these components is essential, the difference between a good quality program and one that is mediocre or poor can usually be attributed to the quality of the staff.

Qualifications

Before hiring anyone, you need to decide what qualifications an employee must have for each particular staff position.

Legal Requirements

The first criterion to be considered is that of the legal requirements imposed by licensing regulations. Some states may not have any such requirements; however, many states do have standards regarding the age of employees, their education in early childhood subjects, and their experience.

Your Own Standards

You must decide whether you want to require your employees to meet only the minimum standards or whether you want to add certain standards of your own regarding education and experience. For example, a state may require only that employees be at least 18 years of age and high school graduates, but you may want your employees to have one or two years of college education, some courses in early childhood subjects, and at least one year of actual experience. You may set your own standards as high as you want.

If you set your standards too high, you greatly limit your field of potential candidates. The salaries that you offer need to be competitive with those offered for other jobs for which these candidates may be eligible. If you can only pay minimum wages, you will need to consider hiring entry-level personnel who have not had much training or experience, but who have the potential to benefit from professional training while on the job. Make certain that such applicants want to continue their professional growth and that you are willing to support their efforts [Sections D58–60].

D2 Job Descriptions

After setting standards for employee qualifications, the next step in hiring new staff is to prepare job descriptions for each position. These descriptions should list the qualifications that you have decided upon, the responsibilities and duties that the employee is expected to meet and perform, and the supervisory staff to whom the employee is responsible. Good job descriptions for the staff decrease the possibility that they will be called upon to assume more duties than they are capable of or that one staff member's job will overlap with or conflict with another's. Good job descriptions also serve as a basis for evaluation of staff performance.

The following are sample job descriptions for the most commonly held jobs at child care centers. There is no separate job description for the director. It is assumed that the director is responsible for all items listed in Section A1, and that your job description can be written from these items.

D3 Job Description for Head Child Care Provider or Assistant Director

The person selected for this position will be responsible for the general supervision and management of a group of 12 to 15 children between the ages of two and five. This person will also assume the duties of acting director at times when the director is absent.

Qualifications

The person selected for this position must be professionally prepared as a child care provider for young children, especially in the field of early childhood education or development, and must be able to meet the requirements of the licensing agency [Section A9]. This person must be a sensitive and mature individual who is able to relate well to both children and adults. This person must have the personality and ability to provide leadership and stability for program continuity.

Responsibilities

Responsibilities will include, but will not be limited to, the following:

- Planning, supervising, and implementing the program for child care in accordance with the policies and philosophy of the center [Sections A14, E26, Part I].
- Gearing the program to the needs of individual children, with concern for their interests, challenges, special talents, and individual styles and paces of learning [Sections C11, E26].
- Considering individual children in relationship to their cultural and socio-economic background.

- Treating children with dignity and respect [Section D9].
- Helping children become aware of their roles as integral members of a group.
- Being responsible for the ordered arrangement, appearance, decor, and learning environment of the child care center [Sections C10–11].
- Conducting parent/caregiver conferences on children's adjustment and behavior [Section F33].
- Assisting the director in explaining the program to visitors [Sections E13, J1].
- Assisting the director in supervising the child care staff, ensuring the smooth coordination of all activities, and directing staff and children inter-relationships [Section D42].
- Assisting the director in staff-training activities, demonstrations, and staff evaluations [Sections D50, D64–68].
- Assisting the staff in the effective use of parent/caregiver child care assistants [Section F22].
- Assisting the director in the ongoing evaluation procedures needed to assess the developmental levels of the children.
- Assisting the director and staff in family-center relationships [Part F].
- Attending all staff meetings and recommended training programs and being responsible for one in-service staff meeting each year [Section D50].
- Attending meetings and conferences of professional organizations appropriate for early childhood education, sometimes as a representative of the center in place of the director [Section J6].

D4 Job Description for Child Care Provider

The person selected for this position will be responsible for the general supervision and management of a group of 12 to 15 children between the ages of two and five.

Qualifications

The person selected for this position must be professionally prepared as a child care provider of young children, especially in the field of early childhood education or development, and be able to meet the requirements of the licensing agency [Section A9]. This person must be a sensitive and mature individual who is able to relate well to both children and adults.

Responsibilities

Responsibilities will include, but will not be limited to, the following:

- Planning, supervising, and implementing the program for child care in accordance with the policies and philosophy of the center [Sections A14, E26, Part I].
- Gearing the program to the needs of individual children, with concern for their interests, challenges, special talents, and individual styles and paces of learning. [Sections C11, E26]

- Considering individual children in relationship to their cultural and socio-economic background.
- Treating children with dignity and respect [Section D9].
- Helping children become aware of their roles as integral members of a group.
- Being responsible for the ordered arrangement, appearance, decor, and learning environment of the child care room [Sections C10–11].
- Assuming an equal share of the joint housekeeping responsibilities of the staff [Section D55].
- Attending all staff meetings. Planning and implementing one staff training meeting each year [Section D50].
- Participating in recommended training programs, conferences, courses, and other aspects of professional growth.
- Implementing methods for effectively utilizing the services of child care assistants [Section F22].
- Planning and implementing methods of establishing a positive liaison with children's parents and caregivers [Sections F4, F10, F25].
- Conducting parent/caregiver conferences on children's adjustment and behavior [Section F33].
- Assisting in the ongoing evaluation procedures needed to assess the developmental levels of the children.
- Assisting in public-relations events sponsored by the center [Part J].

D5 Job Description for Assistant Child Care Provider

The person selected for this position will be responsible for assisting a child care provider in the general supervision and management of a group of 12 to 15 children between the ages of two and five.

Qualifications

The person selected for this position must be at least 19 years of age and in the process of becoming professionally prepared to be a child care provider for young children and meet the requirements of the licensing agency [Section A9]. This person must have a warm and friendly personality, be sensitive to the feelings and needs of others, be able to relate well to children, and be willing to fulfill responsibilities in accordance with the center's educational philosophy [Sections A14, E26, Part I].

Responsibilities

Responsibilities will include, but will not be limited to, the following:

- Assisting in planning and implementing the daily program under the direction of the child care provider [Section E26, Part I].
- Assisting in planning and preparing the child care environment, setting up interest centers, and preparing needed materials and supplies [Sections C10–11].

- Supervising the children when the child care provider is out of the room.
- Helping with general housekeeping tasks [Section D55].
- Assisting the child care provider in any other appropriate ways.
- Maintaining professional attitude and loyalty to the center at all times [Section D9].
- Treating all children with dignity and respect [Section D9].
- Attending all staff meetings and recommended training programs and conferences [Section D50].
- Participating in professional organizations that work for the improvement of early childhood education [Section J6].

D6 Job Description for Volunteer

The person selected for this position will be responsible for assisting the professional staff in the general supervision and management of a group of 12 to 15 children between the ages of two and five.

Qualifications

The person selected for this position must meet one of the following criteria:

a. Be a student in child development, child care, psychology, nursing, or a related field at a local high school, college, university, or trade school.

b. Be a parent, grandparent, or caregiver of a child enrolled in our program.

c. Be a friend of the Community Child Care Center who has volunteered specific services to the center.

The person coming into the program on any of the above criteria must present a warm and friendly personality, be sensitive to the feelings and needs of others, be able to relate well to children, and be willing to support the center's educational and nonpunitive philosophy [Section F12, Part J].

Responsibilities

Responsibilities will include, but will not be limited to, the following:

- Assisting as needed under the direction of the professional staff.
- Maintaining professional attitude at the center at all times.
- Allowing professional staff to deal with problem situations.
- Supporting the philosophy of the program.
- Treating all children with dignity and respect [Section D9].
- If volunteering a skill or talent, presenting a written plan to the professional staff. Upon approval, implementing that plan.

D7 Job Description for Custodian

The person selected for this position will be responsible for the general maintenance of the buildings and grounds and will keep them in a hygienic, safe, and presentable condition. This person will arrange for outside services when necessary to keep buildings and grounds in good repair. This person will work under the day-to-day supervision of the cook-housekeeper.

Qualifications

The person selected for this position must be experienced in the care and maintenance of buildings and grounds, must have a basic knowledge of common household repairs and simple gardening techniques, must be willing to participate in some in-service training in child development, and must be able to relate well to children.

Responsibilities [Section C26]

- Maintaining floors and keeping walls, doors, furnishings, and fixtures clean, safe, operable, and presentable.
- Sanitizing toilets and washbasins daily.
- Keeping entrances, walks, porches, steps, and parking areas swept and free of debris and other obstructions.
- Maintaining electrical fixtures in good working order, changing lightbulbs as needed, and performing minor repairs as needed.
- Keeping toilet tissue, paper towels, and soap dispensers adequately supplied.
- Keeping the garden and grounds neat and attractive at all times. Children will be asked to assist in gardening and other outdoor chores and, on occasion, with some indoor chores as well.
- Helping to keep the kitchen in sanitary condition and assisting in all house-keeping duties in relation to serving food.
- Assisting in setting up and putting away heavy equipment.

D8 Job Description for Cook-Housekeeper

The person selected for this position will be responsible for the general supervision of the nutrition program and all related food services of the center and for the supervision of all custodial services necessary to maintain facilities in a hygienic, safe, and presentable condition. This employee will not be expected to assist in the child care area but may be asked to help with the children if an emergency occurs. All work will be done under the supervision of the director.

Qualifications

The person selected for this position must be an experienced cook, possess a knowledge of basic principles of good nutrition, and have a demonstrated ability to plan for economy in shopping and to plan, prepare and serve balanced meals and snacks. This person will have good personal cleanliness habits, be sincerely interested in working with young children, and display a willingness to pursue studies in child development. In addition, this person will understand the requirements for hygienic plant maintenance and housekeeping and demonstrate ability to supervise the work of others.

Responsibilities

- Planning, making necessary purchases for, preparing, and serving two meals and two snacks per day to all-day children, based on a menu plan for each four-week period, and serving one snack per day to all half-day children.
- Reviewing the food service program with the director and/or nutritionist periodically and coordinating the program with other center activities.
- Providing assistance to staff members for food and cooking experiences they may wish to plan for the children.
- Incorporating birthday parties for individual children into the morning snack for that day, using foods with minimal amounts of sugar.
- Participating in an ongoing in-service training program to expand knowledge of child development in order to understand and meet the needs of children.
- Supervising the work of the custodian and assisting in simple housekeeping tasks during the custodian's absence, especially in relation to food services.
- Performing simple laundry tasks.
- Being responsible for seeing that all doors are locked and all outdoor equipment is put away, and that the building is left in safe condition each day after the last person leaves.
- Providing transportation services in emergency situations.

D9 Job Description: All Staff

The complexities of modern living impose a great deal of stress on everyone, including center clientele and staff. The values of the home and child care center are becoming increasingly important. Therefore, the qualifications for all staff members include personality and character traits that will have a positive influence on the manner in which they will pursue their responsibilities. Give the following job description to each of your staff members. It sets the tone for wholesome interpersonal relationships, professionalism, and standards of excellence. The most common reason for dismissing an employee is a deficiency in one or more of the items in this job description, even though the employee may outwardly fulfill all the responsibilities on the specific job description.

Notice to Staff

You have been selected for your position because of special qualities, talents, or skills that are needed to make up a well-balanced administrative, child care, and support staff. Each member is part of the total staff, and all are dependent upon one another. Relationships are circular, and what affects one affects all. Although specific responsibilities may vary according to your primary job description and your list of individual responsibilities, all staff persons are charged with the total responsibility of working together in a united manner. The goal is to achieve harmony and mutuality throughout the center, with respect, tolerance, patience, honesty, trust, and friendship.

We want you to be proud of your role in this center. You are hereby each charged with the responsibility of seeing to it that the reputation of our program as an outstanding child care and educational environment for children and their families is enhanced and maintained.

Personal Qualities of Each Staff Member

1. **Friendliness**—Maintains a positive attitude toward others, acknowledges the presence of others with a greeting, and is alert to the moods and needs of others.
2. **Honesty**—Is truthful about hours, sick and personal leave, and other center matters. Takes responsibility for own errors, is trustworthy, and respects the property of others.
3. **Voice modulation**—Refrains from use of an abusive, sarcastic, or uncontrolled tone of voice.
4. **Punctuality**—Arrives at work at the specified time and honors the time limits of relief and lunch periods, knowing that others are dependent on one's promptness.
5. **Dependability**—Performs responsibilities as promised. Does not require constant reminders. Uses working hours to do actual work for the center, seeking out tasks to be done, rather than using a lax period to take care of personal obligations.
6. **Integrity**—Cooperates in the maintenance of wholesome interpersonal relationships, free of gossip about co-workers or about child care center families. If there are questions about the actions of a particular staff member, talks directly with that person or discusses the matter, in confidence with the director.
7. **Positive attitude**—Refrains from complaining attitude. Brings complaints to the director or other supervising staff member.
8. **Presentability**—Is poised, well mannered, neatly and appropriately dressed, well groomed, and clean. Follows guidelines of staff handbook.
9. **Patience**—Maintains self-control in dealing with others.
10. **Active and energetic**—Maintains an evident interest in job.

Relationship with Children

1. **Individualization**—Demonstrates concern for the personal differences between individuals in relationship to their needs, interests, development and capabilities.
2. **Knowledgeability**—Plans age level developmentally appropriate activities. Keeps the program operating smoothly with a variety of activities.

3. **Resourcefulness**—Demonstrates creativity and resourcefulness in planning programs and use of materials.
4. **Flexibility**—Is able to work with both individuals and groups of children with equal skill.
5. **Personal manner**—Bends to eye level frequently when talking with a child. Is able to help each child build self-esteem and healthy self-concept.
6. **Professionalism**—When talking to children, uses appropriate language and relates their behavior to growth and development.
7. **Discipline**—Uses nonpunitive methods of discipline and offers guidance in a positive manner.
8. **Responsibility**—Assesses each child's growth, development, and performance, recording some observations for each child, taking special note of changes, and maintaining appropriate records as have been requested.
9. **Relaxation**—Uses stress-reduction techniques in helping children and adults to achieve an inner awareness and calmness.
10. **Tolerance**—Treats all children equally, with respect and empathy. Avoids prejudicial attitudes.

Relationships with Adults, Including Parents and Caregivers

1. **Friendliness**—Maintains a friendly, yet professional relationship with parents, caregivers, and coworkers.
2. **Respect**—Respects others' rights to their individual points of view and ideas.
3. **Integrity**—Maintains confidentiality of information.
4. **Tolerance**—Treats all parents and caregivers equally, not showing favoritism, accepting all at their individual levels. Supports cultural differences in extending the curriculum.
5. **Helpfulness**—Works in a comfortable manner with child care assistants, volunteers, and assistant child care providers, offering guidance in positive ways.
6. **Receptiveness**—Is receptive to the idea of visiting a child in his or her home environment.

Demonstrates Concern for and Awareness of the Total Child Care Center

1. **Safety and health consciousness**—Gives primary consideration to the safety and health of children when planning the environment.
2. **Knowledgeability**—Prepares environments that are appropriate for the particular children involved, both individually and in cooperation with one another. Is able to justify the presentation of a particular environment, material, or activity by explaining its relationship to the educational or personal growth of a child or children.
3. **Orderliness**—Keeps materials, supplies, and equipment well organized to present an attractive, orderly, and inviting appearance to the room or any other area being used.
4. **Carefulness**—Respects the use and care of materials and equipment; is not wasteful.
5. **Responsibility**—Assumes personal responsibility for small problems in the environment that others have neglected or have not been aware of (i.e., trash, lack of water, and so on).

Demonstrates Professionalism

1. **Personal growth**—Is committed to the idea of continued personal and professional growth as a child care provider. Maintains a professional membership in job-related organizations. Pursues personal or formal study and/or reading in the field of child development and education.
2. **Loyalty**—Supports the philosophy of the center and the director.
3. **Realism**—Is able to look at own behavior as a possible cause of the problem when things do not go smoothly.
4. **Confidentiality**—Avoids malicious gossip at all times; respects confidentiality of both written, oral, and observed information.
5. **Cooperation**—Is committed to the concept of team spirit, recognizing the center as one total group rather than a series of separate groups. Generously shares ideas, materials, time, and services, thereby helping other persons to perform their very best.
6. **Responsibility**—Is always ready to share responsibilities with others, to assume others' responsibilities in emergencies, and to put the needs of the center as a whole over petty differences of opinion.
7. **Supportiveness**—Is aware of the center policies and supports them. If not in agreement, knows that policies can be discussed with the director and at staff meetings and reserves those times for doing so rather than spreading discontent among coworkers.

Evaluation

It is suggested that you frequently evaluate yourself on these job requirements. These will form the basis of your official periodic evaluation by the director. You can use the following code:

1—Never or seldom *2—Occasionally*	Weak in this area; need to improve
3—Usually, but not always	Average
4—Most of the time *5—Always*	Strong in this area
6—Outstanding	Help others to achieve this level

D10 Individual Responsibilities

In addition to the regular job description for all staff and the job description for the particular position the employee is filling, each staff member is given a list of "Individual Responsibilities." This list generally contains tasks and obligations that have been arranged between the director and each staff member. These might include housekeeping duties, supervision or responsibility for a particular cooperative task involving several persons, special meeting times, and so on.

Put every agreement in writing. This helps clarify situations when questions arise about who is supposed to do what.

Name *Sue*

In consultation with the director, you have agreed to perform the following tasks for the child care center in addition to your regular obligations.

Monitor outdoor play equipment.
Keep director informed of repair and replacement needs.
Check each day to make sure playground has been locked after use.
Monitor condition of playground in rainy weather.
Get smog report from office daily.

Name *Alexis*

In consultation with the director, you have agreed to perform the following tasks for the child care center, in addition to your regular obligations.

Meet with director at noon every Monday.
Supervise student volunteers.
Prepare staff room needs and orderliness.
Ask various staff room members to do staff bulletin board from time to time.

Name Rod

In consultation with the director, you have agreed to perform the following tasks for the child care center, in addition to your regular obligations.

Open office at 6:00 A.M. daily.
Serve as acting director until arrival of the director.
On day director is absent, serve as acting director until arrival of person who is substituting for the director on that day. If needed, serve as acting director for the day.
Supervise napping program, placement of cots, division of groups, placement of staff, etc. See to it that there is adequate coverage, restful environment, and cooperation between staff members.
Ensure that bedding is sent home for washing at appropriate times.
Ensure that an after-nap program has been organized and that snacks, materials, and other supplies have been prepared by the activity leader.

It should be noted that these responsibilities may change as the year progresses. Jobs are often rotated, thus bringing fresh viewpoints to various situations. There are no hard rules. These types of responsibilities should remain flexible. They are often voluntarily offered by a staff person who may feel strongly about one area of need or another.

D11 Labor Laws

Minimum Wage

Before hiring any employees, familiarize yourself with both federal and state labor laws that may affect the operation of your center.

Contact the U.S. Department of Labor for specific questions in regard to minimum wage. There are special provisions for persons considered to be trainees, apprentices, or students.

Individuals with Disabilities

The Rehabilitation Act of 1973 prohibits job discrimination because of a disability. The Americans with Disabilities Act of 1990 protects qualified applicants and employees with disabilities from being discriminated against in hiring, job training, promotion, discharge, pay, benefits, and any other aspect of employment.

Worker's Compensation Insurance

All states require that employers carry this type of insurance to cover employees who are injured while at work.

Unemployment Insurance

All states have some form of unemployment compensation laws, designed to provide an income to employees who may lose their jobs for economic reasons. This does not apply to employees who are discharged because of misconduct.

Equal Employment Opportunity Is the Law

Executive Order 11246 prohibits discrimination in hiring based on race, color, religion, sex, or national origin, and is known as *affirmative action.*

The laws are not static. Amendments are created from time to time. When in doubt, call your local Labor Relations Board to clarify whether or not the information you want of a prospective employee is nondiscriminatory.

Advertising

All job openings must be advertised in either the newspaper or by posting notices in pertinent areas, so that persons qualified for the position may be aware of them. This eliminates your being able to rely only on personal recommendations or walk-in candidates. It does not, however, preclude your hiring them. Many companies include the term "Equal Opportunity Employer" in their advertisements. For the small center, this may boost the cost of the advertisement. Even so, the wording of the ad must be such that it does not specify gender, race, religion, or other qualifications that may be considered discriminatory. An exception is that Section 702 of the Civil Rights Act (1972) allows religious groups to specify that candidates of a specific religious orientation will be given priority consideration.

Qualifications

Qualifications must be stated so that they cannot be misconstrued as leaning heavily toward one particular race, religion, gender, nationality, or age group; nor may they be stated so that they may discriminate against one particular race, religion, gender, nationality, or age group. Advertisements may not require documents such as photographs, birth certificates, naturalization papers, or any others that may indicate race, gender, nationality, religion, or age group.

The Interview

a. Keep a careful record of all persons interviewed to use as support in case of a discrimination accusation. A tape recording of your interviews is an excellent backup in case of a protest. Be sure to inform applicants that the interview is being taped.

b. Questions asked of all candidates must be uniform. The best practice might be to duplicate the questions ahead of time and give a copy to all members of the interviewing committee. The same questions will be used for each person being interviewed, thus assuring equal opportunity.

c. To refine your selection process, you may ask for points of clarification about any information that the candidate has written on the application form. For example, "Why have you had five jobs in the last three years, as you have indicated on your application?" or "How has your membership in this professional organization helped you to become a better child care provider?" The following list gives some guidelines as to what you may or may not ask or say during an interview.

Name of Applicant

You may ask:	You may not ask:
"Have you ever worked under another name or been convicted of a crime under another name?"	"Has your name been legally changed?" "If so, what was your former name?" "What was your maiden name?"

Address

You may ask:	You may not ask:
"What is your address?" "How long have you been living at that address?"	"With whom do you live?" "Do you own or rent your home?"

Birthplace

You may ask:	You may not ask:
"If I hire you, will you be able to prove that you have a legal right to work in the U.S.?"	"What is your birthplace?" "Where were your parents born?" "May I see some papers that indicate your birthplace?"

Age

You may ask:
"Are you over 18 years of age?"
"If I hire you, can you show me proof that you are over 18?"
"If I hire you, can you submit a work permit if you are under 18?"

You may not ask:
"What is your birth date?"
"When did you complete elementary school?"
"When did you graduate from high school?"
Questions that may indicate an applicant is over 40 years of age.

Religion

You may say:
"These are the hours we would expect you to work."
"We are open five days a week and on some weekends and holidays."

You may ask:
"Do you see that there would be any problem in your being able to work during our hours of operation?"

You may not say:
That your organization belongs to a particular religion.

You may not ask:
Any questions to derive information about the applicant's religion or religious service attendance.
"Does your religion prohibit you from working on certain days?"

Marital Status

You may not ask:
"What is your marital status?"

Children

You may not ask:
"Do you have any children?"
"Do they live with you?"
"Who will care for your children if they are ill?"

Race

You may not ask:
"What is your race?"

National Origin

You may ask:
"What languages do you speak, read, or write?"

You may not ask:
"What is your nationality or national origin?"
"How long have you been in the U.S.?"
"What is your usual language?"

Education

You may ask:
Type and degree of education.
Schools attended.

You may not ask:
Questions about educational background that would not be relevant to the position being interviewed for.

Work Experience

You may ask:	You may not ask:
"What is your work and/or military experience?"	"If you were in the military, how were you discharged?"

Criminal Record

You may ask:	You may not ask:
"Do you have a criminal record? Where? Why?" "Have you ever been convicted of child abuse?"	"Have you ever been arrested?"

Photograph

You may say:	You may not say:
"After hiring you, we will need a photograph of you."	"We need a photograph of you with your application."

Emergency Notification

You may ask:	You may not ask:
"Who should be notified in an emergency?"	"What relative should be notified in an emergency?"

References

You may ask:	You may not ask:
"Do you have any objection to our contacting any of the persons whom you have listed as references on your application?" "Who referred you to this job?"	"Can you give a religious reference?" When checking with former employers, you may not ask questions that elicit information as to race, creed, color, religion, national origin, physical handicap, medical status, age, or gender.

Health

You may ask:	You may not ask:
"Are you physically able to perform the job you are applying for?" "Do you have any condition that may inhibit your performance?" "What can be done to accommodate this limitation?" "Are you able to move heavy equipment and lift children?"	"Do you have a medical disability of any type?" "Have you ever received worker's compensation for illness or injury?" "How is your general physical health?"

Economic Status

You may ask:
"What is your salary history?"

You may not ask:
"Have your wages ever been garnished?"
"Have you ever been bankrupt?"
Any questions about applicant's financial status or credit rating.

Bonding

You may say:
"Bonding is a condition for the job."

You may not ask:
"Have you ever been refused a bond or had a bond cancelled?"

Other

You may not ask:
"What is your height and weight?"
"What is your spouse's name and place of work?"
"Do you have friends or relatives that work for us?"
Related questions.

For suggested interview questions, See Section D16.

D12 Resources for Staff Recruitment

Keep a list of names, addresses, and telephone numbers for staff recruitment. Include employment agencies, job fairs, college and university placement offices, local professional groups, newspapers for classified ads, directors of other child care centers, and persons who have served well as child care assistants.

> Preschool child care providers for established, successful program. Half-day and full-day positions open. Prefer experienced child care provider, but will train person with outstanding personality and good educational background. Must know and meet state requirements. Send résumé to Box 000.

D13 Transmittal of Application

Community Child Care Center

111 THIRD STREET ✿ **TELEPHONE 123-4579**

Dear (applicant name),

Thank you for your response to our advertisement for the position of child care provider in our center. Enclosed is an application for you to complete and return to us at the earliest possible date. Upon receipt of your application, we will telephone you in order to make an appointment for a personal interview.

Sincerely,

Director

D14 Application for Employment

APPLICATION FOR EMPLOYMENT

Job applying for: ____________________________ Full-time _______ Part-time _______

Name: ____

Address: ____

City: ____ ZIP: ____________________

Social Security No.: _________________________ Telephone: ____________________

Other names you have worked under:

____

Last physical exam date: _________________ Last TB test date: ___________________

Do you have any physical condition that may restrict your performance of the job you are applying for?

____

Education:

	Major	Dates Attended	Certificate or Degree	Completion Date
High School				
College/University/Trade School				

Licenses or certificates held, or credentials qualifying you for this employment:

____

Awards, published materials:

____

Page 2

EARLY CHILDHOOD COURSES TAKEN

Course Title/Subject	No. of Units

Special skills or talents you may care to list:

Foreign language: ______

Typing: ______ Swimming instruction: ______ Gymnastics: ______

Computers: ______ Musical instruments: ______ Art: ______

Other: ______

Membership in professional organizations (list):

______

______

______

Experience:

Employer (Name/Address)	Job Description	From/To	Salary	Reason for Leaving

Volunteer or unpaid experience: ______

______

______

Page 3

References:

		Name and Address	Title	Phone No.
Professional (list at least two):	1.			
	2.			
	3.			
Personal (list at least two):	1.			
	2.			
	3.			

Have you ever been convicted of a crime? Yes ______ No ______

When? __________ Where? __________ Why? __________ Outcome? __________

When? __________ Where? __________ Why? __________ Outcome? __________

(Exclusions: Minor traffic violations for which the fine was not over $50; an offense that was settled in a juvenile court.)

Why would you like to have this position? ____

____

____

What do you feel most qualifies you for this position?

____

____

Would you be willing to continue your education by enrolling in certain courses or training programs that may be recommended? ____

D15 Form for Verification of Applicant Experience

Community Child Care Center

111 THIRD STREET ✿ TELEPHONE 123-4579

To (name of person given as reference):

______________________________ is being considered by the personnel committee of our child care center to fill a staff vacancy. Your name has been given to us as a reference. We would appreciate your professional evaluation. The information will be treated with the utmost confidence, and under no circumstances will the applicant be told of the source of any comments. Your cooperation is deeply appreciated.

Sincerely yours,

Director

In your opinion, what is this applicant's ability in each of the following areas:

Staff relationships ______________________________

____

Contact with parents and caregivers ______________________________

____

Understanding of children ______________________________

____

Child care equipment ______________________________

____

Instructional techniques ______________________________

____

Professional conduct ______________________________

____

Professional appearance ______________________________

____

Professional growth ______________________________

____

Page 2

In what way is the applicant known to you? ________________________________

____

During what period of time?____

____

If a former employee, what was this applicant's
- Position? ______________________________
- Salary? ______________________________
- Reason for termination? ______________________
  ____

Comments: ____

____

____

Signature: ____________________
Title: ____________________
Date: ____________________

D16 Interviewing Applicants

1. When reading the resume or application, eliminate any applicants that obviously do not meet licensing requirements. Look for gaps in employment, reasons for termination, frequent moves, and self-disclosures such as criminal convictions.
2. Schedule interviews with the remaining applicants far enough apart to let you spend a sufficient amount of time with each one.
3. Hold the first interview at a time when your program is not in session so that you will be able to give your full attention to the applicant. Conduct the interview in a comfortable and informal setting in order to put the applicant at ease. Consider the appearance, personality, attitudes, and enthusiasm of the applicant. Also consider how the applicant will relate to other staff members, the children, and parents and caregivers. Consider, too, how the applicant will appear to the community as a representative of your child care center. Also review the job description [Sections D2–D4], personnel policy [Section D27], and other pertinent information that will help the applicant know what to expect.
4. During the interview, ask several questions such as the following to determine the applicant's personality and knowledge of child development and educational techniques.
   a. Where do you look for ideas for your curriculum?
   b. If you gather a group together for a session of singing as part of a planned sequence, but none of the children appear to be interested, what action do you take?
   c. If a four-year-old girl spends most of the time wandering around with her thumb in her mouth, not participating in play activities, what do you do?
   d. What do you do if a child who has come to child care happily for several months cries bitterly one morning when her parent or caregiver tries to leave?

e. What do you do if a three-year-old child decides that purple paint is for decorating arms and hands?

f. What do you do if a parent or caregiver complains that something must have happened at the center because his or her child doesn't want to go anymore?

5. Invite the applicant who seems to meet your standards to visit the center when child care groups are in session.
6. The applicant's second visit to the center should be spent as a child care assistant for one hour if it can be arranged without inconvenience. This should be followed by another personal interview, reviewing the applicant's attitudes.
7. If you are unable to decide which of two applicants to hire, schedule a third interview. At that time, each applicant will be more familiar with you and more at ease, thus giving you a better chance to assess those attributes you consider as most important.

Additional Sample Interview Questions

1. Describe yourself. What kind of person are you?
2. Describe your current or last job.
3. How would (name of your last boss) describe you? What would he or she say is best about you? Worst?
4. Tell me about your failures and successes. What was learned from your failures? What was learned from your successes?
5. Describe your experiences with children.
6. Can you tell me some differences between a three-year-old and a seven-year-old?
7. How would you rate your organizing abilities?
8. What would a typical daily schedule for you look like?
9. What is your philosophy about discipline?
10. If you ever disagreed with a parent or caregiver, how did you resolve the differences?
11. Who do you admire, and why?
12. What are your most important values? How did you acquire them?
13. Tell me about a time when you did something good for someone.
14. What would you do if:
    - a child accuses another of cheating at a game?
    - a child's personal belonging is missing from his or her cubby at the end of the day?
    - one child is biting another child?
15. Describe the ways in which you would involve parents and caregivers in the child care program.
16. What do you do in your spare time? What are your hobbies or interests?
17. Why do you want to work with children?
18. How do you deal with stress?
19. What would you do if someone accused you of child abuse?
20. Have you ever been reprimanded at work? For what?

D17 Selecting an Applicant

In reviewing applications, you should consider the applicant's experience and education. It is valuable for children to experience a variety of caregivers, thus reaping the benefits of various generations and experiences.

Qualified Applicants

The child care field is attracting increasing numbers of men and women with nurturing qualities and good educational backgrounds. The availability of highly qualified applicants may eventually help to raise the overall pay scale for both men and women. By the same token, these persons quickly become overqualified for their level of pay and seek work elsewhere, thus ever diminishing the availability of qualified applicants.

Personality

You must evaluate the personalities and ego strength of your applicants and learn if they are willing to work toward continued professional growth. You will also have to weigh their personalities against their work experience to determine whether strength in one area can offset a possible weakness in another.

The Candidate's Own Child

Many applicants who have preschool children may expect to bring them to the center with them. This is not always a satisfactory arrangement, but it can be worked out—usually by having the child in the group of another child care provider.

Social Situations

In considering new staff members, there may be certain social situations that will be almost beyond your control. For example, your best friend's daughter may be seeking child care employment, but you do not consider her a qualified applicant. You may hire the wife of the chairperson of the board or a brother of a leading financial contributor to the organization that sponsors the center. These persons may have very nice personalities, but may turn out to be poor child care providers, even though their educational qualifications meet your standards. You may feel that for the good of the program they should not be on the staff.

Each situation will have its own set of variables. Consider all aspects before hiring someone who is closely connected either directly or indirectly with the governing body. If you hire such a person, make it clear that your personnel policy and provisions for trial employment (probation) apply the same as they do to other staff members. Be prepared for hard feelings should the employee perform unsatisfactorily.

D18 References

To aid in your selection of an employee, you must check references. Unfortunately, today it is difficult to receive pertinent information about how applicants may have performed. Former employers will only tell you information related to hire and termination dates, salary and if the former employees are eligible to be rehired. You must get written permission from the applicant to contact previous employers. Personal references are not as valuable because the applicant won't normally list someone who will speak negatively about them. Personal references, however, can be helpful if you ask whether there are any other people you may contact to ask about your applicant's abilities and work with children.

Once you have called to speak to someone who knows the applicant's abilities, listen to the tone of his or her voice and attitude conveyed. A former supervisor will add a smile behind his or her voice when speaking about a good or excellent employee. The voice tone regarding a problem employee may be hesitant or reluctant. Ask for any other names of people who may be able to tell you more about the applicant. Document all reference information that you obtain in order to determine your selection.

You can also solicit written references once you have selected a candidate. Usually these take a while, and the person may have worked for you for several weeks before you receive written responses. At that time, and while the person is still serving a probationary period [Section D27], you may want to reevaluate your selection if the information that you receive is negative.

The following are sample telephone and written reference check questions.

1. Can you please verify the dates of employment and the position held?
2. How would you describe (applicant name)'s (values, character, personality)?
3. Tell me how (applicant name) related to (parents, caregivers, children, other adults).
4. What were his/her skills like when interacting with children?
5. How did he/she respond to supervision?
6. How did he/she deal with stress?
7. Are you aware of any problems (applicant name) may have had that might interfere with his/her ability to perform this job (Tell the reference what the applicant has applied for)?
8. During the time you worked with (applicant name), did you ever observe anything that would make you uncomfortable recommending them for a position working with children?
9. Would you hire this person to care for your own children?
10. Would you rehire this person?

You may meet with resistance in getting this information, depending on the policies of the agency that you have contacted. However, do not fail to verify that the person to whom you are speaking is the reference that was given. Never tell an applicant that he or she was not hired due to poor references. You may tell them that information provided on his/her application or resume was unable to be verified.

D19 Notifying Applicants That Position Has Been Filled

Community Child Care Center

111 THIRD STREET TELEPHONE 123-4579

Dear (applicant name),

Because of the large number of applications we received in response to our recent advertisement for a child care provider, we have been unable to interview all applicants personally. At this time the position has been filled. However, we will keep your application on file for six months and will notify you if we have another opening.

Sincerely,

Director

D20 Notifying Applicant Who Was Not Hired

Community Child Care Center

111 THIRD STREET TELEPHONE 123-4579

Dear (applicant name),

The position for which you applied has now been filled. Thank you for the time you spent with us during the selection process. We appreciate your many fine qualifications and will keep your application in our current file for one year.

Sincerely,

Director

D21

Notifying Applicant Confirming Employment

When an applicant is hired, it is courteous to make a personal phone call telling that person of your decision. You can then invite the new employee in to pick up a contract and other necessary papers, or you may want to send a confirming letter.

Community Child Care Center

111 THIRD STREET TELEPHONE 123-4579

Dear (applicant name),

The Personnel Committee of our center met yesterday and selected you to fill the vacancy on our child care center staff. Congratulations, and welcome to our group!

I will call you soon to make arrangements for a personal conference in preparation for your job. In the meantime, please sign and return the enclosed contract [Section D26] within five days. I am also enclosing a copy of a Fingerprint Disclaimer form [Section D22], which must be notarized. This form will be removed from our files when we receive your actual fingerprint clearance. Also enclosed is a medical form to be completed by your physician [Section D23] and a health disclaimer [Section D24].

Attached to the contract is our personnel policy and staff handbook, in order that you may become familiar with some of the policies of our center.

Sincerely yours,

Director

Enclosures:
Contract
Health form
Health disclaimer
Fingerprint disclaimer
Personnel policy
Staff handbook

D22 Fingerprinting and Criminal History Checks

In 1990, national legislation was passed called the Child Care Worker Employment Background Check. This legislation requires that fingerprints and criminal history checks be done on all individuals applying to work or come in contact with children, in order that persons who have been convicted of child abuse or child sexual abuse be kept out of the field. Criminal history checks may not always be effective in screening potential abusers; however, they are a step in the hiring process that should never be overlooked.

Call your local police department, sheriff's office, or licensing agency to initiate the criminal history check process. They will give you information about how to go about getting the fingerprinting done and where to send it to be checked. It may take from three days to three months to receive this information. The information released may also vary from state to state. You may get only conviction information, open arrests within a given time, all convictions, or only crimes relating to the delinquency of a minor.

In the meantime, for your own protection, you may opt to hire the applicant with continued employment contingent upon a cleared criminal history check. A good practice is to hire employees on a probationary period [Section D27]. This time period allows for the return of references, criminal history checks, and your personal observations of the person while he or she actually works for you. Have new employees sign a disclaimer like the one below. Keep in mind that all criminal history information is very confidential, and only one or two appropriate employees at your center should have access to that information.

Community Child Care Center

111 THIRD STREET ✿ TELEPHONE 123-4579

I, ______________________________, solemnly swear that I have never been convicted of a crime and do not have a record of child abuse or of child sexual abuse. I understand that I do not need to include in this statement any conviction for a minor traffic violation in which I paid $50 or less in fines.

Signed: ____________________

Date: ____________________

Notarized by:

____

Date: ____________________

D23 Employee Medical Report

Each new employee should be required to give you a statement from a physician regarding his or her health. Use the form that follows:

Community Child Care Center

111 THIRD STREET TELEPHONE 123-4579

Name of applicant: ____________________ Date of birth: ____________

Position applied for: ____________________ Working hours: ____________

Duties and responsibilities will include: ______________________________

____

Some lifting of young children and some picking up and moving of furniture and equipment may be required. Since we are vitally involved with the wholesome emotional growth of the children, we require good mental health of our employees. In your opinion, is this applicant free of disease or serious mental or emotional problems that would be detrimental to children and adults with whom the applicant will be working? ______________________________

____

In your opinion, is this applicant free of any physical challenges that would prevent the performance of the above-listed duties? ____________________

____

General physical condition: ______________________________

Evidence of a negative tuberculin test is required.

Type of test: __________ Date of test: ______ Result: ____________

Date of examination

____

____

Signature of physician

____

Address

____

D24 Disclaimer

Until the medical report is received from the new employee's physician, you should have a disclaimer signed, relieving you of any liability should the employee be performing tasks that a physician would forbid and that may lead to illness or injury to the person. A disclaimer can be a simple statement like the following:

Community Child Care Center

111 THIRD STREET TELEPHONE 123-4579

I, ______________________________, declare that I am physically and mentally fit to perform the functions as a ________________________,
(specify type of job)
including moving and/or lifting heavy equipment and lifting young children. I am free of disease and of any physical restrictions that would interfere with the performance of my duties.

Signed: ______________________________

Date: ______________________________

[This may or may not be notarized.]

Witness: ______________________ Date: ______________________

Witness: ______________________ Date: ______________________

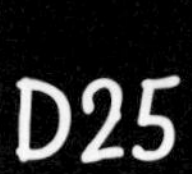

Lifting Ability

For your own protection against possible liability, you may want to have new employees sign a declaration similar to the following:

Community Child Care Center

111 THIRD STREET ✿ TELEPHONE 123-4579

HEAVY LIFTING RELEASE

I, ______________________________, declare that I have not in the past had an accident that restricts my ability to lift a heavy load (60 pounds or less); nor do I presently have a physical condition that restricts my ability to lift a heavy load.

Further, I understand that if a load of over 60 pounds is to be lifted, I will get assistance and not attempt to lift the load by myself.

Further, I hereby release the (name of center) from any liability in connection with my lifting a load or child weighing 60 pounds or less by myself.

Signature: ______________________________

Date: ______________________________

D26 Staff Contract

Community Child Care Center

111 THIRD STREET ✿ TELEPHONE 123-4579

EMPLOYMENT AGREEMENT FOR ______________________________

You are invited to become/continue as a member of our staff for the year beginning ______________and ending ______________.

Your position will be that of ______________________________________,

with responsibilities according to your job description, the personnel policies of the center, the provisions of the staff handbook, and any other agreement made between you and the director of the center, that has been attached to your job description and signed by you.

(You will be paid at the rate of _________ per hour.)

Your salary has been set at the rate of ______________ per year to be paid in bimonthly increments of _______________ each pay period.

Your hours have been set to be from no later than _________ A.M. until at least __________ P.M. on every day the center is open, with the exception of days on which you are on leave.

You are expected to make yourself available for staff meetings and/or in-service training meetings, occasional evening meetings, and pertinent center events. Pay for these occasions has already been taken into consideration in setting your annual salary.

(optional)

As a new employee, you will be on a ____________ month period of probation, during which time the position may be terminated by either party on giving a two-week notice of such termination.

Date: ___________________ For the center: ______________________

Director

I have read the above agreement and agree to abide by the provisions thereof to the best of my ability.

__________________________ ____________

Signature of employee Date

__________________________ ____________

Signature of director Date

D27 Personnel Policy

(Article XII of the School's Operating Policy [Section A14])

The Development of Personnel Policies is critical to the proper functioning of your center. Your staff needs to know about their rights and responsibilities. Having personnel policies can help you specifically state what the employee can expect from you as his or her employer. These policies also spell out to the employee his or her rights. They can free up the director from involvement in any resolutions and help reduce procedural errors. The following personnel policy has been compiled to set the tone for wholesome interpersonal relationships, professionalism, and standards of excellence. You may want to add, delete, or change some of the items to fit your own needs.

A. Salaries

Salaries are to be set for each employee according to agreement among the employee, the director, and the Personnel Committee, subject to the approval of the Board of Directors [Section A11]. Salaries will be based upon abilities, training, length of service, education, experience, and job responsibilities. Payments will be made on the fifteenth day and the last day of each month, or on the working day that falls closest to those days.

Salary increases shall be commensurate with increased enrollment, income, duties, and responsibilities of any employee, upon agreement between the director and the Personnel Committee of the Board of Directors. These increases will follow closely the salary schedule attached hereto [Section B12].

B. Vacation Pay

No deductions from pay will be made for regular program vacations and holiday closings. Year-round employees will receive one week's vacation, with pay, during the summer months.

C. Pregnancy Disability

Staff is eligible for pregnancy disability at the date of hire. Pregnancy leave can be taken up to four months unpaid, along with any vacation and/or sick time during the leave. This leave is in addition to family/medical leave.

D. Family/Medical Leave

Staff becomes eligible for family/medical leave after 1,250 hours have been completed during 12 months of continuous employment. Twelve weeks unpaid leave may be taken for family care or medical purposes due to

1. a serious health condition of the employee's child, parent, spouse;
2. his or her own health condition; or
3. pregnancy; the birth or adoption of his or her child.

Accrued vacation or sick time may be used as part of family/medical leave. Seniority continues to accrue while on family leave; however, sick time and vacation time does not accrue. Upon returning to work after the completion of the leave, the staff will return to the same or comparable position unless business dictates otherwise.

E. **Sick/Personal Leave**

One day a month, sick or personal leave shall be allowed with full pay. Leave shall not be cumulative from year to year. At the end of a program year, unused sick/personal leave shall be compensated for on the following basis:

8 or more days remaining: 2 days off with pay

6 or 7 days remaining: 1 day off with pay

3 to 5 days remaining: 1/2 day off with pay

F. **Hours**

Child care providers shall work from four to eight hours daily, depending upon individual contracts. Child care providers are expected to attend staff meetings of one-half to two hours weekly [Section D50]. Time for such meetings and for program preparation is built into the salary schedule. All salaried persons may be called on for a reasonable amount of extra time at no extra pay in emergency situations, in preparation for meetings, open house, or other special events, and in connection with individual responsibilities as an employee of the Community Child Care Center. The director shall be on call at any time in connection with responsibilities of the position.

G. **Compensatory Time (Overtime)**

Staff persons are not offered comp time (i.e., paid time off in lieu of overtime pay) because of the extremely strict federal and state laws governing this practice.

H. **Insurance Benefits**

All employees shall be covered by Social Security, Worker's Insurance Compensation, and Disability Insurance. As a nonprofit corporation, the center is not required to carry State Unemployment Insurance Compensation. All employees shall be given the option of enrolling in the health and accident policy of the Community Child Care Center. Employees shall be notified of the benefits of the insurance sponsored by the National Association for the Education of Young Children [Section J10].

I. **Probationary Period**

All new employees shall serve a six-month probationary period, at the end of which time the employment will be considered permanent or will be terminated. The director shall schedule regular periods of observation during the probationary period, with ongoing feedback to the employee [Sections D62–64]. Two weeks' written notice either from the center director or from the child care providers must be given in case of termination. Legally, no reason needs to be given if dismissal occurs during the probationary period.

J. **Termination Notice**

If a person is not to be rehired for the following year, written notice of termination of employment shall be made at least two weeks prior to the expiration of the current contract [Section D41].

K. **Retirement Plans**

Employees shall be encouraged to participate in the retirement plan as offered by the National Association for the Education of Young Children and shall also be encouraged to open an IRA account. They shall also have the option of diverting a portion of their salary to a tax-sheltered annuity, which has been arranged by the Community Child Care Center through an insurance company.

L. In-Service Training

Regardless of their previous education and experience, employees will be expected to continue the study of and training in preschool techniques and early childhood education practices in order to keep abreast of new research and knowledge. This continued study and training may take place on the employee's own time outside of regular working hours, and as recommended by the director.

Methods used may include, but not be limited to, in-service training classes at the center [Section D52], parent/caregiver meetings [Section F10], study of current books and other literature, attendance at recommended professional conferences and meetings, membership in recommended professional organizations, and attendance at recommended meetings and workshops of those associations, and enrollment in pertinent courses offered at nearby colleges and universities [Section D58].

M. Costs of Training

The center shall make a partial reimbursement of the tuition charged for enrollment in college or university courses that have been recommended by the director [Section D58]. This reimbursement shall range from 25 to 50 percent of the tuition, depending upon the number of staff members participating in courses concurrently, the expense of the course, and the availability of funds within the budget. Tuition shall be paid in the form of a loan to the employee. During the second year of continued employment following the completion of the course, the loan shall be written off as an expense. Should the person voluntarily leave employment prior to a one-year period, the amount loaned will be deducted from the person's final paycheck.

Costs are also shared for attending educational conferences that may be recommended by the director. Child care providers shall be allowed a predetermined amount each year to be applied toward attending such conferences. However, as with tuition costs, this sum shall be deducted from the final paycheck if the person leaves the center's employ within one year of the conference.

N. Periods of Employment

Employment periods shall be based on yearly needs within the limitations of the budget and in accordance with individual contracts. Generally, child care providers who do not work year-round will start to work approximately one week before the opening day of the new term in the fall and will terminate their employment approximately two days after the closing date in June. Staff members who work during the summer term are employed on a year-round basis.

O. Breaks

All staff persons shall have a 15-minute relief period during each four hours of work. Adequate supervision of children will be arranged.

P. Health Examination

A health examination shall be required at the time of initial employment, including a tuberculin test [Section D36]. Additional examinations may be requested at the discretion of the director, and at any time in the future that the employee's health appears to be in question.

Q. Supervision

The staff will be responsible to the director of the Child Care Center. In the director's absence, the staff will be responsible to the acting director. The director will be responsible to the Board of Directors.

R. Job Descriptions

Each member of the staff will be given a job description that will be applicable to the position covered by the contract [Sections D3–8]. In addition, each member of the staff shall be given a job description that will be applicable to all staff [Section D9]. Also, each member of the staff will be given a job description that will be applicable only to selected specific center-wide responsibilities for that particular employee [Section D10].

S. Contracts

Each employee shall be given a yearly contract setting forth the terms of employment [Section D26].

T. Staff Meetings

Attendance at regularly scheduled and emergency staff meetings outside of regular working hours is expected and will be paid for [Sections D50–51].

U. Personnel Differences

In the event of lack of agreement on procedure between members of the child care staff, the director will make the final decision. In the event of lack of agreement on procedure between members of the child care staff and the director, the director may ask the chairperson of the board to arbitrate and will abide by the chairperson's decision.

V. Amendments

Any changes, revisions, or amendments to the personnel policy will be presented to each staff member at least ten days before offering a new contract.

Note to Reader

Naturally, circumstances vary from one center to another and from year to year. Therefore, you should change the wording of this policy statement and make appropriate additions or deletions to reflect the circumstances at your center.

The following is a list of additional personnel issues that could be addressed in your personnel policies:

Dress Code Policy
Procedures for Staff Absences
Statement of Professionalism
Ethical Code of Conduct
Sexual Harassment Policy
Drug Free Policy
Education Reimbursement
Reimbursement Procedures
Travel Expenses
Health and Safety Procedures
Organizational Chart
ADA Requirements

Community Child Care Center

111 THIRD STREET ✿ TELEPHONE 123-4579

Acknowledgement of Receipt of Personnel Policies

I understand that the Personnel Policies and Procedures Handbook provides information concerning my employment with the Community Child Care Center and its guidelines.

I understand that I must familiarize myself with the information in the handbook and follow the rules, procedures, and guidelines set forth.

My signature below indicates that I have received the Community Child Care Center Personnel Policies and Procedures Handbook, and I have read and accepted the above acknowledgments.

____
Employee name (please print)

____
Employee signature

Date ________________

This page is to be torn out of the Personnel Policy Handbook and put in employee's personnel file.

D28 Staff Leasing or Temporary Service

An employment service available to small businesses is that of staff leasing or temporary employment services. Although there are many such plans, they will generally work in the following manner:

1. You advertise for and select an employee who meets your needs.
2. You determine the salary or hourly wage.
3. You contact the leasing company and turn the employee over to them.
4. They will determine benefits and take-home pay with the employee, according to which benefits they opt for.
5. The employee then works for you but is technically an employee of the leasing company, who handles all paychecks, insurance, deductions, employee relations, and, if necessary, dismissal if you so request.

The benefits of such a program are twofold:

1. For the center director:

   You do not have to hire someone to generate salary checks, with all of the calculations for deductions. You do not have to file quarterly payroll reports.

2. For the employee:

   More benefits are available for less money. The leasing agency handles so large a number of employees that they can obtain group discounts on such items as medical insurance, dental plans, life insurance, educational allowances, pension plans, and credit union services.

The cost of this type of service is paid for by you, at a small percentage above gross-salary rate.

You will find these leasing or temporary employment companies listed in the telephone books under *employment agencies*.

D29 Notifying Parents and Caregivers of Change in Staff

As soon as a new child care provider is hired, send a notice to parents and caregivers to inform them of the change. It is especially important that parents and caregivers understand that the change will be made with minimal disruption to the program. The following is a sample letter:

Community Child Care Center

111 THIRD STREET ✿ **TELEPHONE 123-4579**

Dear Parents and Caregivers:

One of the nice things about a program like ours is the opportunity that the child care providers have to increase their professional understanding and abilities.

Since our program is in a constant state of change and growth, because it is flexible and humanistic, and because it is based on the needs and interests of the individual, child care providers learn and grow as much as children do—maybe even more. And sometimes it becomes necessary for them to move on in order to share what they have learned here with others.

And so it is with mixed feelings of sadness and pleasure that we announce that Anna Bates has accepted a full-time child care position at Kennedy Child Care Center. We are grateful for the many contributions that she has made to our center during her six years with us.

Anna will be replaced by Elly Delgado, who will also serve as Assistant Director. Elly has child care credentials and has participated in our program on a regular basis ever since her oldest daughter—now eleven—was in our child care center eight years ago! She has had three children in our center and has participated as a child care assistant, so she is not only familiar with the center, but has a working knowledge of our program. We are pleased that she will be with us next year. She will work with Anna until the end of the year, so there will be no sudden, traumatic change for the children (or the director, for that matter!) to deal with. Thanks to all of you for your understanding.

Sincerely,

Director

D30 Personnel Action Sheet

Position: ______________________

Name: ______________________ Phone: ______________________

Address: ______________________ ZIP: ______________________

Working hours: ______________________

Working salary: ______________________ Starting date: ______________________

Increases:

Amount of Increases	Rate of Increase	Date Effective	New Title (if any)

D31 Director's Staff List

Name and Address of Staff Members	Telephone	Date of Birth	Position

D32 Substitute Child Care Providers

Substitute child care providers are an important part of your staff. They should be invited to participate in as many staff meetings as possible, perhaps even being paid for their time.

Have two substitutes available for general call. They should come to about every fourth staff meeting and be paid for attending.

In addition, several qualified parents or caregivers can act as substitute child care providers when your regular substitutes are not available. Only those qualified parents and caregivers who have shown outstanding ability as child care assistants should be used as emergency substitutes.

Substitutes are paid an hourly rate, depending on length of service, responsibilities, and so on. Parents and caregivers who fill in for a child care provider are given a choice between receiving tuition credit or being paid at the same rate as substitutes.

D33 Substitute's Folder

Each child care provider prepares a folder of information and suggestions that a substitute can study for a short time, and then be ready to step into a child care group. Contents of the folder may include

- a copy of the Child Care Assistant's Handbook [Section F17].
- a schedule for a typical day, with a copy of a suggested lesson or play plan [Section I6].
- a list of children's names, with pertinent comments that will help the substitute approach each child as an individual.
- name tags ready to pin on each child.
- a special flannelboard story that children have not seen before.
- the names of two or three of children's favorite records, plus a note as to where you keep them.
- a special art project, such as a collection of paper shapes with which children can make collages. (Include triangles, squares, and circles, some of which have had their centers cut out. Let the substitute know what kind of paper and paste to use.)
- suggestions for two or three of children's favorite stories and finger games.
- the words to two or three of children's favorite songs.

The substitute should not be made to feel that the things listed in the folder must be done. Its main purpose is to provide information about the children, along with some extra resources to use if needed. By the same token, child care providers who know ahead of time that they are going to be gone and are anxious to have the materials in the folder used, are responsible for preparing the folder in such a way that the substitute will be readily motivated to do so. They should also include a personal note, such as that on page 169.

Community Child Care Center

111 THIRD STREET TELEPHONE 123-4579

Dear Substitute:

Welcome to my child care room and thank you for coming. I hope that you will find my play plan and the materials in this folder useful. I am especially eager for you to read the individual evaluation list that I have made concerning each child. If you need to know where something is, ask Jenny or Tim. They are my best "finders." Billy sometimes needs to be given some special little job where he can be away from the other children for a few moments. He is generally good at straightening out the contents of a drawer, washing a tabletop, or taking a note to another room. Please give him a special task that makes him feel important. Do this if you notice that he is beginning to get a little belligerent with the other children. Elinor has been very weepy lately. There has been a lot of illness in her family. I hope that you will find time to give her a little extra hug once in a while. She likes to be asked to help. All in all, this is a delightful group of children. Please enjoy your day with them and thank you again for your help.

Sincerely,
Child Care Provider

D34 List of Available Substitutes

Keep a list of people who are available as substitutes posted in the office.

Name and Address of Substitute	Telephone	Days Available	Rate of Pay	Comments

D35 Record of Employee Absences

Name: ______________________________

Date	Reason for Absence	With Pay	Without Pay

D36 Employee's Tuberculin Test Record (Required by the Community Child Care Every Other Year)

Date of Most Recent Test

Name	20 ___	20 ___	20 ___	20 ___	20 ___

D37 Checklist for Personnel File

The personnel file of each employee should include

___ application for employment [Section D14]
___ reference letters [Section D15]
___ health examination and record [Section D23]
___ heavy lifting release [Section D25]
___ criminal record disclaimer [Section D22]
___ tuberculin test record [Section D36]
___ sick leave report (of previous years) [Section D35]
___ personnel action sheet [Section D30]
___ staff member's requests for partial reimbursement of educational fees [Section D61]
___ self-rated evaluation [Section D67]
___ director's evaluations [Sections D65–66]
___ job description [Sections D2–9]
___ college transcripts
___ fingerprint clearance [Section D22]
___ child abuse index check [Section D22]
___ receipt of personnel policy form [Section D27]
___ ethical code of conduct [Sections D56–57]

Note: Individual contracts are kept in a confidential file in the larger budgeting file.

D38 Availability for Reemployment Questionnaire

Community Child Care Center

111 THIRD STREET ✿ **TELEPHONE 123-4579**

Dear (employee name),

The current year is now drawing to a close. Your contributions to the center have been appreciated and I hope that you are planning to continue as a member of our staff.

To assist us in our assessment of our fall needs, please indicate on the lower portion of this form whether or not you will be available to continue on our staff for the forthcoming year.

Please return this form within five working days.

_____ I will be available for employment for the forthcoming year.
_____ I will NOT be available for employment for the forthcoming year.

Signed: ___________________________
Date: ___________________________

D39 Notification of Intention Not to Rehire

If you have a staff member whom you do not expect to rehire, you should give that person notice of your intention at the earliest possible date. In any event, this should be done at least two weeks before you notify other members of the staff that you wish to rehire them. Termination notice should be given in a one-to-one conference with the staff member involved.

This notification should not come as a shock to the staff member. If you have developed an ongoing evaluation procedure and wholesome staff relationships [Sections D42, D64–66, D68], the staff member should already have had some indication of your intentions.

You must, of course, give a valid reason for your decision. But do so in a way that will highlight the person's strengths. Make as many suggestions as you can for alternative employment. Also, tell the person exactly what to expect from you in the way of references and in the way of time off for job interviews. Above all, be kind, gentle, and helpful.

Sufficient reasons exist for not rehiring any staff member who

- has become ineffective at the center because of family or personal problems.
- has taken a second job that reduces the ability to devote adequate time to fulfill the obligations of this job.
- has personality clashes with other staff members that seem to indicate difficulty in working harmoniously with other adults.
- has evaluation reports that consistently indicate unsuitability for work with preschool children [Sections D64–68].
- gossips with other staff members and with parents and caregivers, habitually revealing intimate facts about other people [Sections D9, D63].
- has been dishonest on the application for employment [Section D9].
- has been insubordinate to the director or other supervisorial employees [Section D9].
- has been discourteous to other employees or to visitors to the center [Section D9].
- has demonstrated physical or mental disability that adversely affects job performance [Section D23, D63].
- has difficulty communicating with parents and caregivers [Section F2].
- is addicted to narcotics [Section D9].
- has been convicted of a felony or misdemeanor involving moral turpitude [Section D22].
- has abused sick leave or personal absence privileges [Section D9].
- is consistently late [Section D9].
- has been negligent in the supervision of children to the detriment of their safety and well-being [Parts G and H].
- has accepted a gratuity of some kind from a parent or caregiver in return for special treatment of his or her child [Section D9].
- has accepted a gratuity or some other special consideration in connection with special treatment of another employee [Section D9].
- has indicated reluctance to continue this employment [Section D63].
- has violated one or more provisions of the "Job Description: All Staff" and/or the employee's individual job description [Section D9].

D40 Dismissal of an Employee

There are steps that should be taken, should you plan on dismissing an employee, that may prevent a possible future lawsuit by the person being dismissed. It is assumed that you are considering dismissing the employee because of an infraction of that person's job description. Exceptions to this would be the commission of one or more of the items listed on page 173.

To be fair to the employee, and to protect yourself from possible lawsuits, use the following checklist when considering discharging an employee:

______ a. Document (write down and date) specific incidents of negative performance.

Who was involved?

What time was it?

Where did this incident take place?

What was the cause?

What was the infraction?

There should be at least three or four such incidents prior to dismissal.

______ b. Ask yourself in each instance:

Was the infraction something that I would overlook in other employees, or was it something that I would consider cause for dismissal if others were involved in similar incidents? Have I avoided being discriminatory?

______ c. Have an evaluation conference with the employee.

______ d. Bring up the points that you feel may be grounds for dismissal.

______ e. Listen to employee's point of view/explanation.

______ f. Consider any mitigating circumstances.

______ g. Is the infraction one of which the employee was aware?

______ h. Is it in violation of the employee's job description?

______ i. Is it due to possible misinterpretation of the job description?

______ j. Let the employee know that you disapprove of the particular action that you are protesting.

______ k. Put the employee "on notice," giving fair warning that repetition of the action may be grounds for dismissal.

______ l. Document the conference, including date, time, and location. Write down key points and any particular statements that you feel would be relevant if the exact wording were given in court.

______ m. Document reports by others.

______ n. Record periodic observations.

______ o. If the infraction is repeated and there is no doubt in your mind that you have given the employee fair warning, that you are being unbiased, and that you have documented one or more infractions, write a letter to the employee stating your reasons for dismissal.

D41 Letter for Dismissal of Employee

Community Child Care Center

111 THIRD STREET ✿ TELEPHONE 123-4579

Date: Today's date
To: Name of employee

From: Your name

You are hereby notified that your services will no longer be required by this center as of __________________ (as of today, two weeks from today, and so forth), date of __________________. You will be given two weeks' pay from today's date.

This discharge is due to your failure to abide by the terms of your employment, as follows:

Job description states:

1. ____
   (Include statement in full.)
2. ____
3. ____

In fact, on __________ (date) you were observed . . .

Further, on __________ (date) you stated to me that you . . .

Further, on __________ (date) you . . .

Enclosed is a letter of recommendation as to your child care skills. Perhaps this will help you find a position in a center that is more in tune to your personal philosophy. Even though we are no longer going to employ you, I do want to thank you for the many hours of hard work that you have contributed to our program.

A letter of recommendation might read as follows:

> **Community Child Care Center**
>
> 111 THIRD STREET TELEPHONE 123-4579
>
> To Whom It May Concern:
>
> ______________________________ was employed by this child care center as a child care provider from ______________ to ______________ (dates). She (he) was well liked by the children and demonstrated many good child care techniques (or "many good qualities"). She (he) contributed many good ideas to our program, although her (his) philosophy differed somewhat from that inherent to our program.

Note: Use of the word *philosophy* could mean that the employee was consistently abusive of sick leave and had poor attendance, that the employee was overly punitive with the children, that the employee did not get along with other staff persons, and so on. Your goal should be to replace the person on your own staff, not to prevent that person's future employment by another staff.

D42 Staff Management

Maintaining a harmonious relationship with staff members is of utmost importance. It is one of the best ways to promote good relationships among them. Though it is desirable to become good friends with your staff, it is also wise to remember that you are the boss and must not let friendship interfere with what you feel is best for the program. You will more easily win the cooperation of your staff if

- you frequently show your approval of their actions and ideas.
- you supervise all employees equally and not just those who are floundering. Operate on the assumption that everyone deserves acceptance, praise, recognition, acknowledgment, and attention.
- you delegate authority with fairness and in accordance with an individual's special talents.
- you base your personal relationships on honesty and trust.
- you remain readily available to them and show that you are sincerely interested in their needs.
- you allow for free expression of feelings.
- you set realistic objectives and discuss their purpose with them.
- you respect individual differences.

- you give serious consideration to their suggestions.
- you never talk down to them.
- you give generously of your time.
- you think in terms of helping each individual develop leadership qualities.
- you remember at all times that you are serving as a model.
- you support them in family-staff relationships.

For good staff relations, it is important that you consider the comfort and convenience of the staff. Here are a few suggestions:

- Maintain a separate staff lounge, if possible, with a mirror, cot, and armchairs.
- Provide a place for staff members to keep their personal belongings, so that they will not be accessible to children or visitors.
- Prepare a staff bulletin board on which to post announcements concerning opportunities for professional advancement, opportunities for meeting with other preschool or child care employees, and interesting social events.
- Be sure to make a substitute available for relief periods if the child care provider has no assistant, even if that substitute has to be you.
- Be sure that coffee, tea, juice, and snacks are available for those who would like to have them during a break.
- Permit staff members to use the telephone any time they are not supervising the children. Give them time away from the children to handle emergency calls.

D43 Orientation for New Staff Members

1. Spend some time with each new staff member, discussing the educational philosophy and goals of the center and reviewing a copy of the Employee's Handbook.
2. Tour the facilities with new staff members to give them an opportunity to make a more detailed inspection of the child care rooms and equipment [Part C].
3. Introduce new employees to other members of the staff. If possible, arrange to do so at a breakfast, luncheon, or regularly scheduled staff meeting [Section D44].

D44 Orientation of New Staff Members Hired Midyear

1. A child care provider hired during the center term should report for work at least one week before the other child care provider leaves, if possible, in order to begin training under the staff member who is leaving.
2. Spend some time with the new staff member, discussing your educational philosophy and the goals of the center.
3. Give the new staff member an Employee's Handbook and explain it carefully [Section D45].
4. If the new child care provider has not had the opportunity to train with the employee who is leaving, arrange for a tour of the facility and an opportunity to make a detailed inspection of the child care room and equipment [Part C].
5. Introduce the new child care provider to other members of the staff. If possible, do it at a regularly scheduled staff meeting [Section D43].
6. Allow the new staff member to observe others in the child care environment if the child care provider to be replaced has already left and cannot be observed.
7. Review with the new child care provider all center records concerning each child in the group.
8. Give the new staff member a brief rundown on other children in the center, pointing out details that might be useful because of open child care rooms.
9. Give the new child care provider a little background information on the parents and caregivers, as you have come to know them. [Part F].
10. Give the new child care provider enough of your time to provide needed help, but don't spend any more time in the child care room for the first three or four days than is necessary for giving that help. The new staff member will have plenty to do at first, getting to know the facilities, people involved, procedures, materials, and equipment, without having the added pressure of constant supervision.
11. Give the new child care provider an opportunity during relief periods and after child care each day to meet with you for mutual exchange of information and ideas and for individual in-service training on your part.
12. Notify parents and caregivers of any change in the staff [Section D29].

D45 Employee's Handbook

The Employee's Handbook is made up of the items listed below:

- Program calendar [Section A19]
- Director's statement of goals [Section A14]
- List of board members [Section A11]
- Copy of operating policies [Section A14]
- Rules for playground [Section C5]
- Fire and emergency procedures [Section H10]
- Child care assistant's handbook [Section F17]
- Parent/caregiver handbook [Section E25]
- Sample of enrollment forms [Sections E8, E15]
- Names and addresses of staff members (including telephone numbers and birthdays) [Section D31]
- Current room assignments [Section D46]
- Salary guide [Section B12]
- Application for partial reimbursement of fees for college courses [Section D61]
- Current staff regulations and additions to personnel policy [Section D27]
- Self-rated evaluation form [Section D67]
- Plot plan of center, showing relevant locations [Section A8]
- Information on child abuse and neglect [Sections G41–43]

D46 Child Care Provider's Room and Group Assignment Sheet

The following room and group assignments will be in effect for the coming year:

Name	Room No.	Age Group	Position

D47 Child Care Provider's Notice of Child's Withdrawal from Program

________________________ has been withdrawn from our program as of
(Name of child)

____________________. Please remove this child's name from your roll and turn all
(Date)
records in to me.

____
Director

Reason for withdrawal:

____

____

D48 Receipt for Keys

Community Child Care Center

111 THIRD STREET TELEPHONE 123-4579

Please read the following statement before signing for keys:

The loaning of a key signifies the trust we have placed in you, and charges you with the responsibility of respecting that trust. You may not at any time allow another person to use or duplicate your key unless asked to do so by the director. Report the loss or misplacement of your key immediately. Please acknowledge the receipt of the key by signing below.

RECORD OF KEYS

Signature of Employee	Key #	Dates Loaned	Dates Returned	Witness to Signature

RECORD OF KEY NUMBERS

No. of Key	Use

D49 Temporary Group Roll

The following is a list of the children who are registered and assigned to your group for this year. Please do not enter these names in your roll book until after the third week, in case any changes are made.

Date: ____________________ Group: ____________________

Name of Child	Age as of 9/1	Days Assigned																				

D50 Staff Meetings

Holding regularly scheduled staff meetings will help you maintain a comfortable atmosphere at the center. These meetings give you and your staff an opportunity to express yourselves freely. In particular, staff meetings

- help individual staff members preserve a sense of stability and assist the staff as a whole to maintain a sense of unity.
- provide an opportunity to review past achievements, current procedures, and discuss the need for new procedures.
- present an opportunity to air grievances.
- offer an opportunity to share techniques.
- provide an opportunity to develop friendships between staff members.
- help individual staff members develop and maintain self-confidence.
- help staff members make personal assessments of their own strengths and assist them in developing their professional skills.
- help staff members function freely within the framework of center policy and regulations.
- handle emergency situations.
- maintain an in-service training program that will keep the staff up-to-date on current issues in early childhood education.

Procedures for Staff Meetings

It is important to set a regular time for staff meetings and stick to it. For example, the staff can meet every Monday at noon. On the first and third Monday of each month, you can have a two-hour business meeting and in-service training session. On the second and fourth Mondays, a short business meeting can be held to take care of any pressing needs.

Remind each staff member about the meeting on the preceding Friday. Give each staff member a general outline of the topics that may be discussed. At the same time, give staff members an opportunity to talk about any subject they may want to discuss.

AGENDA FOR STAFF MEETINGS

Date: ______________ Time: ______________ Present: ______________

Special topics for discussions: ______________

Time Allotted	Topic	Facilitator	Outcome

Routine Items to Be Included

1. *Business*
   Enrollment
   Attendance
   Supplies
   Disbursements
   Petty cash
2. *Children's Routines*
   Arrivals
   Health check
   Nutrition
   Restroom use
   Resting
   Dismissal time
3. *Staff*
   Responsibilities
   Division of tasks
   Professional growth
   Complaints
4. *Individual Children*
   Problems, needs
   Interests
   Special talents
5. *Feelings and Emotions*
   Adult
   Child
6. *Child Care Assistants*
   Parents and caregivers
   Student teachers
   College students
7. *Individual Parents' and Caregivers' Needs*
8. *Curriculum Experiences and Goals*

Topics that might be discussed under the various items listed on the staff meeting agenda:

1. **Business**
   a. Enrollment
      - Current status enrollment
      - Plans for enrolling additional children
      - Projection for future enrollment
      - Deferred enrollments
      - Children on the waiting list who have not been registered
      - Enrollment representation
        ratio of boys to girls
        ethnic groups
        economic groups
        children with special needs

   b. Attendance
      - Report on the attendance in each room
      - Discuss the possibility of changing the days of children who attend part-time to balance daily attendance

   c. Supplies
      - Needs
      - Quantity
      - Quality
      - New items
      - "Found" materials
      - Homemade materials
      - Projection for future needs

   d. Disbursements
      - Petty cash
        Staff members turn in receipts for reimbursements.
      - Bills
        A brief discussion is sometimes held over the current state of purchasing and of the budget.

2. **Children's Routines**
   a. Arrivals
      - Arrival time
      - Children who arrive too early
      - Children who arrive too late
      - The importance of a parent or caregiver signing the child in and waiting for the health check
      - Greeting the child upon arrival
      - Parents and caregivers standing around the desk talking when they first arrive in the morning and overwhelming children who are coming up to have their throats checked

   b. Health checks
      - Importance of
      - Techniques of
      - Importance of touching the child during the health check (this gives the child a physical welcome before the day's activities begin)

c. Nutrition
   - Review of techniques
   - Review of foods
   - Review of needs
   - New ideas
   - Allergies

d. Restroom use
   - Importance of taking two-year-olds to the restroom at regular times during the day
   - Importance of cleaning basins after use
   - Being aware of children who have gone to the restroom and have not returned after a few moments

e. Resting
   - Techniques for
   - Importance of
   - Music for
   - Quiet activities
   - Timing of

f. Dismissal time
   - Parents or caregivers who come too early
   - Parents or caregivers who come too late
   - Having the child ready to leave
   - Having the child's materials ready to be taken home
   - Sign-out sheets
   - The child who hasn't been called for
   - Parents or caregivers who have come on time but who have stood around for some time chatting with each other while their children are running around

3. Staff

a. Responsibility
   - Room environment
   - Setting the stage
   - Bulletin boards
   - Keeping room in order
   - Locking doors
   - Keeping cupboards clean
   - Repair needs
   - Adjustment of lighting
   - Adjustment of ventilation
   - Adjustment of heat
   - Public relations agent for the center
   - Professionalism
   - Interpersonal relationships
   - Sick leave
   - Time off for personal reasons
   - Loyalty
   - Dependability
   - Honesty
   - Good grooming
   - Trust
   - Punctuality

b. Division of tasks
   - Review distribution of shared tasks
   - Evaluation of how shared tasks are being performed
   - Additions to shared tasks
   - Timing of shared tasks

c. Professional growth
   - Books
   - Organizational activities
   - College and university courses
   - Visiting other centers
   - Career advancement
   - Career opportunities
   - Projection into the future
   - Visiting other groups within the center
   - Professional conferences, workshops
   - Professional classes
   - Membership in professional organizations

d. Complaints

   This is the time to encourage staff members to evaluate center procedures, interpersonal relationships, and other areas of their jobs in order to discuss any complaints openly and honestly.

4. Individual Child

a. Problems and needs
   - Social relationships
   - Emotional problems
   - Physical problems
   - Intellectual problems or needs
   - Simple screening tests
   - Discussing a child's problem with the child's parents or caregivers
   - Referrals
   - Record keeping

b. Interests
   - Learning centers
   - Special interests of individual children
   - A child who doesn't seem to be interested in any special thing

c. Special talents
   - Artistic talents
   - Musical talents
   - Social maturity
   - Athletic abilities
   - Leadership abilities
   - Ability to organize
   - Neatness, orderliness
   - The child who can read
   - The child who is unusually adept at mathematical concepts
   - The child with special needs
   - The physically challenged child

5. Feelings and Emotions

a. The value of being able to express feelings and emotions without feelings of recrimination

b. The universality of feelings (a child's feelings are the same as an adult's)

c. Encouraging parents or caregivers to express their honest feelings

d. Letting the child know that it is all right to express feelings; helping to channel those feelings into legitimate means of expression

6. Child Care Assistants

a. Parents and caregivers

- Review of items in Parent/Caregiver Handbook
- Encouraging parents or caregivers to serve as assistants
- Scheduling parents or caregivers in various child care rooms
- Problems of the parent or caregiver who prefers to socialize rather than assist

b. Student teachers

- Giving responsibilities
- Rotating of room assignments
- Evaluation of student teachers' work

c. College students and/or student teachers

- Orientation for college students
- Responsibilities of college students
- Observations by college students
- Evaluations of college students

7. Individual Parents or Caregivers

a. Personal relationships

b. Parent-child or caregiver-child relationships

c. Assistance in the child care room

d. Volunteer assistants

e. Involvement of those who do not assist

f. Communication

8. Curriculum Experiences and Goals

a. Learning centers and goals

b. Art experiences and goals

c. Music and movement experiences and goals

d. Science experiences and goals

e. Mathematical experiences and goals

f. Language experiences and goals

g. Listening experiences and goals

h. Problem-solving experiences and goals

i. Social experiences and goals

j. Emotional expressions and feelings

k. Outdoor experiences and goals

- Playground activities
- Gardening activities
- Wheel toys
- Misuse of equipment
- Neighborhood walks
- Field trips

D51 Sample Minutes of Staff Meeting

Community Child Care Center

111 THIRD STREET ✿ TELEPHONE 123-4579

DATE: February 5

STAFF MEMBERS PRESENT: Entire staff

AGENDA

1. Supplies, petty cash
2. Identification cards
3. Arrival times
4. Report of class at university
5. Needs of individual children

Minutes prepared by: Doris

Following a 20-minute lunch and conversation period, the meeting was called to order by the director at 12:00 P.M. The minutes of the previous staff meeting were read and approved.

1. Supplies on-hand and needs for the coming weeks were discussed. Supply requests were turned in. Petty cash purchase receipts were turned in and settled.
2. Staff identification cards were distributed to each member.
3. As is usually the case each year, some of the parents and caregivers have started bringing their children earlier and earlier. Parents and caregivers have been informed that the staff members need the "before center" time for preparing their rooms and materials. A reminder will be sent to parents and caregivers in the newsletter later this week [Section F36].
4. Ms. Bennett gave a report on the last two sessions of the class in early childhood education she has been taking at the university.

A. Fingerpainting on plastic surfaces and allowing the child to make monoprints from the completed painting.

B. A discussion followed on the values of fingerpainting, such as the release of tension, eye-hand coordination exercise, tactile awareness, and—especially when accompanied by recorded music—rhythmic coordination of the entire body.

C. Steps and climbing apparatus were discussed. Even two-year-olds can learn to handle the difficult steps in some buildings. They must be reminded to always hold on to the rail.

D. A discussion was held on letting children handle their own battles as much as possible. If two children get involved in a disagreement, try to get their attention so they will know you are nearby to protect them from their loss of control—but try to give them time to regain full control at their own pace. This will lead to self-growth for the child. Remind them to "use their words."

5. The director called for a discussion on needs for individual children. Billy's child care provider suggested that he would do better with the two-year-old group. The director will observe him, give him some simple tests [Section I24], and then call his father in for a conference to discuss the matter with him. The situation is quite delicate, because the child has an unusually mature vocabulary for his age. The problem may be perceptual rather than developmental.

The meeting was adjourned a little early because there was a great deal of extra work to be done in preparation for the Valentine's Day Party to be held on February 14.

D52 In-Service Training

Techniques

The following are strategies that you may employ for in-service training at your center:

1. A presentation by someone especially knowledgeable in a particular area. The presenter might be the director, one of the staff, or a guest speaker.
2. Small group discussion.
3. Role-playing.
4. Demonstration of a technique, method, or procedure that participants can practice.
5. A workshop. Everyone uses certain materials or learns/practices a new skill.
6. Films, slides, audiotapes, videotapes.
7. Visiting other centers.

Topics

Because the child care and preschool exists for the benefit of young children, the training program for your staff members should deal with subjects that will add to their knowledge. Although in-service training is an ongoing process during the course of the day, specific topics should be selected for training meetings. These topics can then be explored further during the following weeks. Here are some important topics:

Health and safety
Personality of the child
Sensory-motor development
Auditory and visual perception
Theories of development
New ways to use old materials
Old ways to use new materials
Animals in the child care center
Stereotyping of sex roles
Cultural diversity
Stress reduction
Movement activities
Mental health resources
Professionalism
Anti-bias curriculum
Left-right brain hemisphere integration
Ongoing child-evaluation/assessment
Emotional growth of the child
Social growth of the child
Visitors in the child care room
The child care room environment
Family-staff relationships
Spaces in the learning environment
Cooking and mathematics
Combined families
Inclusion
Sexual abuse and responsibilities
How to keep from being sued
Confidentiality and ethics
Child abuse indicators and reporting

D53 Plan for In-Service Training Session

Purpose of Meeting: To compare "learning centers" with "learning circles."

Because the Community Child Care Center tries to avoid having an entire group gather together for learning circles, we will explore, experience, and evaluate techniques for substituting other methods for the learning circle. Participants will role-play various learning situations, compare their own reactions to those possibly experienced by young children, develop ideas for expanding self-learning opportunities for the child through the use of carefully planned learning centers, and formulate plans for the experimental use of some of these ideas.

Schedule

12:45–1:00 All participants will join in setting up a variety of learning centers, equipping the centers with toys, games, and materials that the participants themselves have never actually tried.

1:00–1:45 All participants will actually use the learning centers, work the puzzles, build with blocks, use the manipulative toys, and experience textural materials.

1:45–2:00 The participants will take a 15-minute break, during which time a dessert will be served. The purpose of this social exchange is to take the participants' minds completely off the previous "learning" and teaching experiences. The leader will keep the conversation completely away from the center.

2:00–2:30 The participants will discuss what they learned, felt, and remember from their experience with the learning centers.

Chart for Staff Assignments

A chart such as the one that follows enables the director to know at a glance the number of staff at work during any time period, and whether a substitute is needed. The chart also gives a quick indication of assignments for parent, caregiver, or student volunteers, as well as "floating" assignments. When there is the same staffing daily, only one such chart is necessary. But in the case of different assistants daily or for certain days of the week, additional charts will be needed.

DAY:	DATE:												
NAME	7:00–8:00	8:00–8:30	8:30–9:00	9:00–11:30	11:30–12:00	12:00–12:30	12:30–1:00	1:00–2:00	2:00–3:00	3:00–4:00	4:00–5:00	5:00–6:00	Total*
Joyce	✓	✓	✓	✓	Lu	nch	✓	✓					x6
Gary	✓	✓	✓	✓	Lu	nch	✓	✓					x6
Sammy		✓	✓	✓	✓	Lunc	h	✓	✓	✓	✓		-8
Alyce		✓	✓	✓	✓	✓	✓						-5
Marge			✓	✓	✓	✓	✓						-4 1/2
Pete			✓	✓	Lu	nch	✓	✓	✓	✓	✓	✓	-8 1/2
Evie			✓	✓	✓	✓							-4
Karen Sue			✓	✓	✓	✓							-4
Karen M			✓	✓	✓	Lu	nch	✓	✓				-5 1/2
Pam					✓	✓	✓	✓	✓	✓			x4 1/2
Julie					✓	✓	✓	✓	Lunch	✓	✓	✓	x5 1/2
Sandy						✓	✓	✓	✓	✓	✓		x5
Linda			✓	✓	✓	✓	✓						x4 1/2
Parent or caregiver				Forbes	✓								(3)
Parent or caregiver				Holt	✓								(3)
Parent or caregiver				Petsi	✓								(3)
Parent or caregiver				Volks	✓								(3)
Parent or caregiver													
Student		Terri	✓	✓	✓								(3 1/2)
Student				Cindy	✓	✓	✓						(4)
Student					Susie	✓	✓						(1 1/2)
Student									Janice	✓	✓	✓	(4)
Substitute													
Other													
Total staff	2	5	11	16	16	10	11	8	6	6	5	3	
Total children	18	32	32	93	93	68	68	52	50	56	48	21	

X= hourly pay   O= nonpayroll   – = salaried

D55 Shared Responsibilities

There are a number of things to do before children arrive each morning. These duties are shared by all members of the staff. Staff members also clean things up and put them away at the end of the day. If all persons do their jobs, there will be no ill feelings about these responsibilities. Jobs are rotated frequently, and upon the request of any staff member, tasks will be reassigned. Use the following list to keep track of who is responsible for what.

RESPONSIBILITY	NAME
Unlock storage sheds and playhouses	____________
Lock up storage sheds and playhouses	____________
Prepare juice and snacks	____________
Clean up juice and snacks	____________
Check storage room for appearance and supplies	____________
Prepare paints and paper for artwork	____________
Clean up paint supplies	____________
Prepare refreshment tray and make coffee	____________
Clean up refreshment tray and coffee maker	____________
Check walks and entrances for trash	____________
Check toilets and trash basins for cleanliness	____________
____________	____________
____________	____________

In addition to the general duties shared by the entire staff, each child care provider has a number of other daily tasks to perform. Child care providers keep their own rooms in order, straighten their own cupboards each day [Sections C15, I1], help keep the storage room orderly [Section C16], and keep their bulletin boards freshly posted [Sections F27, I8]. They also take roll each day, post a plan for the use of child care assistants [Section F22], and set up learning centers before children arrive [Section C11].

Playground supervision is another shared responsibility. Child care providers at the Community Child Care Center know that there must be one professional staff member supervising the outdoor activities at all times. At the initial planning meeting each year, child care providers get together and work out their own schedule for this task.

Professional Conduct

This announcement is given to new staff members.

Community Child Care Center

111 THIRD STREET TELEPHONE 123-4579

As a member of the staff of the Community Child Care Center, you are expected to conduct yourself in a professional manner at all times. We want you to become friends with each other, with your children, and with the parents and caregivers of the children. But we also want you to remember that you are an example that others look to for guidance.

1. You must dress neatly and in good taste.
2. You are expected to be punctual, dependable, tactful, and helpful.
3. We want you to be responsive to the children and to their parents and caregivers; however, retain your poise at all times.
4. You are expected to treat all information regarding members of the child care community (including children, parents, caregivers, staff, student teachers, volunteers) with strict confidence, and to avoid gossip at all times.
5. Let your children's parents and caregivers know that you take pride in your work—and conduct yourself in such a way as to convey that attitude through the care with which you pursue your daily activities.

Have fun! Being professional in your conduct does not imply the need to be stiff and formal. Don't forget to have fun with your children. These are little kids that we're working with. Don't be afraid to let them know how much you really do enjoy the reality of their presence. Let them know you can share in their laughter—just as readily as you can share their feelings when they have been hurt and are crying. Let them know that you can enjoy their view of the world.

D57 Confidentiality and Ethics

Child care providers and staff working in the center will be privileged to confidential information as they work with children and their families. A strict code of ethics must be maintained to ensure the private nature of divulged information.

Confidentiality of Records

1. Keep all records about children and families locked up overnight.
2. Often files are kept in two areas—one with confidential family information, to which only child care providers and administrative staff have access; the other, with material such as emergency release information, to which any staff person can have instant access.
3. A decision must be made as to who has access to various records. This should be put in writing.
4. Children's files should not leave the office, except when signed out by a specific child care provider for a specific purpose. The sign-out sheet should state: child's name, reason for use, date and time taken, and date and time it will be returned. Records should never be removed from the premises unless needed for a court case.
5. Personnel files are also confidential. Staff members, however, have a right to ask to see their own files at any time. This should always be done in the presence of the director or acting director. Personnel files should be locked files.
6. Payroll records are also confidential, available only to the bookkeeper and the director. Staff persons, however, may ask to see their own payroll record at any time. These should be kept in locked files.

Note: It is recognized that many small centers may not have locked files. Traditionally, many directors of small programs have their records in a basket, a cardboard box, an attaché case, or other portable container, since they often do much of their work at home. Whatever the arrangement, a small portable file WITH A LOCK can be purchased for a few dollars to keep confidential papers from prying eyes.

Ethical Issues

1. Get written permission to photograph children. Get additional permission if you use these photos in your flyers, advertising, or for any other purpose.
2. Tape-record or videotape children only if you have written release to do so. Tape-recording should be treated with the same confidentiality with which you treat written files. This rule would not apply to the tape-recording that sometimes goes on in child care for purposes of language development, play acting, and other curriculum experiences. Such recordings, however, should be kept within the context of child care activities and not surreptitiously given to others to use for research or any other purpose unless done with the express permission of the parents or caregivers of children involved.
3. Furnish information to other parties only if you have written permission from the person about whom (or about whose child) the information is requested.

4. When to break confidentiality: When a child is endangered, either in areas of health, neglect, or abuse, you may need to report certain heretofore confidential facts without permission.
5. When children impart information to you that implies abuse or neglect, you are legally obligated to report the information to the appropriate authorities.
6. Avoid discussing one family with another family in the area or in the center.
7. Both children and adults have the right to be corrected in private. Do not do so in front of other staff persons, volunteers, visitors, parents, caregivers, or students. Incorrect behavior should be discussed privately with the persons, whether adults or children, who are directly involved.
8. Children have a right to display feelings. If they lose control, they have the right to be allowed a private place for expressing their emotions—without an audience—but with an adult nearby to give reassurance when needed.
9. It is unethical to pursue one's personal business while being paid to supervise a child or group of children.
10. Questions that you have regarding policy or personal matters of a child's family should be asked of the supervisor or director rather than of another child care provider or assistant.
11. Children should not be required to participate in any activity or to abide by a policy that is not good for them. (An example of this would be trying to force a child to taste a certain food.)
12. Persons working with children should refer to their supervisor or the director any parent/caregiver requests for information that could be used to inappropriately discipline a child.
13. Personal information about families, such as a newly instituted separation or divorce, an arrest, a serious illness, or perhaps a job loss, should be divulged to other staff persons only to the extent of what they need to know to support the child. Those who seldom have contact with that child may not need to know family details. Careful judgment must be made by the director in all such instances.
14. Avoid repeating stories about their families that children tell you. Although the stories may have some foundation in truth, they are often distorted. They should be treated as privileged information. You may want to make a written note of them for your own use, but you must be certain that they are kept even more confidential if written down.
15. Avoid judging a family or imposing your own values on a child if there is a difference between your beliefs and that of the child's family. Acting in the "best interest of the child" can be a guideline, but only if the best interest is not to expect a child to live with the school's values if they are in direct conflict with the values the child's family is imparting. This may be evidenced in small ways, such as your allowing a boy to dress up as the "mother" and the family stating, "We absolutely do not want our three-year-old to pretend he's a girl."
16. Most problems of ethics are self-resolved if gossip is avoided at all costs—again, with the exception of cases of child endangerment.

D58 Professional Growth of Staff Members

Part of your responsibility to your staff is to encourage them to continue their professional growth, even if it means advancement out of your center. Growing children respond best to growing adults. Therefore, encourage your staff members to attend educational conferences and take college courses selected from an approved list that you give them. A professional bulletin board can be maintained for posting all relevant course announcements, notices, and bulletins. Your child care providers should also be aware of employment and advancement opportunities, salary variances, and academic preparation. The following lists should be helpful in this regard.

D59 Record of Professional Growth

Name: ______________________________

Workshops, Institutes, Courses, Lectures, etc.	School/ Organization	Presenter/ Instructor	No. of Hours	Date Completed	Comments

Membership in professional associations (include offices held):

Organization	Date	Renewals	Contributions

Lectures given, articles contributed, professional activities, or volunteer contributions to the field of early childhood education and child care:

____

____

D60 Career Preparation and Advancement Guide

In-Service Training

Practical experience in a preschool or child care center as an aide or assistant to a teacher or child care provider, usually coupled with in-service classes and/or staff meetings covering many of the skills and techniques used in working with preschool and child care groups.

Child Development Associate (CDA)

Members of this profession are specialists in child care, drawn largely from persons who are skilled in early childhood education and development, but who do not necessarily hold college or university degrees or credentials. Criteria are flexible, based on an individual's education, field training, demonstrated competencies, and personal qualifications. It is anticipated that this newly developed professional field will provide a vast core of specialists in preschool training who will work under the supervision of a credentialed teacher. This program is administered by NAEYC [Section J7].

Preschool Certificate

Generally requires approximately 30 college units in preschool education and related courses. Usually issued by a community college. These units may be applied to an associate in arts degree.

Associate in Arts Degree

Granted by two-year institutions to students who have completed 60 or more lower-division units of a prescribed course sequence in general education and a major. The credits may be applied to a bachelor's degree or for a terminal course in a vocational field.

Bachelor of Arts (or Science) Degree

Granted by a four-year institution after completion of a specified curriculum of lower- and upper-division courses with a subject major.

Teaching Credential

A license by a state department of education to teach in the public school system. Some states issue special credentials for working in children's centers licensed by the department of education.

Master of Arts or Sciences Degree

Issued by a university or college to a graduate student upon completion of course work and other requirements.

Ph.D. Degree

Conferred by a university to a graduate student who has completed specified course work, written an acceptable dissertation, and met other requirements.

Each higher level of training opens up advancement opportunities within the center or in other areas beyond the program. Jobs within the center include aide or trainee, assistant child care provider, head child care provider, assistant director, director, or supervisor. Opportunities in related areas include the positions of consultant, researcher, administrator, college instructor, demonstration teacher, proprietor of a center, infant-development specialist, and home and family-living teacher (in secondary schools). Some people with preschool experience find advancement in fields of special interest, such as art, dance, music, science, language arts, and so on.

Salaries of preschool staff members vary greatly according to state regulations, the type of program, the child care provider's educational background and experience, the amount of funds for the center, the child care provider's responsibilities, and the community in which the center is located. Salaries are subject to minimum-wage regulations.

D61 Request for Partial Reimbursement of Educational Fees

Some centers will defray a percentage of the cost of college courses taken by staff members. A form such as this one can be used when applying for reimbursement.

Date: ____________

I plan to enroll in the following course at ______________________________________,
for which I will request a partial reimbursement of fees.

Name of course: ____

Number of units: ________ Semester: _______ Quarter: _______ Fee: _______

Instructor: ____

Dates: ___________________________ Times: _________________________

Reasons for selecting this particular course:

____

____

I understand that should I leave your employ within 12 months, the amount advanced will be deducted from my final paycheck.

Signed: ________________________

Approved: ____________ Date: ____________ Amt. of reimbursement: ____________

Not approved: ________________ Date: ____________________

Reason for disapproval: ____

____

D62 Constructive Criticism of Staff Members

In spite of carefully made plans [Section D42], there are bound to be differences between you and members of the staff from time to time. When these differences occur, review the following suggestions:

Be Objective

From time to time you may be critical of

- the way in which a staff member conducts an activity.
- the way in which a staff member handles a particular child.
- the interference presented by a personal problem of a staff member.
- the staff member's relationship or attitude toward parents or caregivers.
- the staff member's relationship or attitude toward child care assistants or aides.
- the staff member's attitude toward extracurricular responsibilities.

Your role as director requires you to keep a critical eye on the way staff members handle their jobs. However, it is of utmost importance that you remain objective in handling these problems.

Give Yourself Time

Except in emergency situations, give yourself a little time to evaluate the problem before speaking to the staff member involved. This time will help you to gain a true perspective of the incident and allow you to choose the best action to take.

Be Gentle

In suggesting a one-to-one meeting to the offending staff member, be as gentle and kind as possible, being sure to point out some of the positive things the staff member has been doing.

Establish a Basis for Mutual Understanding

Your first task is to tell the other person exactly what your criticism is and why. Assure that person that you believe in open and honest two-way communication in discussing the problem.

- Listen very carefully to the staff member's point of view.
- Try to bring out subtle, but important extenuating factors related to the staff member's attitude and to your own criticism.
- Help the staff member clarify feelings and actions.
- Try to look at the problem from the staff member's point of view.

Be Constructive

- Help the staff member find an alternative method by offering several suggestions.
- Offer to help the staff member make the change.
- Continue to be supportive at all times.

Be Discreet

Your criticism is between you and the person involved. Be discreet. Do not involve other staff members.

Be Fair

If other staff members have done the same thing you are criticizing this staff member for, be fair.

- Let the staff member know that you are also going to speak to the other person or persons about the problem.
- From time to time, a problem of conduct does not have to be discussed with an individual staff member at all—but with the group as a whole at the next staff meeting.
- If more than one person is involved, a group meeting might be in order.
- If necessary, an emergency staff meeting can be held.
- In such a case, discretion is very important so that no one individual is "put on the spot" in front of others.

Be Gracious

Let your staff know—and show it by your actions—that you, too, are open to criticism. Let them know that you do not consider yourself infallible and that they are not jeopardizing their positions by disagreeing with your methods.

Be Courageous

If there is continuous open disagreement or mutual criticism between you and a staff member, be courageous. Do not let sentiment prevent you from dismissing that person at the earliest possible date [Section D39].

D63 Personal Problems of Staff Members

Occasionally you will find that a staff member is troubled by a personal problem that is being reflected in his or her work. In a child care setting where feelings and emotions are so important, troubled feelings are hard to cover up. You, as the director, need to be tuned-in to your staff so that when such situations occur, you can be helpful. It is one of your responsibilities to give your staff understanding and support whenever they need them. How do you help a troubled staff member without causing embarrassment, loss of pride, or lessening of self-confidence?

Arrange a Conference

You can arrange a conference—in private and without interruptions. Invite the person to lunch, or send a note asking if the two of you can meet after the children leave to discuss some mutual problems. (The problems are mutual, since the staff member's problems become child care problems for both of you.)

People always like to hear good things about themselves. Start every conference with reassurance of the person's contributions to the program, the center, and the children. It is sometimes difficult to get a person to express his or her feelings about a personal problem—or even to reveal that he or she has a problem, for that matter. Encouragement and reassurance are needed.

Sometimes it helps to start out by relating some minor problem of your own, pointing out that you know it doesn't begin to compare in importance or seriousness with the other person's problems. If you already know what the personal problem concerns, you might be able simply to state that it sometimes helps to discuss a problem with someone else and that you would be happy to listen.

If the person is very secretive about personal problems, your task will be harder. You might be able to say, "You seem to have been rather tense lately at the center. I thought you might be having some personal problems that have been upsetting you. Perhaps talking about them will ease your tensions a little." You might even take an approach that says, in essence, "I'm not trying to pry into your personal affairs. But I thought that just having some time to talk together might help you feel better."

Listen

Once the person has revealed the problem, your primary task is to listen. Perhaps a member of the family is dying or suffering from some serious physical problem. There really isn't anything you can do except help the person express hidden feelings.

If the problem concerns personal relationships with a spouse or some other member of that person's family, you might suggest outside counseling. Sometimes a person only needs reassurance that the problem really isn't so unusual and that it will probably work out in time. Whatever the problem is, just remember that what you are offering your employee is the assurance that you are ready and willing to listen, that you are interested, and that even though the problem may be an uncommon one, you appreciate the seriousness of it and want to do whatever that person feels is helpful.

Loneliness

Loneliness can be a very real problem for a staff member and can seriously interfere with the smooth functioning of a child care group. Sometimes a staff member's only contact with people outside of the home are those that take place at the center. This staff member can sometimes be helped by your offer of friendship, but there are other ways within the center, too. Be sure to provide ample opportunities for social interchange between staff members so that one person doesn't feel isolated. Be sure you have provided opportunities for staff members to work in pairs on different program projects (changing the pairs around frequently), so that all staff members have the opportunity to get acquainted with each other.

Lack of Education

If a lack of education is the basis for a staff member's problem, only direct action will help overcome it. You must be ready to reassure that person that teaching ability on the preschool level does not depend on education alone. If a lack of education is a problem, and if the staff member is a strong person and really wants to improve, you can suggest studying at home or enrolling in a nearby high school or college.

Personal Appearance

If the problem concerns personal appearance, a gentle, kind, and positive exchange of ideas is called for. Problems caused by personal appearance can sometimes be helped through an in-service training program on grooming. This is a good time to call in an outside speaker to address the entire staff. This method spares the individual the embarrassment of hearing about his or her shortcomings directly.

Staff Member's Own Child

Problems may be due to a concern for the staff member's own child, particularly in relation to the child's health or behavior. The greatest concern will probably be the child's rate of learning or behavior at the center. Here you can give the staff member a number of positive suggestions. Above all, be reassuring. Help the staff member learn to accept the child as an individual, appreciate the child's unique abilities, and put less emphasis on weak points. Do your best to help this staff member overcome any feelings of guilt and self-recrimination.

Marital Disputes

In case of marital disputes, the person may only need reassurance about job status. Assure the staff member that a change in marital status will not affect the job—as long as related problems, such as care of children, sufficient income, and other variables don't interfere with job satisfaction.

Seriousness

The types of problems that beset your staff members will be as many and as varied as in any cross section of a community. What you may consider trivial may be of great concern to someone else. Never belittle another person's concerns.

Time Off

Sometimes you may have to give some time off—a few days, or even an extended leave of two or three months. In fact, if the problem is interfering greatly with the person's functioning as a child care provider, you may even suggest a leave of absence for the balance of the program. Suggestions involving leave must be made with great care. If you are sincere in wanting to help, you must consider your reason for suggesting leave. If it is to give the person time to settle some personal affairs, the offer is valid. If it is given because you hope that the person's attitudes, emotional responses, or personality will change, then you are on the wrong track. You can't change people. You must accept them as they are and help them make the fullest use of their abilities while helping them overcome their problems.

Respect

Throughout the conference, you must at all times show your respect for the other person. Show that you respect that person as an individual, that you respect the person's ideas, and that it is normal to have strong feelings about the problem. At all times, remember that what you are doing, in essence, is being a friend. As a friend, you must establish a basis of trust, because without a sense of mutual trust, the entire conference is pointless. You are offering friendship; you are not offering yourself as an expert. Rather, you are offering a means to determine whether or not the problem can only be helped by calling on the services of an expert, or whether just the fact of your friendship and trust will ease the tension enough so that the problem will not interfere with the job.

Personal Priorities

Sometimes the problem may be a simple one of a staff member being so overextended in professional studies that there is little energy or patience left for the job. Such a person should be encouraged to reevaluate personal priorities.

Financial Difficulties

If the problem concerns financial difficulties, listening by itself can't be very helpful. Here you must offer some practical suggestions in order to be of any use. Some people react so strongly to financial problems that their day-to-day functioning can be seriously hampered.

General Discontent with the Job

If the staff member's problem is one of general discontent with the job, termination should be brought about as quickly as possible if problems causing the discontent cannot be resolved [Section D39]. Only those staff members who are willing to accept a job as not being ideal will help your center grow and come somewhat closer to the ideal. Discontent on the part of a staff member can only become infectious and cause misunderstandings and discontent in others, assuming, of course, that you have not created a situation in your center in which the person has a legitimate right to be unhappy.

Professional Help

If, after giving careful consideration to the individual who has a personal problem, you are unable to establish a basis for helping that person, be prepared to seek professional help yourself for further guidance.

Terminating Employment

A final word of caution: If the problem is seriously interfering with the staff member's functioning in a positive manner, you must consider terminating employment.

D64 Evaluating Child Care Center Employees

When evaluating employees, all reports on permanent employees should be filed one month before the expiration of their current contract. Reports on probationary employees must be filed at the completion of their probationary period. You, as the director, will complete the evaluation report for each employee [Sections D65–66]. In addition, the employee will complete a self-evaluation form. Then the two of you should confer privately in accordance with procedures established by the Personnel Committee of the Child Care Board. If you, as director, are dissatisfied with the employee's self-evaluation, you might need to go over it again together. In the event that you feel your assistant director has greater knowledge of an employee's abilities than you do, ask the assistant director to fill out the report and conduct the conference. However, as director of a center, you are responsible for being aware of the progress and performance of each employee.

If an employee is dissatisfied with the evaluation you have completed, that person can request an appeal for review of the rating in conferences with the director and the chairperson of the Personnel Committee. This request is to be made in writing within ten days after the original evaluation was signed.

D65 Employee Evaluation

To be completed by the director:

Community Child Care Center

111 THIRD STREET TELEPHONE 123-4579

NAME: ______________________

DATE: __________ STATUS: Probationary ________ Permanent ________

PERIOD COVERED BY EVALUATION: ___________ Age group: _____

In evaluating your work at this time, I find your performance to be as follows:

Child care room environment:

____

____

Curriculum activities:

____

____

Communication with other staff:

____

____

Relationship to children:

____

____

Communication with parents and caregivers:

____

____

Responsibilities to director and administrative staff:

____

____

Other:

____

____

Signed: ______________________
Director

I have read the above evaluation.

Signed: ______________________
Employee

D66 Procedure for Staff Self-Evaluation Form

1. The staff member fills out self-evaluation form [Section D67].
2. The director fills out the same form.
3. The director meets with the staff member and they compare their ratings and come to some agreement on each item. Your purpose in making this evaluation is to help staff members recognize their strengths more than their weaknesses, so that they can build on those strengths to become better child care providers.
4. The director completes a summary of the evaluation in duplicate, one copy of which is kept by the staff member.
5. The director and the employee each sign them.
6. The evaluations are filed away in the employee's file.

SUMMARY OF STAFF MEMBER'S EVALUATION

Summary of Evaluation: ____

____

____

____

____

____

Date: ______________

Staff Member's Signature: ______________________________

Director's Signature: ________________________________

Recommendations: ____

____

____

____

____

____

D67 Staff Self-Evaluation Form

In addition to the evaluation made by the director [Section D65], it is important that staff members evaluate their own performance. The Community Child Care Center asks its employees to evaluate themselves according to

- job description: all staff
- job description for their particular position

The following form can be used for this purpose:

SELF-EVALUATION OF EMPLOYEE

NAME: ______________________________

DATE: ______________________________

RATINGS: NEVER | OCCASIONALLY | USUALLY | MOST OF THE TIME | ALWAYS | OUTSTANDING

The following self-evaluation is based on my job description:

1. Have I demonstrated friendliness toward others?
2. Have I been trustworthy about hours, leave, property, and center matters?
3. Have I been careful to modulate my voice appropriately?
4. Have I been punctual in work time, relief times, and lunchtimes?
5. Have I been dependable, not taking care of personal business at work?
6. Have I avoided malicious gossip about other staff members? Parents or caregivers? Children?
7. Have I avoided complaining attitudes, going to supervisory staff with my concerns rather than to other employees?
8. Have I always been professionally presentable?
9. Have I maintained self-control in dealing with others?
10. Have I maintained my interest in my job?

Abilities in connection with the program:

1. Have I planned for the personal differences between children?
2. Have I planned age-appropriate activities for children?
3. Have I demonstrated creativity and resourcefulness in planning?
4. Have I been flexible in working with both individuals and groups?
5. Have I used techniques to build the self-esteem of children?
6. Has my demeanor been professional, nonpunitive, and positive?
7. Have I fostered exploration, investigation, imagination, and creativity?
8. Have I been responsible in assessing each child's growth, development, and performance, recording some observations for each child?
9. Have I utilized stress reduction to help maintain a relaxed environment?
10. Have I treated all the children equally, with respect and empathy?

Wholesome relationships with adults, including parents and caregivers:

1. Have I maintained a friendly, yet professional relationship with others?
2. Have I shown respect for others' points of view and ideas?
3. Have I maintained the confidentiality of information?
4. Have I avoided showing favoritism to some parents and caregivers?
5. Have I supported cultural differences in our program?
6. Have I offered positive guidance to child care assistants, helpers, and volunteers?
7. Have I been receptive to the idea of home visits? (optional)

Concern for and awareness of total center:

1. Have I been alert to safety and health needs within the environment?
2. Have I been able to justify the presentation of a particular material or activity in relation to the growth of a child?
3. Have I maintained materials, supplies, and equipment in an orderly and inviting manner?
4. Have I respected the use and care of materials and equipment? Have I avoided being wasteful?
5. Have I assumed personal responsibility for small problems rather than taking the attitude that "someone else will take care of it"?

Demonstration of professionalism:

1. Have I continued my professional growth as an educator or child care provider? Have I maintained membership in job-related organizations?
2. Have I supported the philosophy of the center and the director?
3. Have I been realistic in recognizing my own behavior as the possible cause of a problem when things don't go smoothly?
4. Have I avoided gossip and respected the confidentiality of written, oral, and observed information?
5. Have I been willing to share ideas, materials, time, and services with other members of the staff?
   Have I been committed to the concept of team spirit?
6. Have I been willing to share responsibilities with others and to assume others' responsibilities in emergencies, putting the needs of the center as a whole over petty differences of opinion?
7. Have I remained aware of center policies and openly supported them? Have I reserved disagreement about policies for discussion with the director and at staff meetings rather than spreading discontent among coworkers?

D68 Child Care Observation and Evaluation

In addition to the self-evaluation by staff members of their own performances, it is the director's responsibility to provide an evaluation of each child care provider's room.

The following form may be used by the Community Child Care Center for performing room observations and evaluations. Notify staff members in advance when an evaluation will occur. Following the evaluation, a written copy of the results is given to the staff members. A follow-up conference with the director is made to discuss results and plans for future professional growth.

CHILD CARE ROOM EVALUATION

Name: ______________________________ Date: ________________

Arrangement of Environment:

Child-oriented _____ Comfortable _____ Safety-focused _____
Health-focused _____ Needs improvement _____
Comments: ____
____

Play/Learning Centers:

Challenging _____ Static _____ Too many _____ Too few _____
Age-appropriate _____ Relevant _____ Creative _____ Safe _____
Comments: ____
____

Appearance:

Neat and orderly _____ Aesthetic _____ Sloppy _____
Confusing to the eye _____ Shopworn _____
Comments: ____
____

Display Areas:

Aesthetic _____ Shopworn _____ Out of season _____ Timely _____
Visually thought-provoking _____ Activity-oriented _____ Relevant _____
Child-oriented _____ Adult-oriented _____
Comments: ____
____

Stress Level:

Calm _____ Organized _____ Chaotic _____
Out of control _____ Rushed _____ Overstructured _____
Comments: ____
____

Activities:

Age-appropriate _____ Safe _____ Healthful _____ Group _____
Individual _____ Balanced between quiet and active _____
Choices made available _____ Self-pacing _____
Flexibility in timing _____ Inflexible _____
Comments: ____
____

(continued)

(page 2)

CHILD CARE ROOM EVALUATION

Child Care Style:

Learning goals understood by the child care provider_____
Goals of each activity clear to children _____
Comments: ____
____

Staff-Child Interaction:

Appropriate _____ Limited _____ Very little _____ All children _____
Some children _____ Very few _____ Circulates around the room _____
Observes _____ Facilitates _____ Participates _____ Distracted _____
Alert _____ Withdrawn _____ Daydreaming _____
Gossips with other adults _____ Aware _____ Solicits feedback _____
Offers feedback _____ Challenges _____ Stimulates _____ Empathic _____
Asks probing questions _____ Open-ended _____ Knows when to pull back _____
Individualizes _____ Anticipates _____
Comments: ____
____

Discipline:

Clearly articulates expectations _____ Uses appropriate language _____
Modulates tone of voice and manner _____
Takes steps to prevent inappropriate behavior _____
Avoids punitive attitudes _____ Anticipates problems _____ Is fair _____
Unprejudiced _____ Consistent _____ Uses reminders _____
Avoids making threats _____ Gives choices _____
Overlooks small annoyances _____
Knows when it is appropriate to intervene _____
Points out natural consequences _____ Points out logical consequences _____
Provides renewal time (time for renewing inner feelings) as opposed to time out _____
Helps children use words, discuss differences, and solve their own problems _____
Avoids "police officer" role _____
Comments: ____
____

Summary: ____
____

D69 Use of Memo Forms

Communication among staff members and between the staff and parents and caregivers is vital for a smoothly operating child care center. Because verbal messages can easily be forgotten, use an official memo form. Print the memo on a small sheet of paper of a color other than white. In addition to the memo form, use a "Staff Member's Requests and Notes" form on a paper of a different color, as well for one-way communication from the staff to the director.

Staff Member's Request and Notes to the Director

To: Director

From: ______________________ Date: ______________________

Supplies needed: ______________________

____

Repairs needed: ______________________

____

Assistance needed: ______________________

____

Suggestions: ______________________

____

D70 Monday Memo

The ideal situation is to be able to send a memo around to the entire staff at the beginning of each day. However, with the many responsibilities of greeting parents, caregivers, children, and staff, taking telephone calls, arranging for substitutes, answering questions, and taking care of other "beginning of the day" business, the director does not always have time to put a memo together until mid-morning. One solution to this problem is to rely on the Monday memo. This can be a memo that has been started the previous week and completed, if necessary, early on Monday morning. Make copies ready for most staff members to pick up when they sign their time sheets upon arrival. To assist in the process, try the following procedure:

1. On Friday, send a questionnaire to all staff, asking:
   "What would you like included in next Monday's staff memo?"
   a. ______________________
   b. ______________________
   c. ______________________
   "(Please include any special events planned for your class for next week. Please return this form before 1:00 P.M.)"

2. Either you or a secretary can add the items on Friday afternoon.
3. Early Monday morning, make any additions that may have arisen.
4. Duplicate and distribute the memo.

D71 Monday Memo—Sample

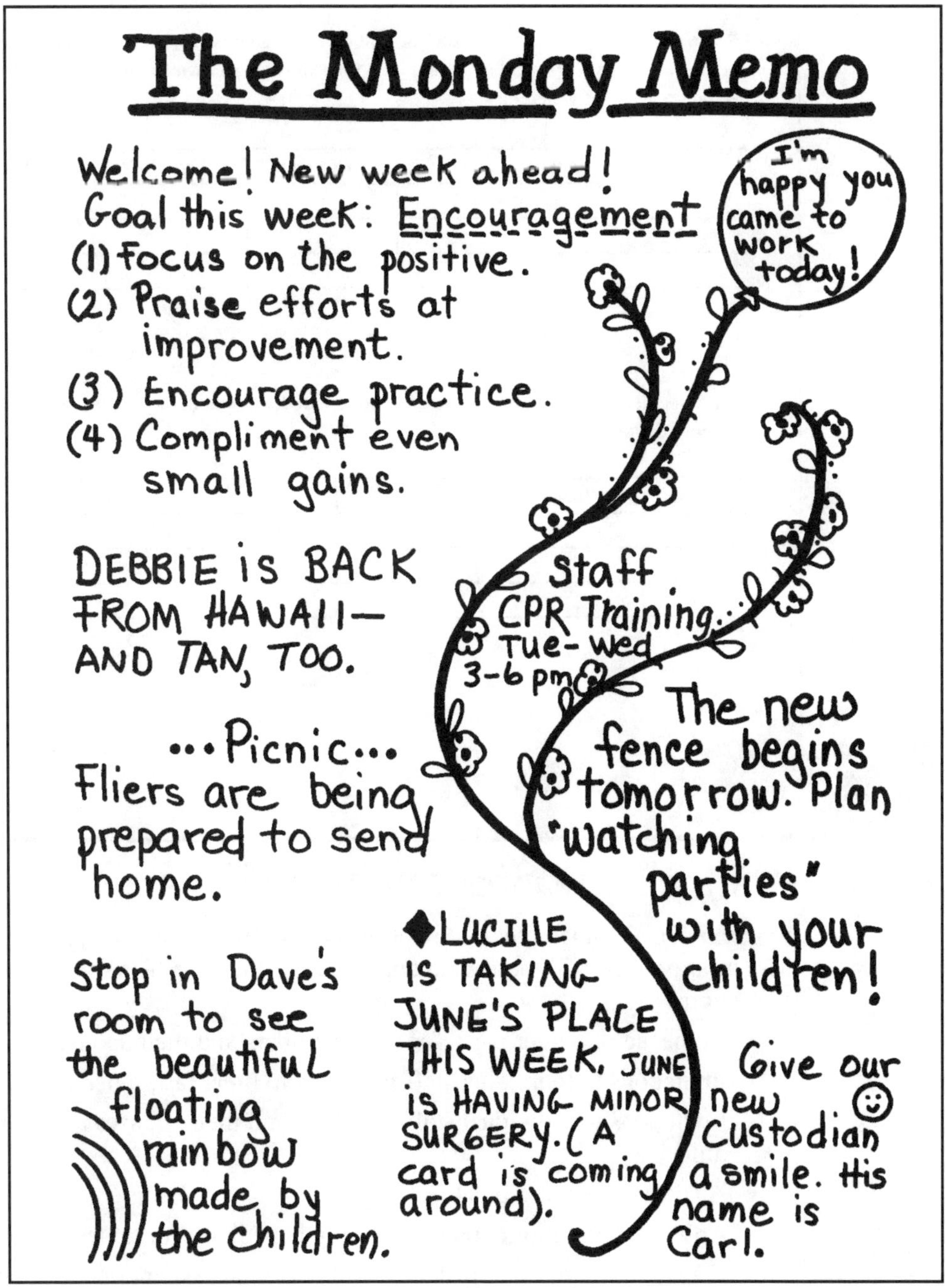

The Monday Memo

Welcome! New week ahead!
Goal this week: Encouragement
(1) Focus on the positive.
(2) Praise efforts at improvement.
(3) Encourage practice.
(4) Compliment even small gains.

I'm happy you came to work today!

DEBBIE IS BACK FROM HAWAII—AND TAN, TOO.

Staff CPR Training Tue-Wed 3-6 pm

...Picnic...
Fliers are being prepared to send home.

The new fence begins tomorrow. Plan "watching parties" with your children!

Stop in Dave's room to see the beautiful floating rainbow made by the children.

♦ LUCILLE IS TAKING JUNE'S PLACE THIS WEEK. JUNE IS HAVING MINOR SURGERY. (A card is coming around).

Give our new custodian a smile. ☺ His name is Carl.

D72 Room Needs for Next Year

MEMO FROM: Director　　　　Date:
TO: Staff
RE: Supplies needed for next year

Please list below any items that you recommend we purchase for the next program year. Include anything you would especially like to have for your own room as well as things that would be good for general use.

Item	How Many?	Why Do You Want This Item?

RE: Repairs needed for next year

Please list below those items that need to be repaired, repainted, or possibly replaced because of poor condition.

Item	What's Wrong with It?

Signed: ____________________

D73 Maintaining Contact with Staff

If you have maintained pleasant relationships with staff members, you can enhance these relationships with personal contact during the year. The following is a list of suggestions:

- Barbecue or dinner party for staff members and their spouses
- Invitations to individual staff members to breakfast, lunch, or a cup of coffee
- Invitations to individual staff members and their spouses to join you for dinner
- A come-as-you-are breakfast
- An invitation to join you on a buying expedition for the center
- Letters and cards sent to staff members while you are on vacation trips
- Telephone calls just to chat

D74 End of Year (Nine-Month Schedule)

FROM: Director
TO: Child care provider
RE: End-of-year duties

____________________ will be the last day for most children to attend the center until next fall. You will be expected to come to work on ______________ and ______________ (list as many days as necessary), when you will be expected to perform the following tasks:

1. Return all expendable supplies to the storage room. This refers to such items as paste, paints, crayons, paper, and so on.
2. Complete Supplies Needed form list [Section D72].
3. Remove all items from open shelves and put them away.
4. List items that need to be repaired or painted.
5. Attend a final staff meeting on _____________ at 9:00 A.M., at which time you will turn in your roll books and other center records. At this meeting, you will be given an opportunity to review the past year, discuss plans for the next year, and indicate areas of the program you feel need improvement. If you can put these feelings in writing, it will be more expedient for all.
6. Take your personal belongings home with you.

D75 Welcome Letter to New Staff Members

Community Child Care Center

111 THIRD STREET TELEPHONE 123-4579

Date

Dear (employee name),

With this letter, we welcome you as a member of our staff and assure you that you will be considered just as important to our center community as those who have been with us for one or more years.

We want you to meet with us at the luncheon we have scheduled for the first Wednesday in September at the Lakeside Inn so that we might become better acquainted.

Please don't hesitate to call me if you have any questions at all about planning for the program year. The staff and I will do everything we can to help you to feel at home.

Very sincerely yours,
Director

D76 Advance Planning Letter to Staff for New Program Year

TO: Staff
FROM: Director
RE: A few items to help you make plans

September 4 NEW STAFF	Between 9:00 A.M. and noon, I will have an orientation meeting for new staff members. At noon, you are all invited to be my guests at the Lakeside Inn for a get-together pre-term luncheon. This will be a social meeting, giving us the opportunity to talk informally about ourselves and what we've done during the summer. I have arranged for substitutes so the summer staff can attend.
September 5 PAYROLL STARTS; PLANNING CONFERENCE	Today we get down to business, and you go on the payroll. We will have a planning conference from 9:00 A.M. until noon. Those of you who wish may stay to begin your room preparations.
September 6 PICNIC	Today we are having a picnic lunch from 11:00 to 2:00 with the children and their families at Lakeside Park.
September 7 SUPPLIES; CONFERENCES	Child care room supplies will be distributed. Please plan on meeting with me individually for half an hour sometime today or Monday.
September 10 BULLETIN BOARDS; GROUP LISTS	Please complete the arrangement of your room environment, including bulletin boards. Temporary group lists will be available so you can work on name tags for your children.
September 11 OPEN HOUSE	New children's Open House. Their parents and caregivers will be advised to visit between 9:00 A.M. and noon and to plan on staying for approximately 30 minutes. You do not need a planned program.
September 11 PARENT/CAREGIVER SPAGHETTI DINNER	Parent/caregiver meeting 6:00 to 9:00 P.M. [Section F5]. This will be a do-it-yourself spaghetti dinner and will take the place of the usual orientation meeting. It will give parents and caregivers an experience in "learning through doing," establish an informal basis for camaraderie, and provide staff members with an opportunity for getting to know parents and caregivers on a one-to-one basis.
September 12	This will be the last day of the program for summer children.
September 13	This will be the first day of the program for fall children.
September 14	Regular schedule for children will go into effect.
September 17	Staff meeting general business [Section D50].

Special Announcement
Lakeside College is conducting a graduate seminar in Language and the Preschool Child, Friday evening and all day Saturday, September 14 and 15. Undergraduates may enroll by permission of the instructor, which I can obtain for those of you who are not eligible for graduate standing. Prof. John Sharkey is the lecturer. He is fantastic! I strongly urge each of you to attend. The center, of course, will pay half of the registration fee. Call me at once if you are interested.

Enrollment

1 Letter for Re-Registration for Currently Enrolled Children
2 Re-Registration Application
3 Advertising for Enrollment Application and Brochure
4 Schedule for Advertising
5 Letter to Currently Enrolled Families Soliciting Assistance in Enrolling New Families
6 Newspaper Announcements
7 Telephone Inquiries for Information or Application
8 Application for Enrollment of New Children
9 Waiting List
10 Deferred Enrollment
11 Letter in Response to Receipt of Application for Deferred Enrollment
12 Letter in Response to Telephone Inquiry Confirming Appointment to Visit
13 Initial Visit to Discuss Enrollment
14 Contract
15 Financial Agreement with Parents and Caregivers (Short Form)
16 Letter in Response to Receipt of Application for Next Program Year
17 Identification and Emergency Information Cards
18 Preadmission Report by Physician
19 Personal Information Folder for Child
20 Permission to Participate in Center Activities and Receive Emergency Medical Care
21 Medical Authorization and Release Form
22 Notification of Changes in Child's Record
23 Picking Up Children at the Center
24 Letter of Welcome to Child's Family
25 Parent/Caregiver Handbook
26 The Daily Program (Supplement to Handbook)
27 Room Assignment Card
28 Orientation of Child to the Center and Separation from Parent or Caregiver
29 Separation of Parent or Caregiver from Child
30 Director's Checklist for Completion of Registration
31 Making Room Assignments
32 Assignment of Days
33 Request for Change in Day Assignment
34 Car Pools
35 Bus Service
36 Group Roll
37 Summer Program

Letter for Re-Registration for Currently Enrolled Children

Community Child Care Center

111 THIRD STREET ✿ TELEPHONE 123-4579

Dear Parents and Caregivers,

Very shortly, we will be starting an advertising campaign for the enrollment of children for the forthcoming program year. In order to help us determine the number of openings we can anticipate, please complete and return the enclosed re-registration application [Section E2].

This application can be used for younger brothers and sisters whom you wish to enroll for next year as well. If you need additional blanks, please let us know. We wish to remind you that we offer a reduction in tuition fee for a second or a third child in a family on our rolls at the same time [Section E25].

Please note that there will be a re-registration fee [Section E25]. You do not have to pay this fee at this time unless you wish to do so. It may be deferred until you pay your June tuition on or before June 1.

If you do not plan to send your child back to our program next year, please sign the space provided for this information.

Very sincerely yours,

Director

E2 Re-Registration Application

Name of child: ____________________ Date of birth: ____________________

Address: ____________________ Telephone no.: ____________________

____

Number of days per week for enrollment: 2 ________ 3 ________ 4 ________ 5 ________

I will bring my child at about __________ A.M. P.M.

I will pick my child up at about __________ A.M. P.M.

Interested in serving as a classroom assistant? Yes ________ No ________

The registration fee must be paid on or before June 1.

Registration fee: ________ Paid herewith ________ Bill me ________

Signed: ____________________

Date: ____________________

I do not plan to send my child back to the Community Child Care Center for the coming program year for the following reason(s):

____

Signed: ____________________

Date: ____________________

E3 Advertising for Enrollment Application and Brochure

Advertising in local daily newspapers, monthly or biweekly journals, military publications, and neighborhood papers is a good way to increase enrollments. A few well-placed advertisements during the year can keep the name of the child care center in the public mind. In making up an ad, list only essential information, and include some clue to your type of program. Run the ad on Monday or Tuesday, when the newspapers contain less advertising than on other days of the week. This makes it more likely that people will notice the ad and enables those who are interested to follow up on the ad before your center is closed for the weekend. For example:

15th YEAR SERVING THE COMMUNITY
Community Child Care Center
111 Third Street • Telephone 123-4579
Ages 2–6 half or full day
Individual Guidance • Creative Learning Experiences
VISIT ANYTIME!
between 7 A.M. and 6 P.M.
Applications for enrollment are now being accepted.

Two or three times a year, run classified ads for one-week periods in order to reach people who rely on them as a means of obtaining information. Here is another example of what can be run:

Community
CHILD CARE CENTER
Loving care, ages 2–6 years, half or full day, limited openings. Telephone 123-4579. Visit anytime 7 A.M. – 6 P.M.

One of the most desirable places to advertise, with the highest return in proportion to the amount spent, is in the yellow pages of the telephone directory. Display ads are very expensive. Consider, instead, an in-column display, which adds a low charge to your monthly bill but gives you year-round exposure.

COMMUNITY CHILD CARE CENTER
Half- and full-day programs—ages 2-6
Extended day care to age 8
Monday to Friday 6 A.M.-7 P.M.
Parent/caregiver participation optional
Individualized guidance—fun
Inquire about our
"Magical Summer" program
111 Third Street 123-4579
Parents and caregivers always welcome

Another form of advertising is a brochure that can be given to people who inquire about the center. Brochures can also be placed in pediatricians' offices, libraries, YMCAs, YWCAs, offices, and similar places. The brochure can be designed in a tri-fold or half-fold format. These formats make it easy for display.

A HAPPY CHILD CARE CENTER
Appropriate play experiences that contribute to the physical, social, emotional, intellectual, and aesthetic development of the child.

A MEANINGFUL CURRICULUM
Learning centers and motivational activities that build important foundations for future reading skills and other academic pursuits.

A PROFESSIONAL STAFF
Carefully selected for their educational background, child care training, experience, and sensitivity to the individual needs of the young child.

PARENT/CAREGIVER PARTICIPATION (OPTIONAL)
To increase parent and caregiver knowledge of child growth and development. Credit earned by participants may be applied to their child's tuition.

Community Child Care Center

111 Third Street • Telephone 123-4579

NONPROFIT • NONSECTARIAN • INTERRACIAL

MONDAY–FRIDAY
2, 3, 4, and 5 days per week
Ages 2 to 6 years
Half or full day
All-day care: 6 A.M. to 7 P.M.
Extended care available for children under 8 years of age.
Nominal Fees
State Licensed

"Our doors are always open to parents and caregivers."

E4 Schedule for Advertising

Name & Address of Publication	When Issued	Ad Deadline	Rates	Dates to Be Used

E5 Letter to Currently Enrolled Families Soliciting Assistance in Enrolling New Families

Community Child Care Center

111 THIRD STREET TELEPHONE 123-4579

Dear Parents and Caregivers,

We are now interviewing families of prospective new children for the forthcoming year.

We hope that you will tell your neighbors, business associates, and other interested friends about our program. We have approximately 30 openings for next term. These will be filled on a first-come, first-served basis.

We are enclosing a few brochures for your use [Section E3]. We would appreciate your giving these to any interested family who may want to consider our program for their child. Please invite them to telephone for an appointment to come and visit.

Thank you for helping us in this respect.

Very sincerely yours,

Director

E6 Newspaper Announcements

An excellent way of introducing your new center to the public or keeping the public aware of your already established center is to send news releases to the local papers any time you have an event. You can use this method of announcing parent/caregiver meetings, field trips, potluck dinners, and other special events. Even the announcement of reopening for a new program year can be made in the form of a news release, as in the example on page 221.

Preparing a News Release

In preparing a news release, you might ask your local newspaper if they have certain guidelines they want you to follow. Otherwise, these general guidelines can be used:

1. *Use your letterhead.* If you do not have printed stationery, type the name and address of your center in the upper left-hand corner.

2. *Under the name of the center, type your name and telephone number.* After your name, you could add "Contact Person."
3. *In the upper right-hand corner, type FOR IMMEDIATE RELEASE or FOR RELEASE ON ___________ (give date).*
4. *Write your news story double-spaced, with 1 1/2" to 2" margins.*
5. *Start out with a concise description:*

   Who

   What

   When

   Where

   Why

   Who to call for further information

   Since this might be the only part of the story that the paper will print, be sure that you give the critical details.
6. *Further expand on the initial description with other information regarding the news item.*
7. *If you use more than one page, write the word* more *at the bottom of each page to indicate that the story is continued on the next page.* It's best to limit yourself to one or two pages.

The following is an example of a news release:

Community Child Care Center

111 THIRD STREET ✿ TELEPHONE 123-4579

NEWS RELEASE

For immediate release

Contact: (Name of director)
Re: Start of 15th year

The Community Child Care Center has announced that it will be starting its fifteenth program year on September 11. The center offers a half-day and a full-day program and utilizes parents and caregivers as child care assistants, which enables some families to enroll at reduced rates. Interested families are invited to telephone for an appointment to discuss the possible enrollment of their child. The center is located at 111 Third St. For further information, call the director.

Photographs

Accompany your news release with a photograph when appropriate. For example, when announcing a guest speaker for a parent/caregiver meeting, include that person's photograph. When having an "open house" event, include a photograph of children participating in an art activity or climbing a piece of equipment in the playground.

When submitting a photograph, use an 8" x 10" glossy enlargement. Be sure to include names of any people in the picture. Include a brief description of what the photograph depicts. Newspapers will sometimes use just the photograph with that brief description, instead of the accompanying news article.

If you want to have the photograph returned to you, be sure to have your name and address on the back of the actual photograph, with a request to "please return."

Do not use a photograph of any child unless you have obtained permission to do so from the parents or caregivers. Your center can ask for a blanket permission from parents and caregivers at the time of enrollment. Out of courtesy, however, also notify the parents and caregivers individually any time you plan to use a photograph in which their child appears.

E7 Telephone Inquiries for Information or Application

The way in which the telephone is answered often gives people their first impression of your center.

Use these guidelines:

1. Be friendly and helpful.
2. Answer the caller's questions briefly. If extended answers are sought, ask the person to come in for a visit or to leave a name and phone number so you (or the director) can call back.
3. Send the information requested promptly.

The following letter is in response to inquiries for information:

Community Child Care Center

111 THIRD STREET TELEPHONE 123-4579

Dear Parents and Caregivers,

Thank you for your interest in our child care center. The enclosed brochure [Section E3] briefly describes our program.

We urge you to visit us to observe our child care groups in session [Section E13]. Plan to bring your child with you when you visit. We are open to visitors daily; however, we limit the number of persons who visit on any one day [Section J1].

Since the number of children enrolled in our center is limited by the provisions of our state license, we suggest that you visit us soon so that we can ensure a place for your child.

Very sincerely yours,

Director

This letter is in response to telephone inquiries requesting applications:

Community Child Care Center

111 THIRD STREET TELEPHONE 123-4579

Dear Parents and Caregivers,

Thank you for your interest in our child care center. Here is a brochure [Section E3] and the application for enrollment [Section E8] that you requested.

Upon receipt of the application form and your registration fee, we will place your child's name on our enrollment list. At that time, we will send you additional registration material that will be necessary to complete your child's enrollment.

We will send you an invitation for a visit and a personal interview before we hold our fall orientation program [Section F5].

Very sincerely yours,

Director

E8 Application for Enrollment of New Children

Program year: ________

Name of child: ______________________ Date of birth: ________________

Address: ______________________ Telephone: ________________

____

Name(s) of parent(s) or caregiver(s): ______________________

____

Parents' or caregivers' employment: ______________________

____

Recommended by ______________________

Number of days per week for enrollment: 2 ______ 3 ______ 4 ______ 5 ______

I will bring my child to the center at ________ A.M. P.M.

I will pick up my child at the center at ________ A.M. P.M.

Interested in serving as a child care assistant? Yes _____ No _____

Tuition schedule is attached [Section B17].

A registration fee must accompany this application. Paid: $________

Signed: ________________

Signed: ________________

(parent or caregiver signatures)

Date: ________________

For center use only:

Approved: ______________________ Date: ________________

____

____

E9 Waiting List

When a center has been in operation for over 15 years, thus building a good reputation, a waiting list is often established. Enrollment inquiries are received year-round, and sometimes long waiting lists are generated. These lists can become unwieldy.

Every four months, send an inquiry to people on the list, telling them you still don't have any openings and asking if they wish to continue to wait. This will help make your waiting list more manageable. The following form can be used for this purpose:

Community Child Care Center

111 THIRD STREET TELEPHONE 123-4579

Re: ______(child's name)______________

Your child has been on our waiting list since ______(date applied)______. We still do not have any openings and cannot anticipate when we may. Your wait may be from a few weeks to a few months.

If you still want to keep your child's name on our list for future enrollment, please sign and return the enclosed postcard. If we do not hear from you within ten days, your child will automatically be removed from the list.

Sincerely,

Director

Enclosed card:

Please keep ____________________________ on your waiting list until ____________________.

Signed: ______________________
(parent or caregiver)

E10 Deferred Enrollment

The names of some children on the waiting list are marked "Priority." These are brothers and sisters of children already enrolled or of children who had previously been enrolled. For these children, follow a procedure called *deferred enrollment.* Here is how it works:

1. The parent or caregiver fills out all of the usual enrollment forms, obtains a physician's pre-admission report, and pays the registration fee.
2. The child's name is listed on the rolls, marked *D.E.* (deferred enrollment).
3. If the child has a brother or sister in the center, the parents or caregivers are already on the mailing list. If it is a brother or sister of a former enrolled child, the family's name is added to the mailing list as though the child were already enrolled. Persons who have deferred enrollments are invited to bring their children to visit often.
4. When an opening occurs in the child's age group, the child is taken off the deferred list and begins attending on a regular basis.

E11 Letter in Response to Receipt of Application for Deferred Enrollment

Community Child Care Center

111 THIRD STREET TELEPHONE 123-4579

Dear Parent or Caregiver,

We have received your application for enrollment for your child and the enrollment fee. Your child's name has been placed on our deferred list. We will notify you just as soon as we have an opening in one of our groups.

In the meantime, we cordially invite you to visit with your child for brief periods of time during the next few weeks while you are waiting for a place. Thursdays are the best mornings to visit, since we do not have quite as many children enrolled on that day as on others. The best time is between 9:30 and 10:30. We have found such visits to be helpful in gradually orienting your child to our program. We suggest that you keep these visits casual, thus avoiding some of the anxiety your child may be feeling about attending the center.

Enclosed is our parent/caregiver handbook [Section E25] for your use in knowing more about our current policies.

Very sincerely yours,
Director

E12 Letter in Response to Telephone Inquiry Confirming Appointment to Visit

Community Child Care Center

111 THIRD STREET TELEPHONE 123-4579

Dear Parent or Caregiver,

Thank you for your interest in our child care center. The enclosed brochure will briefly describe our program [Section E3].

As you requested, we have made an appointment for you to visit on _______(date)_______, so that you may observe our child care groups in session. The best time to visit is between 9:15 and 11 A.M. when you will be able to observe without being interrupted by the comings and goings of parents and caregivers bringing their children to the center and picking them up for lunch.

We are looking forward to meeting you and your child.

Very sincerely yours,

Director

E13 Initial Visit to Discuss Enrollment

When parents and caregivers visit your center with their child to discuss enrollment, you will be their host or hostess and guide. After welcoming them to the center, take them on a brief tour of the child care facilities and grounds. This tour may be conducted by an assistant if you are busy at the time. Following the tour, invite them to visit their child's prospective child care room for a brief time. This visit will enable the child to explore the room environment firsthand. Parents and caregivers are urged to allow the child to choose an activity, observe the others, or voluntarily join in the play or explore the materials. Sometimes the child will enjoy selecting a toy or game and playing with it quietly near his or her parents or caregivers. The child usually enjoys participating in a snack period with the other children.

A hesitant child will frequently enjoy visiting on the playground more than in the child care room. The child feels a little freer there, and some of the outdoor equipment may be familiar.

After the parents or caregivers have visited the room or playground for a while, invite them into your office for a personal interview. Offer some coffee, tea, or juice. Answer questions parents or caregivers have. Discuss center policies [Section E25]. During the interview, try to interest the child in playing with something that will keep his or her attention away from the conversation. Or perhaps the child can accompany another adult outdoors or into a child care area. If not, perhaps an assistant can distract the child long enough for the parents or caregivers to discuss any special problems pertaining to the child's ability to benefit from the program. You may also choose to ask parents or caregivers to come back for another interview without the child.

Observe the child's attitudes and listen to what the parent or caregiver tells you to determine whether or not the child is ready for the preschool experience. If it is mutually agreed that the child will benefit, give parents the various registration forms to fill out in your office and request the registration fee at this time. Also, take the time to explain all center services, policies, and expectations. After you thoroughly explain these and answer their questions, give them the contract to take home to read and sign.

Ask parents or caregivers to return the contract and registration forms as soon as possible in order to complete the enrollment process. They will need enough time for a visit to a physician to get the medical report filled out [Section E18]. Also give them a copy of the parent/caregiver handbook [Section E25] to further acquaint them with school policies and procedures, as spelled out in the contract.

Contract

The contract shown on page 230, called an Admission Agreement, can be drawn up for your Community Child Care Center. You can use this form as a guide and make any changes you need so that the agreement is appropriate for your center.

Whatever form or wording you use, remember that the purpose of this agreement is to let parents and caregivers know exactly what they are getting and, at the same time, exactly what they will be paying for. In this sample agreement, parents and caregivers know exactly what is expected from them in addition to price considerations. Also, the services listed can be used as evidence in case of a dispute as to whether or not you are offering the services required by the licensing agency.

In order for a contract to be binding, it must include the following items:

1. **Parties:** (Included in introductory paragraph, page one, and the third line in A under "Basic Services") This means the names of the parties to the agreement: The center and the person who is responsible for the child and is enrolling the child in the center.
2. **Terms of Contract:** "Term" means the period of time covered by the contract (when it begins and when it ends).

3. **Cost or Price, including Due Dates:** Prices should include those for regular services and any charges you may have for optional services. (In this example, separate fees are charged for tuition and child care before and after the hours of the morning session.) Prices should be followed by a statement concerning delinquency, including dates and costs, if any. Also include a statement of your refund policy [Section E25].

   In order to appropriately list fees, the services provided must also be listed. These should include those required by your particular licensing agency, as well as any optional services provided that are not required but are permissible by law. The services listed here include those listed in the California Department of Social Services regulations.

4. **A Lawful Subject Matter:** Terms of enrolling a child in a care facility and the services provided by that facility are lawful subject matter according to the statement of licensure given at the beginning of the agreement [Section A8].

5. **Signatures of All Parties Involved:** The Admission Agreement should also include a statement of notification in case of a change of rate or a change in basic or optional services. This statement should include that parents and caregivers will be sent a written notice in case of such change, and that such notice will be sent in advance of the proposed change [Section B17].

Community Child Care Center

111 THIRD STREET ✿ TELEPHONE 123-4579

ADMISSION AGREEMENT

The COMMUNITY CHILD CARE CENTER, 111 Third St., Any Town. Phone: (555)123-4579 (hereinafter referred to as the "center") is a child care facility operated by the Community Service Club (at the same address), a nonprofit corporation. The center is licensed by the state Department of Social Services, Community Care Licensing Division, pursuant to sections of the state Administrative Code 00 Division 0. (Substitute the name of your state's licensing agency and the code under which it is licensed.)

A. BASIC SERVICES

The center shall provide the following basic services for

__________________________ __________________________

(name of child being enrolled) (birth date)

whose parent or guardian is

__________________________ __________________________

(name of person enrolling child) (relationship)

1. Half-day program between 9 A.M. and 12 noon for _______ days per week as prearranged, excluding days the center is closed.
2. Child care between _____ A.M. and 9 A.M. Yes ____ No ____
3. Child care between 12 noon and _____ P.M. Yes ____ No ____
4. Child care between 5 P.M. and 7 P.M. Yes ____ No ____
5. The child shall be furnished a healthful midmorning snack. Such a snack shall also be furnished midafternoon for children who are at school after 3:30 P.M.

(continued)

ADMISSION AGREEMENT, page 2

6. The child shall be given assistance with personal care as needed.
7. The child shall be provided with an opportunity to nap between 1:00 P.M. and 3:00 P.M. on a cot or mat provided by the center.
8. The child shall be placed in a group of peers based on age and/or special needs as determined by the staff.
9. The child shall be involved in a program of play and learning experiences that are appropriate for the ages of children enrolled in the center. A balance of active and quiet play is provided for, with individual and group activities geared toward the emotional, social, physical, aesthetic, and individual growth of young children.
10. The center shall assume responsibility for the child after the child has passed the legally required morning health inspection and has been signed in by a parent, guardian, or designated representative of the child's parents or guardians. The center shall retain responsibility until the child is signed out by a parent, guardian, or designated representative of the child's parents or guardians.
11. The child shall be administered physician-prescribed medication only upon the written request of the child's parents or guardians. The center shall not administer a nonprescription medication unless it is accompanied by a physician's request to do so. The center shall have no responsibility of any kind whatsoever for failure to provide requested prescription medication nor for adverse reactions caused by the administration of such prescription medication.
12. The center shall give appropriate first aid to hurt children. A parent or guardian shall be contacted if it is the judgment of the staff that immediate medical attention is necessary. If it is further the judgment of the staff that if the injury is of an emergency nature, paramedics shall be called to the center and a parent or guardian shall be contacted.
13. An ill child shall be isolated and given appropriate care until called for by a parent, guardian, or designated representative.
14. The center shall notify the child's parents or guardians of a suspected exposure to a communicable disease.
15. The center shall make every effort to safeguard personal belongings brought by the child, but shall not be responsible for lost or broken items.
16. The director or any other staff members shall report to Children's Protective Services or the Police Department (or other specified agency as provided by individual state laws) as required by the state Penal Code (quote section for your state) any suspicion of child abuse, sexual or otherwise, neglect, or endangerment of which they may become aware.

ADMISSION AGREEMENT, page 3

B. PAYMENT PROVISIONS

1. In accordance with the statement of fees in the Parent/Caregiver Handbook
   a. nonrefundable registration fee shall be paid upon enrollment.
   b. the registration fee is due each May for children who plan to continue in our program. It shall be applied to summer enrollment as well.
   c. tuition and accommodation fees shall be paid on the first day of each month, except in September, when they shall be paid on the first day of the program, and for the summer session. A five-day grace period shall be allowed for payments, following which the account shall be considered delinquent.
   d. partial tuition credit shall commence with the second consecutive week of absence.
   e. partial accommodation credit shall commence with the second consecutive week of absence.
   f. refunds of unused tuition and fees shall be given upon two weeks' notice of withdrawal from the program.
   g. refunds of unused tuition of accommodation fees shall be given if this agreement is terminated, as provided for in Section (D).
   h. no credit shall be given for days the center is officially closed. Tuition is the same for each month, except then it is prorated in September and in June, according to the opening and closing dates of the program.
2. Tuition may be partially offset by participation by the child's parents or guardians, as specified in the Parent/Caregiver Handbook.

C. OBLIGATIONS OF PARENTS OR GUARDIANS

1. A parent or guardian shall furnish requested medical information not more than ten days after enrollment.
2. A parent, guardian, or designated representative of the child's parents or guardians shall bring the child to the center building upon arrival, wait for a health inspection, and then sign in on the appropriate register.
3. A parent, guardian, or designated representative of the child's parents or guardians shall sign the child out on the appropriate register before taking the child from the premises.
4. The parents or guardians shall notify the center when someone other than those named on the emergency information card will be calling for the child.
5. The parents or guardians shall provide the child with a nutritious lunch if the child is to be at the center after 12 noon. Contents should follow guidelines, as specified in the Parent/Caregiver Handbook.
6. The parents or guardians shall provide the child with two small sheets and a blanket or other covering to use during nap periods if the child stays at school after 1:00 P.M.
7. The parents or guardians shall see that the child is dressed appropriately when brought to the center, following the guidelines in the Parent/Caregiver Handbook.

ADMISSION AGREEMENT, page 4

8. The parents or guardians shall notify the center of the child's possible exposure to a communicable disease.
9. The parents or guardians shall notify the center when the child is absent.
10. The parents or guardians shall give two weeks' notice or forfeit two weeks' tuition and fees, in case of withdrawal from the program.
11. The parents or guardians shall abide by the parking rules of the center.
12. The parents or guardians shall notify the center when the child will not be called for at the time specified when signing in.
13. The parents or guardians shall respect the nonreligious nature of our program.
14. The parents or guardians shall refrain from reprimanding children of other families while on the premises.
15. The parents or guardians shall come to the center for conferences when asked to do so by a member of the center's staff.

D. TERMINATION OF THE AGREEMENT

This agreement shall be terminated if any one or more of the following occur:

1. The program year has come to an end.
2. Death of the child.
3. Serious illness of the child, preventing attendance.
4. The parents or guardians of the child allow their account to become delinquent.
5. Failure of the parents or guardians to honor the obligations listed in this agreement or in any rules, regulations, or manuals promulgated or provided by the center.
6. The center in its sole and unfettered discretion determines that it is unable to meet the needs of the child.
7. The center in its sole and unfettered discretion determines that it is not in the best interest of the program or other children enrolled at the center to have the child in attendance.
8. Failure of the child's parents or guardians to cooperate with the center which the center determines in its sole and unfettered discretion is serious enough to warrant termination.

PROCEDURE

In exercising its discretion under numbers 5, 6, 7, and 8 above, the center may require the child and/or the child's parents or guardians to attend conference(s) with center personnel regarding the matters that potentially warrant termination of the agreement. The child's parents or guardians may request a conference with center personnel regarding the matters that potentially warrant termination, but the center shall have no obligation to grant any such request.

The center's director or staff shall have the sole right and responsibility to determine any disputed factual matters regarding termination of this agreement.

ADMISSION AGREEMENT, page 5

E. MODIFICATION CLAUSE

This agreement may be modified whenever any of the circumstances covered by this agreement changes. Such modification may only be made in writing and must be signed and dated by the parties involved in order to be binding and effective. Oral modifications are not binding under this agreement and shall not be enforceable under any condition.

F. OTHER

This provides that:

The parties to this agreement are aware of the (name of licensing agency)'s right to interview the child and the center staff, and to inspect and audit all records maintained by the center, without securing the prior consent of anyone. The parties are also aware of the licensing agency's right to observe the physical condition of the child, including conditions indicating abuse or neglect, and to have a licensed medical professional physically examine the child. (Be sure to check carefully and include only the rights provided by the laws in your particular state, if any such laws exist.)

SIGNATURES TO AGREEMENT

For services listed in this agreement, and in accordance with the terms of this agreement, I agree to pay Community Child Care Center the monthly sum of

Tuition: ____________________

Accommodation: ____________________
(child care)

Total: ____________________

or prorated amount thereof during the months of September and June. I further agree to pay the registration fee of $____________________.

I agree to cooperate with the general policies of the center; to perform the obligations of parents or guardians set forth in this agreement; and to abide by the rules, regulations, and manuals promulgated and provided by the center. My signature below indicates that I have read the terms of this agreement and the rules, regulations, and manuals promulgated and provided by the school. It further indicates that I have had this material explained to me and that all my questions have been satisfactorily answered.

Parent or guardian: ________________________

Parent or guardian: ________________________

Dated: ________________

____
Director

Dated: ________________________________

E15 Financial Agreement with Parents and Caregivers (Short Form)

Community Child Care Center

111 THIRD STREET TELEPHONE 123-4579

Dear Parents or Caregivers:

Please read and sign this agreement.

I hereby agree to comply with the rules and regulations of the Community Child Care Center regarding fees, attendance, health, parking, clothing, and other items specified in the parent/caregiver handbook issued by the center each year. I am aware of the scheduled holidays.

As indicated on the contract that I have signed, I hereby agree to notify the center two weeks in advance of withdrawal, should such event occur, or pay the difference.

I have read the statement to the effect that no refund of tuition can be given after May 1 of each year, or after August 1 for the summer term.

Signed: ______________________________
(parent or legal guardian)

Date: ___________________ Signed: ______________________________
(parent or legal guardian)

Witnesses:

___________________________ Date: ______________

___________________________ Date: ______________

E16 Letter in Response to Receipt of Application for Next Program Year

Community Child Care Center

111 THIRD STREET TELEPHONE 123-4579

Dear Parent or Caregiver:

We have received your application for registration for your child and the registration fee of $00. Your child's name has been placed on our rolls for the beginning of the fall term.

We suggest that you do not discuss the program at length with your child, thus avoiding some of the anxiety your child may be feeling about attending the center. We will help you plan an orientation to our program so that it can be done with the greatest benefit to all involved [Section E28].

Research has indicated that the word *send* has a meaning of finality to a young child. For example, you "send a letter to a friend," but you never see that letter again, or you "send that dog out of our yard." Perhaps when discussing the program, it would be better to use terms such as "we are taking Sartha to preschool" rather than "sending her to preschool."

We will soon ask you to come in for an interview. At that time, we will review center policies and give you a contract to sign with the registration forms to complete the paperwork for school entrance. With these will be a handbook and an orientation schedule, which will have suggestions for clothing that we feel to be appropriate for preschool.

If you have any questions regarding our center or your child's enrollment, please do not hesitate to telephone me.

Very sincerely yours,

Director

E17 Identification and Emergency Information Cards

Identification and Emergency Information (Side 1 of card)

Name of child: ______________________________

Last First Nickname

Date of birth: ______________

Address: ______________________________ ZIP: ______________

Phone: ____________________ E-mail address: ______________________

Mother or caregiver: ______________________________

Employment: ______________________________

Phone: ______________ Hours: ________ E-mail address: ______________

Father or caregiver: ______________________________

Employment: ______________________________

Phone: ______________ Hours: ________ E-mail address: ______________

Persons authorized to pick up child:

______________ ______________ ______________

______________ ______________ ______________

(Under no circumstances will child be released to anyone not known to the center without authorization from parents or caregivers.)

Note: It is legal for either parent or caregiver to pick up a child unless we have a copy of a court order restricting visitation.

Persons to be Called in Case of Emergency (Side 2 of card)

(Be sure to include someone who will usually know your whereabouts.)

Name: ____________________ Relationship to child: ______________

Address: ______________________________ Phone: ______________

Name: ____________________ Relationship to child: ______________

Address: ______________________________ Phone: ______________

Child's physician: ______________________________ Phone: ______________

Emergency hospital preference: ______________________________

Custody arrangements (Please indicate where child will be):

Mon. night: ____________________ Tues. night: ____________________

Wed. night: ____________________ Thurs. night: ____________________

Fri. night: ____________________ Weekend: ____________________

Center use only

Date of interview: Date of child's visit: Starting date:

Group assignment: No. of days per week: Hours:

E18 Preadmission Report by Physician

______________________, whose date of birth is ____________________, has been enrolled in our center. Groups meet from two to five times weekly, from ___________ A.M. to ___________ P.M., in groups of from 12 to 15 children, under the supervision of a professional child care provider and an assistant. The daily program involves both vigorous and quiet indoor and outdoor play, including the use of climbing equipment. A midmorning snack is served—usually fruit juice and crackers.

Does this child require special attention, medication, or routines or have any physical condition that may have to be taken into consideration in planning for the child's time at preschool?

____

In your opinion, is this child physically and emotionally able to participate in a preschool program like the one described above?

____

Has this child received any of the immunizations listed below? When?

Diphtheria	________	Rubella	________	Polio 1	________
Pertussis	________	Rubeola	________	Polio 2	________
Tetanus	________	Smallpox	________	Polio 3	________
Other	________		________		________

Date of last tuberculin tests: ______________________ Results: _______________

Date of most recent examination: ______________________________________

____

____________________________ Date: ____________________________________

Physician's signature

E19 Personal Information Folder for Child

Community Child Care Center

111 THIRD STREET TELEPHONE 123-4579

Family and Social History

Name of child: ______________________ Date of birth: __________
Address: __________________________ Home phone: __________
Mother (or guardian): ______________________ Age: ________
Father (or guardian): ______________________ Age: ________

Marital Status of Parents and Caregivers

Married ____________ One parent or caregiver household ________
Living together ____________ Living separately ____________
Separated ____________ (How long?) Divorced ____________ (How long?)
Stepfather ____________ (How long?) Stepmother ____________ (How long?)
Remarks ______________________________

If Child is Adopted

Age of adoption: _______ Does child know he or she is adopted? __________
Custody/visiting arrangements: ______________________

Brothers and Sisters of Child

Name: ____________ Date of birth: ________ Grade in school: ______
Name: ____________ Date of birth: ________ Grade in school: ______
Name: ____________ Date of birth: ________ Grade in school: ______
Name: ____________ Date of birth: ________ Grade in school: ______

Other members of the household (include relationship and age): __________
____

If both parents or caregivers are away from home during the morning, please state arrangement for child's care when not at the center: ______________________
____

Does child have room alone? ______ If not, with whom? ____________
Who has cared for child other than parents or caregivers? (State whether adults or teenagers)
____

(continued)

Has child had group play experience? ____________ Where? ______________________
Does child have neighborhood playmates? Specify: ______________________________
When and with whom does child watch TV? ______________________________

Developmental History of Child:

Age at which child

crept on hands and knees _____ sat alone _____ walked alone _____

named simple objects _____ repeated short sentences _____ slept through the night _____

began toilet training ________

Word child uses for urination _______

Bowel movements _______ Usual time for B.M. _________

Does the child dress self? ________ Undress self? _________

Is child right- or left-handed? ________

What time does the child usually eat breakfast? _______ Lunch? _______ Dinner? ______

Eating problems? ______ Is family vegetarian? ______

Other dietary restrictions: ______________________________

What time does child usually go to bed at night? ________ Awaken? ________

Does child sleep well? ________

What are child's favorite indoor play activities? ______________________________

Outdoor play activities? ______________________________

Does child play with water? ______ Go barefoot? ______

Does child have any special fears that you are aware of? ______________________

Does child have any speech problems? ______________________________

Does child have any other problems that we should be aware of? ________________

____

What method of behavior control is used in you home? ______________________

____

What is child's usual reaction? ______________________________

How would you describe your child's personality? ______________________________

____

____

____

____

____

Health History of Child

What illnesses has the child had? At what age?

Chicken Pox _______ Mumps _________ Scarlet fever ________
Measles _______ Diabetes _________ Hepatitis ________
Other ____

Does child have frequent colds? Explain: ______________________

____

Tonsillitis? ______________ Earaches? _____ Stomachaches? _____

Does child vomit easily? ______________________

Does child run high fevers easily? ______________________

Has child had any serious accidents? Explain: ______________________

Is child allergic? ___________ If so, how does it usually manifest itself?

Asthma _______ Hay fever _______ Hives _______ Other _______

Do you know what the allergy is caused by? ______________________

Has child ever been to a dentist? ______ Has child had vision tested? ______

Hearing tested? ______ Does child wear corrective shoes? _____

____

For Center Use Only

Illness _____ Date _______ Illness ______ Date _______ Illness _____ Date ____
Illness _____ Date _______ Illness ______ Date _______ Illness _____ Date ____

Accidents: ______________________

Other health information: ______________________

Cumulative record

Name of child: ______________________ Date of birth: ________________

Date started child care: ______________________

Attendance record

Excellent _________ Good _________ Irregular _________ Poor _________

Health Record while in preschool

Excellent _________ Good _________ Fair _________ Poor _________

Comments on child's progress: ______________________

____

____

____

E20 Permission to Participate in Center Activities and Receive Emergency Medical Care

I hereby grant permission for my child to use all equipment, to participate in all center activities and to leave the center premises under the supervision of a staff member for neighborhood walks or field trips in an authorized vehicle.

I hereby grant permission for the director or acting director to take whatever steps may be necessary to obtain emergency medical care. These steps may include, but are not limited to, the following:

1. Attempt to contact a parent or guardian, the child's physician, or the persons listed on the emergency information form.
2. If we cannot contact you or your child's physician, we will do one or both of the following: (a) Call another physician or paramedics (b) Have the child taken to an emergency hospital in the company of a staff member.
3. Any expenses incurred under 2, above, will be borne by the child's family.
4. The school will not be responsible for anything that may happen as a result of false information given at the time of enrollment.
5. The school WILL NOT assume responsibility for a child who has not been signed in upon arrival for the day.

Signed ____ Date ________
(mother or legal guardian)

Signed ____ Date ________
(father or legal guardian)

Witness ______________ Date ________ Witness ______________ Date ________

E21 Medical Authorization and Release Form

Use the form below to obtain consent for emergency medical care. Please note the clause allowing the child to be released to you when care is no longer required. Without the clause, a hospital must keep a child until a parent or guardian arrives, even if treatment is complete.

Community Child Care Center

111 THIRD STREET TELEPHONE 123-4579

MEDICAL AUTHORIZATION FOR ________________________________
(name of child)

The undersigned, who are the parents or guardians having legal custody of the above-named minor, hereby authorize the above-named child care center into whose care the above-named minor has been entrusted, to consent to any X-ray examination, anesthetic, medical or surgical diagnosis or treatment, and hospital care to be rendered to said minor under the general or special supervision and upon the advice of a physician and surgeon licensed under the provisions of the Medical Practice Act, or to consent to an X-ray examination, anesthetic, dental or surgical diagnosis or treatment, and hospital care to be rendered to said minor by a dentist licensed under the provisions of the Dental Practice Act.

The undersigned further authorize the above-named child care center to have the above-named minor released into the custody of its representative, should hospital care no longer be required.

This form is to be used ONLY in an extreme EMERGENCY, when said parents or guardians cannot be or are unavailable to be contacted.

Dated: ___________

______________________________ (parent or legal guardian)

______________________________ (parent or legal guardian)

E22 Notification of Changes in Child's Record

Community Child Care Center

111 THIRD STREET TELEPHONE 123-4579

To: All Parents and Caregivers

From: Director

Please keep this form with your handbook and your program calendar [Section A19]. If a change occurs that should be noted on your child's records, please complete this form and send it to the center immediately. Upon receipt of this notice, we will make the requested change and will send you another form in case you have further changes at some future date.

Changes being requested (please check appropriate items):

_________ Change of address
_________ Change of telephone number
_________ Change of mother's or caregiver's place of employment
_________ Change of father's or caregiver's place of employment
_________ Change (or addition to) persons to whom child may be released
_________ Change of marital status or living arrangements
_________ Other: ______________________________

Item to be deleted: ______________________________
Item to be added: ______________________________
2nd item to be deleted: ______________________________
2nd item to be added: ______________________________
Effective date for above changes: ______________________

Signed: ______________________
Date: ______________________

For center use only:
Change noted and made by
______________________ Date: ____________

E23 Picking Up Children at the Center

Occasionally, someone unknown to you or not listed on the identification form may attempt to pick up a child. In such instances, it is extremely important that you do not release the child without first contacting one of the parents, caregivers, or one of the people to be called in case of emergency [Section E17]. Be sure that your children's parents or caregivers are aware of the fact that they must send you a note, either with their child or with the person who calls for the child, authorizing that person to pick up the child. Compare the signature on such a note with that in your files to make sure that they are the same. You may sometimes be called on the phone by a parent or caregiver authorizing you to allow someone else to pick up the child that day. Do not accept such telephone instructions unless you can identify the calling party without question. If you have any doubts, you might verify the request by calling the other parent or caregiver, or some person listed to be called in case of emergency. If you are not certain about releasing the child, do not take the risk. It is better to stay at the center with the child until you locate someone on the release form than to risk the liability of allowing that child to leave with an unauthorized person.

E24 Letter of Welcome to Child's Family

Community Child Care Center

111 THIRD STREET TELEPHONE 123-4579

Dear Family of ________________________________:
(child's name)

Welcome! You are a Community Child Care Center family now. We would like to extend an open invitation to you to drop in often for informal visits. This will give us the opportunity to become acquainted with your entire family and will allow us to provide optimum learning opportunities for your child. Our doors are always open to you.

Informality is the key. We place great value on freedom to be oneself—for adults and children alike. We offer a relaxed and casual setting geared to the needs and interests of each child and each parent or caregiver who is a part of our center. We try to take into consideration individual differences, special abilities, and family cultural patterns.

We will have special days for families, but don't wait for invitations. Visit us often—even for five minutes. Know, with your child, that preschool is a good place because you have been there and have seen it firsthand.

We thank you for allowing us to join with you in providing for the care, loving, and nurturing of your developing child. We look forward with eagerness to the year ahead.

Yours most sincerely,
The director and staff

E25 Parent/Caregiver Handbook

Age groupings are generally based on the child's age as of September 1 of each year [Section E31]. Groupings are flexible and a child may be moved from one group to another to meet special needs. All but the youngest group intermingle freely throughout the day according to individual interests, needs, differences, and capabilities [Section E26].

All staff members are active in our state and local professional early childhood associations [Sections J6]. The director is a member of and active in the National Association for the Education of Young Children, a member of a local private schools association, and a member of ACEI (Association for Childhood Education International).

All staff members are experienced early childhood child care providers or educators. All participate in a continuous program of in-service education and studies for professional advancement in order to remain alert to the ever-changing needs of today's families and to the findings of current research [Section D52].

The center is open to all children, regardless of race, nationality, or creed, who may benefit from our type of program. The child must be at least two years of age, but does not have to be toilet trained (make changes appropriate to your center's age requirement) [Section I9], and must not be over kindergarten age. The center is nonprofit, nonsectarian, and nonpolitical [Section A14].

All that we expect of the children is that they come to our program, be themselves, and have respect for others. *What we expect of parents and caregivers* is that you read the operating procedures in this handbook and in supplemental notes and newsletters that we may send you from time to time [Section F36]; and that you feel free to be a part of the center, offering suggestions, comments, and constructive criticisms as well as financial and moral support [Part F].

1. Financial Arrangements

Tuition is based on the actual costs of operating the center divided by the number of children enrolled. Fees for the coming year, based on a nonprofit budget, are

DAYS PER WEEK	PRESCHOOL TUITION	ADD FOR CHILD CARE: 6–9 A.M.	6–12 P.M.*	(EVENING HOURS) 12–5 P.M.*	5–7 P.M.	OTHER	TOTAL
2	$00	$00	$00	$00	$00	$00	_____
3	$00	$00	$00	$00	$00	$00	_____
4	$00	$00	$00	$00	$00	$00	_____
5	$00	$00	$00	$00	$00	$00	_____

*Fee includes lunch

Fees for a second or third child from the same family at the same time will be 15% less than these. Tuition is payable in advance. The center depends on each month's tuition to pay its current expenses [Section B14]. Since many of our bills are payable between the first and the tenth of the month, all fees are due prior to the month of attendance. Unless you have made other arrangements with the director of the center, please pay each month's tuition on or before the first day of that month.

Credit for Absences

1st week of absence: No credit
2nd consecutive week: 20% of daily fee
3rd consecutive week: 50% of daily fee
4th week and more: Full credit

Registration Fees

A registration fee of $00 is payable when you enroll a child for the first time; $00 is due for each succeeding year of enrollment, or for each additional child in the family who is enrolled.

Vacation and Holiday Credit

No credit on tuition is given for scheduled holidays and vacation periods.

Payment in Case of Withdrawal from Program

Each child is enrolled for the entire year or the balance of the program year. Two weeks' prior notice, or two weeks' tuition, is payable upon child's withdrawal from the program before April 30. No refund of tuition can be made after May 1. Any child in the program as of that date will be charged tuition through the close of the program in June.

Makeup Days for Absences

We are licensed to handle a certain number of children per day, distributed among the various child care groups in specific numbers. Therefore, we cannot automatically grant opportunities to make up all days lost as a result of absences. If a child has a prolonged illness, however, we will make every attempt to allow for some extra time at our center.

Overtime Charges

There will be an overtime charge for children not picked up at their regular dismissal time. Consistent lateness after 7:00 P.M. will be cause to ask you to withdraw your child from the program. [Some child care centers charge a minimum of $5.00 for the first 15 minutes or any part thereof. They then may charge $1.00 for every minute late after that.]

2. The Health and Safety of Your Child [Parts G and H]

Your child's health is a matter of major importance to all of us. Upon enrollment, you must file a health form signed by a physician [Section E18]. We also require that the child have certain standard immunizations and a tuberculin clearance. A daily health inspection is given upon each child's arrival at the center. The person bringing the child must wait until the inspection is over before leaving the premises [Section G16].

Your child may be sent home if any symptoms of illness appear during the day. In such cases, your child will be immediately isolated from the others and you will be contacted [Sections C14, G16, E20].

Keep your child home if he or she

- has a fever or has had one during the previous 24-hour period.
- is taking an antibiotic.
- has a cold that is less than four days old.
- has heavy nasal discharge.

- has a constant cough.
- is fussy, cranky, and generally out of sorts.
- is just tired. Rest at such times may prevent the development of serious illness.
- has symptoms of a possible communicable disease. (These are usually sniffles, reddened eyes, sore throat, headache and abdominal pain, plus a fever.) Please notify the center at once if the child has a communicable disease.

Your child may come to the center

- if a cold is over, but a minor nasal drip remains.
- if there has been an exposure to a communicable disease, but the center has been notified so that the incubation period can be discussed and it can be determined on what dates your child should stay home [Section G28].

Tuberculin tests are required annually of all staff members and participants. We urgently recommend that all parents and caregivers also have a test each year.

In case of accidental injury [Sections G1, G10], we will make an immediate attempt to contact a parent or caregiver. If we can't reach you, we will call the child's physician. If necessary, we will also call an ambulance or paramedics. Until the arrival of a parent or caregiver, the physician, an ambulance, or paramedics, the director or an assistant will be in charge and make all decisions about the care of the child. You will be expected to assume responsibility for any resultant expense not covered by our insurance. The center will maintain a parents' or caregivers' signed consent form agreeing to this provision [Section E20]. It is to your child's benefit that you keep the center up-to-date on phone numbers, emergency numbers, and other pertinent information [Section E22].

Dismissal Time

Because the avoidance of fatigue is important to your child's well-being, we urge you to call for your child on time.

3. Authorization to Pick Up Child

No child will be released to a person not authorized by a parent or caregiver to pick up the child. We must have written or verifiable verbal authorization for changes in this respect [Sections E17, E22].

4. Child Care Assistance by Parents and Caregivers

Child care assistance for credit is a key component of our program [Section F12]. Two or three periodic orientation/training meetings will be held for persons wishing to earn tuition credit in this way [Sections F15–16]. There are also other ways to earn credit. We are always in need of minor repairs. Parents and caregivers can be helpful in this area. If you are willing to help out, please notify us.

5. Volunteers

In addition to those tasks for which credit is earned, we are always in need of volunteers [Sections F25–26]. We need and urge your voluntary assistance in planning trips, programs, public relations activities, recruitment of future enrollments, and other activities. We always need extra parents and caregivers to accompany us on trips.

6. Ways in Which We May Be of Help to You

When you enroll your child in our program, we assume the responsibility of giving you assistance with special needs in relation to your child's adjustment, growth, and development.

A. *Conferences* in relation to your child's progress will be arranged upon request [Section F33].

B. *Assessments* can be administered for developmental profile purposes. Your child may be referred to persons for special services pending the outcome of the assessment [Section I24].

C. *Parent/caregiver education programs,* in addition to those we ordinarily offer, will be set up on any pertinent topic at the request of three or more parents or caregivers [Sections F10, F26, F28].

D. *Your own child* will be given maximum consideration as an individual. We will look after your child's health and safety while he or she is at the center and present a planned program geared to what we believe to be developmentally sound and educationally beneficial [Section A14(IV)].

7. Parent/Caregiver Room

A special alcove has been set aside for use as a gathering place for parents and caregivers [Section F11]. You are welcome to visit with us often, to visit with other parents and caregivers, to use our library on child care and early childhood education, and to join us for refreshments. Open 9 to 12 daily.

8. "Experiencers"

Areas are set up from time to time for parents and caregivers to join the children or other parents and caregivers as "experiencers" [Section F26]. A variety of materials are provided with which you may experiment, create, use your imagination, invent, try out, and discover the types of feelings and emotions that the children experience as they pursue activities in an environment geared toward self-learning and self-discovery.

9. What to Wear to School

Think of your child's comfort—and provide simple clothing that is free of complicated fastenings. Think of the messy art materials and other messy activities—and provide clothing that is washable. Think of our playground—and provide clothing that is sturdy. Think of the changeable weather (and the fact that even though the sun may be bright and warm at 9:00 A.M., it might be cold and cloudy at 10:00 A.M.) and dress your child appropriately. Provide sweaters and jackets, even on the first sunny fall days. It's much easier to remove an unneeded item than be without.

Think of your child's comfort and provide your child with long pants from at least mid-October through about mid-April, although they are appropriate during other months as well.

Think of how you would feel playing outdoors in wet, cold, and windy weather. For your child's own comfort, provide suitable head covering when needed. A lightweight sweater should be worn under raincoats. Avoid sending sweaters or jackets with drawstrings. Drawstrings can cause possible choking incidents.

Finally, think of our collection of unlabeled, unclaimed clothing—and put labels on all outer garments, including hats and boots. If you do not have commercial labels, use adhesive tape. We keep a supply at the center for such use.

No open sandals, please (dirt, gravel, granite, sand, stubbed toes).

Child Care Assistants [Sections F12–24]

When you are working as a child care assistant, wear comfortable clothing, something that will not be ruined if it should get some fingerpaint on it, and be sure that it is warm enough. Bring a sweater. Our rooms are usually quite comfortable, but the wind blows sharp on many of the days when we play outdoors. Remember, too, that most of our playground surface is made of decomposed granite and sand [Section C8]. Tennis shoes or other comfortable walking shoes are more comfortable than open sandals or high heels.

Extra Clothing

If your child is prone to having toilet accidents, it is a good idea to leave a complete extra set of clothing at the center. Remember to change the size along about January or February.

We will appreciate contributions of large sizes of underwear, long pants, and undershirts that your child might have outgrown. We need sizes 4, 5, 6, and 8.

10. Car Pools

We help parents and caregivers find others with whom to form car pools [Section E34]. Car-pooling is tricky, and we offer the following rules to help make it a mutually beneficial and pleasant experience. When your children are to be picked up,

- have them ready. Wait with them. Take them to the car. Open the car door.
- be home to receive the children upon their return.
- let the driver see that you know your children are home.
- if your child is ill, notify the driver early enough to avoid an unneeded trip to your home on that day.
- if your child is not ready, wave the driver on and take your child yourself on that particular day.

Only take as many children in a car as you have seat belts. When it is your turn to drive,

- arrive at the center no earlier than 6:00 A.M.
- never leave children unattended in the car—even for a few minutes.
- if a disturbance occurs, pull to the curb. STOP. Then deal with it.
- if no one is at home to receive a child, take that child home with you. It will be the parents' or caregivers' responsibility to track the child down.

Check your car for safety. Always, always, always lock doors. Drive carefully. Do not hurry. Life is more precious than time.

Staff members are not allowed to drive children to or from the center except in emergency situations.

11. Nutrition

We serve a midmorning snack, usually juice and crackers [Section I18]. Parents and caregivers are welcome to send other snacks to be shared by their child's group. Suggested snacks are apple wedges, orange sections, raisins, celery or carrot sticks, flavored gelatin, and so on. Occasionally your child will have the opportunity to cook or otherwise prepare special food for a snack or a meal.

12. Birthdays

We celebrate birthdays during snack period. Please do not send cakes or full-size cupcakes. We have children who eat only the tops, children who eat only the bottoms, and children who eat everyone else's crumbs. We prefer that you send cookies or miniature cupcakes (muffin tins filled only enough to produce a cookie-size cupcake). These are easier to handle and are greeted by children as a special treat. Your child's child care provider will add special stories, songs, candles, and so forth, to make this a special time for your child.

13. Toys from Home

Except for toys that are needed in the very opening days to help ease your child's transition from home to our center, we ask that you leave your child's toys at home or in your car. If an item is brought to the center, we cannot be responsible for it. It must be shared and it must have the child's name on it. If you have a book that may be of interest to all the children, we appreciate this being shared with the group, but we ask that it be left for several days. We also appreciate occasional special music for curriculum enrichment. However, because we do not use tape or compact disc players every day, we suggest you discuss it first with your child's child care provider.

No Guns, War Toys, or Other Toys of Destruction

These items are taboo in our center. A child must have a means to express feelings of aggression. We suggest clay to pound (manual dexterity), a hammer and saw to use (good for visual-motor perception), a punching bag to hit (to vent anger while developing perceptual abilities), and fingerpaints (to soothe jangled feelings while practicing a developmental rhythmic movement).

The following is a recommended list of toys to encourage creativity, dramatic and active play, and intellectual and social growth.

Suggestions for Toys

FOR CREATIVE EXPRESSION

Paper: Drawing paper packaged
Construction paper, assorted colors
Roll of white butcher paper (18", 45.75 cm, wide) to cut as needed

Markers: Watercolor (avoid those marked "permanent"), Broad-tip and fine-tip

Fingerpaint, plasticine (clay), and play dough

Scissors (blunt edge for children under five)

Glues and pastes of several kinds

Tool sets (or buy individual tools and make your own sets) with wood scraps

Mosaics (cardboard or wood for back, glue, and items to glue on can be found in arts/crafts stores)

Jewelry-making materials

Opaque watercolors (excellent for home artwork), good brushes, and watercolor paper

Weaving sets

Crayons and chalk

Craft kits (commercial)

Sewing materials

Pastels

Rubber stamp sets

FOR DRAMATIC PLAY

Dolls, accessories

Puppets

Grocery store items

Commercial sets of farm, circus, service station

Sets of cardboard boxes of varying sizes

LEGOS®, Tinker Toys®, Lincoln Logs®

Blocks

Hospital/nurse/doctor sets

Miniature cars, people (avoid those that encourage violence)

Refrigerator carton to make into a house, room, or store

Costumes and accessories

Walkie talkie

Cooking materials, play foods

FOR ACTIVE PLAY

Sports equipment

Boxes and cartons, as above

Trampoline or mattress to jump on

Scooter

Wheel toys

Musical instruments (good quality, please)

Balls

Pogo sticks

Skates

Hula hoops

Yo-yos

rollerblades

FOR INTELLECTUAL AND SOCIAL DEVELOPMENT

Science things: Magnets, magnifiers, microscopes, chemistry sets, or other science sets

Fishbowl or aquarium—with fish, of course

Plants, seeds

Books

Magazines/subscription

Puzzles

Manipulative games, blocks

CD player

Computer/software, age appropriate

Computer games

Electronic games

Electronic kits

Construction kits (models)

Board games

Solitaire games

Play money

Watch

Cash register

Calculator

Tape recorder

Pets (lots of doggies and kitties at the pound)

CAUTION:

Avoid toys that are flimsy, have sharp edges, that have misleading or exaggerated statements, that are so packaged that you can't check out the quality, or that are only for looking at.

14. Arrival and Pickup

Arrival. The center's hours of operation are from 6 A.M. until 7 P.M. Children registered for full-day child care may arrive between 6 A.M. and 9 A.M. Children signed up for part-time preschool only must arrive at 9:00 A.M. Preschool class hours are from 9 A.M. until noon. Please bring your child to the center on time. A child may feel uncomfortable about arriving after everyone else has become involved in play activities.

Pickup. If you know you are going to be detained, please notify the center immediately so that we can reassure your child. There is an overtime charge, but we are flexible. If saving ten minutes means risking an accident, please drive safely—and plan differently next time. If you are more than ten minutes late at noon, we will provide lunch for your child and charge accordingly. Because the center has no provision for care after 7:00 P.M., consistent lateness after that hour will be cause for dismissal.

E26 The Daily Program (Supplement to Handbook)

When children enter their child care room in the morning, they are greeted by their child care provider and then given the freedom to explore various learning activities and interest centers that have been prepared before their arrival [Section C11]. These centers are changed from week to week, day to day, and sometimes from hour to hour. Paint. Clay. Collage. Musical instruments. Wood construction, with real carpentry tools. Blocks. Books. Dolls to bathe. Suitcases to pack. Flour and salt with which to make "play dough." Special things for special days—and each day is a special day. There are enough interest centers and activities going on at one time that the child is motivated by knowing they are there. Always something new or some way that is new. But always, enough things remain the same to provide the security and comfort of familiarity. Learning centers are not arranged for ease of movement and convenience of use, but rather for maximum challenge to the body and mind.

A child care provider is always nearby to lend support when needed—to help children when they momentarily lose control of materials, equipment, or even their emotions. A child care provider is always nearby to answer a question, offer a challenging statement, or make an asked-for suggestion—in keeping with each particular child's current level of achievement, interest, ability, and needs.

Sometimes a brief period of whispers. A quiet time. Relaxation. A savoring within of good feelings. An involvement time when there is a very special closeness between child and child. And between staff member and child. A love time. A child's time. A magic time.

Perhaps a story. Or quiet music. Or a gradual approach to a rhythmic activity and dancing time of crawling and jumping and growing like flowers or blowing like the wind. Or we go outdoors to run, climb, jump, walk on narrow boards, or balance on square boards that can be rocked to and fro. Time to grow. Time and room to explore, to experiment, to discover. Time to play. Time to be a child.

A Goal-Directed Program

At our center, you will see

- no lines to stand in. Only games to play.
- no elementary school games. Only preschool games.
- no patterns to follow. Only materials with which to create.
- no complicated, abstract meanings that the child cannot comprehend. Only ideas and things to talk about, relate to, compare with, match, fit into, try out, reinforce, invent, discover, and enjoy.

Yet, at all times children are being continuously challenged by specific learning goals that we have set for them.

- In order to begin to read and perform other academic tasks, the children must first gather meaning from the world and develop an awareness of concepts.
- In order to gather meaning from the world, children must have many satisfying sensory and sensory-motor experiences—they must touch, feel, smell, hear, see. Perceptual development follows. This is how children interpret their sensory experiences, which is a prerequisite for developing their minds.

Our program is geared toward helping children develop habits of observation, questioning, and listening. It gives them an awareness of their own feelings and their right to express those feelings by sometimes channeling them into other means of expression. They learn that they are free to make choices, and that as long as they stay within the limits of consideration for people and things, they do not always have to conform. An open-ended program prepares children to use their intellectual and creative abilities in future learning tasks.

To Our Parents and Caregivers

- We want you to know, to understand, and to discuss with us our goals.
- We want you to look often into our busy, happy, noisy, creative child care rooms and see your child at play.
- We want you to realize the validity of that play and the importance of what is being learned.
- Parents, caregivers, and staff members together can help your child develop his or her full potential.

HAVE A HAPPY YEAR!

Room Assignment Card

This card is given to parents and caregivers to inform them about their child's room assignment. Parents and caregivers hand the card to the child care provider who keeps it on file, referring to it for details about the child. The child care provider may use the back of the card for notes about the child. These notes are not progress records, but facts about the child's personality and behavior.

Community Child Care Center

111 THIRD STREET TELEPHONE 123-4579

Room Assignment Card

Name of child: ______________________________

Day care provider: ____________________ Room: ________

Address: ______________________________ ZIP: ________

Telephone: ______________ E-mail address: ______________

Date of birth: ______ Starting date: ______ Days: ______ Hours: ______

These persons are authorized to pick up this child:

1. ______________________ Relationship ________
2. ______________________ Relationship ________
3. ______________________ Relationship ________

Permission in file for

Playground equipment ______ photographs ______ field trips ______

Allergies: ______________________________

Brothers/sisters: ______________________________

Other: ______________________________

(Reverse side of Room Assignment Card)

Notes: ______________________________

____

____

____

____

Jot down any information that will help you in your relationship with the child; for example, if he or she is left-handed, musical, a poor eater, or interested in jungle animals.

E28 Orientation of Child to the Center and Separation from Parent or Caregiver

Starting preschool is an exciting experience for a young child—but it can also be a difficult one. Whatever the personality of the child, however eager he or she may seem to feel about the new situation, there will be a moment when the child suddenly realizes that the parent or caregiver is not going to be there. The apprehension that accompanies this realization is a normal reaction. Most children have little difficulty adjusting to preschool after they have made an initial visit with a parent or caregiver.

Nevertheless, it is important to introduce the child to the center in a way that will make this first separation from the parent or caregiver as easy as possible. Here are suggested ways to do this.

Child's Orientation

1. *Introduce the child to the program gradually.* First, have the child come for a series of three or four brief visits, and later for one or two full-session visits. On the child's first regular day, and on as many of the following days as necessary, a parent, caregiver, or other adult friend or relative should stay in the room.
2. *Adults who stay more than one day should gradually move out of the room—* they may sit right outside the door for a while and later move to the parent/caregiver room. They should be encouraged to keep busy with reading or some other absorbing activity to keep from focusing their attention on the child. When children sense that they are not being closely watched, they will usually start to relax.
3. *Never allow a parent, caregiver, or other adult to sneak away without saying good-bye to the child.* Ask the parent or caregiver to say good-bye and then leave quickly and unhesitatingly without looking back. Tell the parent or caregiver ahead of time that if the child cries at the moment of separation, the crying will seldom continue for more than a few minutes after the parent or caregiver is out of sight. When children cry, let them know that you understand how they feel, but tell them that their crying makes the other children cry, so it is better for them to cry in your office or some other area out of the room. If children have been given time to get acquainted with the child care provider, they will usually be happy to stop crying and get back to the room with which they have already become familiar. Sometimes, children who have not cried all morning (or all day) will start in when parents or caregivers come to call for them.
4. *If the separation seems to be unusually difficult for both the parent or caregiver and the child, arrange to have an adult other than the parent or caregiver bring the child to the center in the morning.* The separation difficulty usually takes place with only parents or caregivers. After being brought a few times by someone other than the parent or caregiver, the child may become able to face the separation with ease. Suggest that the child be picked up a little early on the first few days at the center. Sometimes the child does fine until other parents or caregivers arrive for their children. Apprehension may then begin as to whether the child, too, will be picked up.
5. Explain to parents and caregivers that it is normal to go through a period of adjustment during so big a change in the child's life. Tell them that you try to prevent trauma by anticipating the many difficulties that may arise. Even if no difficulties arise, it is good to be prepared. It is usually better to find out at the very beginning if the child is going to have some difficulty with the separation. Sometimes on the first day, the child will be so absorbed with the toys and the environment that there won't even be an awareness of being separated from the parents or caregivers. Frequently in such an instance, the adjustment must be made sometime later—any time from a few days to a few weeks. It is a normal part of a child's wholesome growth in learning to accept change and being away from home.
6. Help parents and caregivers understand that children's emotions are similar to those of adults. This helps an apprehensive adult have more wholesome empathy for the child's problems of separation. Remind the parent or caregiver to give the child some extra time, personal (physical) contact, and love during the opening few days of preschool. Suggest that the parent or caregiver not question the child about what he or she did during the first days. Suggest, too, that others in the family be cautioned not to do so. Allow the beginning days of preschool to be gentle, casual, and nonthreatening by not constantly reminding the child of it at home—but by responding to questions or comments directly from the child.

E29 Separation of Parent or Caregiver from Child

It is sometimes just as difficult for parents and caregivers to face separation from children on the first day of preschool as it may be for children to separate from parents and caregivers. Patiently help parents and caregivers recognize these feelings and reassure them that it is a normal reaction.

If necessary, review with parents and caregivers the center program; the health and safety precautions; the opportunities for children to learn, grow, and have fun; the opportunities for individual care and attention; and all the other details about the overall staff planning for children's adjustment. Reiterate the plan of always having parents and caregivers stay with children on their first morning, and for as long as is necessary for children's integration into the program.

Introduce parents and caregivers to your library and encourage them to read one or two books about the values of early childhood education. Ask parents and caregivers to help one or two others prepare some art materials for later use—or perhaps sort some puzzle pieces, cut out some pictures from magazines, or alphabetize some lists of names. Whatever the job, when two or three parents and caregivers work together in such activities, their tensions are relaxed and their confidence in the center is strengthened.

Encourage conversation between parents and caregivers. Ask two or three parents and caregivers of children who are already in the program to converse with reluctant parents and caregivers. Such conversation brings about feelings of friendliness that lead to increased confidence. Give parents and caregivers as much of your extra time as they need during the period of adjustment to separation.

E30 Director's Checklist for Completion of Registration

Child	Registration Fee	Emergency Card	History Folder	Permission Form	Financial Agreement	Health	Car Pool	September Tuition
Dani B.	✔	✔	✔	✔	✔		✔	✔
Jackie C.	✔	✔	✔	✔	✔	✔		

E31 Making Room Assignments

Even though you may be licensed for 16 children per room, limit the number of children per day in the two-year-old group to 12, giving an adult-to-child ratio of 1:6. A ratio of 1:8 is recommended for older groups.

When taking enrollment each spring, prepare a roll sheet for each child care group. Since some children do not attend five days a week, the number of openings must be determined on the basis of spaces available, rather than on the number of children on the roll. Sixteen children per day times five days per week equals 80 spaces available in each of the older groups.

Group: Marge's (4-4 to 4-9 in September)

A. NAME OF CHILD	B. Age Next September	C. New or Returning	D. Number of Days Per Week	E. Child Care Hours
1. Sara Boyd	4-4	new	5	1:30-5:30
2. Pat Dunlap	4-5	new	5	1:30-4:30
3. Ryan Foster	4-4	ret.	3	12-1 only
4. Christine Ginanotta	4-7	ret.	5	7-1
5. Deborah Houghman	4-9	ret.	5	7-4
6. Karlene Hyatt	4-4	ret.	5	8-5
7. Dani Jordan	4-8	ret.	4	8-5
8. Maureen Kushner	4-6	ret.	3	--
9. Jason Lavitt	4-4	ret.	5	9-6
10. Rebecca Ledbetter	4-6	new	5	7-5
11. Stevie Mancini	4-9	ret.	4	7-6
12. Brian Smothers	4-8	ret.	3	--
13. Curtis Shaw	4-5	ret.	3	7-9 only
14. Todd Tarlton	4-5	ret.	5	--
15. Ross Young	4-4	ret.	4	8-9 only
16. Kimberly Allison	4-8	ret.	3	--
17. Kevin Tull	4-7	new	5	7-5
18.				
19.				
20.				
21.				
22.				
23.				
24.				

Total spaces available = 80 (16 children per day times 5 days per week)

The roll sheet lists children's names, their ages (in years and months) as of the following September, whether they are new or returning, and the number of days per week that each child will attend. The total of days per week (Column D) shows how many spaces have been filled for each group. In the illustration, 72 spaces are filled. This leaves eight spaces, which can be filled by enrolling one child for five days per week and one for three days (total = eight), or any other combination that will add up to eight.

After groups are filled, continue to interview prospective families until you have approximately eight or ten children on the deferred enrollment list [Section E10]. As the year progresses, first fill openings from the limited number of children on deferred enrollment. Gradually, begin to move the more mature children in each group to the next older age group, so that by spring you are only enrolling two- or three-year-olds as openings occur. This ensures a continuous stream of younger children with a potential for returning to the program for the ensuing two or three years.

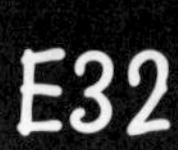

E32 Assignment of Days

Community Child Care Center

111 THIRD STREET **TELEPHONE 123-4579**

To:	All Parents and Caregivers	Date:
From:	Director	Child:

In accordance with the policy of the Community Child Care Center, your child has been assigned the following days, which are the same days that other part-time children in your area are attending:

M _____ T _____ W _____ Th _____ F _____

If you feel that you must request a change, please submit the request on the attached form and return it to the office. No changes will be made before October 1. Please follow the assigned schedule until then. Bear in mind that in order to fulfill your request, we must find someone with the days you request who will be willing to change to the days you have been assigned. Thank you for your cooperation.

Also attached is a list of other persons who live in your general area. We have asked Susan Weiser to help organize car pools. She will contact you to find out your wishes in the matter. If you do not receive a call from her, please call the number listed on the car-pool list. If you have any questions regarding your assignment, please telephone the center.

E33 Request for Change in Day Assignment

Name of child:
Address:
Telephone no.:
Days previously assigned (Check): M _____ T _____ W _____ Th _____ F _____

Days to which change is requested:
M _____ T _____ W _____ Th _____ F _____

Reason for requesting change:
____
____
____

For center use only:
Change effected as of ____________________

Approved by ____________________
Date: ____________________

E34 Car Pools

Community Child Care Center

111 THIRD STREET TELEPHONE 123-4579

Dear Parent or Caregiver,

The persons listed below will have children coming to the Community Child Care Center at the same time as your own child. May we suggest that you contact one another if you are interested in forming a car pool. If you are not interested in joining a car pool, please keep this list anyway. There may be a time during the year when you may want to contact someone living close to you.

Name	Address	Telephone	E-Mail Address

______________________________ has volunteered to assist you in getting into a car pool and will get in touch with you.

Sincerely,

Director

E35 Bus Service

Community Child Care Center

111 THIRD STREET TELEPHONE 123-4579

Dear Parents and Caregivers,

Beginning Monday, September 28, the ABC Transportation Company will provide bus service to and from our center for children who live within the city limits. Pickups will be made at your home between ___ A.M. and ____ A.M., depending on your location. Fees will be nominal, but will vary according to the distance you live from the center and the number of days per week you wish to use the service.

If you are interested in this service, please sign and return the enclosed application. The bus company will call or send a representative to your home to complete arrangements and arrange for the payment of fees, which will be made directly to the company.

Sincerely,

Director

APPLICATION FOR BUS SERVICE

Name of child: ____________________________

Address: ____________________________

____

Nearest cross street: ________________________

Days of week attends program:

M _____ T _____ W _____ Th _____ F _____

I am interested in transportation service on the days indicated. I need service

only to the center ________________

only from the center to home __________

both ways ________________________

Signed: ________________________

Date: ________________________

E36 Group Roll

The child care provider is given a temporary roll to use until final assignments, final enrollments, and requests for changes have been taken care of. The permanent roll is not used until October 1. The Community Child Care Center has devised its own roll form for each child care provider to record children's attendance.

Name of Child	Days Assigned M	T	W	T	F	Age in Sept.	Age in Dec.	Age in Mar.	Address	Telephone
Dani B.	✔		✔		✔	4-1	4-3	4-6	278 W. Diamond	243-0462
Cooky H.	✔		✔	✔		4-0	4-2	4-5	13210 S. 19th Ave.	243-2341

Month of ________ Year: ________

1	2	3	4	5	6	7	8	9	10	11	12	13	14	15	16	17	18	19	20	21	22	23	24	25	26	27	28	29	30	31

To: Staff
From: Director

Subject: Marking group roll

Please use the following notations in marking the roll book each day.

Present ___•___ Absent ___A___ Does not attend that day ___–___ Holiday ___X___

I will expect you to bring your roll book to the staff meeting each Monday, so I can get a quick picture of the attendance in each group.

E37 Summer Program

Many children need child care during the summer. However, many families go on vacation, and some parents and caregivers who work do not do so during the summer because they have several children at home. You must determine well ahead of time what your enrollment will be for the period from June to September so you can arrange to have the required number of staff persons available.

A summer enrichment program can be offered for children ages two through twelve in order to keep staff employed during the traditionally slower summer months, to maintain income level during the summer, and to provide continuing care for children who need such care year-round. Encourage children from outside your center to attend your summer program.

Consider providing multicultural studies with other activities in both the preschool and elementary programs. Creative activities, tumbling and gymnastics, play production, conversational Spanish, computer and Internet exploration, and similar activities can be included to provide a day-camp type of experience, while still providing needed child care. Swimming can be offered and arranged for at a nearby YMCA or YWCA, with lessons and bus transportation paid for by parents and caregivers. On the next page is a sample of a flier for a summer program. Send this letter to parents and caregivers to determine the number of children who will be attending your summer program.

Community Child Care Center

111 THIRD STREET TELEPHONE 123-4579

Dear Parents and Caregivers,

In order to plan for the summer term, we must know the number of children who will be attending. Please complete the form below and return it immediately to indicate your plans. We will appreciate the return of this form whether or not you are planning to send your child to the summer term.

We would like to take this opportunity to remind you that special activities, as noted in our newsletter, have been planned for the summer months. There will be a greater emphasis on long-term projects, dramatics, and arrangements for swimming lessons at the Y for those who are interested.

Sincerely,

Director

- -

Name of child: ______________________ Group: ________

is planning ______ is not planning ______ to attend the center this summer.

IF ATTENDING: Starting date: __________ (if after June 20) Ending date: __________ (if before Aug. 30)

Vacation dates during this time: ______________________

I have enclosed $00 for the registration fee. ________

______________ Date

______________ Signature of parent or caregiver

Community Child Care Center

MAGICAL SUMMER
OF
LEARNING & FUN

MINI-DAY CAMP for children
Ages 2 1/2–12 years

JUNE 20–
AUG. 30
M–F
9 A.M.–1 P.M.
Child care
6 A.M.–7 P.M.

LOCATED AT

------------------------------ CLIP HERE ------------------------------

Yes! ____________________ is interested in the MAGICAL SUMMER program.

Please send registration information to

____

_______________________________________ ZIP ______________

Telephone: ____________________ E-mail address: ____________________

Parents and Caregivers

F1 Today's Parents/Caregivers

Preschools many years ago were usually founded by small groups of mothers who wanted a 2 1/2-hour-a-day program, two or three days a week, in which their children could play with one another while they shopped or cleaned house.

With the emergence of changing families and homes headed by single parents or caregivers, the child care center director must weigh carefully all relationships with parents and caregivers. The standard formats for meetings, clubs, and conferences, although given in the pages that follow, must be constantly modified, added to, and taken away from to meet the wide range of needs of such a diverse group as today's parents and caregivers. Our job is that of serving these families—whatever their family makeup, whatever their lifestyle. Their needs are great, and we are privileged to play so important a role in this very crucial time of their children's lives. Our goal must be to bring a stabilizing influence to all their lives by being reliable, trustworthy, and sensitive to their changing needs. Our greatest tool is communication.

F2 Communicating with Parents/Caregivers

Communication comes in many shapes and forms. These include, but are not limited to, the following:

1. **Telephone Inquiry**
   A natural exchange of information begins with the first inquiry made by the parent or caregiver [Section E7]. Be certain the telephone skills of your staff are exemplary. Information must always be conveyed in a positive, supporting manner.
2. **Letters Regarding Enrollment and Information**
   Parents or caregivers will form opinions about your center in advance on the basis of the written information you send out. Be sure that such information conveys warmth, personal interest, and enthusiasm. Be certain that all communications are neat and attractive. Use illustrations when possible.
3. **Admissions Interview**
   The mutual exchange of information continues when parents and caregivers visit the center to discuss children's admission to your program and to observe child care groups [Section E13]. Each visitor should be treated as though he or she is the most important person who has ever come to your center. (After all, your job depends on parents and caregivers bringing their children.) With such an attitude, you may not only ensure the enrollment, but you will also make new friends.
4. **Orientation Meetings**
   Helping parents and caregivers understand your procedures will keep down anxiety about their children's first days in the program. [Sections F2–8].

5. **Parent/Caregiver Contact**
   Helping parents and caregivers get to know one another will encourage them to become active members of your center's community [Sections F5, F28].
6. **Family–Staff Contacts**
   Providing opportunities for parents and caregivers to become acquainted with staff members heightens their confidence in your program. Throughout the year, child care providers will have many opportunities to share information and ideas with parents and caregivers, which will add to their mutual understanding of the children [Section F10]. Frequently these exchanges will be in the form of telephone communications.
7. **Parent/Caregiver Meetings**
   These gatherings may be educational, social, or both. When opportunities are provided for the exchange of ideas, there is increased understanding of mutual concern by the people involved [Sections F10, F28].
8. **Conferences**
   You may hold scheduled, planned conferences, or you may arrange spontaneous meetings whenever individual concerns arise. Either the parent or caregiver or the child care provider may request such a conference. One-to-one meetings, such as in the parent-staff or parent-director conferences, frequently provide a way to clear up misunderstandings before they become serious to any parties involved [Sections F23, F31–33].
9. **Written Communication**
   An ongoing program of written communication between parents and caregivers and the center is especially important for those parents and caregivers who are unable to visit the center or attend meetings. These may take the form of
   a. newsletters and memos [Section F36].
   b. bulletin boards for parents and caregivers [Section F27].
   c. informal notes from the child's child care provider to parents and caregivers.
   d. informal notes from the director to parents and caregivers.
   e. reports of accidental injury [Sections G8–9].
   f. incident reports.
   g. monthly calendars.
   h. the Parent/Caregiver Handbook [Section E25].
   i. written evaluation of the child.

F3 Self-Evaluation Chart for Principles of Communication

The following is a self-evaluation chart to achieve greater personal awareness about your communication skills.

	NEVER	OCCASIONALLY	USUALLY	MOST OF THE TIME	ALWAYS
1. Do I listen to what the other person has to say? *Communication must be two-way—otherwise there is none. Even if one person is doing all the talking, it is two-way if the other person is listening with care and interest.*					
2. Do I state my position in clear, concise terms? *Communicating will be more meaningful and can be brought to a conclusion more quickly if you clarify at the beginning the specific topic for discussion and your position in relation to that topic.*					
3. Do I use professional, but understandable vocabulary? *Your purpose is to get the message across or to elicit a response or commitment from the other party. This can be more readily accomplished if you don't scare the other person off by using professional jargon.*					
4. Do I speak in a way that lets other people know that I appreciate their viewpoints and opinions even though they differ from mine? *By respecting the right of the other person to have his or her own view of things, you are reinforcing that person's capacity to respect you.*					
5. Am I gracious in my response to compliments? *When receiving a compliment, it is complimentary to the other person to show your appreciation with an immediate "thank you," allowing the other person the pleasure of knowing he or she has been acknowledged. Avoid apologizing.*					
6. Do I show my appreciation for constructive criticism? *We don't always appreciate constructive criticism until some time after we have received it. It is a good idea to acknowledge the criticism immediately and to tell the other person that you appreciate his or her interest and that you will give it your consideration.*					
7. Am I tactful in my response to criticism that is not constructive? *When receiving such criticism, it is wise to attempt to retain a basis for communication with the person doing the criticizing. Try to establish a basis for continued communication, in an attempt to keep criticism from becoming gossip and becoming a cause for concern to parents, caregivers, or staff members. Let the person know that you appreciate the interest shown and that you would like to take the matter under consideration and discuss it further between the two of you.*					
8. Do I direct the conversation to other topics when gossip or disparaging remarks are introduced? *Gossip can be very detrimental to a center. Discourage it whenever possible. Never indulge in even the smallest bit of gossip yourself, so you can serve as a positive model to others.*					

Planning Meetings with Parents/Caregivers

Use this checklist for planning the various meetings you will have with parents and caregivers throughout the course of the year.

Item	
Purpose of meeting	Orientation of new parents and caregivers
Goals of meeting	Explain orientation procedures, center policies, introduce staff, get acquainted.
Time and date of meeting	Tuesday, Sept. 10, 7:30 p.m.
Notification of parents and caregivers	At staff meeting, Sept. 5
Preparation of agenda	√
Arranging for refreshments	√ (staff)
Newspaper publicity	
Planning for place of meeting	√
Arranging environment	Doris & Elly
Table decorations	Jack
Seating	Custodian has been notified.
Projector and screen, if needed	
Tape or CD player, if needed	
Other equipment	
Janitorial arrangements	√
Tape recorder/PA system	Sarah Johnson will operate it.
Other:	

Parent/Caregiver Orientation Meetings

Parent/caregiver orientation meetings will be among your most important responsibilities as director of a child care center. They are held for several purposes, which may include the following:

1. **Discussing center policy with parents and caregivers** [Sections A14, E25]. If you have an average daily attendance of 80 children brought to your center by about 50 parents and caregivers (considering those who are in car pools or who ride buses), and a staff of 15 adults each day, including your child care assistants, that means you have 145 people to be accounted for during the first hours of each day. A clear understanding of center policies will help to keep all of these people from stepping on one another's toes. It will also save much time in answering questions, telephone inquiries, and complaints when there is a clear understanding of all rules and regulations about the center.

2. **Explaining the educational philosophy of your center** [Sections A14 (IV), C11, E26, F17].
This will be an ongoing responsibility throughout the year. Parents and caregivers who send their children to your center have a right to be informed of the program's educational philosophy which, in essence, will be whatever your philosophy of education is. Since education is an ever-changing force in our society, it calls for constant interpreting and reinterpreting to those who are not directly involved in administrating it. Acknowledge in advance that not everyone subscribes to the same philosophy that you do, but that your goal is to do what is good for their children, and that you believe you can achieve that goal with your methods.
3. **Introducing parents and caregivers to the entire staff, and especially to the people who will be their children's child care providers.**
This will be the basis for what you hope will be a growing and positive relationship throughout the year. Let the parents and caregivers know of your pride and confidence in your staff in order to instill the same confidence in them. This will help make the year a successful one.
4. **Acquainting parents and caregivers with your plan for their children's gradual orientation to the center** [Section E28].
You may wish to add other reasons for holding parent/caregiver orientation meetings that apply to your particular circumstances, such as bus schedules.

F6 Invitation to Parent/Caregiver Orientation Meeting

Community Child Care Center

111 THIRD STREET ✿ TELEPHONE 123-4579

Dear Parents and Caregivers:

You are invited to an orientation meeting for parents and caregivers of our new children on Tuesday evening at 7:30 P.M. The meeting will take place at the center and will last approximately two hours.

Since we will be a child care community of 110 children, ten regular staff members, and at least 200 parents and caregivers—not to mention grandparents, aunts, uncles, college students, other visitors, and personal friends—we need some mutual understanding in order to keep from stepping on one another's toes.

To ensure that your child will realize maximum benefits from our program, we want you to understand our goals, procedures, guidance policies, and basic educational policy.

We therefore consider it important that at least one parent or caregiver, preferably both, attend this orientation meeting. We are notifying you of the date in advance so that you can make arrangements.

Very sincerely yours,
Director

F7 Agenda for Parent/Caregiver Orientation Meeting

Time		*Facilitator*
(3 min.)	1. Welcome	Director
(5 min.)	2. Explanation of purposes and goals of meeting [Section F4].	Director
(30 min.)	3. Explanation of center policies and review of Parent/Caregiver Handbook [Section E25].	Assistant director #1
(10 min.)	4. Explanation of center educational philosophy [Sections A14, C11, E26, F5, F17].	Assistant director #2
(10 min.)	5. Introduction of staff members.	Director
(3 min.)	6. Explanation of the "gradual admission" process [Section E28].	Child care provider of two-year-olds
(10 min.)	7. Questions from parents and caregivers.	Staff
(20–30 min.)	8. Refreshments, socializing, and visiting child care rooms.	Staff

F8 Tape-Recording Parent/Caregiver Orientation Meeting

Strongly encourage attendance at parent/caregiver orientation meetings, at least on the part of one parent or caregiver. But remember that there are usually circumstances that prevent some well-intentioned persons from attending. For this reason, you should tape-record each meeting and make arrangements for those who did not attend to come in and listen to the recording.

Invariably, there will be some parents and caregivers who neither come to the meeting nor come to listen to the tape recording. These same people may complain because they don't know what's going on at the center or feel they are never notified of events. Bear in mind that these parents and caregivers really want what is good for their children or they wouldn't be sending them to your program. Be tolerant, understanding, and helpful. Try to develop a friendship and do what you can to help them feel that they are a part of your center's community.

F9 Alternate Times for Orientation Meetings

It is difficult to get acquainted with parents and caregivers who work or go to school and, therefore, barely have time to bring the child in the morning. It is your responsibility to find ways other than the casual daily contacts or enrollment interview to become acquainted with them. Meetings should be made as inviting as possible.

Community Child Care Center

111 THIRD STREET TELEPHONE 123-4579

INVITATION TO PARENTS AND CAREGIVERS OF ALL CHILDREN

Dear Parents and Caregivers:

You are cordially invited to attend an orientation meeting and spaghetti dinner at the Community Child Care Center on Tuesday, September 14, from 6:30 P.M. until 9:00 P.M. If you can't get here in time for dinner, we urge that you plan on arriving by 7:30 P.M. to attend the rest of the meeting. We want to get acquainted with you, and we want you to have this chance to get acquainted with us.

Note: Child care will be provided by reservation.

Community Child Care Center

111 THIRD STREET TELEPHONE 123-4579

INVITATION TO PARENTS AND CAREGIVERS OF ALL CHILDREN

Dear Parents and Caregivers:

You are cordially invited to attend an orientation meeting on Wednesday, September 15, between 7:30 and 9:00 P.M. Whether or not you have had a child in child care before, we urge you to attend this meeting so that we may get off to a wonderful start of an exciting new year together. Please return the enclosed sheet indicating whether you and/or your spouse or partner will be able to attend the scheduled meeting. We will serve dessert and coffee.

Note: Child care will be provided by reservation.

(Please sign the applicable sections and return this form.)

I will ______ will not ______ attend the spaghetti dinner on Tuesday, September 14.

Signed: ______________________________

I will ______ will not ______ attend the orientation meeting for parents and caregivers on Wednesday, September 15.

Signed: ______________________________

An alternative meeting will be arranged for those parents and caregivers of new children who cannot attend either of these meetings.

F10 Planning and Implementing Parent/Caregiver Education Meetings

One way that your Community Child Care Center can help parents and caregivers in their jobs as "child raisers" is by providing a planned program of parent/caregiver education meetings throughout the program year. There are many ways to handle these meetings:

1. Regularly scheduled monthly meetings or parent/caregiver club meetings.
2. Timely scheduled meetings planned according to specific interests and needs of the parents and caregivers.
3. A series of meetings at various times of the year with a central focus or theme.
4. Meetings to report on educational conferences that members of the staff have attended.
5. Special meetings for the orientation of new program education practices or changes.
6. Lunch meetings can be especially effective with working parents and caregivers. Set aside a two-hour time period. Those who bring their lunches eat with their own children while other children are outdoors playing. The staff socializes with parents and caregivers after they have eaten.

The following pages show examples of letters announcing various types of parent/caregiver education meetings.

Parent/Caregiver Education Meeting with Child's Child Care Provider

Community Child Care Center

111 THIRD STREET ✿ TELEPHONE 123-4579

Dear Parents and Caregivers:

We have planned a series of meetings that will enable you to meet in a group with your child's child care provider. At these meetings, discussion will concern some of the learning experiences your child has been participating in and what is planned for the coming months. We will also discuss ways in which you may follow up on center activities in your home to further enhance your child's development. You will have a chance to exchange ideas with other parents and caregivers who have children in the same child care group.

The meeting for your child's group will be on Tuesday, November 18. You may come from 7:30 to 8:30 A.M. or from 7:30 to 8:30 P.M.

We feel this meeting is important. Please arrange your plans now so that you will be free to attend next Tuesday morning or evening.

Very sincerely yours,

Director

Note: Child care will be provided.

Instituting a Parent Discussion Series

Community Child Care Center

111 THIRD STREET ✿ TELEPHONE 123-4579

To: All Parents and Caregivers

From: The Community Child Care Center

Subject: Parent/Caregiver Discussion Group

As we are all aware, being a parent or caregiver is an important job. Sometimes, getting together and discussing problems and exchanging ideas about child training can be very beneficial. Therefore, we have planned a series of parent/caregiver discussion meetings for just this purpose.

Starting on Thursday evening, April 27, at 7:00, we will have a weekly discussion group for a six-week period. The topics will be subjects that you, the parents and caregivers, choose to discuss.

A staff member will direct each meeting. Each session will last for one hour. We will meet in Room 12 at our center. We're counting on your attendance, participation, and support.

Please sign the enclosed form indicating your intention to attend. Also, indicate any subjects you would like to include as topics for discussion. The meetings will be held April 27, May 4, May 11, May 18, May 25, and June 1. Please come.

P.S. Child care will be provided.

Registration for Parent/Caregiver Discussion Group

Yes, count me in.

I will attend the parent/caregiver discussion group on April 27, and as many of the other meetings as I am able to.

Parent/caregiver ______________________________

Parent/caregiver ______________________________

Topics I would like to hear discussed:

____

____

____

____

Parent/Caregiver Education Meeting

Community Child Care Center

111 THIRD STREET TELEPHONE 123-4579

To: All Parents and Caregivers

From: Community Child Care Center

Subject: "Night to Howl" (Nonpunitive Discipline)

Discipline is always a ready topic for discussion among parents and caregivers—and among staff members as well.

Please join us for "Night to Howl," at which a panel of parents and caregivers of eight of our children will answer questions confidentially. We want them to share their own ideas—and we are hoping they won't be influenced by spouses, friends, or anyone else.

Participating parents and caregivers will be

__________ __________ __________ __________

__________ __________ __________ __________

They'll be expecting you.

Procedure for Parent/Caregiver Panel

1. Invite eight parents and caregivers to participate. Try to select representatives from different occupational, economic, and cultural groups.
2. Inform parents and caregivers that you will give them the questions they will be asked to answer on the day before the meeting. You want the answers to be spontaneous and representative of their own ideas, not the result of research. That is why you are not giving them the questions further in advance.
3. Give each participant the entire list of questions in advance, marking off the question you have assigned to him or her.
4. On the night of the meeting, you can ask participants to role-play some of the incidents from the featured questions.

Sample Questions for Parent/Caregiver Panel

1. What do you do when your child uses offensive language?
2. What do you do when your child has a tantrum or expresses hatred?
3. What do you do if your child is willfully destructive?
4. What do you do when two or more children start quarreling?
5. What do you do when your child displays stubbornness?
6. What do you do when your child refuses to go to sleep?
7. What do you do when your child is continually dawdling?
8. What do you do when your child endangers his or someone else's life by such actions as playing with matches or running into the street?

F11 Parent/Caregiver Corner

An alcove adjacent to the director's office can be set aside as a parent/caregiver corner. Place several comfortable chairs around a large coffee table. Provide fruit juices, coffee, tea, and baked goods on a nearby cart. Have available a good collection of books of interest to parents and caregivers. Encourage them to borrow the books for home reading. Have this announcement posted on a nearby parent/caregiver bulletin board.

I Took a Book

Name	Title of Book	Dates	
		Out	Ret'd

Encourage parents and caregivers to share with you and your staff the books and articles they have read. Their suggestions can be posted on the bulletin board and mentioned in newsletters sent to children's homes [Section F36].

Parents, caregivers, and staff should be encouraged to contribute other items of interest, such as magazine articles on innovative educational techniques, a piece of sculpture from their home, or an interesting plant. Place various creative art materials, challenging puzzles, or games on a nearby table for parents and caregivers to use.

The parent/caregiver corner is a lively and relaxing corner and adds much to make children's families feel welcome. This area greets parents and caregivers as they bring their children to the center each day.

In addition to the parent/caregiver corner, have a small conference room available when you need privacy for a confidential discussion with a parent or caregiver. But for the most part, you will find that what you gain in warmth, friendship, and close rapport with parents and caregivers by not allowing yourself to be isolated will more than offset the feeling that you will occasionally have of being "surrounded." It's all part of your job. You can make it an exciting part by extending a feeling of welcome to everyone who comes in.

Greeting the Parent/Caregiver and Child

When parents and caregivers arrive each day, the director greets them cordially along with their children. If they do not have to go to work or school, the director can invite families of children to stay a while and chat with other parents and caregivers. If they wish to talk to you, ask them to either visit in the child's room or sit down and have a cup of coffee or tea until you finish greeting other parents, caregivers, and children. You will then be able to give them your full attention. In the meantime, some other parents and caregivers might join the first and you will find yourself hosting a genial group who, in enjoying your hospitality, develop more positive feelings about the center.

If a parent or caregiver is waiting to talk with you, be sure to do so before becoming involved in some other activity. If you have a previous appointment, talk briefly with the parent or caregiver, evaluate the concern, and, if necessary, set up a time for a conference either later that day or on another day.

Working parents and caregivers are given opportunities for immediate conferences, early-morning or late-afternoon appointments, or whatever will help them in relation to their working schedules and family obligations.

F12 Parents/Caregivers as Child Care Assistants

By using parents and caregivers as child care assistants, your Community Child Care Center is able to enrich its program in many ways. Primarily, parents and caregivers take the place of paid child care aides. Their presence in your center lends warmth and a feeling of home child care rapport, as well as a rapport between staff members, parents and caregivers, and children that develops when people work closely together.

Tuition Credit

Tuition credit can be given to parent/caregiver child care assistants at a rate that is 25 percent less than the hourly minimum paid for an assistant or aide. You can apply this savings to higher salaries for your child care staff. At the same time, families with limited incomes can reduce the amount of their tuition enough to make it easier for them to send their children to child care. Most of your assistants will be nonworking parents or caregivers whose children attend part-time. You might have some eager participation by working parents or caregivers who come on their days off. Many parents and caregivers like to assist at their child's child care center because of the experience and knowledge they acquire, rather than for the tuition credit. Not only does the parent or caregiver learn, but the child care staff, by working so closely with many different parents and caregivers, is constantly acquiring new ideas and insights they might otherwise miss.

Benefits to the Child

The child always benefits when there is a close communication between the center and members of the child's family. However, when a parent or caregiver assists in the child care room, the child has the experience of a close and ongoing relationship with a warm and understanding child care provider and learns to respond positively to supervision by a wide variety of adults. The same thing happens when students from nearby schools and colleges or other volunteers from the community assist in the program as well [Section J2]. Have your parents and caregivers help in child care groups other than those of their children. As the year progresses, you can gradually move them into their children's rooms.

Health Clearance

Before a parent or caregiver can assist in the child care environment, the parent/caregiver medical report [Section F14] must be completed and placed in the center's files. In addition, you must have on file evidence of a negative tuberculin test. In many communities, the county or city health department will perform such tests free of charge. Some communities may charge a small fee for sending a report.

Training Sessions

Parents and caregivers must attend one or more training sessions before actually assisting in child care [Sections F15–17]. At these orientation meetings, the director must outline the goals of the center and explain how you work toward those goals. Attendance at these meetings is compulsory. One meeting can be held in the fall and one refresher meeting in January or February. Child care should always be provided for parents and caregivers who attend these meetings.

Career Development

Many participating parents and caregivers, both men and women, have developed interest in early childhood education and begin to take relevant college courses, acquire units, start substituting in the public schools, and eventually become professional teachers or child care operators.

F13 Invitation to Become a Child Care Assistant

Community Child Care Center

111 THIRD STREET TELEPHONE 123-4579

Dear Parent or Caregiver:

In order to keep tuition costs at a minimum, to provide you with an opportunity for firsthand knowledge of what is going on at your child's child care center, and to extend your knowledge of good principles of early childhood education, the Community Child Care Center will again offer its parents and caregivers the privilege of serving as a child care assistant.

As stated in our parent/caregiver handbook, tuition credit is given for each day you help out. It is applicable to the tuition due the month following service to the center.

If you are interested in participating, we must have on file a medical report from a physician, including a record of a negative tuberculin test. This test may be a chest X-ray or an interdermal (skin patch) test. These may be obtained from the County Health Department at a nominal fee or from your own physician.

Enclosed is a form to be used by your physician in reporting to us. Licensing regulations require that we have this report on file before you are permitted to assist in the center. Also enclosed is a reservation for an orientation meeting. Please return this reservation if you plan to participate in this program.

Very sincerely,
Director

Parent/Caregiver Medical Report

Community Child Care Center

111 THIRD STREET TELEPHONE 123-4579

______________________________ is planning to serve as a child care assistant at the Community Child Care Center. Duties and responsibilities will include: ____

____.

Some lifting of young children and some occasional assistance in the moving and carrying of furniture and equipment may be required, necessitating good physical health. Since we are vitally involved with the wholesome emotional growth of children in our care, we require good mental health of our child care assistants. In your opinion, is this person free of any disease, serious mental or emotional problems, or physical issues that would need to be given consideration in assigning any of the above duties? ____________________________

____

Evidence of a negative tuberculin test is required.

Type of test: __________ Date of test: __________ Result: __________

Date of examination:

_______________ ______________________________

(Signature by physician)

____

(Address)

F15 Reservation for Orientation Meeting for Child Care Assistant Program

Community Child Care Center

111 THIRD STREET ✿ TELEPHONE 123-4579

Dear Parents and Caregivers:

An orientation–training meeting for parents and caregivers who will serve as child care assistants will be held on Monday, September 8, from 10:30 A.M. until 3:00 P.M. Child care will be provided. Please bring a sack lunch for yourself and your child. One or two refresher meetings will be held during the year. Attendance is required for all who wish to participate in this program. Tuition credit will be given to each person who attends this meeting. Please notify us of your desire to participate by returning the enclosed reservation form.

Very sincerely yours,
Director

☐ I plan to participate as a child care assistant at the center.

☐ I will be able to attend the orientation–training meeting on Monday, September 8.

☐ I will bring __________ child (children) to be supervised during the meeting.

Signed: ______________________________

☐ I plan to participate but cannot attend because

____

☐ I will attend a make-up meeting when it is scheduled.

Signed: ______________________________

F16 Director's Orientation Meeting Agenda for Parents/Caregivers as Child Care Assistants

Purpose of Meeting: To familiarize parents and caregivers who will serve as child care assistants with the center's rules, regulations, procedures, and techniques.

Objectives: To review the assistant's handbook in detail, to experience the use of creative materials, to help parents and caregivers understand what is expected of them, and to give them a basic introduction to skills and techniques that they will find useful.

10:30–11:30 A.M.	Review each section of the child care assistants handbook, giving special emphasis to professional conduct, ways to handle undesirable behavior, and ways to be of realistic assistance to busy child care providers [Section F17].
11:30–12:00 P.M.	Mary Powell, who has served as a child care assistant for three years, will speak to the group about techniques she has found particularly useful, with emphasis on how to be supportive to child care providers.
12:00–12:30 P.M.	Lunch (sack lunches brought by parents and caregivers; the center will provide beverages).
12:30–1:30 P.M.	To a musical background, participants fingerpaint on the Formica tabletops, brush paint on large sheets of paper spread on the floor or pinned to the walls, and use rhythm band instruments. The last five minutes of this period will be spent cleaning up, also to music. This activity emulates actual child care experiences.
1:30–2:00 P.M.	Demonstration of storytelling techniques, using a story on the adult level but with all the suspense and interest that a child experiences in following a simple plot on a child's level.
2:00–2:30 P.M.	Evaluation and review. Discussion of feelings that were experienced during the workshop sessions.
2:30–3:00 P.M.	A tour of the child care areas to examine the supply cupboards, storage rooms, playground storage, key hooks, and so on.

You may also choose to hold these meetings in two consecutive sessions of two-and-a-half hours each, instead of one four-and-a-half hour session. The activity part of the training can then be conducted on a separate day from the handbook review. Whether to hold one long or two short sessions should depend on the availability of parents and caregivers.

F17 Handbook for Child Care Assistants

Arrival and Departure

On participation days, please be at the center by _________ A.M. Sign in at the desk and then go directly to your assigned room. If you have a purse, wallet, or bag, ask the child care provider to lock it in the closet. When you leave, ask the director for a credit check to save and turn in for tuition credit.

Techniques in Child Care

What you bring to the children in your child care group is not always apparent to the casual observer. Set the stage in order to guide children unobtrusively. Through adult guidance and association with their playmates, children are being prepared for self-control at the pace they can absorb.

They become aware of their own worth, both as individuals and as members of their peer group, while learning to respect the rights of others and to conform to minor regulations. Attempt to maintain an atmosphere of freedom, friendliness, and creativity. Mostly, adults should stay in the background, but are ready to help if they are needed.

Setting the Stage

1. Place materials where they are inviting for creative expression and cooperative play.
2. Be ready to take children's cues for new play, games, or activities.
3. Arrange learning centers neatly [Section C11].
4. Vary the arrangements from time to time.

Creating a Favorable Climate

1. Tense children cannot participate freely. Help them relax by being interested in them.
2. Speak slowly, simply, and quietly. Smile freely, and bend down to children's eye levels.
3. Do not feel you must be busy all the time, but you must be constantly aware of what all the children are doing—and be ready to step in when needed.
4. Relax and enjoy yourself. We appreciate your presence.

Setting Limits: Why and How

1. Setting limits gives children the security of knowing that their strong emotions will not lead them to do things that they will later regret. Children know an adult will take the responsibility of stopping unacceptable behavior until they are able to do so for themselves.
2. Teach children about safety, care of property, good health habits, and consideration for others.
3. Allow children to make as many decisions as possible within the necessary limits.
4. Explain the rules in a cheerful, sympathetic manner to make them understandable and acceptable to children. Avoid repetition. Say what you have to say once after first being sure that children are paying attention. Be consistent, firm, and fair.
5. Enforce the rules in a positive, nonpersonal way.
6. Understand the reasons for a child's behaving in a disruptive manner (such as hitting, kicking, biting, throwing things, defying, or running away). Behaviors may be caused by any of the following:

fear	jealousy	loneliness
fatigue	confusion	hyperactivity
anger	need for toileting	overstimulation
curiosity	boredom	sleepiness
insecurity	shyness	embarrassment
hunger	illness	other ______________

Children may also be trying out negative behavior, because the need to fight controls is normal at certain stages of development.

Handling Difficult Situations

In spite of the limits you set, difficult situations will arise.

1. Remain alert to the total situation. Attempt to foresee and forestall trouble. Redirect an uncooperative child to another activity. Redirect the entire activity into a more wholesome direction.
2. Allow children to work out their own solutions. Encourage shy children to stand up for themselves. Encourage aggressive children to verbalize. Encourage all children to "use your words."
3. Help children understand one another's actions.
4. Treat toilet accidents casually.
5. Try to ignore improper language. Sometimes you can say, "talking nicely." (The use of gerunds such as "talking," "waiting," or "sharing" usually gets an immediate response.)
6. Do not allow children to strike you. Restrain them gently and say, "I don't like to be hit."
7. If one child requires too much adult attention, that child should be temporarily removed from the group. Do so gently without punitive action. Your purpose is to help the child. Call this period "Renewal Time," or another term you feel is appropriate, and say, "Let me know when you feel better inside." (Time to renew feelings.)
8. When in doubt, it is sometimes best to do nothing unless health or safety is involved.

Giving Directions

1. Be sure you have the child's attention.
2. Give positive directions that leave the child no choice of interpretation.
3. Give a choice of three things when possible. (It's easier to make a choice from three items than from two.)
4. Warn ahead of time before changing an activity.
5. Never plead, threaten, or strike (even your own child).
6. Invite participation—never force it.
7. Direct the child to a new activity when the present activity is completed.
8. Use a quiet voice as much as possible. Physically get down to the child's level when talking with him or her.

Professional Attitudes

1. Never discuss a child when other children, parents, or caregivers are present.
2. Never discuss children within their hearing.
3. Do not discuss one parent's or caregiver's handling of a situation with another parent or caregiver. Refer the matter to the child care provider or director for interpretation.
4. Please do not talk among yourselves in the child care room or on the playground.
5. You will have a 15-minute break each morning.
6. Do not at any time leave children unsupervised, either indoors or out, even for a few minutes.

Painting

Put aprons on the children. Print their names on their papers with crayon. Allow children to select their own colors from those that have been made available for that day, and allow children to use their own painting techniques, methods of painting, and so on. Invite all children to paint, but never force them. Use buckets of water for rinsing paint off hands when finished. A small amount of soap may be added to the water.

Juice Time

In the older groups, put out the midmorning snack and allow children to help themselves [Section I18]. Put up cards with simple drawings to let children know how many of each item they may take. Occasionally, they need to be reminded verbally. Vary this procedure from time to time with little tea parties, one group serving another group, one person serving others, and so forth. The child care provider will tell you when to vary the procedure, or you may volunteer a planned change yourself.

Cleanup Duties

Juice pitchers must be washed daily. Put leftover juice back in the refrigerator. If you are asked to get juice out of the refrigerator, use the opened bottles first.

Bike Playground

Each child care provider should have a key to the bike storage shed. You may be asked to take the bikes out or put them away. Please handle them with care. Bikes get much wear and tear. There is a nail on the upper right-hand corner of the roof where the lock is kept when not in use. Children may not use the bikes to bump into a person or thing.

Safety Rules

1. Gates must be closed at all times.
2. Children may throw only balls or beanbags. Objects such as sticks, sand, rocks, and toys are not thrown.
3. No objects are allowed on the slide. Children may slide only in a sitting position, facing forward.
4. Children may climb around the brick wall holding onto the fence. They may not climb over the fence.
5. Going up or down the stairs, children must walk single file, holding the rail.
6. When indoors, children must walk rather than run.
7. Children must always hold on when using any moving play equipment.
8. Report to a staff member at once any broken boards, nails sticking out, or any other needed repairs.
9. Children are not allowed to go out of the play areas except when walking between playgrounds or when accompanied by a staff member.

Storytelling

Select your story according to the understanding and age of the group. Older children like stories with a plot and stories with humor. Younger prefer familiar stories and simple picture books. Teach children that stories may also come from books without pictures. Know the story and enjoy it yourself. If you happen to have a favorite that you can tell well, use it every time. If you like it, the children will like it, too, no matter how often they hear it.

Have an ample supply of storybooks, flannelboard stories, and colored chalk for blackboard stories. Feel free to use your ingenuity.

If the story just isn't going over, drop it and switch to another activity—perhaps finger games, quiet songs, or whatever you do well. If you are going to read a story, look it over first and be familiar with it. Whatever approach you use, remember that it isn't the story that counts; it's you. Involve yourself with the group. Be a part of it. Talk *to* the children—not *at* them.

Age Characteristics in Play

Children under Two Years of Age

Physical, cognitive, and social-emotional development are the three main domains of development for a young child. During the first two years, a child's growth is rapid.

The newborn physically exhibits various reflexes that later are replaced by voluntary movements. As they mature, infants can roll over, creep, crawl, stand, and learn how to walk. They will begin to interact with the environment. As a sign of cognitive growth, any objects that they find will be put in their mouths as they explore how they work.

At around six to nine months of age, infants begin to understand that objects can exist even though they may not be able to see them. Crying is the first means of communication, and later they begin to use words. Each infant is born with his or her own unique temperament. This temperament sets the stage for social-emotional development. Infants will become attached to caregivers and show separation anxiety when people who are important to them leave. They become interested in their own abilities and will begin to show an interest in other children.

Toddlers (2 to 3 1/2)

Toddlers play as individuals, have short interest spans, and need much freedom of activity. They learn by repetition and experimentation. They are learning to handle their bodies in basic developmental movements. They must be free to practice and become more agile and sure of their equilibrium. They must learn about space and their relation to space. They are fast-growing and ever-changing.

In quiet activities, they enjoy handling materials—feeling clay, painting indiscriminately on large pieces of paper, listening to simple songs, and generally just feeling things, moving, touching, smelling, handling, listening, and so on.

In free-play activities, these children like to play near others, but are not usually ready to share and take turns until they are a little older. Your job is to see that they don't misuse the toys with which they are playing, and that they put one thing away before picking up another.

At 9:50 A.M., take younger children to the toilet. Do not force any child to use the toilet. You may say, "It's your turn now." If the child refuses, quietly say, "Well, then just wash your hands for juice time."

Older Children (3 1/2 to 6)

As children grow, their interest span shows a definite increase. They are beginning to be able to pursue activities for longer periods of time, concentrate more fully, and follow directions more quickly.

By the time children are four years old, they have begun to share play with other children. They still require much freedom in choice and use of play materials. Their motor coordination is maturing more rapidly, and they are developing a fluidity of movement—they are much more able to move easily from one activity to another and from one place to another.

In quiet activities, they are able to make objects and name them. They like to build and make things. Dramatic play becomes important to many children in this age group, and we encourage it. Children are imaginative, creative, and experimental—and they flourish when given opportunities to use these qualities.

Children are distinct individuals. Child care becomes more interesting when you can appreciate children's differences, value their ideas, and relate to them as individuals. Remember that children in the older groups participate in a free-flow, flexible schedule, with much autonomy as to where and with whom they spend their time [Sections E26, I3–7].

School-Age Children (6 to 12)

The school-age child's physical development begins to slow down; he or she will grow two to three inches per year. Fine and large motor skills are steadily improving. Be aware of any hearing or vision problems that may occur. Encourage parents and caregivers to check their children's hearing and vision on a regular basis. School-age children begin to think more logically and can process and recall information more readily. Their memory improves, as well as their language and grammar skills.

Friendships are very important to school-age children. They develop feelings of empathy and compassion. Their self-esteem is affected by their self-concept. Encourage school-age children to participate in activities that will help them master their skills. Give them opportunities to assist you in setting up activities. Develop peer group activities, such as clubs or work groups.

F18 Room Assignments

Parents and caregivers should be assigned to rooms other than those containing their own children, at least for most of the year. This frees both parents and caregivers and children to pursue their own experiences without the pressure of too strong a concern about what the other one is doing. As the year progresses and the child becomes fully at ease with the environment and with the other children and adults, the parent or caregiver may be occasionally allowed to help in the same room. Usually, the parents and caregivers, too, have become accustomed to the routines of the center by then and are able to be of assistance, while at the same time enjoying the opportunity to see their own child "in action." Room assignments must remain flexible so assistants can relieve one another.

Assignment of Days

For parents who assist on a regular weekly basis, there is no problem as to the assignment of days. However, those who assist from one to three times a month must sign up for their days in advance. When regularly assigned days are cancelled or changed, makeup days can be arranged according to calendar openings. Use a regular appointment book calendar to keep track of the schedule or use a blank form like the following.

OCTOBER

Sunday	Monday	Tuesday	Wednesday	Thursday	Friday	Saturday
	1 Brown Palmer	2 Garcia Patty W.	3 Kathy John P. (music)	4 Wolfgang Hamilton (garden)	5 Gould O'Neal	6
7	8 Brown Palmer	9 Garcia Patty W.	10 Kathy John P.	11 Wolfgang Hamilton (garden)	12 Gould O'Neal	13
14	15 Brown Palmer	16 Garcia	17 (music) John P. Stella	18 Wolfgang Hamilton (garden)	19 Gould O'Neal	20
21	22 Brown Palmer	23 Garcia Patty W.	24 Kathy John P. (music)	25 Wolfgang Maria	26 Smith Hamilton	27
28	29 Brown Palmer	30 Garcia Patty W.	31 Kathy			

F19 List of Child Care Assistants to Call as Substitutes

Each parent or caregiver can be given a list of the names of all other parents and caregivers who assist in the child care. If a parent or caregiver finds it necessary to be absent on an assigned date, it is that person's responsibility to telephone other assisting parents and caregivers to find a substitute.

	Days Child Attends					
Name	M	T	W	Th	F	Telephone

F20 Participation Verification Form for Child Care Assistants

Name	No. of Days per Month	Best Day	Phone	Health Form (Date)	TB OK on File (Date and Source)

Evaluation Form for Child Care Assistants

Evaluation Form for Child Care Assistants

Name of parent or caregiver: ________________________________ Date: ____________

Participation in ____

Comments: ____

____

____

Would I be pleased to have this parent or caregiver as a regular weekly helper?

Yes ______ No ______

F21 Issuing Credit

Each time a parent or caregiver completes an assignment, the director or an assistant can issue a credit ticket. Use smooth, lightweight cardboard for this purpose. It is the parent's or caregiver's responsibility to pick up the credit ticket and return it with the next tuition check. The ticket can read as follows:

COMMUNITY CHILD CARE CENTER
PARTICIPATION CREDIT COUPON

This amount may be deducted from your next payment: $ ______________________

This coupon must be attached.

Name: ____

Date of Participation: ____________________________ Approved by: __________

F22 Supervising Child Care Assistants

Once the parent or caregiver has been assigned to a particular room, the child care provider of that group is responsible on that day for supervising the assistant. The child care provider keeps a sheet posted where parents and caregivers can refresh their memories about what is expected of them. Here is an example of such a note:

Welcome! I'm glad to have you as an assistant today.

The cleaning supplies are in the first cupboard over the sink.

The snack supplies are in the second cupboard.

Special books, tambourine, and roll book are in the third cupboard.

Office supplies, scissors, pushpins, and other such items are in the first drawer.

Today, the children will participate in the following activities:

Date *Tuesday*

Time	Activity	Special Instructions
9-10:30	Learning centers Play (indoors or out)	Supervise painting area. Supervise children while I'm on yard duty (10-10:30).
10:30	Judy's birthday Children can get their own snack from the tray.	I'll tell her favorite story while you take a 10-minute break.
11:00	Accompany Mrs. Jackson and eight of our children on a hike to the top of the hill.	

F23 Misunderstandings

Even when there is good rapport between staff and child care assistants, there may be occasional areas of disagreement. This is normal human behavior. It the director's responsibility to use his or her skills to ease the tension. If possible, help the child care provider find some way to resolve the difficulty by working out some type of compromise with the parent or caregiver—or by deferring to the parent or caregiver (as the "customer") until some other basis for understanding can be reached.

Reasons for Misunderstandings

Determining the reason behind certain actions or certain types of unexpected responses can help those involved to resolve their differences. Some common (and normal) reasons for differences between a child care provider and a child care assistant may include

- an unconscious rivalry between the child care provider and a very strong-minded parent or caregiver.
- an overly sensitive reaction to a comment or action that may unwittingly put one of the persons involved on the defensive.
- a misunderstanding of a comment or an action.

Techniques for Resolving Differences

1. Arrange for some time outside of the child care for the persons involved to meet and try to reach a basis for better understanding.
2. Offer a compromise.
3. Meet individually with the persons involved, and try to help them understand why the other person has a different point of view.
4. Always stress that adults, as well as children, should be allowed the freedom of emotional expression to retain an atmosphere of naturalness. As long as doing so does not interfere with the smooth functioning of the center, it is legitimate to express one's feelings.
5. Try to find a humorous note to inject into the situation to relax the tension.
6. If hostile feelings between a particular parent or caregiver and a child care provider seem to persist, assign the parent or caregiver to a different child care provider.

Director's Responsibility When Differences Occur

Whatever techniques the director chooses to use, the overall responsibility is to help each person involved reestablish self-esteem and self-confidence, both of which may have been shaken by the disagreement.

When a Child Care Assistant Is Ineffective

From time to time you may encounter an enthusiastic assistant who is unsuited to child care. This situation presents a delicate problem, because each volunteer has been promised the right to assist. The director must find some way of redirecting the parent or caregiver to another, more suitable task. Here is an example of how one such problem was solved.

One child care assistant panicked whenever she was asked to supervise even a small group of three or four children. She was emotionally unable to relieve the child care provider for a break. This woman was an excellent bookkeeper. Gradually, some of the office bookkeeping was turned over to her. Once a week, she spent two-and-a-half hours bringing the center's financial records up-to-date, preparing statements, and making a meaningful contribution to the center's community.

F24 Reminders for New Assistants

Community Child Care Center

111 THIRD STREET ✿ TELEPHONE 123-4579

Dear Child Care Assistants:

For many of you, helping out at the center is a totally new experience. Your child will probably adjust long before you do. We think it will help you to adjust more quickly if you realize the valuable contribution that you have made to the center by participation. The staff depends a great deal on having someone in each room to assist each child care provider. Your presence means that a wider range of experiences is available to the children because of the extra supervision available. It means greater freedom for each child because your presence serves as an added safety precaution.

Each day is different. We do most special activities for two consecutive days so that all children have an opportunity to participate. But certain activities may never happen to come along on the days when you're at the center. So if you're curious, switch days occasionally.

We operate on the principle of organized free choice. The child care rooms are set up by the child care provider in advance to guide children toward specific learning goals. But within the present structure, children are free to use the materials in their own ways, move at their own pace, and select their own experiences.

The flexible curriculum featured at our center is not an easy type of program for the novice to catch on to. Please feel free to ask questions about things that you would like to have clarified.

The child care center staff and assistants are responsible for everything above floor level. Besides children, this includes the furnishings, built-ins, walls, and so on. Cleaning supplies are kept in the first cupboard in each room. Sponges should be taken out, moistened, and kept ready on the counter. You can help us by seeing that countertops and tables are kept clean. Although children learn that we expect them to put away whatever they have "taken out" to use, there are many times when an adult needs to step in and help.

Although you are primarily at the center to assist with the children, the more you can do for the child care provider in helping with housekeeping, the more time there will be to devote to preparing for ongoing experiences. Putting things in cupboards, hanging up sweaters and jackets that have fallen down, straightening out bookcases—whatever you see that needs doing—all help.

As an assistant, your responsibility to children is to lend support when needed and help them retain control of their emotions, the tools they are using, and the materials they are working with.

We do have limits. Children are not allowed to do anything that is harmful to themselves, to others, or to the materials and equipment. But they are also encouraged to use imagination, inventiveness, originality, and individuality. They are encouraged to move, talk, and be themselves.

You, too, are encouraged to use your imagination, inventiveness, originality, and individuality. Tell us about your special talents and interests. If you have an idea you want to try out, tell the child care provider. This is your center, too. And on the day you assist, you are a member of the staff.

So relax and enjoy yourself.

Sincerely,
Director

F25 Other Areas of Assistance

Parents and caregivers assist the center in many other areas of the program in addition to helping in the child care rooms. To help reduce the cost of maintenance and repairs of furnishings, toys, and equipment, parents and caregivers who are handy with tools are encouraged to do minor repair work in return for tuition credit. Parents and caregivers may also work as office assistants, stenographers, or clerical workers, as the need arises.

Not all assistance in the child care center by parents and caregivers is done for tuition credit. Many times, we ask for volunteer assistance. At the beginning of each year, send the following questionnaire home to all parents and caregivers:

Community Child Care Center

111 THIRD STREET TELEPHONE 123-4579

To: All Parents and Caregivers

From: The Staff

From time to time, we need volunteer assistants to help us enrich our child care education program. Please indicate in which of the following areas you would like to help:

___ Computer instruction
___ Photographing or videotaping children at play
___ Repairing toys and equipment
___ Painting toys and equipment
___ Coordinating and assisting with field trips
___ Providing transportation for children on field trips
___ Helping with weekly shopping needs
___ Helping to plan parent/caregiver meetings
___ Helping to organize a parent/caregiver club
___ Helping with public relations activities
___ Helping children with gardening
___ Helping children with cooking
___ Playing a musical instrument for the children
___ Helping to plan an open house
___ Organizing family picnics
___ Other (specify): ______________________________

____

Please give this note to your child to return to us. Your child knows that many parents and caregivers assist in the center and will be delighted to give us a note with your name on it as an assistant.

____
(signature)

Keep track of who did what for the center in case you want to ask them to do it again. Here's a form you can use for this information:

Summary of Parents and Caregivers Who Have Volunteered for Various Tasks

Item	Name	Phone	Best Day	Number of Days per Month
Computer instruction				
Photography				
Tape recordings				
Repairs				
Painting				
Field trips				
Shopping				
Parent/caregiver meetings				
Parent/caregiver club				
Public relations				
Gardening				
Cooking				
Musical instrument (specify)				
Open house				
Family picnic				
Other				
Other				

F26 Involving Parents/Caregivers

Many parents and caregivers do not have the desire or the time to participate as a child care assistant or a volunteer for special events. Because the advantages of family-center involvement are so important, implement several plans to encourage parents and caregivers to participate.

1. From time to time, place a table near the front door where the parents and caregivers can't help but see it upon arrival in the morning. Place materials on this table that challenge immediate participation. A sign may read:

   STAY A WHILE AND HELP YOUR CHILD SOLVE ONE OF THESE NEW AND DIFFICULT PUZZLES.

   STOP AND HELP YOUR CHILD MAKE A FUNNY HAT FOR THE PARADE.

   HELP YOUR CHILD MAKE A THANKSGIVING TURKEY.
2. Put up a large mural from time to time right inside the entrance to the center with paints, brushes, collage materials, and so on, to be added to by parents and caregivers when they bring their children in the morning—or when they come to pick them up.
3. Encourage parents and caregivers to organize various hobby, study, or social groups to meet at the center. You can organize sewing groups, gourmet cooking groups, exercise classes, book groups, and many others. The ideas for these groups come from parents and caregivers. The director supports these groups by helping them organize—sending out notices, providing meeting places and, when necessary, finding a parent or caregiver to provide leadership. If no such parent or caregiver is available, you can either try to find an interested and willing leader from the larger community, an interested staff member, or you may have to provide the leadership yourself.
4. It is more difficult to promote interaction with parents and caregivers who work, but their involvement is perhaps even more important than others to the child's maximum development of wholesome feelings of love and security and overall family unity. Evening meetings with a speaker are sometimes considered a chore for working parents and caregivers. Mealtime activities are the most appreciated and the most attended. Therefore, throughout the year, schedule a series of breakfasts, lunches, dinners, and picnics for children and their families. These get-togethers can be timed so as to accommodate the hours and needs of the majority of working parents and caregivers.

F27 Parent/Caregiver Bulletin Board

Set aside an area for a bulletin board specifically to post information for parents and caregivers. Select a spot where parents and caregivers can easily see it as they enter or leave the center. Right above the sign-in sheet or in the parent/caregiver room are good places. Here are a few suggestions for items for the board:

- Newspaper clippings about children, education, and family life.
- Photographs from newspapers and magazines that would be of interest to parents and caregivers of young children.
- Cartoons on the subjects of children, teachers, schools, and family life.
- Helpful hints, such as: "Put a small mark with a pencil or a piece of adhesive tape inside the right heel of each pair of your child's shoes to help him or her learn the difference between left and right."
- Program calendar [Section A19]. A running list of the various happenings of the week.

- Newsletters [Section F36]. It's a good idea to keep the previous newsletter posted, too. That means you always have at least two of them up.
- Child care room sayings. Keep one little section for mounting an ever-changing collection of "cute sayings" by the children.
- Curriculum charts. Be sure to keep these posted where parents and caregivers can readily see them. You might place a red checkmark next to an item when your group has finished it. This gives interested parents and caregivers a quick overview of the kinds of curriculum events that have been going on.
- Health Department notices, indicating clinics and immunization schedules.
- Mental health clinics or other available resources.

You can also post the following kinds of things on the bulletin board:

- Names of parents and caregivers who help in various ways.
- List of car pools.
- Announcements of educational meetings and conferences that you plan to attend.
- Any special announcement for your children's parents and caregivers, such as items to bring for craft projects, procedures for signing out, and so forth.

In addition to the "special" items you post each week, be sure you always post a copy of the general schedule [Section I7] you follow and copies of the curriculum charts you use.

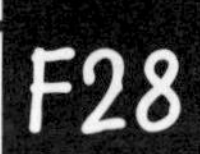

Parent/Caregiver Club

An officially organized Parent/Caregiver Club can be a valuable method of involving parents and caregivers in the operation of the center and the education and care of their children. Many centers use the Parent/Caregiver Club as a method of handling parent/caregiver education programs. This is based on the assumption that if parents and caregivers plan their own programs, they will be more likely to support them.

Possible Objectives of a Parent/Caregiver Club

1. To interest and involve parents and caregivers in the child care center's program.
2. To educate parents and caregivers concerning the center's curriculum and child-rearing techniques.
3. To emphasize the importance of the parental and caregiver role.
4. To develop understanding between the home and the center.
5. To provide an opportunity for parents and caregivers with common concerns to meet with each other and share experiences.
6. To develop friendships among parents and caregivers.
7. To raise funds for special projects.

Possible Disadvantages of a Parent/Caregiver Club

1. Directors who are unsure of their role may feel conflict with strong parent/caregiver leadership.

2. If the chairperson of the Parent/Caregiver Club is not strong and active, then the director may have to take on the chairperson's responsibilities, which increases the director's workload.
3. The Parent/Caregiver Club may plan activities but leave the details to the director to handle.
4. Unless the responsibilities of the director and Parent/Caregiver Club are well defined, there may be some duplication of work.
5. In some center communities, parents and caregivers may feel too involved in other activities to join yet another club. You should survey your parents and caregivers carefully to make sure enough of them are interested to warrant your efforts.

How to Start a Parent/Caregiver Club

1. Obtain permission, if necessary, to start a Parent/Caregiver Club from the board or sponsoring agency.
2. Find out if parents and caregivers are interested in such an organization. You can use the following letter to determine this information:

Community Child Care Center

111 THIRD STREET TELEPHONE 123-4579

Dear Parents and Caregivers,

A number of parents and caregivers from our center have expressed their interest in forming a Parent/Caregiver Club in order to share common concerns, learn more about the needs of young children and how they can best be met, and become more involved in the program curriculum. If you are interested in helping to establish such a club, please sign your name and return this form to the director's office.

Sincerely,
Director

- -

☐ I am interested _____ not interested _____ in establishing and participating in a Parent/Caregiver Club.

☐ I am interested in serving as the chairperson of a Parent/Caregiver Club.

☐ I am interested in serving on a committee to plan for the organization of the Parent/Caregiver Club.

____

(signature of parent or caregiver)

3. If the response to your inquiry is sufficient, organize a committee of interested parents and caregivers to plan for the organization of the club.

4. Set the time for the planning committee meeting and inform the committee members.

Community Child Care Center

111 THIRD STREET ✿ TELEPHONE 123-4579

Dear Mr./Ms. ______________________,

You have been selected to serve on a planning committee to organize the Community Child Care Center Parent/Caregiver Club. The first planning meeting will be held at ____________________________________ at 6:00 P.M. on Monday, ____________________. The Community Child Care Center will treat you to dinner.

Thank you for your interest and cooperation. It you will be unable to attend, please let me know.

Sincerely,

Director

5. Plan the agenda for the meeting.
   - Select a planning committee chairperson.
   - Develop objectives for the club.
   - Plan for the selection of the club's chairperson.
   - Determine how to present the club plan to other parents and caregivers.

Project Ideas for a Parent/Caregiver Club

- Work parties to repair and build equipment
- Family picnics to get better acquainted
- Fund-raising projects for scholarships

  art fair

  bake sale

  community open house
- Parent/caregiver education meetings [Section F10]
- Parent/caregiver study groups
- Field trips [Section I11]
- Baby-sitting exchange
- Children's clothing exchange
- Encounter groups
- Dramatic presentations
- Public policy, legislation affecting families and children

Definition of Responsible Parties for Parent/Caregiver Club

The Parent/Caregiver Club, though organized and run by parents and caregivers, is directly responsible to the director of the center. The Parent/Caregiver Club in no way runs the center, makes policy, or otherwise assumes any of the administrative functions of the center. All functions, plans, and programs undertaken by the club will be evaluated by the director as to whether they fall within the boundaries of center policy and goals. For example, since the center is nonpolitical, no political functions will be sponsored by the club. Since the center is nonsectarian, no religious functions will be assumed by the club. Since the center is nonprofit, any funds raised by the club will be earmarked for specific purposes, such as scholarship funds, educational programs, or community relations. At no time will funds be raised for the purpose of adding to the capital assets of the center [Section B14].

F29 Parent/Caregiver Involvement: A Self-Evaluation Study

Involving the child's family in your program is one way to create a climate that is attuned to the needs of children and staff. Parents and caregivers can bring gentleness, warmth, friendliness, and helpfulness—and they can receive the same things in return. The following list enables you to evaluate what you have done and helps you discover areas you may have overlooked.

Have you

- let parents and caregivers of your children know you are sincerely interested in them as individuals?
- shown interest in the family as a whole, not just the child?
- shown interest in their personal interests and problems?
- asked for their suggestions and opinions?
- stressed opportunities for developing social relationships with other families in the area?
- followed up each written communication or invitation with a call to those who have not responded?
- enlisted the aid of parents and caregivers to contact other parents and caregivers and help involve them in the program?
- sent information home to motivate parents and caregivers to reinforce children's child care experiences?
- enlisted the aid of parents and caregivers in gathering free materials, either from their own scrap collections or from neighborhood business firms?
- held workshops in which parents and caregivers can come together informally?
- offered programs to help parents and caregivers know more about the developmental needs of children?

- asked parents and caregivers to suggest topics for study groups, workshops, trips, and programs?
- invited parents and caregivers to come to the center to see photographs of their own children, see work done by their children, and hear tape recordings made in the child care rooms?
- sent out newsletters at regular intervals?

The Reluctant Parent or Caregiver

After you have developed a good program of parent/caregiver involvement, you may still find that some children's parents and caregivers are reluctant to participate. In that case, your task is to be helpful and understanding.

Perhaps a parent or caregiver is shy and would do better if you visit three or four times, perhaps taking another parent or caregiver with you to get acquainted. Perhaps a parent's or caregiver's personal problems and pressures require a great deal of emotional energy, leaving none for outside interests. Here again, gentle assistance and sincere friendship can be helpful. Everyone responds to friendship—even the reluctant parent or caregiver.

F30 Request for Notes from Home Regarding Child's Mood or Behavior

write us a note, please

Community Child Care Center

111 THIRD STREET TELEPHONE 123-4579

Dear Parents and Caregivers,

Young children are very vulnerable to their environments and to those people in their lives to whom they feel close. Sometimes there are occurrences in the home, especially among the adult members of the family, that may disturb or temporarily upset the child. Perhaps there has been a quarrel, an illness, unexpected visitors, or financial difficulties that have been discussed within the child's hearing. All these kinds of things create tension, to which the child may react.

Tension-creating incidents are not necessarily unpleasant. Perhaps someone is planning a trip, or welcome visitors are expected and being prepared for, or new furniture or carpeting is arriving, or the carpenter is coming to see about building some new cabinets. Perhaps a big dinner party is being planned or has taken place. All these kinds of things may cause the child to be emotionally keyed up and may cause a quicker reaction than usual to otherwise normal incidents.

It may be that the tension-creating incident was really a very minor thing that you may even have trouble recalling: the car keys were missing for five minutes, the milk was sour at breakfast, one piece of toast burned, or you had to rush to make a 9:15 A.M. appointment. Perhaps it was just the adult members of the family discussing the latest newspaper headline, or the TV set that didn't work, or the newspaper that wasn't delivered.

Whatever the incident, you may have unwittingly imparted unusual feelings of tension in your child. Perhaps, in fact, you dealt with your own tensions by being short tempered or overly stern.

Sometimes it might not have been anything anyone else did at all. Children can become upset simply because they don't like the colors of their clothes, or because they have new shoelaces in their shoes when they wanted to keep the old ones.

It is difficult, at best, to understand the workings of young children's minds. We do know, however, that their feelings, their tensions, and their emotions are real. They are the same as the feelings, emotions, and tensions we experience.

Whatever the cause, whatever the incident, if you notice that your child seems unusually tense—or if you know there was indeed an unpleasant situation that day—please try to let us know about it. Write us a short note and tell us about it so we may give your child the understanding that may help to calm some anxieties.

Very sincerely yours,
Director

F31 Common Complaints from Parents/Caregivers

Someone hit my child (or bit, kicked, scratched, spit at, pushed off a bike, and so on).
Someone almost put my child's eye out.
Someone has been teaching my child nasty words.
Someone wanted to watch while my child was going to the toilet.
Someone took my child's cracker—or toy, or nickel, or turn.
My child doesn't have any friends at the center.
My child doesn't do anything at preschool.
My child doesn't want to go to child care anymore. Something must have happened.
My child never paints.
My child doesn't like to rest.
My child said the child care provider was not in the room most of the time.
I think the child care provider is too strict with my child.
I think the child care provider is too lenient with my child.
I think the child care provider doesn't realize that my child tires easily.
I think the playground equipment is too dangerous.
I don't think there is enough equipment.
I want my child to have a workbook.
My child isn't being taught the alphabet.
My child is ready to learn to read.

F32 Handling Complaints from Parents/Caregivers

You will receive complaints or hear about them indirectly, no matter how fine a program you conduct and no matter how expertly you supervise and handle the children. Hopefully, these complaints won't turn you off to the job before you develop the necessary techniques for handling complaints. Perhaps the following ideas might be of help to you:

1. Remember at all times that no matter what a parent or caregiver may say or how a parent or caregiver may act, the most important person in the entire center in the parent's and caregiver's estimation is his or her own child. This is as it should be. Respect the fact.
2. Remember that the parent or caregiver is paying you to provide a service. When people pay for services, they have the right to voice complaints if they are not completely satisfied with the type of service they are receiving.
3. Resist the temptation to "dodge" the complaining or overly concerned parent or caregiver with an "Oh, that pest" kind of attitude. Put yourself in his or her place and try to realize that what that person is really asking for is help and guidance.
4. Don't hesitate to acknowledge that a situation might be dangerous. Agree to observe and discuss the possibility of changing a procedure or replacing certain equipment. At the same time, you can explain to a parent or caregiver that even though something may look dangerous, your experience (and that of others) has shown that it is not [Section C5].
5. When a staff member is being criticized, you have the delicate problem of supporting your staff while recognizing that the parent or caregiver may have a legitimate complaint [Sections D42, D62–63].
6. Acknowledge that accidents do happen; children do get hurt. This is why we have constant supervision and many safety rules [Part H]. Emphasize that when a group of children is playing together, there is always some risk involved. Let the parent or caregiver know that your staff's responsibilities include allowing the child to participate in as many learning experiences as possible, trying to make those experiences good ones, while trying to protect the child from getting hurt—both physically and psychologically. You might even review with the parent or caregiver the principles of how the child learns through play [Section E26].
7. Have your staff direct all complaints to you, so you can take the time to handle them in a way that reflects the center's philosophy [Sections A14, E26]. A staff member might say, "Well, that is a serious problem. I think you should talk to the director about it." Ask staff members to tell you about any complaint so you can anticipate a parent or caregiver coming to you. If the parent or caregiver does not then come to you, sometimes it is wise for you to casually bring up the subject at an opportune moment—or if it is really a very serious problem, ask the parent or caregiver to come in to talk with you. Although such difficulties are usually better discussed in a one-to-one conference, some parents and caregivers may feel a sense of guilt about making a complaint and might therefore feel more comfortable by first discussing the problem on the telephone.

8. Many complaints can be handled by clarifying to the parent or caregiver what is normal behavior for a preschool-age child. Constant education and reeducation of parents and caregivers will lessen the number of complaints you receive.
9. Whatever you do, always remember that you are not expected to please everyone at all times. Be gracious, considerate, and helpful. But at the same time, stand up for the principles you believe in and use parent/caregiver education to try to get others to understand them.
10. Use the following principles as a guide when handling complaints:
    a. *Listen carefully.* Sometimes, a person just needs an opportunity to air his or her feelings.
    b. *Repeat what you have heard the other person say, trying to summarize it in one sentence.* For example, "You seem to be saying that Krista's child care provider is unfriendly because she doesn't always greet Krista at the door, and you feel this is the reason why Krista doesn't like preschool."
    c. *State the changes that you think the parent or caregiver would like to have made.* For example, "You would like Krista's child care provider to greet Krista immediately when she comes to preschool."
    d. *State what you will do, while supporting your staff.* "I will talk to Krista's child care provider. Sometimes even the most perceptive child care provider might overlook the importance of something like this."
    e. *If you know what the child's problem really is, this might be the time to bring it up.* Bring issues up only if you sense the mood of the parent or caregiver is right for it. "Would it be possible to bring Krista to the center just a little earlier each day? Sometimes, when she arrives as late as she does, all of the other children are involved in their play activities and she may feel somewhat left out."

F33 Parent/Caregiver Conferences

The best person to confer with a parent or caregiver is the person who knows the child and the parent or caregiver the best. It might be the director, the child's child care provider, or even both. A child care provider who has not had a great deal of experience working with parents and caregivers can sometimes say something that might alarm them, causing them to withdraw their child. Because retaining pupils is important in a private child care center, you should avoid this possibility.

If the director has daily contact with parents or caregivers and children and is mainly responsible for evaluating children, then the director should confer with parents or caregivers. The child care provider and director should hold the conference together whenever feasible. The following suggestions will be helpful when you meet with a parent or caregiver to discuss a child's progress or a special problem:

1. Be prepared for the conference. Take note of specific behavior and situations of which the parent or caregiver should be aware.
2. Open and close the conference on a positive note.

3. Help parents or caregivers bring up the concerns they have about their child and the center. A good question to begin with is, "What does Kevin tell you about our center?"
4. Do not alarm parents or caregivers needlessly. If there is a real problem, you must tell them about it; but if at all possible, emphasize that it is a common problem of children this age. If the problem concerns the child's behavior, tell parents or caregivers that it is the behavior you disapprove of and not the child.
5. Do not make parents or caregivers feel guilty by implying that it is their fault the child has problems.
6. Help parents or caregivers come up with suggestions that may help the child.
7. Parents and caregivers usually ask for the child care provider's advice because they feel that he or she is an authority. Don't fall into the trap of giving only one suggestion. Parents and caregivers usually will try what you recommend and then come back and report that it doesn't work. If parents or caregivers press for suggestions, always give two or more possibilities while emphasizing there may be many other ways of handling this problem. Say, "I can tell you what some parents or caregivers have found helpful."
8. Arrange the conferences at a time and place where you will not be interrupted.
9. Do not waste parents' or caregivers' time. Stick to the subject and close at a preset time. A 30-minute conference is usually adequate.
10. End the conference with a summary statement emphasizing the suggestions that were made for the child care provider and parents and caregivers to work on. Set a time when you will reevaluate the situation.

It is not always necessary to meet with each parent or caregiver to report general progress. You can give parents and caregivers a choice about whether or not they would like a conference by putting the following announcement in the newsletter. You can also post a notice in a conspicuous place at the center.

Parent/caregiver conferences will be held during the month of November.
Please call the center for an appointment.

PARENT/CAREGIVER CONFERENCE TIMES

If you would like to meet with the director and your child's child care provider, please sign your name beside one of these appointment times.

Nov. 6
3:00
3:30
4:00
4:30
5:00
5:30

If the child care provider feels that a special parent/caregiver conference is needed to discuss a problem, then the child care provider or director should personally talk to the parent or caregiver about arranging a conference time rather than sending home a notice.

Parent/Caregiver Conference Report Form

Use a form for keeping records of conferences with parents and caregivers. Here is a sample of a completed form:

Name of child: Lisa Moore

Person giving conference: Director Date: 10/2

Parent/caregiver present: Mother Age of child: 3 1/2

Reason for conference: Lisa's adjustments at the center

Items to be reported to parent or caregiver:

ADJUSTMENT TO CENTER: Lisa was hesitant and withdrawn for the first few weeks. A real change appeared in her behavior after I made a home visit. She is now a little more confident. She knows what she would like to play with and goes directly to that item.

MOTOR DEVELOPMENT: Uses her body well. She runs, jumps from the three-foot-high box, walks on the six-foot balance beam, and has good control stopping and guiding the tricycles. She can copy a circle and square and can copy a cross in three out of four tries.

SOCIAL DEVELOPMENT: She smiles, laughs, and talks to the adults in the room, but she does not seem confident in her relations with her peers. She plays well alone but will stop playing when another child comes next to her. However, she enjoys watching them.

INTELLECTUAL DEVELOPMENT: Speaks clearly, but still is substituting some letters, such as "th" for "s." She asks questions of adults and actively explores her environment when an adult is near. She recognizes the numerals and can count up to ten objects. She is working on the recognition and sounds of letters. When asked what a plumber does, she announced, "Picks plums."

FAVORITE ACTIVITIES: Sandbox and dolls.

CHILD CARE PROVIDER'S GOALS FOR THE CHILD: Help her feel more comfortable with other children by helping her find someone to be her special friend.

Parent/caregiver comments:

Ms. Moore felt the observations of Lisa's development were similar to what she had observed at home. However, Lisa does play with another girl in the neighborhood without being hesitant, so Ms. Moore was somewhat surprised that Lisa was still hesitant with others at the center. She said if there was any child Lisa seemed to have more contact with than others, she would invite the child home to play with Lisa. (I suggested Angie Hill.)

Child care provider's summary:

Ms. Moore was very relaxed and pleasant. She appeared eager to learn about Lisa and help in any way she could. I assured her that Lisa's hesitancy in social situations was to be expected and that I would report back to her next month, after Angie had been invited to her home to play.

F34 Parent/Caregiver Day-to-Day Record Keeping for Evaluation of Child

Record keeping is done primarily for the purpose of teaching us to look objectively at our own children. The director keeps developmental records, noting the month-to-month progress of each child at the center. This progress is noted only after comparing notes with other staff members, in order to be as accurate as possible. These records are used as a reference for parent/caregiver conferences.

Many parents and caregivers are now keeping a day-to-day record on their child, working together with the center. Others would like to do the same, but do not quite understand how to go about it.

Suggest that parents and caregivers write down each day the outstanding moments of that day. Ask them to note the following kinds of things:

Did your child throw a tantrum? Why? What did you say? What did your child say or do? What preceded it? What followed? How did you handle the situation? Or did it handle you?

Or perhaps your child doesn't want to go to sleep at night. *When does your child go to sleep? Does your child ever want to nap or go to sleep early? When does your child awaken? What do you do just before bedtime? How do you finally get your child to sleep?*

Or perhaps your child was unusually good today and, for the first time, helped clean up after lunch without a peep. *What did you talk about at lunch? Breakfast? What did you say just before lunch? Was the house quieter than usual? Noisier?*

Some days you may not find anything to write. On others, you may find a great deal. But after a few weeks, read the notes over. They will help you figure out why certain things happened the way they did. Often you will be able to see a definite pattern of desirable and undesirable behavior and find a direct relationship with some home situation or some specific event. They will help you see more clearly—into yourselves and into your child. They will also help you learn to handle a crisis objectively, and even understand why there was a crisis in the first place.

F35 Home Visits

Home visits are recommended

- after the child has enrolled in the center, but before the first day of attendance, so he or she becomes familiar with the child care provider and feels less hesitant about going.
- during the first few weeks he or she attends the center. This helps the child adjust to preschool.
- when a child expresses an interest in having a child care provider see his or her home, bedroom, puppy, and so on. This shows the child that the child care provider cares and takes a personal interest in his or her special things.

- any time during the program year for the child care provider to gain a better understanding of the children by observing them in their homes, as well as becoming better acquainted with both of their parents or caregivers.

Remember that a home visit is a social event and not a substitute for a parent/caregiver conference. The child's behavior should not be discussed if the child is present. The visit should be casual, friendly, and short.

When children become ill or get hurt at child care, their knowledge that you know where they live and have been to their homes often relieves some of their anxiety while they are waiting for their parents or caregivers to arrive.

F36 Newsletters

Send a monthly newsletter to each center family. Include items such as the following:

- Reminders of center policy (such as name tags on clothing or punctuality), events on the program calendar, changes in procedures, and information about contributions needed.
- Helpful hints on child rearing; information about new books and articles on parenting or child care; listings of items of interest such as a good park, an educational TV program, or bargain clothing.
- Information on home projects, such as art and food activities, words to songs and finger games that children are learning, notices about classroom activities, and comments or drawings by children.

An example of a newsletter is shown on the following page.

Community Child Care Center

111 THIRD STREET ✿ TELEPHONE 123-4579

Vol. No 123 NEWSLETTER October 19

WHAT ARE THEY LEARNING?

• As you buy various fall fruits (oranges, apples, melons, etc.), compare the colors with your child. Discuss the various tastes. Which kind is the sweetest? Which is the juiciest? What are the seeds for? (Try planting some of the seeds.)

• Put out a pan of water and experiment with floating and sinking objects. Color the water with a drop of yellow food color. After a while, add blue.

• Blow bubbles. Make a bubble blower out of an empty thread spool. (Use soapsuds—not detergent.)

• Make a "bubbler." Fill an empty bottle 3/4 with water. Add from one teaspoon to two tablespoons (depending on the size of the bottle) of mineral oil. Be sure to leave some air space at the top. Slowly turn the bottle upside down. First the air, then the oil, will bubble to the top. A narrow bottle works best.

• Looking for something to do? Cut out all the red pictures in a magazine. Cut out pictures of things that move, things that make a noise, and so on. (Don't worry about the lines—just learning to manipulate small scissors back and forth is quite an achievement for a preschool child. Lines can come later.) Tear paper scraps to paste onto paper plates. Make placemats out of paper or cloth. Decorate them with crayons.

CLOTHING

We want to remind you not to send your child to our program in dress clothes. PLAY is the WORK of childhood. At our center, children have opportunities to play with many different types of equipment and to explore and experiment with many different kinds of exciting tools and materials. They mix their own paint, build airplanes, and construct buildings. They play with mud, sand, and water. They climb and jump and roll on the grass and play on the floor. Although they sometimes wear aprons, children WILL get dirty. Please send them in play clothes so they will be able to involve themselves freely with the many learning experiences provided.

We will soon be sending you your calendar for the next eight weeks. We will send reminder notes for various scheduled events. Please keep it handy to refer to when you are making your plans.

School Will Be Closed on Monday

October 23
Veterans Day

Join us for a cup of coffee on Wednesday morning, Oct. 25, 9–10 A.M., to find out about the sound game our preschool children are learning about. We think this is the best way to prepare children for reading. We would like to have you watch a demonstration class, and then we'll explain it to you.

$$

TUITION FEES

As stated in the handbook, tuition is payable in advance unless other arrangements have been made. May we remind you that next month's tuition will be due on Friday.

$$

THREE COLLEGE STUDENTS	Kathy, Joan, and Tricia are assisting regularly in our child care groups this month.

OPEN-TOED SANDALS are dangerous to wear when running and jumping outdoors. We ask that you send your child to our program in shoes, not sandals. Tennis shoes are great for our ground surfaces.

Boo!
Halloween

Halloween at our center will mean experimenting with the colors orange (yellow + red), black, and white. It will mean pumpkins and jack-o'-lanterns. (What kind of face does it have? Is it smiling? sad? Is is scary? funny? What color is the inside of the pumpkin? What happens to the inside flesh when we cook it? What would happen if we plant the seeds? Maybe we'll plant some and find out!)

Halloween will also mean a funny hat parade. If you like, you can make your child's funny hat at school on Thursday or Friday, Oct. 26 or 27.

- Please do not send masks to the center.
- Please do not send costumes to the center.
- Please do not send candy to the center.

And please, please, remember the young age of your child and keep Halloween simple at your home. Overstimulation, overeating, and overreacting always lead to many absences from the program on the days immediately following Halloween.

Dr. Samuel Adams
of State Teacher's College

He will speak on the topic of "Nonpunitive Discipline," a subject of considerable interest to parents and caregivers of preschool children. Refreshments will be served.

Friday, November 6 at 7:30 P.M.

F37 Evaluation by Parents/Caregivers

From time to time, it is useful to ask parents and caregivers to evaluate your program from their points of view. This form may be used for such an evaluation:

Community Child Care Center

111 THIRD STREET TELEPHONE 123-4579

Dear Parents and Caregivers:

We are continually making efforts to improve our program, in order that we may offer the very highest quality of service to your child. In order to help us in this respect, please complete the following questionnaire and return it to us. We assure you that your comments will be taken into careful consideration in planning our future course.

1. Do you read the newsletters we send home? Yes _____ No _____
2. Do you find them of value? Yes _____ No _____

Please comment: ____

3. Have you received periodic communication from your child's child care provider? Yes _____ No _____

Comment: ____

4. Do you feel the center safeguards your child's health? Yes _____ No _____

Comment: ____

5. Have you been appropriately notified of minor injuries that your child has received at the center? Yes _____ No _____

Comment: ____

6. Have your educational expectations been met? Yes _____ No _____

Comment: ____

7. Are the center policies as outlined to you at the time of enrollment consistent with what is actually practiced? Yes _____ No _____

Comment: ____

8. Would you recommend our program to your friends? Yes _____ No _____

Comment: ____

Please let us know if you would like to talk to us about some of the issues you presented here.

Name: ______________________ Child's name: ____________________

Phone number: ________________ Best time to reach you: ____________

Health

G

G1

Emergency First Aid and Procedures

During enrollment, families must provide you with emergency information and the consent you will need if their children experience emergency illness or injury. This information should be updated once every year. As a director of a facility that cares for children, you are required by your state licensing agency to be trained in pediatric first aid and CPR. Some states require that all staff must be trained in first aid and CPR as well. Check with your local licensing agency about your training requirements. You should always inform parents and caregivers about your emergency first aid procedures. Let them know that you must be trained in first aid and CPR; and in an emergency, you follow these procedures.

1. Take all complaints of illness or injury seriously. Assess the child's health.
2. Keep calm. Notify the director immediately. Notify center nurse if there is one, or a designated first aid assistant if there is one.
3. Call 911 or appropriate emergency help, then parents and caregivers, in that order. Call the child's physician, if necessary.
4. Administer first aid and/or CPR, if necessary.
5. Emergencies must be taken care of in this order:
   a. Breathing has top priority. Clear airway.
   b. Stopping any bleeding has second priority.
   c. Treat for shock after the breathing and bleeding have been dealt with.
6. Do not move child if there is a possible injury to the back or neck.
7. Check the child's emergency card for name of physician, hospital preference of parents or caregivers, and any special instructions. You may need to contact them or any person they listed to call in an emergency.
8. Continuously reassure the child.
9. If the child has stopped breathing, call the fire department for resuscitator, while someone gives mouth-to-mouth resuscitation.
10. Ice packs are made of small household sponges, which are wetted, encased in a double plastic sandwich bag, and frozen.
11. Complete an incident report to send home with the child [Section G8]. If a physician needs to be seen, complete the more detailed accident/illness report [Section G10] in duplicate. One is to be sent home; one is for center files.
12. If a parent or caregiver cannot be contacted, try other numbers on the emergency card. As a last resort, call police.

G2 First Aid Kit

In your first aid cupboard, keep two lunch pails that can serve as first aid kits. One is for general use and the other is to take on field trips. Your cupboard should be higher than those used by the children, and the door must always be kept closed. Each child care room should have a box containing several sizes of bandages, small gauze pads, and sealed packages of alcohol wipes or antiseptic to take care of minor cuts, scratches, and abrasions. Have a similar kit to take out to the playground. Any vehicle used to transport children must also carry a stocked first aid kit. In addition to the first aid kit, also include a bottle of water, soap, coins for a pay phone, and a first aid handbook.

First Aid Kit Supplies

ON HAND	NEEDED	
_____	_____	Box of nonporous disposable gloves
_____	_____	Small bottle of antiseptic soap or hydrogen peroxide (an easy-to-use, safe antiseptic)
_____	_____	Gauze squares (1", 2", 3", 4")
_____	_____	Self-adhesive bandages (spots, patches, oversized, 1/2", 3/4", 1", 2", 4")
_____	_____	Adhesive tape (several sizes)
_____	_____	Absorbent cotton (rolls and balls)
_____	_____	Tweezers (for splinters)
_____	_____	Needle (for splinters)
_____	_____	Scissors (small, good quality)
_____	_____	Scissors (cuticle)
_____	_____	Thermometer (disposable ones are available, electronic ones save time, forehead strips may be used)
_____	_____	Triangular bandages (36" x 36" or 24" x 24" to use for slings)
_____	_____	Splints (cardboard)
_____	_____	Safety pins
_____	_____	Syrup of ipecac (to induce vomiting in case of accidental poisoning [Section G6])
_____	_____	Paper cups
_____	_____	Calamine lotion or vinegar
_____	_____	Burn ointment
_____	_____	Mineral oil
_____	_____	Small bulb syringe
_____	_____	Bee sting kit
_____	_____	Ice packs
_____	_____	Eye dressing
_____	_____	Sealable plastic bags for soiled materials
_____	_____	Pencil and notepad

In the freezer compartment of the refrigerator, keep about one dozen 2" and 4" pieces of sponge that have been soaked in water, wrapped in a plastic bag, and frozen. These can be used as ice packs.

Emergency Telephone Numbers

Fill in the appropriate numbers and post this sheet by your telephone.

TO CALL	TELEPHONE
Emergency	
Paramedics	
Fire	
Police	
Poison Control	
Ambulance	
County Health Department	
City Hall or Air Pollution Control District	
School Physician or Public Health Nurse	
Hospital Address: Directions to get there:	

Reasons for Calling an Ambulance or Paramedics

1. Ambulance drivers and attendants have first aid training. They also handle many accident cases and therefore have practical experience in treating many kinds of injuries.
2. First aid can be given to children even before they are taken to a hospital.
3. First aid can be given to children while they are on the way to a hospital.
4. Ambulance drivers and paramedics have access to important medical information and services. If there are a number of hospitals in the area, they can select the one that is best equipped to handle specific types of problems. They have access to the nearest Poison Control Center and can obtain valuable information on antidotes and first aid precautions while they are on the way to the accident.
5. If an accident occurs at your center and the parents or caregivers are not there to release a child, the ambulance driver or paramedics will usually notify the police, thereby covering the legal aspects of transporting a child from the center to the hospital.
6. If an ambulance or paramedics are called, and it is then determined that the child does not need hospital care, many ambulance companies will not charge

for the "dry run" to the center. If the problem is taken care of before they arrive, the company should be notified, so the driver can turn the sirens off. The ambulance driver will usually continue to the center to check on the situation and to verify that the ambulance is no longer needed. Please note that some ambulance services are required to transport children to the hospital when called, even if the child does not need hospital care. Check with your local ambulance service for any regulations.

7. It is recommended that you contact the nearest ambulance company and paramedics and become acquainted with the services offered.

G5 First Aid Procedures Handbook

Develop a first aid manual and keep it with the first aid kit in the office. Each child care provider should also have a copy in his or her room. Wear nonporous, disposable gloves when coming in contact with blood, body fluids, feces, nasal and eye discharge, saliva, urine, and vomit. Discard contaminated materials in a sealed plastic bag. Always wash your hands.

Common Minor Cuts, Abrasions, Splinter Wounds, or Other Skin Punctures

1. Wearing gloves, attempt to control any profuse bleeding.
2. Cleanse the wound with a sterile gauze pad, hydrogen peroxide, antiseptic soap, and water.
3. Allow to dry and cover with a self-adhesive bandage.
4. Check your records to make sure the child has had a series of three tetanus immunizations and a booster shot.
5. Small splinters, if they are easily accessible, can be removed with sterile implements. If a splinter proves difficult to remove, leave it alone. Complete an accident report and recommend that the parents or caregivers contact the child's physician.
6. Puncture wounds should always be reported, even if they are seemingly minor, so that parents or caregivers may consult the child's physician regarding the possible need of a tetanus booster.

Bruises and Bumps

1. Immediate application of an ice pack for the first 15 to 30 minutes will both relieve the pain and reduce the swelling or the possibility of swelling. You may also use cold compresses made from the larger-sized gauze pads.
2. If a bump is severe, have the child lie down.
3. If the injury is to the head, the child should lie down with his or her head slightly elevated. Watch for sleepiness, some memory loss, nausea, vomiting, or convulsions. Other symptoms of serious injury may be weakness, or fluid or blood seeping from ear, mouth, or nose. If the child appears to be momentarily stunned at the time of injury, there may be a concussion. If you suspect a concussion, bring the child to the hospital or call 911 for ambulance service. Otherwise, someone should remain with the child. If during this period there

seems to be a loss of consciousness, get medical help immediately. Treat the child for shock if indicated. When the child has been attended to, the parents or caregivers should be called immediately.

Shock

Shock is usually caused by too little blood circulating through the body because of serious injury, either internal or external. The symptoms are profuse cold sweating; extreme paleness; and possibly a very rapid, barely perceptible pulse; nausea; dizziness; rapid breathing; thirstiness; and gasping for air. A child in shock should be handled with gentleness and care.

1. If the child is not unconscious, elevate the feet slightly, except in case of head, neck, spine, back, or chest injury, and loosen all clothing.
2. Turn the child's head sideways if he or she is vomiting.
3. Cover the child with a warm blanket and use a hot water bottle or heating pad to help keep the body warm.
4. Give the child small sips of water unless he or she is unconscious.
5. Have someone notify the child's parents or caregivers immediately. Someone should be with the child at all times.

Bleeding

Loss of blood can weaken a child. A child who has been bleeding should be kept as quiet as possible.

Bleeding from an open wound. The first thing to do is to apply a sterile gauze pad or other dressing over the bleeding area, pressing firmly (use gloves). While you are maintaining the pressure, have someone else place a bandage or some adhesive tape firmly over the dressing to hold it in place. If the bleeding continues, call 911 immediately. Try to keep the body part that is bleeding higher than heart level, if possible. Contact the child's parents or caregivers at once.

Nosebleeds. Common nosebleeds may occur from time to time in the child care center. Have the child sit in a chair with head bent forward. The head can be down on the arms, which are resting on a tabletop. Pinch lower end of nose closed to stop the bleeding and provide an opportunity for a blood clot to form (use gloves). Tell the child not to blow his or her nose. Apply an ice pack to the back of the neck. If the bleeding has not stopped at the end of 15 minutes, call the parents or caregivers and ask them to contact their physician. After the bleeding has stopped, the child must be watched for after-effects from the loss of blood, such as fainting or shock. The child should sit upright and limit activities for approximately an hour following the nosebleed.

Scalp wounds. Scalp wounds frequently bleed more profusely than wounds in other parts of the body because the scalp has many blood vessels. A common impulse is to wash such a wound. *Do not do so.* Rather, apply direct pressure to the wound with a sterile pad until medical help is obtained. If pressure does not stop the bleeding, apply pressure over the temporal artery directly in front of the upper part of the ear on the same side of the head as the wound.

Fainting

A child may faint from being overheated, overtired, or frightened. Lack of air or a blow to the head may also cause fainting. Whatever the reason, it is actually due to a sudden lessening of the blood supply flowing to the brain. Fainting is usually preceded by dizziness and a blurring of vision. Breathing will be very shallow and the child may break out in a cold sweat. A child who has fainted will usually be very pale, but in rare instances it is possible for the face to be flushed instead. If pale, the child should lie down without elevating the head until the color of the skin returns to normal. If flushed, have the child lie down with the head slightly higher than the rest of the body until the skin color returns to normal. Apply a damp cloth to the forehead.

Eye Injuries

Foreign substances. One of the most frequent emergencies you will have to take care of in the child care center is removing foreign substances (usually sand) from a child's eye. You or whoever else administers first aid in your center will soon become expert in handling this problem. Wash your hands before examining the child's eye. *Never use dry cotton or pointed instruments of any kind when treating the eye.* If specks are on the lower lids, you can grasp the lashes and turn the lids up in order to remove the substance with a clean piece of wet gauze or clean cloth. If the substance is on the upper lid, grasp lashes and pull the lid down over the lower lid. The tears formed may wash it out. Sometimes you can stand behind the child while holding the lid of the injured eye open. Splash running water into the eye. This is a good remedy for sand in the eyes. If the substance cannot be easily removed, medical attention should be obtained immediately, especially if anything appears to be embedded in the eyeball. If in doubt as to what to do, cover the injured eye with a moistened gauze pad and have the child sit or lie quietly in order to avoid as much movement of the eye as possible. Any other injury to the eye should be examined by a physician as soon as possible. Don't allow the child to rub the eye.

Chemical burns to the eye. If a chemical substance gets into the eye, such as household cleaning material or art material, flush the eye with at least a quart of water. If the material is quite caustic, continue to flush with water for at least 15 minutes. The child should be taken to a physician as quickly as possible after the initial irrigation.

Punctures. Any time an object penetrates the eyeball, no attempt should be made to even examine it. *Call the paramedics.* A physician and the child's parents or caregivers should be contacted immediately. Quick action is important in such cases.

Bites and Stings

Insect bites and stings. Find the stinger. Do not pull the stinger, as it may break off. Try to remove the stinger by scraping it out with your fingernail or a credit card. Apply ice to relieve the pain. Watch the child for possible secondary reactions, such as shock or fainting. If the child is known to be allergic to insect bites or if the observed reaction to such a sting seems to indicate a possible allergy, the paramedics should be notified immediately. A paste of baking soda applied to the bite may help. In an emergency, a paste of mud can be used. Notify the parents or caregivers.

Animal bites. Wash thoroughly with antiseptic soap, using a moistened gauze pad to cleanse the area. Rinse thoroughly, preferably with clean running water for a few minutes. Dry with a sterile dressing and keep covered. Notify the parents or caregivers. If they are not available, notify the child's physician immediately. Notify the local health department, which will see that the animal is quarantined.

Human bites. If the skin is broken, wash area with soap or hydrogen peroxide. Apply a sterile dressing. Use an ice pack to alleviate pain. The parents or caregivers may want to notify a physician.

Snakebites. Get child to hospital as quickly as possible or call 911. Wash wound and keep the injured area still. *Keep the injury lower than the heart.* Do not apply ice, cut the wound, or apply a tourniquet. Keep the victim still until ambulance arrives. Use a snakebite kit if available, but only if it is impossible to get to a hospital.

Scorpion stings and black widow spider bites. If possible, apply a tourniquet for five minutes. Apply ice. Call paramedics and parents or caregivers immediately.

Tick bites. Cover the tick with oil or petroleum jelly. Within a few minutes it will loosen its hold so that it can be removed with a tweezers. Be sure that all of it is removed. The area should be washed thoroughly with antiseptic soap and water.

Foreign Bodies in the Throat

Choking on small obstructions or food particles, such as popcorn, is an occasional cause of death in small children. The child should be held upside down. This can be done by having the child lie facedown on a table with head and shoulders hanging down toward the floor. Slap the child vigorously on the back between the shoulder blades. If that doesn't work, try the Heimlich maneuver. Be prepared to give artificial respiration if the child's breathing seems to stop. Call 911 at once. Then call the parents or caregivers. Suggest medical attention, even if the symptoms have subsided.

Burns

Minor burns. Flood with cold water for ten minutes or wet with a cloth or towel, or even an article of clothing. Do not apply ointments. For severe burns in which blisters or other symptoms develop, have the child lie down and watch him or her for possible shock. Submerge burned area in cold water or wet with cloth as above. Do not break blisters. Notify paramedics and the parents or caregivers immediately. Treat for shock, if necessary. Do not try to remove clothing from areas that have been burned. For third-degree burns, call paramedics. Cover burned area with clean cloth or sheet until they arrive.

Sunburn. If the child seems to be showing signs of sensitivity to or burning from the sun, take him or her indoors immediately. Sunburn can be a second-degree burn that may require medical attention. Watch for signs of blistering and fever. Calamine lotion or vinegar can be used to soothe the skin. Use these only in cases of mild sunburn that do not require medical help. Notify the parents or caregivers if the child seems ill.

Chemical burns on parts of the body other than the eye. Flood with water immediately. Then call 911. Flooding can be done in a shower or with a garden hose. Use buckets of water if a hose is not available. Clothes can be left on to save time. Continue washing with cool water until the ambulance arrives.

Blisters (from causes other than burns)

Do not attempt to treat blisters, except to cover them with a protective bandage. If a blister has broken open, clean it with soap and water and apply a sterile dressing. If a blister looks infected or inflamed, notify the parents or caregivers. Suggest medical treatment.

Heat Exhaustion

This can occur when a child has been playing in direct sunlight for a long period of time without rest or fluids. It can also be caused by overexposure to indoor heat. It will especially affect a child who is in poor physical condition. Symptoms include dizziness, nausea, staggering, and clamminess. The child may look very pale and perspire heavily. The pulse is usually weak and the breathing is shallow. Have the child lie down without a pillow in an area where there is plenty of circulating fresh air. Use a hand fan, if necessary. Cover the child with a blanket. Get the child to drink some water, and then call paramedics and the parents or caregivers.

Heat cramps are similar to heat exhaustion, but they affect the stomach muscles. Give the child plenty of water to drink.

Sunstroke. Symptoms include dizziness, headache, nausea, and irritability. The mouth and skin are dry. The body is hot (rather than cold, as in heat exhaustion). Instead of profusely sweating, the face is dry. Get the child into the shade or a cool place as soon as possible. If the air is not circulating, use a hand fan. Apply cold cloths to the head. Loosen the clothing and wrap the entire body in a wet sheet, sprinkling cold water over the sheet from time to time. Give the child cool drinks such as water, juice, or soft drinks. Do not give the child a stimulant. Call paramedics and the child's parents or caregivers at once.

Frostbite

Symptoms of frostbite include severe pain, if the hands or feet are frostbitten, and a grayish skin color (caused by ice in the tissues) of the affected areas. Do not rub the frostbitten area. Place the child in a warm room, but not close to intense heat. Thaw the frostbitten part by bathing it in warm water. Give the child a warm drink.

Asphyxiation

This occurs when the child cannot obtain oxygen or when an excessive amount of carbon dioxide has been inhaled. If it is caused by some weight on the child's chest, try to remove the weight so that the natural breathing apparatus can take over. If it is caused by an injury to the chest, do not move the child. Use mouth-to-mouth resuscitation. Call paramedics.

Choking or strangling on an object. Remove object from mouth, if possible. If this is not possible, stand behind the child, put your arms around the child's midriff, and squeeze with a quick, hard jerk. Repeat if necessary. Give artificial respiration if breathing does not resume. Place a very young child facedown on your lap and hit between the shoulder blades four times. If this doesn't dislodge the object, turn the child over on his or her back and give three or four thrusts of your hand into the lower chest area.

Drowning. Call 911 and administer CPR.

Gas inhalation. Call 911. Remove the child from gaseous area.

Exposure to noxious fumes. Remove the child from the area. If breathing has stopped, call 911 and administer CPR.

Broken Bones, Sprains, and Similar Injuries

Do not move the child. The child should be kept warm and lying down. Watch for shock. Apply emergency treatment for shock, if necessary. Call 911 and then the parents or caregivers. If a bone is showing through the skin, place a sterile pad over it. Do not try to examine or cleanse it. If the injury is a sprain, apply ice to it. If the injury is to the nose, elevate the head slightly and loosen the clothing around the neck. Ice can be applied to the back of the neck but not to the nose. If the injury is to the mouth, jaw, or teeth, call 911 at once and then the child's parents or caregivers.

Convulsions or Grand Mal Seizures

Convulsions cause loss of consciousness and violent, spasmodic twitching of the muscles. These symptoms are sometimes followed by a stupor and an apparent loss of awareness to surroundings.

Grand Mal Seizures

1. Remain calm. The seizure is painless to the child.
2. *Do not try to restrain the child.* Nothing can be done to stop the seizure once it has begun. It must run its course.
3. Clear the area around the child to prevent injury from hard or sharp objects.
4. Don't force anything between the teeth, despite what you may have heard in the past. If the mouth is already open, a soft cloth can be placed between the side teeth to minimize biting of the tongue.
5. Call 911 if
   - an attack is immediately followed by another.
   - the seizure lasts longer than ten minutes.
   - the child's health record and history show no indication of epilepsy.
6. When the seizure is over:
   - Notify the parents or caregivers and the child's physician.
   - Allow the child to rest.
   - Explain to the other children that the seizure is not contagious and is nothing to fear. Explain that it is simply a temporary loss of body control.

Severed Limb, Finger, or Toe

Call paramedics. Put the severed part in clean plastic bag. Place ice in another plastic bag and place the first bag into the ice-filled bag. Place the bags in a protective container. A dishpan or soup pot (if large enough) will do. When the paramedics arrive, be sure to send the severed part with the child when he or she is being taken to the hospital. If an object is impaled in the wound, do not remove it. Bandage around the wound to keep the object in place. To stop the flow of blood, put a sterile dressing over the wound and apply pressure.

Chest Penetration

If an accident has caused an opening in the chest, the sound of air being inhaled will be heard. Bubbles of blood will be seen as the child exhales. If something has become embedded in the chest, do not remove it. Call the paramedics or an ambulance. Take the following emergency measures:

1. Try to seal the opening by pressing firmly with a folded piece of cloth held in the palm of the hand. The cloth can be wrapped in aluminum foil for sterility, with a sterile gauze pad under the improvised pad.
2. The child should be lying down, with the upper part of the body and the head slightly raised. The body can be turned slightly toward the side with the wound.
3. If necessary, while you are waiting for paramedics, the pad can be taped down to be airtight. If this is very painful, another pad of cotton can be placed over the pads before applying the tape.

Electric Shock

One person can turn off the main electric switch while another tries to separate the child from the electrical conductor with a piece of dry wood. Do not touch the child's body until it is totally separated from the source of electricity to avoid having the current spread to you. Take the following steps:

1. Call the paramedics or ambulance.
2. Apply mouth-to-mouth resuscitation if the child is not breathing.
3. If the heart is not beating, use CPR (cardiopulmonary resuscitation). Only a person trained in this procedure should use it.
4. Child should be lying down, partially on side, facedown. Place one leg so that the knee is bent slightly. Bend the elbow on that same side. Turn the child's face toward that side. Place the other arm straight above the head.

Stomachache

Suggest use of toilet. Check for too tight a belt. Give nothing to eat or drink. Take a temperature. If the child has a fever, sharp pains, nausea, or diarrhea, parents or caregivers should be called and the child sent home. A heating pad or hot water bottle held to the stomach may alleviate the pain.

Headache

This should be taken seriously. Check for fever. Have the child rest quietly. If the headache persists, call the parents or caregivers.

Tooth Injury

If tooth is chipped or broken, the child must be taken to a dentist as soon as possible. Place cold compresses over the face in the area of the tooth injury. Save any tooth fragments. Take the child to the dentist immediately, along with the tooth fragments. If a tooth gets knocked out, find the tooth. Rinse it with water, but DO NOT clean it. Do not handle the tooth by its root. Place it in a cup of milk or water. Call the parents or caregivers to take the child and the tooth to the dentist immediately.

Hyperventilation

This is brought on by "overbreathing," usually when the child is under great stress. Symptoms include dizziness; possible tingling sensation in mouth, lips, hands, or feet; and difficulty in breathing. The child gasps for air. Having the child breathe in and out of a paper bag will usually alleviate this condition. The child should breathe in deeply and exhale slowly a few times.

If breathing does not return to normal, seek medical assistance for additional diagnosis of problem.

G6 First Aid Procedures for Poisons

In spite of precautions you may take, the inquisitiveness of young children will sometimes lead them to consume substances that are poisonous. Assume each of these situations to be serious and summon medical aid immediately. If you are in doubt about what treatment to give, or if you do not know what the child has swallowed, call an ambulance service. It will contact the nearest poison control center and advise you while they are on their way to help. These are the primary treatments recommended:

1. Have someone call an ambulance, a doctor, and the parents or caregivers, in that order, while you begin first-aid procedures.
2. Try to identify what the child has taken. Save urine, stools, and whatever the child vomits, as well as anything remaining of what the child has swallowed. Save the container from which the substance was obtained.
3. Induce vomiting, *except as noted in items 5, 6, and 7 below.*
    a. Tickle the back of the throat; touch it with your finger.
    b. Give the child a glass of warm water with one tablespoon of dry mustard, baking soda, or even soapsuds (not detergent).
    c. Syrup of ipecac is recommended by many physicians. It should be administered according to directions on the bottle. It will usually cause vomiting in about 15 minutes. Repeat the dose once if the child has not vomited in 20 minutes.
4. Give an antidote to dilute the poison. If the antidote is unknown, use milk. If milk is not available, give water. If the pulse is weak and the heart is beating irregularly, give warm tea.
5. Do not induce vomiting or give liquids if the child is in a coma or having convulsions. If the child vomits voluntarily, place him or her on the side so the respiratory muscles are not restricted.
6. Do not induce vomiting if child has swallowed a substance containing kerosene products of any kind. Vomiting may cause the kerosene to get into the lungs, which can be fatal. It is safer to let it remain in the stomach until medical treatment can be obtained.
7. Do not induce vomiting if the child has swallowed a corrosive substance, such as a household cleaner, bleach, or polish. Vomiting will cause further damage.
8. Keep child warm until medical help arrives.

Food Poisoning

Food poisoning can be very serious to a small child. Preventive measures are of utmost importance. Take the following precautions:

- Refrigeration equipment should be in good working condition to maintain temperatures below 45°F. Appropriate foods must be kept under refrigeration, even in cold weather.
- Utensils should be cleaned under hygienic conditions, disinfected, and used only in a sanitary manner.
- Persons who handle food (even snacks) should practice good health habits. They must always wash their hands with soap and rinse well after using the lavatory. They must be free of disease or infection.
- Food must be protected from contact with flies and rodents.
- Leftover foods should be covered with both contents and date listed for identification for future use. Outdated foods must not be served.
- Keep plumbing in sanitary condition.
- Do not use contents of damaged or badly dented cans.
- Learn to recognize the symptoms of food poisoning. The child may have eaten contaminated food at home and become violently ill at your center. These symptoms include: severe abdominal pain and cramps, nausea, vomiting, diarrhea, and overall weakness.

If you have any questions concerning possible food contamination or poisoning, telephone the county or city health department at once. In emergencies, call the ambulance service, which will give you advice while on the way to your center.

G8 Notifying Parents/Caregivers of Accidents

Use this simple form for notifying parents or caregivers of common incidents. To minimize the impact on parents and caregivers, call this an "Incident Report." When possible, have your forms printed on NCR paper so one copy can go home and the other placed in the child's file for a permanent record. Be concise, exact, nonalarming, but concerned. Accidents that require a doctor or an ambulance should be reported on the Center Accident Record [Section G10].

Incident Report

Parent or caregiver name: *Meredith Belosky* Date: *April 9*
The following incident occurred at school today at *10:25 A.M.*.
When Sandra paused to talked to another child while we were returning from the playground, her finger got pinched in the door.
Emergency procedures we administered:
We soothed it with ice and comfort. I suggest that you do not comment to her about it unless she brings it up.
Administered by *Miss Jones* Time: *10:30*
If you wish to question me further regarding this incident, please feel free to telephone.

Director

G9 Incident Journal

After filling out the Incident Report, the incident is recorded in a journal, which is kept in the office. Thus, if any parent calls for more information and the person who wrote the report is not there, others can check the journal and verify the details.

Here is a sample of what an incident journal may look like:

Date & time:	**Child:**	**Child care provider:**
4/23 3 P.M.	*Susan Grott*	*Anne*

Incident:
After nap, Susan seemed a little wobbly. She staggered into a table, bruising her hip.
Action:
I applied ice pack, gave TLC.

Date & time:	**Child:**	**Child care provider:**
4/23 3:10 P.M.	*Larry Festin*	*Gary*

Incident:
Larry grabbed truck from a friend; kicked the child's shins. The friend reached over and scratched Larry's face, leaving streaks down cheek.
Action:
Cleansed with peroxide. Applied ice pack. Renewal time for both children.

Date & time: 4/23 3:10 P.M. **Child:** Jenny Sanderson **Child care provider:** Gary

Incident:
(see above) Jenny had red spot on shin.

Action:
Applied ice pack. Note sent home stated both children were fighting with one another. Told to "use words."

Date & time: 4/24 5:15 P.M. **Child:** Jerry White **Child care provider:** Lucille

Incident:
Jerry complained of stomach cramps.

Action:
Since he was being picked up shortly, had him lie down with hot water bottle on tummy. Did not take his temp. Didn't seem warm.

G10 Center Accident Records

Use these forms for accidents requiring a doctor or an ambulance. Complete the Accident Report in triplicate. Give one copy to the parents or caregivers, keep one copy for the files, and keep another copy in reserve if it is needed for the insurance company.

ACCIDENT REPORT

Name of child: ______________________________ Date of accident: ____________

Address: ___________________________________ Time of accident: ____________

________________________ ZIP _____ Phone no. of child: __________

Nature of injury (describe in detail, including how it happened):

Who was supervising the child at the time?

Emergency care administered (include the time):

Administered by ______________________________ Time: ______________

Physician notified, if any: _____________________ Time: ______________

Ambulance called, if any: ______________________ Time: ______________

Where directed: ______________________________ Time: ______________

Which parent (or caregiver) was notified: _____________ Time: ______________

This should be on a separate sheet so as not to jeopardize the center's standing.

EVALUATION OF ACCIDENT (for center use only)

Describe supervision at time of accident:

Describe environment:

How might accident have been prevented?

Have any changes been recommended as result of accident?

G11 Maintaining Health Records

Your first responsibility to the children you enroll in your center is to verify that their physical condition is such that their attendance and participation in your program will not be detrimental to their health. You and the child's child care provider should study very carefully the physician's preadmission medical report on the child and the Health History Form [Sections E18–19], completed by the parents and caregivers. Any health problems should be noted and listed on a separate sheet, copies of which are given to every member of the staff, not just the child's own child care provider. Every staff member should be aware of any child's special needs or problems. You can also include any problems that may affect the emotional well-being of the children.

We also have specific forms that list allergies and special dietary needs [Section G13]. These are posted in each room for the use of assistants, aides, and other participants. These may be for just the one group or for all children at the center, depending on the size of each group and the size of the center.

Forms that list family problems that may affect the child's emotional well-being are filled out individually for each child care provider. This information is confidential and is not shared with other staff members unless it is determined that it would be of benefit to the child [Sections G12, G14].

G12 Children's Health/Emotional Problems

Name of Child	Group	Problem
John S.	1	Congenital hip malformation. Limps, but needs no special care. Is sometimes in pain.
June M.	1	Crossed eyes. Must be watched to make sure that she keeps her glasses on.
Nancy L.	2	Asthmatic. Avoid overstimulation.
Jakar S.	2	Poor motor coordination. Stumbles and bumps into things. Undergoing tests at this time.
Elizabeth S.	3	Enlarged adenoids, breathes heavily.
Tony J.	4	Nervous. Was seriously injured in an automobile accident when only 1 1/2 years old. Is improving.
Maria F.	4	Epileptic. Takes medication, but does not need special care other than awareness of her problem.

Note to Staff:

Please study this list so you will be aware of the physical/emotional problems of these children. Please take these problems into consideration when these children do not seem to be following their normal behavior. This information is confidential and must not go beyond the staff members. None of these children need any special attention other than ordinarily given to each child. Their enrollment has been approved by their physicians. It is hoped that the center environment will give each of them a boost toward an improved state of health.

G13 Allergies and Special Dietary Needs

Child care providers: Please be discreet in the use of this information.

As of October 1

Name of Child	Group	Special Need
Johanna L.	1	No cow's milk. Soy milk in refrigerator.
Billy B.	1	Hyperglycemia. Limited carbohydrates and high protein. He brings milk and lunch from home.
Alicia J.	1	No citrus fruits. Substitute other foods.
Gordon F.	2	Allergic to bee stings. URGENT. Call ambulance. First aid kit in refrigerator.
Chuckie W.	3	Vegetarian. Substitute other foods for meat and fish.
Barbie D.	4	Diabetic. No sugar. Special ice cream in freezer.

G14 Family and Environmental Problems That May Cause Distress

There are frequently factors in the child's life away from the center that may affect his or her physical and emotional well-being. Child care providers should be kept informed of these things that may help them enlarge their understanding of the children in their care. Use the following form to note problems of various children. The head child care provider in a group is given this information to share, as needed with co-workers. It is kept in a confidential locked file.

NOT TO BE POSTED

Family and Environmental Factors You Should Know About

(CONFIDENTIAL)

Group:

Name of Child	Problem
1. John E.	Father working out of town for three months.
2. Sandy R.	Father alcoholic; much quarreling at home.
3. Barry R.	Grandmother living in home; semi-invalid; requires daily treatment.
4. Robbie S.	Mother has broken hip; bedridden temporarily; no outside help.
5. Jennie B.	Parents temporarily separated; friendly, but Jennie very disturbed.
6. Libby F.	Father not living at home; court order to stay away.
7. Sarah F.	Unemployment; financial problems.
8. Tina P.	Joint custody; alternates weekdays w/mother; Fri.–Sun. w/father. Father picks her up on Fri., brings Mon.; carries pillow and suitcase.
9. Terrence L.	Alternates weeks between parents; father remarried w/two small stepchildren; mother not remarried but has new baby. Schedules frequently changed.

Note: Please treat this information with utmost confidence. Use the information to help the child in a way that makes preschool more pleasant and beneficial.

G15 Other Family Circumstances That May Affect Children

These are examples of family problems that have been observed in past years that may affect children.

- Father has moved out after violent scene between both parents. Neighbors were involved.
- Mother has quietly moved to another city. Does not want children.
- Parents separated. Father has weekend visiting privileges. Child never wants to go with father, but father insists.
- Father's job is being terminated. Much tension in the home.
- Mother will require surgery. Grandmother will care for child in her home. Grandmother is very social, does much entertaining, many adults in house all the time, no children in area to play with.

- Ten-year-old sister has developed serious heart condition. Is now bedridden and requires much special care.
- Mother suffered a breakdown during the summer. Child has been taken care of by various relatives at their homes. Mother is fine now, but child is still confused by all the changes that took place. Father has become extremely irritable. Large doctor bills are presenting a problem.
- Mother has remarried. New stepfather takes child many places with him. Child has been overstimulated.
- Family was in serious automobile accident. All spent weekend in hospital. Child is frightened of riding in an automobile. Very tense.
- No English is spoken in the home. Child is reprimanded when he attempts to converse with his two older brothers in English. Family wants children to retain native tongue. Much pressure on child lately.
- Child's dog was badly injured by automobile. Died next to child on way to veterinarian.
- Stepparents or "live-in" friends of parent.
- Joint/split custody.
- Family evicted and living in car until they can relocate.

G16 Daily Health Check

Give each child a health check immediately upon arrival each day. In many centers, this is done by the group child care provider. At your child care center, the director (or assistant director) can take over the responsibility, employing the following routine:

1. The director greets children individually. They open their mouths, with heads tipped back, allowing the overhead lights to take the place of having to use a flashlight. (Children usually assume the director is checking to see if they brushed their teeth.) The director notes any unusual redness, irritation, or patchiness, gently touching the child's throat and neck with the fingertips to check for swollen glands, which may indicate an oncoming illness or may be the result of having recently been ill. If no other symptoms are present, the child will not be sent home just on the basis of slightly swollen glands. But the parents and caregivers will be alerted and both parents or caregivers and staff will observe the child closely for a couple of days and ensure that the child has sufficient rest.
2. Note is also taken of the color and condition of the child's skin, eyes, and overall appearance. Watch for the following symptoms:
   - Watery, inflamed eyes or crusty eyes or eyelids
   - Glazed appearance of eyes
   - Deep cough
   - Inflamed nostrils
   - Heavy nasal discharge
   - Unusual irritability
   - Rash, sores, flushed appearance, clamminess, pallor, or other unusual skin conditions
   - Contagious diseases

3. In spite of immunization laws, the director must also be alert to any signs of contagious disease, such as mumps or chicken pox, especially if they are prevalent in the community at the time. It is sometimes difficult to determine if a child is actually ill. For example, a young child may have an insect bite that raises a tiny blister similar to the first small blister of chicken pox. Or a chubby-faced child with slightly enlarged glands may appear to have the mumps. One good way to check is to have the child turn with his or her back to you. If you can still see swelling, it is possibly the mumps, and you should take the precaution of sending the child home at once and recommending that he or she be examined by a physician. Whenever there is any doubt about the child's health, ask the parent or caregiver to keep the child home for 24 hours.

G17 Other Indications of a Possible Health Problems

There are other indications of a possible health/emotional problems that the entire staff should be alert to, especially if any changes are noted. The following conditions, when observed by a staff member, should be reported to the director. Arrangements should be made as soon as possible to discuss the matter. Referrals should be given for appropriate professional help, if needed [Sections G41–43].

- Sudden pallor of skin
- Sudden flushing of skin
- Unusual number of trips to the toilet for either bowel movements or urination
- Headaches
- Stomachaches
- Crossed eyes
- Poor vision
- Tilting head going up and down steps
- Poor hearing
- Unclear speech (for age)
- Scratching of skin
- Runny nose
- Rubbing of nose
- Wheezing; shortness of breath
- Extreme weight fluctuation
- Clammy, sweaty appearance
- Vomiting or gagging
- Swelling
- Change in appearance of eyes
- Constant sneezing or coughing
- Listlessness
- Sleepiness
- Unusual aggressiveness
- Unusual loudness of voice
- Frequent stumbling, falling
- Temper tantrums
- Tics or grimacing
- Clumsiness
- Abnormal gait; limp
- Convulsions; "blackout" spells

Vision

If your observations indicate the possibility of a child having a problem seeing, the parents or caregivers should be notified immediately. You may have noticed difficulty in picking up small objects, or difficulty in moving through a room without bumping into people and things, or that the eyes seem to be crossed at times.

For preliminary screening of the child who is three or over, you can obtain a Snellen Visual Testing Chart from the Illinois Society for the Prevention of Blindness [Section G45]. Ask a local ophthalmologist to give you the simple basic instructions for using the chart. Also, contact any interest groups in your area that provide vision screening.

When you talk to the parents or caregivers about the child's vision, be prepared to give them referral information and encourage them to follow-up on your report immediately.

Hearing

In children under three, the detection of potential hearing problems is very difficult. Again, observation is one of your best clues. Children who do not seem to be developing speech appropriate to their age, or whose responses to verbal directions are below average, should be suspected of having a hearing deficiency. Check those children who speak with a jargon of their own, using many unintelligible sounds.

By the time children have reached three years of age, they can be tested with an audiometer. This screening test is frequently provided to day care centers by various volunteer organizations. Your local health department or an audiologist will help you get the information you need for local resources.

Other Problems

Your observation of the child's development should extend to all areas. Observe such things as size and growth, movement, responses, behavior, learning ability, sensory awareness, coordination, and social relationships. If you suspect that anything is wrong, you must tell the child's parents or caregivers. They have the right to know immediately if there is even the slightest possibility that their child needs to have appropriate screening tests by qualified professional persons. See Section G45 for referral information that will help parents determine how to get help the child needs.

G18 Epileptic Seizures

It may be that a child is enrolled at your center who has epilepsy or a psychomotor deficiency that has not yet been diagnosed. Such a child may have small seizures that no one has really pinpointed as being an indication of a disease. Child care workers should be alert to the following signs:

1. Frequent spells of staring vacantly into space. Often one says that the child "daydreams a great deal."
2. Lack of response
3. Eyes rolling upward
4. Tic-like movements, such as twitching of mouth or jerking of head, which the child seemingly cannot control
5. Rhythmic uncontrolled head movements
6. Head dropping
7. Purposeless sounds and body movements of which the child is seemingly unaware
8. Chewing and swallowing movements

Any of these symptoms are cause for concern. When two or more have been observed repeatedly, the parents or caregivers should be given an immediate referral to a physician. (See Section G5 for First Aid for Grand Mal Seizures.)

G19 Children with Special Needs

The Americans with Disabilities Act requires child care centers to accommodate children with disabilities. They require that reasonable accommodations be given. Physical changes in your center may include installing ramps, widening doors, and providing restrooms with wheelchair access. You may need to also provide for special physical, emotional, or psychological needs, such as assisting with feeding, performing medical procedures, and providing special dietary requirements.

When a religious organization operates a child care center, it is not required to comply with ADA requirements. If the religious organization leases its facility to an outside agency to run the center, that agency would have to comply. Family child care providers and programs for extended-day child care for school-age children are required to comply with the ADA. Again, these programs are required to make reasonable accommodations unless it demonstrates an undue burden to do so.

When considering admitting a child with developmental special needs, ask yourself the following questions:

1. Does you or your staff have the necessary skills needed to administer the medical duties required?
2. Will the child require more care than you can reasonably accommodate?
3. Will the extra time involved in taking care of the child increase the risk of illness or injury to the other children or neglect their needs?
4. Can your facility be equipped or rearranged to accommodate the health and safety needs of the child?

Understand that you cannot exclude a child because he or she has special needs. You must make a good effort to consider every child on an individual basis. There are circumstances, however, in which you can legally refuse to accept a child. You can refuse if the child poses a direct threat to others, or accommodations would pose an undue hardship, or alter drastically the nature of your program. Before enrolling the child, meet with the child's parents or caregivers, as well as health care providers, to discuss the needs. They will give you the outline of what you will need to perform and how much time it should take. Ask the parents or caregivers to train you on any required medical procedures, and give you written instructions of schedules and eating requirements. Hold periodic meetings with the health care professional and the parents or caregivers to talk over the child's progress and if the special needs are being met.

There are several types of disabilities that can be considered:

Children with Mental Retardation

Slightly retarded children often do well in a child care setting, especially if placed with children a little younger than they are chronologically. They often need no special attention until they get ready to go to elementary school. Then a determination needs to be made as to the most appropriate educational program for them.

Children with Mild Visual Problems

A visually impaired child can participate in the majority of activities in the child care center, with a little extra help from both adults and children when needed.

Children with Mild Hearing Problems

Mild hearing impairment should not interfere with a child's successful participation in a child care program. If the child has more than a mild hearing problem, however, it would be better to utilize the services of the many special programs throughout the nation that will teach the child how to sign and read lips. The child will be given special language training to ensure future integration into classrooms with hearing children.

Children with Special Physical Needs

Again, children with mild physical problems can add an important dimension to a child care center, teaching the other children empathy and helpfulness. In accepting physically challenged children, however, be sure that the facilities are suitable for them (according to what their needs are), and be sure that the children, though possibly needing a frequent helping hand, do not need to have the staff give special therapy.

Children with Emotional Problems

The director must determine carefully whether or not a child is disruptive to an otherwise smooth-running program. If the child responds to direction, a good child care program can often be of great help in teaching him or her to handle the emotions. But if a child needs continuous one-to-one supervision, thus depriving other children of an important element of their supervision, that child should be withdrawn from the program. Often special programs are available in the community for children with exceptional needs. When possible, the family should be given the necessary referral support.

Isolation

If children show symptoms of illness during the day, they should be immediately isolated and a parent or caregiver contacted [Section E20]. If you know that a child will be picked up within a half hour anyway, you may not need to call. If a parent or caregiver is called, expect them to be at the center within 30 minutes to pick up the child.

In the meantime, ill children should be given an opportunity to lie down on a cot, with a staff member nearby. A very ill child might be held by an adult for a while and given comfort. Children who are ill but do not feel like lying down may be given an opportunity to sit quietly in the isolation area and read a book or use crayons, if they wish. Take care to reassure the isolated child that someone will soon be coming to take him or her home. On rare occasions, a very young child may be so upset that the child's child care provider is temporarily released from the room to wait with the child until the parent or caregiver arrives.

If an ill child's parent or caregiver cannot be contacted, or if there is a lack of transportation, the center may contact someone on the Emergency List [Section E17] to pick up the child. If a parent or caregiver cannot be contacted, and no one on the Emergency List can be reached, plan on keeping the child in isolation from the other children until the regular pickup time. If the child is very ill, however, you may have to call the child's physician or paramedics, or take whatever other steps you feel are necessary for the child's well-being and in keeping with the permission slip the parent or caregiver has already signed [Section E20].

G21 Communicable Diseases and Infections

With the rapid growth of out-of-the-home child care in recent years, there has been a growing awareness of the ease with which many infectious illnesses spread. The close contact of young children, especially of those who are not yet toilet-trained and require diaper changing, leads to the spread of bacteria and viruses from one to another.

When any of the children or groups of children have to our knowledge been exposed to a communicable disease, notices are distributed to parents and caregivers. The following is a sample of a letter you can use in such cases.

Community Child Care Center

111 THIRD STREET TELEPHONE 123-4579

Dear Parents and Caregivers,

It is the policy of the center to notify parents and caregivers when there has been a possible exposure to a communicable disease within the center.

On Tuesday, April 2, your child may have been exposed to chicken pox by a child who broke out with the disease that day. While the incubation period for chicken pox can be from 14 to 21 days, onset of the disease is usually on the 14th or 15th day after exposure. We suggest that you watch your child carefully for possible symptoms—usually very small blisters and a high fever.

Sincerely,

Director

Extraordinary care in precautionary measures can greatly minimize the spread of these infections. Post the following guidelines prominently in each room, the restrooms, and other locations throughout the center.

Community Child Care Center

111 THIRD STREET ✿ TELEPHONE 123-4579

PRECAUTIONARY HEALTH MEASURES

1. WASH HANDS THOROUGHLY WITH SOAP AND RUNNING WATER. WASH BETWEEN FINGERS, UNDER FINGERNAILS, BACKS OF HANDS, AND WRISTS. ALLOW SUFFICIENT TIME FOR ADEQUATE RINSING. DRY WITH PAPER TOWEL. WASH FAUCETS WITH SOAP WHILE WASHING HANDS, SO THAT CLEAN HANDS DO NOT PICK UP BACTERIA FROM THEM. TURN OFF FAUCETS WITH PAPER TOWEL. HAND-WASHING SHOULD BE VIGOROUS AND DELIBERATE AS OPPOSED TO CASUAL AND SUPERFICIAL.
   HANDS SHOULD ALWAYS BE WASHED
   - after using restroom.
   - before and after changing a child's diapers or other clothing.
   - before beginning any type of food service, even if it's just handling utensils.
   - before and after inspecting an open sore, rash, scalp (for head lice), or any other type of possibly infectious skin lesion.
   - after helping a child with nose-blowing or handling a child who has vomited.
2. CHILDREN MUST WASH THEIR HANDS
   - when they arrive for the day.
   - after use of toilet.
   - after having diaper or other clothing changed.
   - before handling eating utensils or food of any kind.
   - after blowing their noses.
3. HELP REMIND CHILDREN NOT TO PUT TOYS, OTHER PERSON'S FOOD OR UTENSILS, OR OTHER OBJECTS IN OR ON THEIR MOUTHS.
4. COVER MOUTH WHEN COUGHING, PREFERABLY WITH TISSUE.
5. DISPOSE OF TISSUE IN WASTEBASKET AFTER USE. NEVER REUSE.
6. PLACE SOILED CLOTHING IN A PLASTIC BAG, DOUBLE BAGGED, TO BE SENT HOME.
7. PLACE SOILED DISPOSABLE DIAPERS IN A COVERED PLASTIC-LINED CONTAINER.
8. DISINFECT ALL DIAPERING AND CLOTHES-CHANGING SURFACES FREQUENTLY, USING A COMMERCIAL DISINFECTANT OR ORDINARY HOUSEHOLD BLEACH MIXED WITH WATER. WIPE SURFACE WITH A PAPER TOWEL. DISCARD TOWEL IN PLASTIC-LINED COVERED CONTAINER.
9. REMAIN ALERT FOR AND REPORT AT ONCE ANY SIGNS OF
   - *diarrhea*—two or more loose stools require that the child be sent home. Pay special attention to hand washing procedures.
   - *skin rashes, blisters, lesions, encrusted areas*—may be indicative of ringworm, impetigo, the start of chicken pox, or other diseases. These symptoms may only indicate heat rash (prickly heat), which is not contagious. However, if a contagious condition is suspected, send child home.

G22 AIDS

The panic regarding the disease AIDS may reflect unfavorably on a child who has a parent or caregiver with the disease, or a parent or caregiver who is a carrier of the virus. This panic is further extended toward children who may be found to have the disease or to be carriers of the virus. HIV (Human Immunodeficiency Virus), the vector that leads to AIDS (Acquired Immune Deficiency Syndrome), is *not* transmitted by touching; hugging; kissing; sharing dishes or food; being coughed, cried, or sneezed on; or from toilet seats, urine, stool, vomit, saliva, mucus, or sweat (as long as it is untainted by blood). Three conditions are necessary for the transmission of HIV: 1) The blood must be fresh and a sufficient amount must be present, along with a route of entry into the uninfected person's bloodstream; 2) sharing of contaminated needles through drug abuse (HIV is transmitted most commonly this way), through sexual intercourse, or by an infected pregnant women to her fetus; or 3) exposure to infected blood through transfusions.

Children in group settings often experience bites from other children. Understandably, parents and caregivers are concerned about biting. There has never been a confirmed case of transmission by biting. In order for transmission to take place, the infected child must have fresh blood in his or her mouth and break the skin of an uninfected child. Parents and caregivers worry about fights, but fresh blood-to-blood contact during fighting is unusual.

Many children have no symptoms; therefore child care staff most likely will not know if a child is infected. If the parent or caregiver knows, they have no obligation to tell anyone at the center. Since a child with HIV poses no danger, parents and caregivers of other children do not need to know. If the director is told, she or he has an ethical obligation to keep the information confidential. Children with HIV have the right to attend a child care center. HIV is a disability, and the law does not allow discrimination of a disability. Staff also cannot be fired or removed because they have HIV. To reduce the risk of spreading HIV, all staff should routinely follow the necessary precautions to prevent any bloodborne infection, including hepatitis B:

1. Wear gloves when changing diapers.
2. Wear gloves when cleaning up blood and body fluids.
3. All children and staff must use good hand-washing practices.
4. Wash spilled breast milk on skin immediately with soap and water.
5. Do not allow children to share toothbrushes.
6. Clean up any spills of blood immediately. Wear gloves.
7. Use freshly prepared bleach solution to disinfect any surfaces on which blood or body fluids were spilled.
8. Cover open wounds on children and adults.

G23 Sexually Transmitted Diseases

As with AIDS, reassurance may be obtained from the health department when there are known cases of syphilis, gonorrhea, and other sexually transmitted diseases within the families of any of the children. These diseases are only known to be transmitted through actual sexual contact.

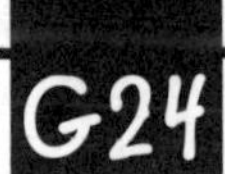

G24 Record of Calls from Parents/Caregivers Regarding Reasons for Child's Absence

Keep a record of why children are absent so that you can be aware of such health problems as a flu epidemic and be on the watch for it at your center.

Name	Group	Date Absent	Who Called	Reason for Absence
John J.	2	11/4	mother	flu

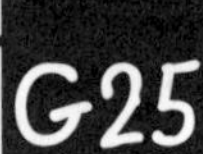

G25 Permission to Reenter Center After Illness

1. After short absences, a verbal interview with the parent or caregiver and a careful morning inspection will determine whether or not the child is well enough to return to the center.
2. After an absence of two weeks or more because of illness of any kind, a physician's permission must be obtained before the child returns to the center.
3. After an absence of two months or more because of illness, a new physician's preadmission form must be obtained.
4. A child may return to the center after chicken pox when all blisters have developed scabs. The scabs need not all be gone.
5. A child who has had mumps can return to the center when all swelling has subsided. If the swelling was only on one side, the child must wait an additional 24 hours to see if the other side will swell.

G26 Request to Administer Medication

At your child care center, medication should be administered to a child only upon written request of the parents or caregivers. The medication must be in its original container with the child's name and directions for use clearly marked. Check with your local licensing agency for regulations on administering medications, whether prescription or over-the-counter. Parents and caregivers are asked to arrange times of multiple doses in such a way that you do not find yourselves administering medication during the first two hours of arrival nor the last two hours before departure. Thus, the majority of medications are timed to be given only at 10:00 A.M. and 3:00 P.M. (if two doses are given). If only one dose, try to have the parents or caregivers time it around noon. By standardizing the times, you will find it easier to handle the process, as opposed to having a steady stream of children receiving medication all through the day.

The following procedures are recommended:

1. Parents or caregivers bring medication. Place it in a locked cupboard. If it needs to be refrigerated, place it in a locked container kept in the refrigerator for that purpose.
2. Parents or caregivers write down request [Section G26].
3. Notes are sent to each child care room, letting each child care provider know if any children are on medication, and what time to send them to the office.
4. All medications are administered by the office staff or director only.
5. Any medications still at the school on Friday are sent home. Ongoing daily medications must be resupplied each Monday.

Form for Request to Administer Medication

Community Child Care Center

111 THIRD STREET ✿ TELEPHONE 123-4579

INSTRUCTIONS: Please fill out columns 1–4 completely in order to ensure that medication will be administered. When it is administered, the individual doing so will write down the time of administration and initial it.

Name of Child	Medication	Requested by	Dose	Time	Given by	Time	Given by

G28 Incubation Chart for Common Communicable Diseases

At your child care center, you can allow a child who has been exposed to a communicable disease to attend your center after the end of the incubation period. On rare occasions, you may want to close the center for a day or two to minimize the chance of an epidemic. Whatever policy you want to adopt, just remember that while most cases of childhood diseases are mild, there are some which are serious enough to warrant every precaution.

DISEASE	SYMPTOMS	INCUBATION PERIOD	DURATION OF CONTAGION	PREVENTIVE MEASURES
Bacterial meningitis	Listlessness, sleeps extensively, acts "dopey," has been sick but doesn't seem to be getting better, may have stiff neck. Bacteria is called Haemophilus Influenza Type B, but is not a flu.	Indefinite	Indefinite	Vaccine is called HIB. Recommended for children between the ages of two and five years. Children in child care centers should be given the vaccine at 18 months, although its effectiveness at that age is not as great as at age two.
Chicken pox	Aching muscles and fever. Small blister-like pimples appear, on which scabs later form.	14–21 days, usually 14–15	Normally 6 days after outbreak	Check with your local health department or physician for the latest information about a vaccine. There is a natural immunity after recovery from the disease.
Common cold	Runny nose, sneezing, coughing, may have watery eyes, listless.	1–2 days	Varies, may attend center if no fever	Hand-washing, good hygiene, when coughing or sneezing keep mouth covered, preferably with a cleansing tissue.
Diphtheria	Grayish membrane on throat and tonsils. Fever; rapid pulse; enlarged neck glands; and sometimes a thick, yellowish discharge from the nose.	2–7 days most common	1–2 days if treated with antibiotics, 2–4 weeks if not	Immunizations during infancy and early childhood, avoidance of contact with anyone who has the disease.
Gastroenteritis, viral (diarrhea)	Diarrhea—loose, soft, watery stools may be light yellow-brown to green-brown, stomachache, feeling of nausea.	2–7 days most common	Varies, may return to center when diarrhea stops	Careful hand-washing with soap.
Herpes, oral (cold sores)	Blisters in mouth, on lips, or near mouth. First open, then develop dark crust. Once a person has had herpes, it may reappear often. No need to exclude from center.	Usually 2–12 days	Variable	Good hygiene, avoid contact with an open sore.

DISEASE	SYMPTOMS	INCUBATION PERIOD	DURATION OF CONTAGION	PREVENTIVE MEASURES
Impetigo	Blisters on skin that open, then develop yellowish crust. Child may attend cemter if under treatment and sores are covered with sterile dressing.	Variable	Most contagious first 24 hours after sores appear	Hand-washing with soap, good hygiene, clean fingernails, avoid direct contact.
Influenza (haemophilus) H flu type B	Headache, sore throat, accompanied by fever.	1–3 days	Varies, may return to center when temperature is normal for 24 hours	A vaccine is available; usually used with children only if they are suffering a chronic disease.
Measles, German (rubella)	Slight fever, swollen glands behind the ears and on neck. Flat reddish-pink rash on the head and/or body. Rash does not itch.	14–21 days	4–5 days duration	Immunization available, required for children before they start child care. (Women of childbearing age who have not had German measles should be vaccinated against it. The disease can cause birth defects.)
Measles (rubeola)	Fever, cough, runny nose, followed by rash in 4 days. Eyes may be very red. Rash usually starts on some part of face and spreads downward. Miniature pimples may appear in mouth prior to outbreak.	7–14 days; usually 9–11	Usually 7–8 days, until rash is gone	Vaccine available. Required before starting child care.
Mumps	Headache, fever, sometimes irritation in the mouth; the salivary glands between ear and chin swell painfully.	11–26 days; usually 17-19	Until the swelling is gone	Natural immunity when young and after having disease. Shots available if physician thinks prevention after exposure is important for a particular individual.
Pinkeye	Eyes are reddened, inner lids may be very red, eyelids may have slight discharge, may become encrusted. (Allergic conjunctivitis is similar in appearance, but is not contagious. When in doubt, a physician should be consulted.)	1–3 days	2–5 days, may return to center when redness and discharge are gone	Good hygiene and hand-washing with soap.
Ringworm	Flat, scaly spots on skin, usually in circular shape, but may be irregular. May have raised borders around them. Borders may be slightly red in color.	4–10 days (skin); 10–20 days (scalp)	Varies, may attend child care if all spots are covered	Good hygiene, hand-washing, avoid contact with infected areas.
Scabies	Tiny red bumps or blisters, severe itching.	First time: 1 month; reinfection: 2–5 days	Varies, may return to center if under physician's care for the infection	Avoiding close contact with someone who is infected.

DISEASE	SYMPTOMS	INCUBATION PERIOD	DURATION OF CONTAGION	PREVENTIVE MEASURES
Scarlet fever	Varies. Usually very high fever; red, sore throat and tonsils, and furred tongue. On second day, a bright scarlet rash appears on the face and gradually spreads over the rest of the body during the 2 days that follow.	1–7 days	Contagious for 24 hours after being treated with antibiotics	Preventive measures unknown. Antibiotics should be administered if contact with the disease is suspected.
Strep throat	Headache, nausea, fever, extreme soreness in throat.	1–7 days, usually 2–5	7–10 days, until all symptoms and soreness are gone	None. Can be minimized by use of antibiotics after exposure.
Whooping cough* (pertussis)	Runny nose, dry cough, and slight fever, as with ordinary cold. Worsens after a few days. Nasal discharge thickens and coughing becomes very severe and occurs in continuous minute-long bouts. After such a bout, child gasps for breath, making a "whooping" sound.	7–14 days	7 days if on antibiotics, 3 weeks if not	Immunization.

* Has not been common in recent years, but panic over vaccine may cause disease to become more prevalent [Section G29].

G29 Immunizations

Periodically, public concern arises out of fear that immunization for certain diseases may be more harmful than the disease itself. Children need immunizations to protect them from certain childhood diseases. Some of these diseases have caused complications and death in children. Before the development of the pertussis vaccine, the death rate from whooping cough was so high that its advantage far outweighs the slight risk of administering it. Vaccines prevent children from getting the following diseases:

- Measles
- Mumps
- Polio
- Rubella (German measles)
- Pertussis
- Diphtheria
- Tetanus
- Haemophilus influenza type B (HIB disease)
- Hepatitis B
- Varicella (chicken pox)

Children must be immunized beginning at birth. Most vaccinations are completed by age two. All children in your care should not be admitted in your center until all necessary immunizations are met. This will protect children in your care from getting infected and protect the infection of others. Children under five years of age are susceptible to diseases because their immune systems have not built up the defenses to fight the diseases. Inform parents and caregivers of their responsibility to immunize their children. Help them find programs in your community that may offer free vaccines, if needed.

The following is a list of vaccinations that are recommended by age two and are given in five visits:

- 1 vaccination against measles/mumps/rubella
- 4 vaccinations against HIB
- 3 vaccinations against polio
- 4 vaccinations against diphtheria, tetanus, and pertussis
- 3 vaccinations against hepatitis B
- 1 vaccination against varicella

Check with your local health department for the recommended childhood immunization schedule. These schedules should be posted at your center and given to families when they enroll their children in your care.

G30 Immunizations: Exemption Form

Families who have concerns about vaccinations are required to furnish your child care center with the following form:

Community Child Care Center

111 THIRD STREET TELEPHONE 123-4579

EXEMPTION FROM REQUIRED IMMUNIZATIONS

Name of child: ____________________ Date of birth: __________

I request that the above named child be excused from the required immunizations for the following reasons:

____

____

Signed: ____________________
(parent or caregiver)

Date: ____________________

Verification (must be by a physician or clergy):

I hereby verify the reason(s) given for the above request:

Signed: ____________________
(physician or clergy)

G31 Health Education of Children

The health program of the Community Child Care Center encompasses the health education of children.

CHECK ONE: YES	NO	ITEM	LEARNING EXPERIENCE
____	____	1. Child care provider explains to children reason for the morning health check.	Children understand the adult's interest in their health.
____	____	2. Child care provider explains why they are being sent home for illness.	Children understand that home care will help them get well.
____	____	3. Child care provider explains why it is important for children to tell an adult if they feel ill or have been hurt at the center.	Children understand that an adult will try to help them feel better. They learn that they are responsible for their own health awareness.
____	____	4. Children make get-well cards for children who are at home sick.	Children develop concern for the welfare of others. Sick children are encouraged by hearing from the center. It develops their ego and sense of self-awareness.
____	____	5. Give children eye tests [Section G17].	Children learn the importance of eye care.
____	____	6. Give children hearing tests [Section G17].	Children learn the importance of ear care.
____	____	7. Children may use a dramatic play kit containing items for playing roles of doctor, nurse, dentist, and ambulance driver.	Helps children to be comfortable in medical situations.
____	____	8. Child care provider takes younger children to toilet at regular intervals and shows the correct use [Section I9].	Children develop the ability to take care of their own toilet needs.
____	____	9. Children learn that they always wash their hands with soap after using the toilet [Section I9].	Children establish habits of good hygiene.
____	____	10. Children are instructed in the use and disposal of cleansing tissues.	Children learn hygienic use of tissues, to cover mouth when coughing, and mouth and nose when sneezing.
____	____	11. Children are taught how to use the drinking fountain.	Children learn not to put their mouths directly on the fountain; learn to control water for proper use.

CHECK ONE: YES	NO	ITEM	LEARNING EXPERIENCE
____	____	12. Children learn the proper way to brush teeth. To the tune of "Here We Go Round the Mulberry Bush," children sing, "This is the way we brush our teeth."	Children learn the importance of taking care of their teeth and the proper way to do so; lessens possible fear of the dentist.
____	____	13. Food is served in a low-stress atmosphere.	Children learn to eat in a relaxed manner.
____	____	14. Children are given opportunities to rest and relax. Child care provider explains why rest is important and teaches relaxation techniques and stress-reduction games.	Children learn the importance of resting and ways to achieve relaxation.
____	____	15. Children learn to recognize their own cots and bedding.	Children learn sanitary precautions of napping only on their own cots.
____	____	16. Children are continuously given lessons on and examples of wholesome nutritional practices.	Children gain knowledge of wholesome nutrition.
____	____	17. Children are given education on proper and improper "touching" and caution in regard to possible sexual abuse.	Children learn about their personal rights.

G32 Tub for Emergency Bathing

A fairly large tub or dishpan, a bar of soap, washcloths, and clean towels should be kept available for emergency use. After a toilet accident, especially in the case of diarrhea, bathing will make the child feel more comfortable.

G33 Posture Development

1. Tables and chairs should be of proper size for age of children. Chairs for two- and three-year-olds should be 10" or 11" high. Tables for this age group should be 18" or 19". Chairs for four-, five-, and six-year-olds should be 12" or 13" high. Tables should be 20" or 21". If you have children of different ages and can only have one size of chair, a 12" height is recommended. Ideally, children should be able to put both feet on the floor while sitting in a chair.
2. Children should not be made to sit for long periods of time.
3. Arrange the room in a way that will encourage children to move around. For example, it is not necessary to place tables right next to the shelves for table toys.
4. Children should be discouraged from sitting on the floor with their feet under them. Legs should be folded in front or spread outward.

5. Provide pillows, rugs, beanbag chairs, and similar items for children to use instead of chairs.
6. Things to observe:
   - How does the child walk? Move through room? Sit? Perform on equipment?
   - How are the child's coordination and manual dexterity?

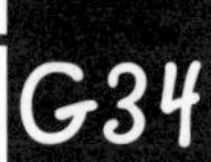

G34 Provisions for Vigorous Indoor Activity During Inclement Weather

When the weather keeps children from playing outdoors, give them an opportunity for some vigorous indoor activities. At such times the rhythmic activity and music programs can be extended, alternating with short rest periods, to give children a chance to run, jump, roll on the floor, rock on their stomachs, spin like tops, hop, and make similar movements. You might encourage children to shout for brief periods. That will make it easier for them to keep their voices at an appropriate level for the indoor environment at other times.

When pursuing vigorous activities indoors, be sure children do not become overheated, overstimulated, or overtired. Allowing plenty of time between each separate activity can help in that regard. When nearing the end of the period, slow activities down gradually before asking children to rest. Allow a "cooling down" time. After the activity period, give children a cool drink and a restful time of quiet activities.

G35 Drinking Water

Active young children frequently get very thirsty. For their physical comfort and for the promotion of good health habits, have drinking water readily available both indoors and out. If you do not have a drinking fountain, you can keep a covered pitcher of fresh water and disposable water cups on hand. The pitcher should be refilled with fresh water at least once an hour. An inexpensive water bubbler for the playground can be attached to any ordinary faucet. Be sure to instruct children to keep their mouths off the fixture. You may also keep bottled spring water at the center. It's expensive, but it's one way to encourage the development of a water-drinking habit in young children.

G36 Precautionary Measures in Dress According to Changes in Weather and Other Health Factors

It is easier to remove an unneeded sweater than not to have one when needed. Sweaters and jackets should be taken off and put on during the day according to changing weather. Several thin layers of clothing give better protection than one heavy one.

Some children perspire freely and are very wet and warm after active physical play or when awakening after a nap. Change children's shirts if necessary; dry their faces, necks, and arms with a towel; wipe their faces with a cool, damp cloth; and have them rinse their hands in cool water for 60 seconds. You may also have them rest quietly for five minutes.

G37 If Parent/Caregiver Wants Child to Stay Inside

Sometimes a parent or caregiver may ask you to keep a child indoors during the playground period. However, your ability to oblige depends on the room arrangements, the total number of children present on a particular day, the number of adults available for supervising the children, and other such factors. Perhaps you can arrange for a child who must stay indoors to visit another room, or look at a book or pursue some other quiet activity in the director's office. One of the advantages of having an open schedule in which children can move freely indoors or out during play hours [Section E26] is that there is always supervision in the child care room.

Sometimes a child will prefer not to go outside on a particular day or at a particular time. Even though it would be good for the child to play outside, children's feelings and moods must be respected. If you are truly dedicated to treating children according to their individual needs and capacities, you will find it easy to make special arrangements to meet those needs.

If someone doesn't want to go outdoors when the rest of the group is going, try to find out why. Perhaps the child is feeling tired and wants to rest or pursue quiet activities. The child may be feeling lonely and wants the security of staying in the room. The child may be coming down with an illness or may simply want to stay inside because of a feeling for completing the rhythm of what had been going on in his or her body and mind. Sometimes children really feel the need to be quiet and alone for just a little while, just as adults sometimes do.

Children who do not want to go outdoors over a long period of time simply because they prefer indoor activities should be told from time to time, "Now it's time to go outdoors." Let them know you understand that they would rather be indoors, but that you think it would be good for them to pursue some outdoor activities for at least ten minutes—or 20, or 30. If you have been flexible and understanding, they will accept your right to make such a request.

If a parent or caregiver does not want a child to go outdoors at all over a long period of time, other action is necessary. The parent or caregiver can be requested to have a new physician's report completed [Section E18], affirming that the child is physically and emotionally unable to participate in outdoor activities.

G38 Rest and Relaxation

Young children respond best to programs that alternate active play with quiet activities [Section E26]. It is sometimes necessary to give a particular child or an entire group some extra rest for brief periods if they become overstimulated. Child care providers often find it difficult to quiet children who have been playing busily and noisily. When they do quiet the children, it is all too often done to give the child care provider some rest or a break, not for the benefit of the children.

Although the purpose of resting is to offset fatigue, both mental and physical, it is of minimum benefit to children's physical health and emotional growth unless they are truly relaxed. They need to be fully involved with the quiet time, the resting period. They need to have help being involved with relaxation.

Relaxation is a skill that can be learned. Child care providers should be given in-service training to remind them of ways to help children become involved with relaxation. Some suggestions to have posted in each room are:

1. Create a restful, relaxing environment.
2. Tell a quiet story.
3. Tell an "eyes-closed" story.
4. Sing soft lullabies.
5. Play gentle music.
6. Ways to rest: head on table, on mats on floor, on cots, on pillows.
7. Play rhythmic movement resting games.
8. Touch children to reassure them; "love" will help them relax.
9. Play finger games; look at books; have quiet conversations.
10. Teach muscle tension ("tight") and relaxation ("loose") by going through the parts of the body, one by one.
11. Obtain a book, such as *Think of Something Quiet* (by Clare Cherry, Fearon Teacher Aids) and do the activities recommended for relaxation.

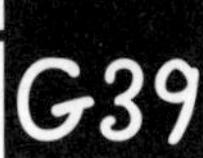

Family Education for Health

Through newsletters, parent/caregiver meetings, center visits, group projects, and other means of communication, families should be encouraged to support the center's program geared toward the development of good health habits for their children. Topics to be addressed might include the following:

- Physical fitness: movement through exercise; vigorous outdoor play, which includes running, jumping, and climbing; and many opportunities to walk.
- Nutritional health
  - Eating a balanced diet [Section K5]
  - Eating a good breakfast before coming to preschool, if breakfast is not served at the center
  - Not eating between meals or at bedtime, except for planned nutritional snacks
  - Not eating unwholesome foods, such as sugar, pastry, chips, cola drinks, chocolate, and so on [Section K5]
- Go to bed early enough to get approximately ten hours of sleep, plus additional rest periods during the day.
- Drink approximately six small glasses of water a day.
- Frequent enough washing and bathing to keep the body clean.
- Some time outdoors each day.
- Practice in relaxation.

Emotional Health of Children

A well-planned program is sensitive to the emotional well-being of the child. The director must recognize signals of possible emotional disturbance, such as those listed here. Staff must be able to recognize these signals, too. It is also important to note any changes from previous levels of functioning.

Checklist for Signals of Possible Emotional Problems

___ Listlessness

___ Frequent temper tantrums

___ Easily distracted from an activity

___ Lack of interest in surroundings

___ Lack of interest in other children

___ Inability to relate to adults

___ Destructiveness

___ Extreme nervousness

___ Extreme irritableness

___ Cries easily

___ Frequently drops things

___ Frequently bumps into things

___ Frequently stumbles

___ Unusually shy, quiet

___ Unusually aggressive, loud

___ Frequently hitting or biting other children

___ Frequently hiding

___ Frequently attempting to run away

___ Inability to relax or rest

___ Inability to move body rhythmically to given beat

___ Excessive need to urinate

___ Excessive thirst

___ Excessively inattentive

___ Overanxious about doing what is expected, or doing things "right"

___ Seldom laughs or smiles

___ Has frequent headaches

___ Has frequent stomachaches

___ Falls asleep during play activities

___ Is unable to locate the various parts of his or her body

___ Is unable to follow directions

___ Is unable to move easily through a room or through an obstacle course

Many of these symptoms may indicate physical problems. Some may be signs that the child has a perceptual-motor problem. However, symptoms that are caused by physical or perceptual difficulty may lead to emotional disturbances unless the adults know what the difficulty is and seek to correct it.

Please remember that many of these symptoms need not be taken too seriously if they are only evidenced on occasion. The child may only be trying to determine what acceptable behavior is and how control can be gained. But when any of these symptoms becomes excessive, there is cause for real concern.

If you have a child in your center who displays any of the foregoing characteristics, arrange to consult with a mental health counselor who would be able to work with you and the staff in the evaluation of this behavior. Inviting such a person to speak at a staff meeting could be a valuable part of your in-service training program.

To maintain an environment and pursue a program of activities and experiences geared toward meeting the emotional needs of children, you should include

- comfortable lighting.
- sufficient space for comfort and safety.
- good ventilation.
- harmonious color planning.

- plants in each room to increase production of oxygen.
- good acoustical planning to minimize the reverberation of sound.
- adequate timing to prevent the need for constant hurrying.
- sufficient supervision to allow for giving consideration to individual needs and interests.
- sufficient planning to eliminate the need for constant restrictions and too many rules.

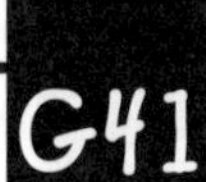

G41 Child Abuse

Harm to or neglect of a child by another person, whether by another child or an adult, is child abuse.

It can happen within all cultures, income groups, and ethnicities. The abuse may cause severe injury to a child and can result in death. There are four categories of child abuse. They are *neglect, emotional/verbal abuse, physical abuse,* and *sexual abuse.* In most cases of sexual abuse, the child knows the offender, and the offender is a member of the child's household in 50% of the cases. In the United States, statistics show that one out of four females are sexually abused as children and one out of ten males have been sexually assaulted before they reach 18 years of age.

Neglect

It is especially urgent that all staff persons be alert to any signs of neglect of a child

- left alone at home or left with a young sibling in charge.
- not bathed or cleaned over a long period of time.
- not fed at home.
- left locked in automobile while parent(s) or caregivers(s) are busy with their own pursuits.
- not given medical attention for serious illness.

Emotional/Verbal Abuse

In determining emotional or verbal abuse, it is difficult today to clarify between verbal abuse by one or more persons in the child's home and the language of verbal abuse picked up from inappropriate television programs.

Look for emotional/verbal abuse if a child

- uses violence and extreme verbal abuse in dealing with others.
- acts out violence and extreme verbal abuse in dramatic play activities.
- is extremely withdrawn.
- is overly aggressive.
- is depressed.
- afraid to go home.
- shies away from physical contact with adults, parents, or caregivers.

Physical Abuse

- Numerous bumps, bruises, cuts, and scratches on body
- One portion of body extremely red, as though struck

- Burn or scald marks
- Numerous breaks, fractures
- Lengthy stories by parent or caregiver about how a particular trauma happened
- Refusal by child to explain how a trauma happened
- Drawing back, retreating, when approached by an adult
- Putting hands up in front of face as though protecting self when approached by an adult
- Dressed in long sleeves or long pants on a hot day
- Bizarre actions which may indicate child has been given illegal drugs
- Any change in normal behavior patterns
- Disagreement between the child's explanation and the parent or caregiver's explanation about the injury

Sexual Abuse

- Reluctance to attend the center or to return home, or to go wherever the abuse may be taking place
- Pain, itching, bleeding, or bruises in genital or anal areas
- Discharge from vagina or penis; blood on undergarments
- Need for frequent urination
- Difficulty or discomfort in walking or sitting or both
- Unusually high interest in sexual matters
- Masturbation in front of others; increased and excessive masturbation
- Overtired, listless, sleepy
- Withdrawn
- Change in relationships with peers
- Inflicts pain on self; accident-prone
- Refusal to eat
- Reversion to infantile behavior
- Renewal of bedwetting; possibly wetting underpants as well
- Evidence of a venereal disease
- Acts out sexual abuse in dramatic play activities with peers, in housekeeping and doll areas, or even through drawings
- Hesitancy to ride a tricycle
- Someone other than parents or caregivers brings child later than usual more than once
- Any change in normal behavior patterns
- Unusual stories told by the child, designed to draw attention by reporting imaginary traumatic happenings at home; this can be a way of saying "help"

Be especially concerned when there are clusters of the above warning signals.

To prevent child abuse from occurring at your center, implement the following policies:

1. Make sure that all employees are fingerprinted and criminal background checks have been done.
2. Provide yearly training on child abuse prevention, CPR, first aid and health and safety practices.

3. Employees are never left alone with a child. There is always another child, parent, caregiver, or staff member present. If you find yourself alone with a child, prop the door open and make sure any windows are not obstructed.
4. Bathrooms are always checked before a child is allowed to use them, especially on a field trip or at a park. Restroom use outside of the child care center must be supervised by a staff member.
5. As children enter and exit the bathroom facilities, they are always in view of a staff member.
6. There are separate bathroom facilities for preschool and school-age children.
7. Document when visible all marks, bruises, scratches, and so on, on children when they enter the facility.
8. Any bruises, scratches, and so on on a child when playing at the facility must be documented and reported to the parent or caregiver.
9. All staff is mandated to report any suspected child abuse. Report all injuries and incidents to your local licensing agency as well as your local child protective services.

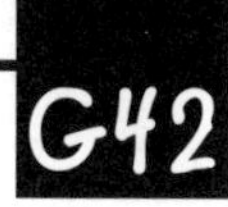

Disclosure and Reporting Abuse

A child may tell you about abuse in various ways. They may give you an indirect hint, such as "My babysitter bothers me," "Daddy hates me," or "Jimmy wears funny underwear." They may try to disguise the disclosure or have strings attached to the disclosure, such as "What would happen if a girl told that she was being molested and they didn't believe her?" or "I have something to tell you, but you have to promise not to tell anyone." However a child chooses to tell you about the abuse, try to find a private place to talk. Make sure that the door is kept open or that you can be observed. Try not to panic. Believe that the child is telling you the truth. Use the child's vocabulary. Reassure the child that it is good to tell and that you will do your best to protect him or her. Determine if the child is in immediate danger and let him or her know what you will do. Report the abuse to the proper authorities. Your role is to investigate the situation. You have a responsibility to report it to the proper authorities. This gets the process rolling for getting help for the child.

You can send home information on abuse and inform the parents and caregivers that the director and other staff members have the responsibility of reporting any suspected cases of abuse. You can also give out a notice similar to the following at time of enrollment:

Community Child Care Center

111 THIRD STREET ✿ TELEPHONE 123-4579

To parents and caregivers of children enrolled in our program:

We want you to know that we are keenly attuned to public concern about the prevalence of child physical and sexual abuse and neglect. You are ultimately responsible for your own child. If you have any questions or doubts about our program or employees, please talk to our director for clarification. Please keep the following information. Note: Insert the appropriate phone numbers for your area.

Situation	Police or Sheriff	City or County Children's Protective Services	State or Local Licensing
If you have reason to believe that a child is being abused, whether the abuser is a family member, friend, neighbor, or casual acquaintance, immediately telephone:			
If you have reason to believe a stranger has sexually abused a child, immediately telephone:			
If you have reason to believe that a child is being abused at a school or child care facility, immediately telephone:			

A portion of the State Penal Code reads as follows [change according to your state codes]: ". . . certain professionals and laypersons must report suspected abuse to the proper authorities. The mandated reporters include . . . child care custodians, teachers, licensed child care workers, foster parents, social workers, medical practitioners, public health employees, counselors, religious practitioners who treat children, and employees of a child protective agency, including sheriffs, probation officers, and welfare department employees." We want you to know that as child care custodians and child care providers, our staff, being mandated reporters, will comply with these provisions.

G43 After Reporting Abuse

If you have reported a suspected child abuse case to the authorities, great care should be taken in helping children and their families through the investigative period. Assure them that your report is confidential. Encourage open communication and efforts to keep one another informed of any progress made. There is often a great deal of red tape involved. Families will need your help. Perhaps you can speed things up by arranging for private counseling immediately while waiting for the official investigation to be completed.

Always keep the attitude that yours is a helping role, not a punitive one.

Resources for Health and Social Services Information Referrals

Be sure to keep a list of people and organizations that can help you with the physical and mental health problems that you will encounter from time to time. This information is only useful if you make it useful. Fill in the spaces in the chart provided for your local resources. Then send out letters to those organizations with which you would like to establish contact. Here is a form letter you can use:

Community Child Care Center

111 THIRD STREET TELEPHONE 123-4579

Name of organization: ______________________

Address: ________________________________

____

Dear Sir or Madam:

Please send me the following information:

What pamphlets, if any, do you publish?

What services do you provide?

Is there a local or state branch of your organization to which we can apply for services or information? If so, please let me know where it is located and whom I should contact.

Very sincerely yours,

Director

Referral Services Resource Chart

Consult the organizations listed on the following pages for help in arranging referrals for children with special problems. You might also find it helpful to fill in the addresses and phone numbers of the local branches of these organizations. For a more complete guide to listings such as these, write to American Public Health Services, 1790 Broadway, New York, NY 10019. They publish *Guide to Services.*

ORGANIZATION	NEAREST BRANCH
Vision American Foundation for the Blind, Inc. 11 Pennsylvania Plaza New York, NY 10001-0000 (212) 502-7600 www.afb.org	Telephone ____________ Address ____________ ____________
Illinois Society for the Prevention of Blindness 407 S. Dearborn Street, Suite 1000 Chicago, IL 60605 (312) 922-8710	Telephone ____________ Address ____________ ____________
Lions Clubs International 300 West 22nd Street Hinsdale, IL 60570-0001 (630) 571-5466 (630) 571-6533	Telephone ____________ Address ____________ ____________
Local ophthalmologist	Telephone ____________ Address ____________ ____________
Hearing National Association for Hearing and Speech Action 10801 Rockville Pike Rockville, MD 20852 (301) 897-8682	Telephone ____________ Address ____________ ____________
Local audiologist	Telephone ____________ Address ____________ ____________
Dental American Dental Association 211 East Chicago Avenue Chicago, IL 60611 (312) 440-2500 www.ada.org	Telephone ____________ Address ____________ ____________
Local dental clinic	Telephone ____________ Address ____________ ____________
Local children's dentist	Telephone ____________ Address ____________ ____________

ORGANIZATION	NEAREST BRANCH
Mental Health National Mental Health Association 1021 Prince Street Alexandria, VA 22314 (703) 684-7722 www.nmha.org	Telephone __________ Address __________ __________
The Arc A National Association on Mental Retardation National Headquarters P.O. Box 1047 Arlington, TX 76010 (817) 261-6003 www.thearc.org	Telephone __________ Address __________ __________
Local mental health association	Telephone __________ Address __________ __________
Local child psychologist	Telephone __________ Address __________ __________
Local child psychiatrist	Telephone __________ Address __________ __________
Psychological testing clinics	Telephone __________ Address __________ __________
Speech National Association for Hearing and Speech Action 10801 Rockville Pike Rockville, MD 20852 (301) 897-8682	Telephone __________ Address __________ __________
Local speech therapist	Telephone __________ Address __________ __________

ORGANIZATION	NEAREST BRANCH
Other Health American Diabetes Association National Office 1701 North Beauregard Street Alexandria, VA 22311 1-800-DIABETES www.diabetes.org	Telephone ____________ Address ____________ ____________
American Red Cross 11th Floor 1621 N. Kent Street Arlington, VA 22209 (703) 248-4222 www.redcross.org	Telephone ____________ Address ____________ ____________
Muscular Dystrophy Association 3300 E. Sunrise Drive Tucson, AZ 85718 1-800-572-1717 www.mdausa.org	Telephone ____________ Address ____________ ____________
National Multiple Sclerosis Society 733 3rd Avenue New York, NY 10017 (212) 986-3240 1-800-FIGHT-MS www.nmss.org	Telephone ____________ Address ____________ ____________
March of Dimes Birth Defects Foundation 1275 Mamaroneck Avenue White Plains, NY 10605 (914) 428-7100 1-888-MODIMES www.modimes.org	Telephone ____________ Address ____________ ____________
National Center for Education in Maternal and Child Health 2000 15th Street North, Suite 701 Arlington, VA 22201-2617 (703) 524-7802 www.ncemch.org	Telephone ____________ Address ____________ ____________
National Safety Council (Local telephone book)	Telephone ____________ Address ____________ ____________

ORGANIZATION	NEAREST BRANCH
National Easter Seal Society 230 West Monroe Street, Suite 1800 Chicago, IL 60606 (312) 726-6200 1-800-221-6827 www.easter-seals.org	Telephone ____________ Address ____________ ____________
United Cerebral Palsy Associations 1600 L Street, NW Washington, DC 20036-5602 (202) 776-0406 1-800-USA-5-UCP www.ucpa.org	Telephone ____________ Address ____________ ____________
Visiting Nurse Association (Local telephone book)	Telephone ____________ Address ____________ ____________
Family Alliance for Children and Families 1701 K Street, NW Suite 200 Washington, DC 20006-1503 (202) 223-3447 1-800-220-1016 www.alliance1.org	Telephone ____________ Address ____________ ____________
American Public Human Services Association 801 First Street, NE Suite 500 Washington, DC 20002-4267 (202) 682-0100 www.aphsa.org	Telephone ____________ Address ____________ ____________
Parents Anonymous 675 W. Foothill Blvd., Suite 220 Claremont, CA 91711-3475 (909) 621-6184 www.parentsanonymous-natl.org	Telephone ____________ Address ____________ ____________
Parents Without Partners 1650 South Dixie Highway, Suite 510 Boca Raton, FL 33432 (561) 391-8833 www.parentswithoutpartners.org	Telephone ____________ Address ____________ ____________

Record of Referrals Made

This record of referrals made will enable you to gather information as to the validity of referrals and the validity of each of the agencies used. It will be of service when a similar problem arises at a future date.

NAME OF CHILD	PROBLEM	REFERRED TO	DATE

Results:

Results:

Results:

NAME OF CHILD	PROBLEM	REFERRED TO	DATE

Results:

Results:

Results:

H

Safety

1 Assuming Responsibility for Children at Your Center
2 Safety Responsibilities
3 Legal Responsibility and Liability
4 Liability Insurance
5 Safety Rules
6 Clothing Safety
7 Hazardous Conditions
8 Safety Evaluation
9 The Accident-Prone Child
10 Emergency Evacuation and Disaster Plans
11 Disaster Drills
12 Air Pollution
13 Security
14 Automobile Safety
15 Transporting Children
16 Street Safety
17 Traffic Game
18 Parking Lot Safety
19 Lead Poisoning
20 Safety Precautions with Toys
21 Safety Precautions According to Age Differences

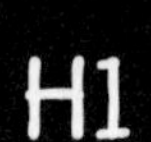

H1 Assuming Responsibility for Children at Your Center

At the time of enrollment, parents and caregivers should be asked to sign certain statements in regard to the center's responsibility for their children [Sections E14, E20]. Parents and caregivers need to be clearly informed that the center will not assume responsibility for children who have not been signed in when they arrive for the day. After they have been signed in, the center and its staff are responsible for them until they are signed out. It is the responsibility of the center to make sure that no child is picked up without a staff member's knowledge and that no child is released to any unauthorized person. Parents and caregivers are also informed that the center cannot be responsible for their children if the information given to the center at the time of their enrollment is false.

H2 Safety Responsibilities

Anticipation
Anticipate possible hazards and take the necessary precautionary and preventive measures.

Supervision
Responsible and adequate supervision is the most important factor in the prevention of accidental injury.

Guidelines
By offering guidelines, including prohibitive rules, you can teach the child some principles of self-protection. All rules must be explained to the child in simple, precise language. The rules will only be effective if the child is helped to understand correct and incorrect actions.

Space
If at least 75 square feet of outdoor space and 35 square feet of indoor space per child are provided, overcrowding will not be a hazard.

Time
Allow plenty of time so that rushing and hurrying do not cause accidents.

Understanding
These principles must be tempered with an understanding of the needs of children. You must avoid getting so caught up in these principles that children are inhibited in their natural tendencies to explore, climb, build vertically, jump, or seek adventure. Children are naturally full of curiosity.

They frequently act on impulse. It is our responsibility to see that we have prepared the center environment so that safety restrictions are minimal and thus more easily emphasized.

Trust
Understanding must be accompanied by a strong sense of trust in children and faith in their ability to recognize your trust, and to respond to it in a positive manner by more readily reacting to required safety precautions. Trust, however, does not in any

way imply that you expect them to have the ability to judge for themselves the safeness of their actions. Such judgment will only come through a combination of responsible and helpful supervision coupled with their growing maturity.

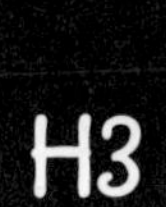

H3 Legal Responsibility and Liability

If the child care facility is owned by a corporation, the corporation is liable in case of legal action stemming from injury to a child. In centers that are not incorporated, both the owners and the staff members or other adults involved can be held liable for accidental injury to a child. In any case, you should be aware that the center will be held responsible for any injury if negligence can be proved. Areas of negligence include, but are not limited to, the following:

- Improper or insufficient supervision, especially if it is less than the legal adult-to-child ratio [Section A8]
- Defective equipment
- Defective building
- Inadequate protective fencing
- Lack of handrails for stairs
- Unsafe ground conditions
- Unsafe floor conditions
- Allowing a child to enroll without a health report from a licensed physician [Section E18]
- Allowing a child to remain at the center if lack of self-control makes the child dangerous to self or others [Section G40]
- Employing a staff member or using the regular services of a volunteer who does not have a health clearance from a physician. (This applies to student teachers, child care assistants, substitutes, and trainees, as well as regular staff.)
- Failure to notify parents, guardians, or a physician when a child is seriously ill or injured [Section E20]
- Failure to have a plan for evacuating the building in case of fire [Sections H10–11]
- Failure to notify staff members of a child's physical, emotional, or health problems that warrant special consideration, such as allergies, epilepsy, hearing or visual problems, recent illness, or family problems [Sections G12–15]
- Misrepresentation in obtaining fire, health, sanitation, building safety, and other permits that are required by state and local regulations [Section A8]
- Failure to provide adequate refrigeration for food as necessary
- Unsanitary conditions, especially in regard to toilets, washbasins, and food-serving facilities
- Failure to vent gas heaters or to screen open fireplaces or free-standing heaters
- Failure to keep locks in good repair on doors and gates that lead to the street

Liability Insurance

Liability in case of accidental injury or possible neglect varies from state to state. A good insurance agent will advise you of your needs, according to law, for an adequate liability insurance plan. Insurance plans should provide protection for the operators of the center, the staff, volunteers, and visitors. Further protection is afforded by a good health and accident insurance plan, which should be spelled out in detail to all members of the center community. Adequate accident insurance coverage will frequently minimize the possibility of legal action in case of unintentional negligence or unavoidable accidents [Section A10].

In reviewing your policies, check to be sure you have earthquake or hurricane insurance if applicable to your area, and even insurance to cover expenses of a possible bomb threat.

H5 Safety Rules

Always tell children about the common dangers that concern them. Try to use words that are simple enough for them to understand, and repeat them often. Safety rules can include the following:

1. Such things as scissors and screwdrivers must be handled with care. They must be carried with the pointed end turned down and the handle pointed away from the body. They must always be put away immediately after use.
2. Sharp objects, small objects, rocks, sticks, toys, and other such items should be kept out of the mouth. They can be dangerous if swallowed. Also, a hole can be poked in the cheek or lip if the child falls down with something sharp in his or her mouth.
3. Only those electrical gadgets that are a part of the learning centers may be handled by children. Wall plugs and electric cords are not to be tampered with.
4. Matches are not to be used by children at any time.
5. Children must stop and look very carefully in both directions before they cross the street. Small children may not cross until an adult says it is safe. They must walk carefully—never run.
6. Playground equipment should be used with care. Explain to children that these rules are to prevent them from getting hurt or from hurting someone else.

H6 Clothing Safety

A good safety program for the child will include the following rules about dressing:

1. Long skirts can be dangerous when a child is going up and down steps or using playground equipment. For example, a child trying to get into a rocking boat might get a long skirt caught under the rocker and be unable to move out of the way safely as it rocks back and forth.
2. Dress clothes can also be unsafe when using playground equipment. Therefore, dress clothes may be worn only indoors.
3. Open-toed sandals often cause children to trip or stub their toes. Therefore, they may not be worn.
4. Shoes must be worn at all times when riding wheel toys.
5. Dress shoes sometimes have very slippery soles. They should not be worn to school unless they have composition or rubber soles.
6. Some rain hats cover the child's eyes. Rainy weather calls for unobstructed vision.
7. Dress clothes may cause children to be so self-conscious about keeping them clean that they become awkward in the use of play equipment.
8. Clothing with loose strings, especially around the neck, can get caught on playground equipment and strangle a child. Do not permit any child to play on equipment if he or she is wearing clothing with loose strings.

H7 Hazardous Conditions

Areas of Concern

Paint

Lead paint is poisonous. Use only lead-free paints. Read labels carefully.

Wax

Highly waxed floors may be slippery.

Spilled liquids

These should be cleaned up immediately. If necessary, you can throw newspapers and a cardboard box or a chair over the liquid until it can be wiped up.

Ice on sidewalk

Sprinkle salt over icy areas.

Sand on paved areas

Keep it swept up to avoid slipping.

Cracks in ground surfaces

Check for cracks periodically and repair any you find.

Garden tools

Do not leave these lying around. Children may trip over them.

Broken equipment

It should not be used until repaired.

Cleansing agents and other housekeeping supplies

These must be kept where children cannot reach them.

Doors, passageways

Keep them free of obstructions.

Rainy-day clothing

Wear bright colors that can be seen by automobile drivers.

Ropes

Ropes should be used only for supervised jump-rope activities.

Puddles

Close supervision is required.

Handrails

Teach children to use them.

Loose boards, protruding nails

Carpentry repairs should be made immediately as needed.

Broken gate

Provide substitute barrier until repair is made.

Clutter on floors

Clutter can be a hazard.

Electrical outlets

These should be covered at all times.

Heaters and fireplaces

Be sure they are screened.

Lighting

All play areas and passageways should be clearly illuminated.

Ball playing

Do not permit it in unfenced areas adjacent to a street. Even the most careful supervision cannot always prevent a child from suddenly darting out into the street to recover a ball.

Unsuitable equipment

Equipment should be geared to the preschool child.

Splintered wood

Sanding should be done as needed.

Paper cutter

Always keep it on a high shelf turned backward so that the handle cannot be raised. Always keep safety latch in place.

Matches

These should always be kept where they are inaccessible to the child.

Ant poison

Use sprays rather than leaving poisonous substances on the ground.

Poisonous plants

See Section C6.

Swimming pool

Even if the pool area is fenced, the gate must be kept locked when the pool is not being supervised.

Uncovered foods

They can be hazardous in warm or hot weather, or when flies are prevalent.

Flies and other insects

Consult a pest control company.

H8 Safety Evaluation

Once a month, assign a staff member to evaluate the safety features of the center. Other staff members should not know who is assigned the task for the month or when the check is being made. This periodic evaluation will help all staff members be more alert and will reinforce the importance of safety measures. (Use the following checklist to check each area.)

Area ______________________________

Is supervision strategically placed?
Is the flow of children being considered from a viewpoint of safety?
Is the equipment arranged in a safe manner?
Are playground rules being taught and reinforced?

H9 The Accident-Prone Child

It is not uncommon to have children enrolled in child care who appear to be accident-prone. It is important to make every effort to determine if there is any underlying physical cause. A child may have poor sensory-motor perception that interferes with receiving the necessary visual, auditory, and other signals to warn of potential dangers. If you feel there is possibility of a motor problem, it is best to document the incidents in the child's assessment and discuss them with the parents or caregivers. Special services should then be referred for the child.

H10 Emergency Evacuation and Disaster Plans

In case of fire, earthquake, flood, bomb threat, power outage, tornado, cyclone, and/or hurricane, there should be a written plan outlining emergency procedures and ongoing training for these procedures. Such plans should prepare for

- the safe evacuation of the premises.
- emergency care of children following the evacuation until they are reunited with their families.
- emergency care of children if confined within the building during a disaster.

The following is a plan that can be used as a guide to formulate procedures meeting the needs of your own area. If your child care center is located in an earthquake-prone area, there is a plan also provided specifically for earthquake preparedness. The same type of planning can be used in preparing for other natural or artificially created disasters.

Disaster Plan for the Community Child Care Center

I. Responsibility

A. Child Care Center

The center will retain responsibility of all children on premises until they are released to a parent, caregiver, or other designated person, or until they have been transported to an official evacuation center, in which case selected staff will remain with children until all have been reunited with their families.

B. Employees

All employees will remain on the premises as service workers, as designated by law. Such employees will be subject to whatever tasks are assigned by the person or persons in charge, and may not leave the premises until the same person or persons give them official permission to do so.

C. Parents and Caregivers

Parents and caregivers should not telephone the center. They should listen to the radio for progress reports on whatever disaster is taking place. Follow official instructions as relayed by officials via the radio. If parents and caregivers are able to reach the center without danger to themselves or without interference with disaster workers, they should come to pick up their children. Children will be released only to parents, caregivers, or other designated persons.

II. In Case of Fire: Life, Alarm, Report, Contain, Evacuate, Evaluate

A. Save Life: Evacuate any persons in immediate danger.

B. Sound Alarm:

1. Use fire-alarm pull stations.
2. Supplement with intercom, bullhorn, megaphone, or voice shouts.

C. Report Fire:

1. Dial 911.
2. Say, "There is a fire at ____(give address)____. The nearest cross street is ____(give cross street)____, and ____(what)____ is burning."
3. Assign one person to meet the fire officials.

D. Use a portable fire extinguisher or wall extinguisher if it is safe to stay in the area while doing so.

E. Contain (slow) the spread of fire and smoke by closing all doors and windows.
   1. Child care providers are responsible for doing this in their own child care rooms and in neighboring child care rooms they know are empty.
   2. Administrative and support personnel do this in all other rooms.

F. Utilities: If the fire is major, assign one person to shut off electricity and gas.

G. Evacuate children and adults to an area well away from the building and safe from traffic.
   1. As soon as the fire is discovered, start the orderly evacuation of the building, as during fire drills.
   2. Child care providers take with them their roll book, if possible.
   3. Administrative or other predesignated personnel check toilets, isolation areas for sick children, and other areas where children might be away from their groups and will be responsible for evacuating these children.
   4. If easily accessible, administrative personnel take emergency files with them, as well as a first aid kit.

H. After Evacuation:
   1. When safe within the predesignated evacuation area, all children and adults must be accounted for.
      a. Child care providers take roll of their own groups.
      b. Director checks with each child care provider to make sure that children and any adult assistants are all accounted for.
   2. Director and child care providers reassure children of their safety.
   3. First aid is administered, if needed.
   4. Building is not reentered until permission is given by fire officials.

I. Evaluation

   Follow the fire emergency with an evaluation by all staff in order to spot areas of weakness or oversight to be remedied for future emergencies.

III. In Case of Earthquakes

A. During the Earthquake and Aftershocks
   1. The gravest dangers may be caused by
      a. falling objects or toppling furniture or structures.
      b. the body being thrown by the shaking.
      c. shattered glass, especially windows and fluorescent lightbulbs. (Windows can be lined with Mylar for protection against glass, which may implode into a room.)
      d. broken outdoor power lines.
   2. When shaking begins, do the following:
      a. Shout, "Duck and cover!"
      b. Children duck and cover as practiced during earthquake drills (Section H11).
         (1) Turn away from windows and drop to knees.
         (2) Get under a desk or table, if possible. If not, children should stand in an interior doorway (see c(2) following).

(3) Clasp hands behind neck, bring arms against head (covering ears), close eyes, and drop head to knees.

(4) Remain silent and hold position for five minutes, or until shaking has stopped, whichever is longer.

(5) If furniture moves, move own body with it, remaining under cover.

(6) Alert children that a loud rumbling noise is an expected part of the earthquake.

c. Adults do the following:

(1) Duck and cover, as do children.

(2) If there is no room under furniture after children have been positioned, stand in an interior doorway. Brace back against one side of door frame, feet slightly forward, knees slightly bent. Cover head, as for "duck and cover," and bend head down slightly, keeping eyes closed. If glass is not shattering, open eyes to monitor children.

B. After the Shaking Stops

The building needs to be evacuated before aftershocks occur, because the initial quake may have caused structural damage that will cause the building to collapse under the stress of additional shaking. When the initial shaking has stopped, allow five minutes to evacuate the premises, hopefully before aftershocks occur.

1. Establish a buddy system, so that each staff member is responsible for one other.
2. By voice shout, check to make sure staff members in neighboring rooms have not been injured. By previous arrangement, have each person shout, "OK in Room ____" or "OK in Mary's room" or some similar agreed-upon phrase.
3. Lead child care group calmly to prearranged evacuation site in an outdoor area as far from power line danger as possible.
4. Take roll book, if possible.
5. Take earthquake emergency kit (bag or box), if possible, containing
   a. large name tags prepared in advance for each child, with name, allergies, and any special medication needs listed on them
   b. small first aid kit, with two days' supply of emergency medication for those who need it daily
   c. two potties, for preschool children, with plastic bags to use as inserts before each use
   d. flashlights with batteries taped to outside for preservation. Batteries need to be checked periodically in emergency kits
   e. writing pad, clipboard, and several pens
   f. a few changes of underpants for preschool children
   g. duty caps (see explanation, section D1, following) with explanation of all duties and color coding, if used
6. Predesignated staff, probably director and office personnel, check restrooms, sick bay, and any other areas where children might have been away from their own groups. Lead these children to safety.

7. In evacuating the building, if damage has occurred to sections of the usual evacuation route, use an alternative route, as practiced during earthquake drills. Be prepared to find doors jammed and rubble in the evacuation exits and routes.
8. In evacuating the building, your goal should be to get all ambulatory persons out. Injured persons who are unable to walk out must be left behind. A search team will come back for them.

C. At the Evacuation Site

Once the evacuation site has been reached, the most important tasks are to account for all persons, give reassurance to the children, and begin emergency duties.

1. Take roll. Report any missing children.
2. Place the previously prepared name tags on children, noting any serious injuries on tags.
3. Account for all adults. Report any missing persons.
4. Give reassurance to children.
5. Combine at least two groups together, to share in supervision and emergency duties.
6. All adults put on duty caps (see explanation, section D1, following).
7. Begin emergency duties.
8. Be prepared for aftershocks. During aftershocks, duck and cover.

D. Emergency Duties

These can be preassigned or can be assigned on the spot. Everyone must be familiar with all emergency duties, location of supplies, and planned procedures, since not everyone may be present when a disaster occurs. Assignments should be made so that if one person cannot perform assigned duties, another can take over. Assignments should also be made, if the number of staff is sufficient, so that two persons work together on each duty—or more, if needed (such as in food preparation and serving). It is advisable that all persons be prepared in advance to serve in any capacity.

Duty caps may be prepared in advance, signifying what task has been assigned to the person wearing the cap. For "on-the-spot" assignments, adhesive-backed tags can be prepared in advance and distributed to the selected individuals to fasten to the cap that has been stored in individual emergency kits. The following team tasks should be assigned:

1. Command Team
    a. Assigns emergency duties, if not prearranged.
    b. Oversees all emergency operations.
    c. Assures that all persons are accounted for.
    d. Monitors communication on a battery-operated radio or cellular phone.
    e. Makes all emergency decisions about which there may be controversy.
    f. Works closely with all other teams.
2. Safety Team
    a. The safety persons are the only ones allowed to reenter the building, assuming it is safe to do so.

b. Searches for missing persons in the building.
   (1) Listens for cries for help, moaning, or sobbing.
   (2) Periodically shouts, "Hello. Are you here?"
c. Checks building for obvious structural damage.
d. Shuts off electrical supply, water, and gas lines. (Tools for these tasks have previously been taped to each shut-off site.)
e. Obtains emergency supplies, if accessible, and places them outside the building for supply team to access.
f. Locks doors, if possible. Otherwise, secures building to prevent entry by others.
g. If an emergency phone call needs to be made, reenters the building to do so, only if a cellular phone is not available. Makes calls on an available cellular phone.
h. Checks water heaters for damage. If containers are available, draws off as much water as possible to conserve emergency bottled water supply.
i. Continuously monitors entire evacuation site for safety of children and adults.
j. Makes final decisions regarding safety.

3. Supply Team
   a. Is in charge of all supplies and distribution of same, including blankets, food, water, and other needed items.
   b. Has the authority to ration supplies as necessary.
   c. Prepares food for consumption and service.
4. First Aid Team
   a. Sets up a first aid area, as previously determined, and assumes supervision of all first aid needs that child care providers cannot handle within their groups.
   b. Provides first aid and administers medication as necessary.
   c. Makes all decisions regarding emergency medical care.
5. Morale Booster Team
   a. Helps to minimize panic.
   b. Plans for group activities, singing, stories, and games.
   c. Distributes books and play materials.
   d. Relays messages from Command Team by use of bullhorn, if needed.
6. Sanitation Team
   a. Sets up a predetermined area for toileting. Uses plastic sheets or tarps to provide for some privacy and for separation of male and female sectors.
   b. Sets up portable toilets, if available, in appropriate locations.
   c. Substitute portable toilets may be set up by the use of buckets, waste baskets, or similar containers. Disposable plastic liners are placed in the container before each use.
   d. Containers can be placed part-way into the ground to adjust to height of children.

e. If portable toilets have not been arranged for in the emergency supplies, pits must be dug into the ground. This should be a narrow pit, allowing children to straddle the opening. After each use, a small amount of dirt is thrown in. Lime will cut down on odor. However, if lime can be stored, portable toilets (or a substitute) can also be stored.

7. Morgue Team

In case of a major earthquake, deaths may result. A prearranged site should be selected for storing bodies.

a. Bodies must be moved to morgue site as soon as possible.

b. Place body in plastic bag, tie, and fasten card to bag. Card should show the name of the person and the time of death.

c. There may be need to reenter the building to remove bodies, as in hot weather, because bodies must be stored in a cool place.

8. Dismissal Team

a. Meets persons who arrive to take children at a designated dismissal area.

b. Locates children for dismissal, while parents and caregivers remain at meeting place.

c. Obtains signatures of persons picking up children after validating their authority to do so by checking emergency cards or by any other available means. Asks for identification material from all persons not readily recognizable by staff members.

E. Letter to Parents and Caregivers

Parents and caregivers should be supplied with a copy or a summary of your emergency plans. Send home the following instructions:

1. Do not call the center.
2. Do not come to the center, unless you are close and radio reports indicate there is no danger in traveling city streets. Children will be released only from a designated dismissal area and only to authorized family members or their representatives.
3. Community disasters will be reported on the radio. Be sure that your family has a transistor radio. Listen to it for directions.
4. Be assured that the child care providers and other center personnel are giving your child any emergency care that may be needed. They, too, are listening to the radio and will be hearing the same instructions as you.
5. The safest place in case of a disaster is off the city streets, out of the way of emergency and rescue equipment.
6. If the building in which the the Community Child Care Center is housed has been designated as one of the community disaster emergency stations, your child will probably be safer here than anywhere else.
7. Do not wander through the evacuation site. Remain at the dismissal area and wait for your child to be brought to you.
8. Please send to the center the following items for use by your child in case of emergency:

____

____

____

(The above list might include blanket, clothing, flashlight, comb, or any other items you may feel you want to ask parents and caregivers to provide. Much depends on what storage facilities you have.)

F. First Aid Supplies

In addition to the first aid kit you have stored for daily use during the operation of your facility, the following items suggest the types of first aid materials that should be stored for use in case of a major disaster:

1. For treating cuts and wounds, include
   a. Assorted bandages, including triangular, elastic, and strips of sterilized torn sheeting
   b. Assorted Band-Aids™ and rolls of adhesive tape
   c. Gauze, pads, rolls, elasticized and regular
   d. Hydrogen peroxide for cleansing wounds
   e. Cotton, absorbent, for cleansing wounds
   f. Cotton swabs
   g. Sanitary pads for compresses
   h. Scissors
   i. Tourniquets
2. For treating sprains and breaks, include
   a. Assorted bandages, as above
   b. Adhesive tape
   c. Splints, cardboard
   d. Instant ice packs
3. Other
   a. Thermometers
   b. Pain relievers: children's aspirin or children's pain reliever
   c. Tweezers
   d. Eyedroppers
   e. Needles
   f. Safety pins
   g. Adult-sized bulb syringe
   h. Inhalers
   i. Alcohol for sterilization
   j. Kaopectate™, for upset stomach
   k. Cough drops, mild cough syrup
   l. Burn ointment
   m. Magnifying glass, for finding imbedded glass
   n. First aid cream
   o. Toothache kits
   p. Water purification tablets

G. General Supplies
  1. Flashlights, with batteries taped to outside, ready for use
  2. Towelettes, premoistened
  3. Paper towels
  4. Toilet tissue
  5. Tissue
  6. Plastic bags, including zipper type, several assorted sizes, including extra large
  7. Pocket knives
  8. Rolls of plastic to use as ground covers, dividers, or plastic tarps
  9. Clear tape, masking tape
  10. String
  11. Rope (enough to set off evacuation site and rope off various sections for separating close groups, if needed)
  12. Buckets
  13. Paper sacks, assorted sizes
  14. Games, books, puzzles, song sheets, balls, and other toys for use by morale workers
  15. Bullhorn and megaphones
  16. Walkie-talkie
  17. Battery-operated radios (at least two)
  18. Candles, with matches
  19. Newspapers
  20. Portable fire extinguisher
  21. Bicarbonate of soda
  22. Cellular phone, or access to one

H. Tools
  1. Shovels
  2. Pickax
  3. Saw
  4. Pliers
  5. Screwdrivers
  6. Brooms
  7. Crescent wrench
  8. Padded sledgehammer
  9. Hammer, nails

I. Food and Water Supplies: Choose from the following items, which should be replaced yearly unless otherwise specified.
  1. Water: Having a supply of fresh water is one of the most important things to have on hand in case of a disaster. Distilled water will keep the longest and does not have to be boiled or purified. Five-gallon commercially purchased bottles require a deposit on the bottle. One-gallon bottles purchased at the market are inexpensive and do not

require a deposit. They are easily handled. Square-shaped containers are easiest to store because they can be stacked. Spring water can be purchased in 12- or 24-packs and are easily stored.

2. Other drinks
   a. Canned fruit juices or fruit boxes
   b. Powdered milk
   c. Coffee, tea bags, hot chocolate mix
3. Vegetables
   a. Cans, institutional size
   b. Soups, institutional size
4. Fruits, cans, institutional size
5. Protein
   a. Peanuts, dry roasted and unsalted
   b. Peanut butter (replace frequently—about every three or four months)
   c. Tuna fish, canned
   d. Chicken, canned
   e. Milk, canned
   f. Beans, canned, to eat with rice for good protein balance
6. Breads and cereals
   a. Brown bread, canned
   b. Instant cereals (oatmeal, Cream of Wheat, Cream of Rice) and boxed cereals
   c. Rice, 3-minute variety
   d. Crackers (in tight tin, changed every two months)
   e. Pasta, canned
7. K-rations or other such emergency foods may be used in place of or as a supplement to the types of foods listed.
8. Other
   a. Condiments
   b. Instant soups
   c. Some dehydrated foods, depending on amount of water storage

   Note: Dry foods can be frozen for 96 hours to kill all eggs, then stored dry without danger of the development of worms or other bugs in the food.

J. Equipment and Supplies for Food Preparation and Service
   1. Paper plates and cups, for hot and cold foods
   2. Plastic eating utensils
   3. Styrofoam cups
   4. Large kettles for food preparation
   5. Alternative cooking arrangement:
      a. Sterno stove w/sterno
      b. Barbecue grill w/coals
      c. Camp stove w/fuel

6. Can openers
7. Cooking utensils, spoons
8. Liquid soap
9. Aluminum foil, heavy-duty
10. Paper towels

IV. In Case of Power Blackout

A. Remain calm.

B. Have children "freeze" where they are until you can obtain alternate lighting from flashlights or candles which have been previously stored for use in case of such an occurrence.

C. If daytime, and weather is nice, evacuate building. Transfer activities outdoors if rooms are too dark to use.

D. If weather is hot and electricity blackout has caused the air conditioner to cease operating, plan for being outdoors, if possible.

E. If it is very hot outdoors, find the coolest area possible where there is adequate shade.

F. If the weather is too cold or rainy, keep children indoors.

G. Utilize available emergency supplies to keep children comfortable.

V. In Case of Flooding

A. If it is safe to remain in the building, as on a second floor, do so unless ordered to evacuate by city officials.

B. Use available emergency supplies to keep children comfortable.

C. If ordered to evacuate building and the grounds are flooded outdoors, wait for official assistance.

D. If assistance isn't forthcoming, get children to the highest possible location.

VI. In Case of Hurricane

A. Normally there will be warnings far enough in advance so that appropriate preparations may be taken, in accordance with advice of local authorities.

B. Listen to a battery-operated radio (should there be a power outage) to keep informed of the progress of the hurricane and to receive instructions from local authorities.

C. Flashlights should be kept available in case of power outage.

D. Your primary efforts should be geared toward uniting all children with their parents and caregivers prior to the arrival of the hurricane.

VII. In Case of Tornado

A. If there is sufficient warning, children can be picked up by their parents or caregivers.

B. Children who are at child care during the tornado warnings should be kept indoors. They should be taken to inner hallways. If there are no such hallways, they should "drop," get under furniture, and cover as they would in an earthquake [Section H10, Part IIIA]. If your building has a storm cellar, children should be taken there until the tornado is over. A door and window should be opened to allow air to move through the building. Care must be taken to stay out of the path of debris blowing through.

C. Keep flashlights available in case of a power outage.

D. Use a portable radio to keep informed of the progress of the tornado and of predictions and/or any special instructions from local officials.

E. Once children are in a protected area, your biggest problem will be one of morale. Children need much more reassurance in times of disaster.

F. Children who are walking to or from the center should get into a ditch or culvert, if possible, to avoid being blown away. This can also be a protection against flying debris.

VIII. In Case of Bomb Threat

A. Follow instructions of police or other officials.

B. Reassure children.

C. If necessary to evacuate building, do so as for fire.

D. Evacuate building, even if you think there is a possibility that the threat may not be authentic.

E. If the threat has been made to you, contact the police department immediately.

IX. Plot Plan

A plot plan should be prepared to use in any major disaster. This should be a simplified drawing of your facility, indicating

- alarm locations.
- fire hose locations.
- escape routes for emergency evacuation. Stairs and exits should be noted.
- possible alternate routes.
- locations for shutoff of gas, electricity, and water.
  (Note: When electricity is shut off, alarm will cease to ring.)
- location of evacuation site.
- high voltage lines, if within block area of facility.

If building is two stories, have a separate plot plan for the second floor. A sample of a plot plan is provided on page 381.

X. Emergency Telephone Numbers

If the emergency is isolated to your location, you may want to use the telephone for various emergency services. In case of a community-wide disaster, use the telephone only in top-priority emergencies. The types of numbers you may find convenient to have on hand are

1. emergency: 911 (List specific numbers of fire department, police department, and paramedics.)
2. physicians to call:
   a. ______________________________
   b. ______________________________
   c. or those on children's emergency cards
3. hospitals:
   a. ______________________________
   b. ______________________________
   c. ______________________________
4. ambulance services:
   a. ______________________________
   b. ______________________________

5. American Red Cross
6. pharmacies:
   a. ______________________
   b. ______________________
7. locksmith
8. health department
9. coroner
10. Poison Control center
11. other:

____

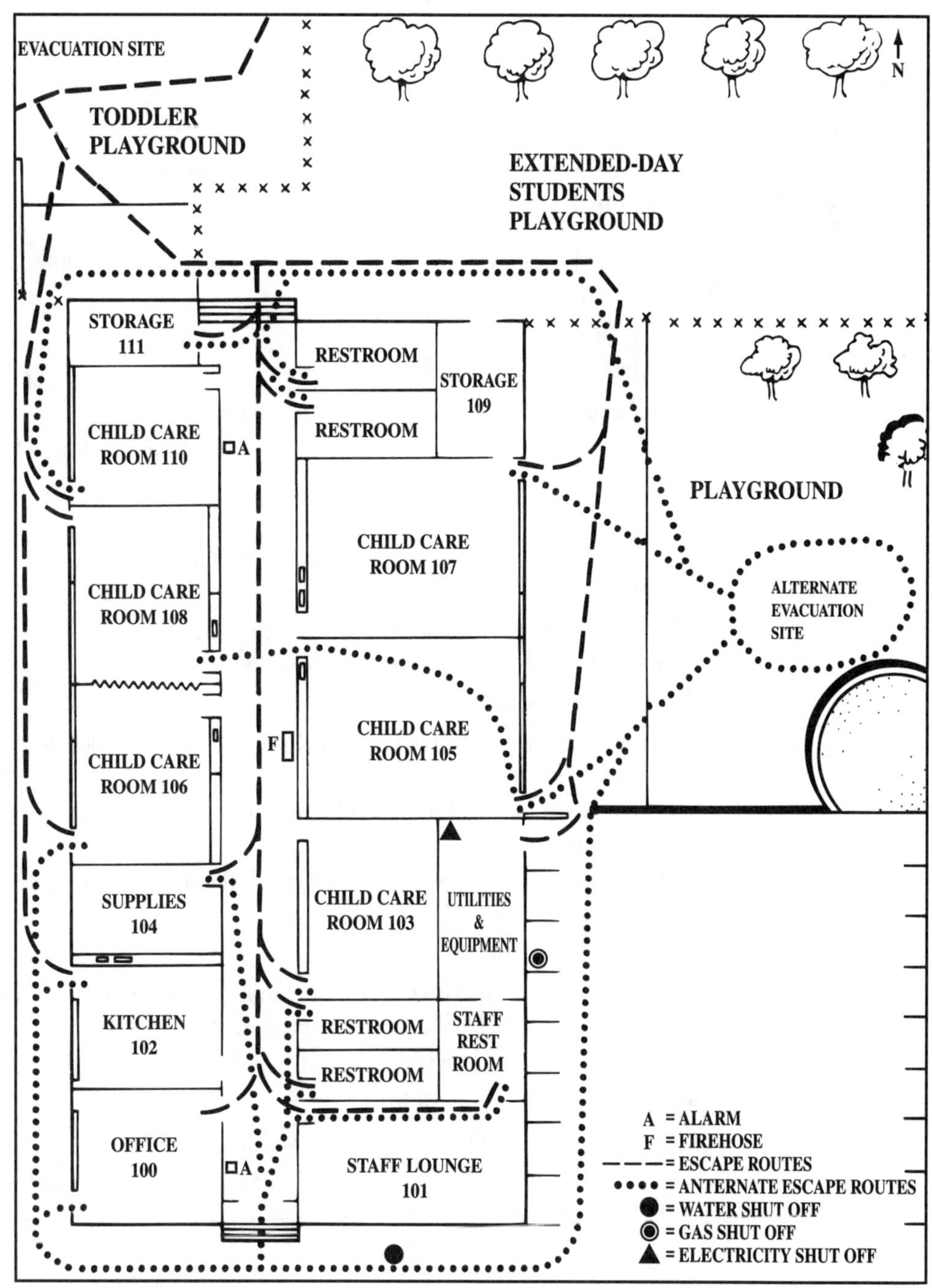

XI. Signals

A. Signal to Leave the Building: Fire alarm bell for five minutes. When the signal sounds, the following should occur:

1. Children immediately follow child care provider to the door and out of the building to a point 200 feet from building.
2. If possible, assistant picks up roll book, closes doors, and follows the rest of the group, giving the child care provider the roll book.
3. Child care provider immediately checks the roll to make sure that everyone is accounted for. (This may also be done by a head count.)

B. Signal to Return: Whistle blown by the director, or three short bells. Upon hearing the whistle or bell, the adults and children will return to the room by the same route by which they exited.

H11 Disaster Drills

The purpose of drills is to accustom children to evacuating a building in a prompt and orderly manner, without panic.

A. Procedure for Fire Drill

1. Signal to leave the building:
   a. Ring one bell intermittently for five minutes.
   b. Supplement the ring by voice shout, checking areas where bell might be missed.
2. Prior to leaving the building:
   a. Everyone simulates the duties assigned them, as listed in the preparation plan, going through the same motions as if it were for a real fire.
   b. Child care providers lead children calmly, but quickly from the building, with the goal of evacuating premises within one minute.
3. When safely outside:
   a. Child care providers check their group rolls, ensuring that everyone is accounted for.
   b. Director checks with each child care provider, complimenting each group on its performance.
   c. Groups wait with their child care providers until the signal to return to the building is heard.
4. Returning to building:
   a. One long, continuous ring signals the return to the building. (This is sometimes done by the director blowing a whistle.)
   b. Children return by the same route by which they exited.
5. After returning to the building:
   a. Everyone evaluates strengths and weaknesses of drill.
   b. Discuss with children what to do in case their clothes catch fire at any time.

- "Stop where you are."
- "Drop to the ground."
- "Roll over and over again until the fire is out."

Practice: STOP, DROP, ROLL many times.

B. Procedure for Earthquake Drill

1. Signal for "duck and cover":
   a. Continuous bell for five minutes indicates an earthquake and the duration of "duck and cover" time.
   b. Supplement the ring of bell by voice shout, "Earthquake!"
2. Duck and cover:
   a. Proceed as in disaster plan for real earthquake.
   b. When bell stops ringing, proceed as for evacuation.
3. Evacuation of building:
   a. Go through all motions as though actually performing tasks outlined in disaster plan.
   b. Calmly lead children from building to evacuation site.
4. At evacuation site:
   a. Child care providers check group rolls, ensuring that everyone is accounted for.
   b. Director assigns duties.
   c. Each person walks through motions of assigned duty, simulating what everyone would really be doing should it be an authentic disaster.
5. At an "all clear" from the director, child care providers lead their groups back the way they came.
6. Upon returning to the room, practice one or two alternate escape routes. Do this individually for your own group.
7. Evaluate with children, and with each other, how drill progressed.

The information in this section delineating procedures in case of disaster must be used by you only as a general guide. Check the legal requirements in your community. Check against your local city guidelines. Always consider that customs change; new, improved products become available; and legal regulations vary.

C. Written Procedures

Using the above information, prepare a written procedure for your own facility, being very specific about duty assignment procedures. List each duty, what is required, and who should fulfill that particular duty.

D. Prearranged Disaster Duty Assignments

These may be made by use of a chart similar to the following:

DISASTER DUTIES FOR FIRE	PERSONS RESPONSIBLE
Alarm, north end of hall	
Alarm, south end of hall	
Call fire department	
Shut off electricity	
Meet fire officials	
Doors and windows not in child care rooms	
Emergency card files, cash and checks	
Fire hoses, if safe to use	
Inspect building to make sure it is empty	
Accounting of all persons in evacuation site	
Give "all clear" to return to building	

DISASTER DUTIES FOR EARTHQUAKE OR OTHER DISASTERS	
Shut off electricity, gas, water	
Safety duties	
First aid duties	
Command duties	
Supplies duties	
Sanitation duties	
Morale-boosting duties	
Morgue duties	
Dismissal duties	

H12 Air Pollution

Air pollution is a very important health problem in most cities. The two most common problems are smog and particulate matter, such as pollen, dust, and soot. Children inhale more pollution into their lungs than adults do because they breathe more rapidly. When they have colds, children usually breathe through their mouths, taking in more pollutants. Because their lungs are still developing, breathing polluted air may cause permanent lung injury. You can protect children in your care from air pollutants by refraining from outdoor activities on days when air quality in your area is 100 or above. Contact a local radio station or newspaper to check on air quality conditions. On smoggy days, schedule your outdoor activity for the early morning and keep any activities away from heavy traffic areas.

H13 Security

The following are considerations concerning the security of the premises and the persons on the premises, including the children for whom you are responsible:

1. Transferring Responsibility of Child to Center and Back

Adhere strictly to the sign-in and sign-out procedures established for your center, as outlined in Sections E17, E22–23, and in the enrollment agreement in Section E14.

a. Signing in:

Be sure the adult bringing the child signs in with a name signature. You must ask for full first and last name. Initials should not be accepted.

b. Elementary-age children:

They may sign themselves in with the permission of their parents or caregivers.

c. When persons come to pick up children:

Be sure to ask for the identification of any person you don't know who comes to pick up a child, even if that person tells you his or her name is on the emergency card or you have had a note or phone call from a parent or caregiver telling you that person will be coming.

d. The center is the responsible party until child is signed out:

If a child has not been signed out, you are still the responsible party, even if the child has been picked up.

2. Children's Protection Program

a. Videotaping children:

Arrange to videotape all children in your program. Each child should be shown from the front and from each side. Let parents and caregivers know that you will have the videotape safely kept in a locked file.

b. Files for important documents:

File a copy of each child's birth certificate and dental records for those families who wish to participate in the program. The center's copy of annual photographs taken of the children are also on file.

c. Distinguishing characteristics:

Parents and caregivers are advised to know their children's blood types; to record any distinguishing marks, such as moles, scars, or birthmarks; and to obtain passports for them, since passports are difficult to duplicate.

d. Helpful facts:

Single parents and caregivers are advised to record as many facts about their ex-spouses or partners as they are able, such as birth dates, Social Security numbers, driver's license numbers, employment records, and related data.

e. Friends and relatives:

Similar information about close friends and relatives may be of use in tracking down a missing child.

3. Children's Belongings

a. Disclaimer to parents or caregivers:

Every safeguard should be taken to protect children's belongings, but you can protect yourself by giving parents and caregivers a disclaimer notice that states that you will not be responsible for the loss or breakage of items brought to school by the children.

b. Tag things if parents and caregivers don't:

Parents and caregivers frequently do not adhere to reminders to put name tags on all outerwear and on any personal belongings brought to the center. An easy remedy is to simply tag everything yourself. It only takes a few moments a day to check jackets and sweaters for name tags. A piece of adhesive tape and a marking pen can quickly solve the problem.

c. Provide name tag order service:

Some centers offer to take orders for professionally prepared name tags for the parents and caregivers to use.

d. Safeguard expensive items:

When children bring expensive toys or other items from home to share, prepare a special place to safeguard those items after use.

4. Staff Protection

a. Space for personal belongings:

All persons working at your center should be provided with a space that can be locked in which they can keep personal belongings.

b. During a disaster drill:

During a disaster drill [Section H11], when the building has been completely emptied, assign one person to remain in the building for security reasons. This is an opportune time for theft.

c. Waiver of responsibility:

Be sure that there is a clear understanding with your staff that the center cannot be responsible for the loss of personal items. This can be part of your employment contract.

d. Buddy system:

It is recommended that no woman enter the building alone before daylight, nor be left alone to close up after dark. Two people can open and close the center at those times.

e. Lighted parking areas:

Make certain there is ample lighting for the persons who close up the center and need to walk to their cars in the dark.

f. Buddy system for parking area:

It is recommended that two persons walk to their cars together, and that they follow all safety precautions before entering their cars. Each should wait for the other to start his or her engine before driving off.

g. Parking closest to building:

Make arrangements for those who stay the latest to park the closest to the building, provided there is adequate lighting.

h. Training for self-protection. Consider various methods of self-protection, such as

- use of mace, if legal in your community (training is necessary)

- use of various electronic protective devices now on the market
- training in some form of martial arts
- carrying an alarm whistle

5. Keys

a. Keys should be distributed with caution.

b. Keys should be signed for when they are given.

c. Periodically check on all keys that have been given out and reconsider whether the persons who have them really need them.

6. Building

a. Entrances:

Since there can be several entrances to the building that houses your child care center, unlock only one door before 8:00 A.M. and leave only one open after 4:00 P.M. That way, you have control over who enters the building when there is minimal staff on hand.

b. Use of buzzer to indicate door opening:

If there is a door that must be opened early and late in the day, and there is some concern over who might enter the building, rig a bell or buzzer to ring whenever that door is used at certain times of day.

c. Visitors in building:

All visitors must sign in in the office. They are given name tags identifying their purpose for being in the building.

d. Unknown persons in building:

Any persons unknown to you that come into the building at any time of day should be asked to identify themselves.

e. Identification a must:

If a person refuses to give you identification, call the police immediately.

f. Asking someone to leave the premises:

If a person refuses to leave the premises when asked, call the police immediately.

g. Grounds:

(1) Unknown persons:

The same precautions taken indoors must be taken outdoors. Any persons unknown to the staff seen on the grounds when the center is open should be asked to provide identification. If you determine they have no business on the premises, ask them to leave. If they do not leave, call the police immediately.

(2) Unknown automobiles:

Take note of any unknown automobiles parked in your parking area or on the street nearby. If anything seems unusual, note the license plate number. If the automobile continues to appear for no apparent legitimate reason, notify the police.

H14 Automobile Safety

Because of the large number of children living in highly urbanized areas where there is a high concentration of vehicles on the streets, safety education and awareness are extremely important. The car pool rules listed in the Parent/Caregiver Handbook [Section E25] should form the basis for automobile safety at your center. Shortly after the start of each year, send home the following reminder:

Community Child Care Center

111 THIRD STREET TELEPHONE 123-4579

To: All Parents and Caregivers

From: Staff

The automobile can be a deadly weapon. It is the leading cause of accidental death for young children in this country. In spite of considerable public education in this area, the situation is not improving. We urge you to reread the car pool rules in the Parent/Caregiver Handbook. The precautions emphasized on that page apply to all drivers.

Here are some of our safety rules. Post them in your car to serve as a reminder each time you drive.

1. Be sure that windows are clear of ice or fog.
2. If it is raining, be sure your windshield wipers are working.
3. Be sure that the brakes are in good condition.
4. Do not start the car until all seat belts are fastened, all children are sitting as far back on the seats as they are able to, and all doors are closed.
5. Be sure there are no distracting quarrels in progress. If a disturbance occurs while driving the car, pull to the curb. Stop. Then deal with the problem.
6. Drive carefully. Stay within or below posted speed limits.
7. Park where the child is in no danger of running in front of another car when getting out of your car. For example, try not to park across the street from the center or from the child's home.
8. The child should get in and out of the car on the curb side only.
9. Do not hurry. A life is more precious than time.

H15 Transporting Children

Automobile crashes are one of the most common causes of injury and death for children. When transporting children in your care, always use an approved car seat. Any child who weighs less than 40 lbs. requires a car seat. All other passengers should use seat belts. Make sure that whoever operates the vehicle has a valid driver's license for that type of vehicle. The vehicle used to transport the children must be licensed and registered according to your state laws. Each vehicle should be equipped with a first aid kit and emergency identification and emergency contact information for all children being transported. On field trips, maintain the proper child-to-adult ratios. Never count the driver as a one of the caregivers. The driver is unable to properly supervise children when driving the vehicle. Therefore, there should be at least one other adult in the vehicle to supervise children. Remember to never allow children to be left alone in a vehicle. For more information about transportation safety, call the National Highway Transportation Safety Administration's Auto Safety Hotline at 1-800-424-9393.

H16 Street Safety

On walks around the center neighborhood or elsewhere, conduct an ongoing program of education for street safety. Children are taught

- to look both ways and make sure that no cars are coming before crossing a street. To help children understand about looking both ways, you may say, "Look for cars coming and going."
- to stand on the curb, where it is easier to be seen by someone in a car, until it is safe to cross.
- to obey traffic signals. From time to time, walk with children to intersections where there are traffic lights. Children learn the meaning of each color. They also learn that even though the green light means go, they must look to make sure that cars have stopped before they start to cross the street.

When taking children on these walks, have one strict rule: Children must always wait for an adult to tell them that it is safe to cross the street. When the group is near a busy intersection, no child is allowed to walk in front of a staff member, and one or more adults stay at the rear of the group where they can see everyone at all times.

To further emphasize the need for pedestrian safety, have signs posted around the center. Have toy traffic signs in the playground as well. In addition, children can play a traffic game, which is described in Section H17.

H17 Traffic Game

In this game, children pretend that they are driving cars. Actually, they are walking, running, and responding to directions that a staff member calls out. Discuss ahead of time where the road will be and the traffic rules:

- All cars must go in the same direction.
- All cars must obey the traffic signals.
- No speeding.
- No bumping.
- No blocking traffic.

Depending on the size of the group, one or two children are selected to be Traffic Officers. Here is a typical routine.

"Everyone start your cars. Warm up the motors. Wait for the signal to turn green. The signal says Go!"
"The yellow light says Wait."
"The red light says Stop."
"The green light says Go."
"You are on the freeway now. You may drive a little faster."
"Now you are downtown. Drive very slow."
"The red light says Stop."
"The green light says Go."
"Flat tire. Pull off to the side of the road to repair it."

Invent variations of your own to add to the game.

H18 Parking Lot Safety

The entire center community should be constantly reminded of the need for caution in the use of parking lots. Use the following reminder:

Community Child Care Center

111 THIRD STREET TELEPHONE 123-4579

Dear Parents and Caregivers,

Parking lots are a source of danger to young children. Please take these precautions:

1. Enter and leave the parking lot with extreme caution. Be on the lookout for wandering children.
2. Always hold your child's hand when going to and coming from an automobile. Do not let your child run ahead of you. He or she might inadvertently run in the path of a car that is just starting to back out.
3. Please do not stand in the parking lot conversing with other adults unless your child is seated safely in the car with doors closed.
4. On our part, we will take walks to the parking lot with your child and discuss safety precautions.

Sincerely,
Director

H19 Lead Poisoning

Lead poisoning is a common environmental health problem among children. The only way you can tell that a child has lead poisoning is to have his or her blood tested. Children under two years of age run a greater risk of lead poisoning because they put their hands in their mouths. Therefore, they are more likely to eat dust, paint, and soil contaminated with lead. Children absorb lead more easily. They can be exposed to lead by eating lead-based paint chips or dust. This happens when they chew on surfaces such as windowsills, or surfaces close to the floor that may contain lead-based paint. Drinking water that has moved through lead pipes and eating food on lead-glazed pottery can also expose children to lead poisoning.

You can help reduce the risk of children in your care being exposed to lead poisoning by washing your children's hands before meals and whenever else possible. Provide lunches and snacks rich in calcium and iron. This will help reduce the amount of lead absorbed from the gastrointestinal tract. Do not store food in opened cans. Use ceramic containers that have labels saying they are made with lead-free glazes. Have your facility evaluated for lead hazards. To receive information on testing, call your local health department, the National Lead Information Hotline: (800) LEAD-FYI, or the National Lead Information Clearinghouse: (800) 424-LEAD.

H20 Safety Precautions with Toys

Avoid toys that break easily. Try to visualize how a particular toy would look if it were broken—injuries can occur when wire, springs, or sharp pieces of plastic are exposed. Do not buy a prepackaged item without first examining an unpackaged sample.

Avoid toys that burn. A good guideline is to avoid all electrical toys for young children. Good toys should spark a child's imagination and creativity. The child's imagination can create the same kinds of things that electricity provides. No toy or part of a toy should burn easily or, if ignited, cause noxious smoke or drip molten material. For example, a plastic ball that seems harmless can easily catch fire if it lands on a gas range or an electric burner.

Avoid all toys that cut or puncture. All edges of a toy, interior and exterior, should be smooth with rounded corners. All exposed metal edges should be properly finished. Hidden spikes and points that can cause puncture wounds should be avoided. For example, sometimes a small, inexpensive toy car has points sticking out from the wheels that could hurt a child who falls on it. Darts of any kind are not toys for children. Neither are archery sets or spring-loaded gun sets with removable suction cups.

Avoid toys that pinch. Many toys have places where small fingers can be pinched, such as slots, holes, or the underside of the fenders of wheeled toys. Windup mechanisms should be enclosed to avoid catching fingers or hair. Toys that have hinges should be examined carefully before purchase. Rocking horses and folding furniture may also present hazards. Examine such items carefully.

Avoid toys that can be swallowed. Very small objects (less than 3/8" diameter) are seldom a problem if swallowed; however, they can be inhaled into the lungs. Removing them requires surgery. Larger objects, when swallowed, may get caught in the windpipe. Check all toys for screws, nuts, bolts, marbles, or other parts that might come loose.

Avoid toys that cause eye and ear injuries. Some toy goggles or space helmets are made of plastic that shatters easily. If the part that you see through on such headgear is made of curved plastic, it can cause eyestrain and may cause the child to get hurt accidentally because of a misjudgment of vision. Some cap and sound guns make more noise than jackhammers. Excessively noisy and loud guns can lead to serious hearing problems.

Avoid toys that cause bumps and bruises. When buying wheel or riding toys, look for large, sturdy, widely spaced wheels and axles near the extreme ends of the vehicle so that it will keep it from rearing up or pitching forward easily. Avoid flimsy wagons that a child can fall out of.

Avoid toys that are toxic or unclean. Materials and finishes used for toys should not cause skin irritation or other allergic reactions, or have a powdery surface that could cause inhalation toxicity. Toys that come in contact with a child's mouth should come in packaging that ensures cleanliness. Stuffed toys, especially, can be contaminated if impure materials are used for the stuffing. Even a toy that is labeled "nontoxic" may have some toxic material.

Avoid toys that can be psychologically harmful. Toys that depict mutilation, human eyeball balls, and war toys are examples of toys that have a potential for causing psychological harm to children. They certainly have no place in a child care center.

Avoid toys that aren't necessary. Too many toys can be just as devastating to the development and emotional well-being of children as too few. By supplementing commercial toys with "found" materials and improvised play centers, you can stimulate children to use their imaginations.

H21 Safety Precautions According to Age Differences

Accidents are the major cause of death among children in this country. Depending on the age of the children, the differences in their developmental stages will affect the safety needs in your center. These needs will vary at different ages. In teaching children to be aware of safety precautions, take care not to be overprotective to the extent that they become timid or afraid of exploration. By teaching children in your care sound safety habits and explaining why they are important, you can develop children's self-confidence and contribute to their self-esteem.

Infant to Two-Year-Old Children

During the first six months of life, children are totally dependent, therefore vulnerable to injury if not supervised at all times. They are not mobile during this time, but are at high risk of Sudden Infant Death Syndrome. When preparing infants for sleeping, place them on their backs or sides—not on their stomachs. Make sure that the mattresses for sleeping are firm and flat. Avoid beanbags, sheepskins, foam sofa cushions, synthetic pillows, or foam pads. Do not overheat the infant. Be mindful that too much heavy bedding or clothing can cause the infant to become overheated. Keep your environment temperature at 70°F or less. Use clean hands when putting an infant to sleep and check the infant's mouth for any food that may remain.

At six to twelve months, infants become actively involved with their environment and the people around them. As a way to explore an object, an infant will pick it up and put the object in his or her mouth. Make sure that objects do not have sharp edges and are appropriate for children to explore. Objects small enough to swallow should be taken out of the environment. Wash the object after the child is done exploring it. The more mobile infant will be able to open any cabinet. Safety latches should be used on all cabinets, doors, and so on. Remove all cleaning solutions, medications, or hazardous chemicals from the infants' environment. Store them on a high shelf in a locked cabinet. Cover all electrical sockets with safety plugs.

At twelve months to two years of age, the children's skills for walking and their abilities to access danger increase. Their balance is somewhat unsteady. They must be supervised closely, but at the same time allowed to explore and master the environment. On a daily basis, the indoor and outdoor environment must be examined for any physical hazards. Remove unsafe equipment, replace broken toys, and give children plenty of opportunities to master their physical skills with close supervision.

Two-Year-Old Children

- This is a climbing age. Place a protective barrier around any area that may be dangerous to climb.
- This is a wanderer's age. Lock all exits that may lead to potential danger.
- This is a take-apart age. Toys should not have parts that can break or splinter easily.
- This is an experimental age. Sharp objects, matches, electrical plugs, and scissors should be kept where children cannot get to them. Either repair or discard splintered, rickety, or rusty objects.

Three-Year-Old Children

- Three-year-olds are always in a hurry. They don't always look where they are going. They know and understand the safety rules you have taught them, but they may be in such a hurry that they will trip over objects on the floor.
- This is an experimental age. Drugs, poisons, cleaning materials, and chemicals should all be kept safely out of reach.

Four-Year-Old Children

- Four-year-olds are eager, quick, and seemingly in constant motion.
- They can understand safety rules and will remind others of them, but they can't be trusted to remember them at all times. Therefore, they still require constant supervision and frequent, firm reminders about such things as running out into the street, watching out for cars coming in and out of driveways, and obeying school rules.
- This is a manipulative age. Give children careful instructions for the use of tools and remind them to put tools back in their proper places after they have finished using them.

Five-Year-Old Children

- Five-year-olds are dependable, conscientious, and anxious to please; however, they are also impulsive, investigative, and full of energy.
- They can help you with the younger children in taking necessary precautions, but since their judgment is still that of a child with a child's limited view of the world, they continue to require adult supervision.

Six- to Twelve-Year-Old Children

The ages of six to twelve are referred to as "middle childhood," or "school-age years." Developmental changes continue to occur but are not as dramatic as they were during the infant and toddler years. They can dress themselves and eat without adult assistance. They show continued improvement in skills learned earlier.

- Watch them on the playground to see how their motor skills are improving. Encourage them to practice and perfect the skills of jumping, balancing, throwing, catching, running, and sequencing foot movements. This will help them master the skills they need without causing physical injury to their bodies. When in an organized game or sport, outline the game rules. This will help to show why rules are important for their safety.
- Children in this age group are more aware of the world around them. Violence on TV is increasing and studies have shown school-age children, when angered, sometimes model aggressive behavior seen on television. Staff must be available at all times to handle violent behavior by communicating with them, observing them at all times, and redirecting their behavior or activity.
- Do not allow plastic play guns of any kind at your center. Plastic toy guns do not teach how extremely dangerous real guns are.

Children's Program

I1 Child Care Room Management

Child care providers are responsible for the management of the child care rooms. This includes being responsible for the daily schedule, materials and supplies, room arrangements, activities, record keeping, and curriculum. Your responsibilities as the director include the following:

1. Providing child care providers with the necessary guidelines to achieve the center's goals in accordance with the philosophy of your program [Sections A14, E26].
2. Providing the necessary tools and support child care providers need to follow those guidelines.
3. Allowing for the freedom of individual expression for each staff member, while ensuring that the staff works in harmony toward common goals.

I2 Opening Days of Your Program

The opening days of your program are very important, because they give you an opportunity to establish a good pattern for the ensuing year. Ask your staff to follow this general outline when planning for the program's opening days.

1. **Orientation to the Center**

   This is begun on the child's first visit [Section E13, E28]. However, it will continue for at least three or four weeks—until children and child care providers get to know one another well. Remember that children have every reason to be apprehensive. The building is an unfamiliar place, the routines are new, and the people involved are all strangers. Children need reassurance that this is a friendly and helpful place.

   - Smile, smile, smile.
   - Speak softly and precisely.
   - Slowly accustom children to your touch.
   - Let children know that you are gentle, interested, and dependable.

2. **Orientation to Activities and Play Materials**

   - Explain to children in a simple, matter-of-fact way how various materials may be used.
   - Ask returning children to show the new ones how materials and equipment can be used.
   - Introduce only a few items each day.
   - Explain the misuse of materials and equipment, as well as their uses.
   - Explain that each thing should be put away before taking out another. If you do this from the first day, the rule will be enforceable throughout the year.

3. **Orientation to Routines**

   Take plenty of time to explain to children the procedures for various routines. Speak slowly and use simple terms.

4. **Orientation to One Another**

   Names. Using children's names frequently is one of the important ways that you can make orientation to the center as pleasant as possible. See that each child has an easily readable name tag to wear during the first weeks. Say children's names often, in as pleasant and gentle a voice as you can. Help children learn each other's names as well.

   - A good introductory name game is to clap the syllables of each person's name. For example: Má-ry´ Ben´-nett´. Repeat two or three times for each child.
   - Play "leader." Stand across the room and call a child to come to you. That child calls another child to come. Continue until all children have been called.
   - Roll a large ball to one child, calling out his or her name. That child then rolls the ball to and calls the name of another child, and so on.
   - Improvise similar "leader" games.

   Addresses. Let the children know that you know where they live. This makes them feel more comfortable and secure.

   Telephone Numbers. Let the children know that you also know their telephone numbers. Play telephoning home with each child.

5. **Health and Safety Rules and Procedures [Parts G and H]**

   In order to establish an atmosphere in which children can have true freedom to set their own paces, establish health and safety rules early. Always enforce the rules. Do so pleasantly, but firmly.

6. **Behavioral Problems**

   Carefully review the section on behavior in the child care assistant's manual [Section F17]. Refrain from punitive measures when trying to help children solve behavioral problems. Your purpose is to help them retain control of their emotions and actions, not to stop them from expressing feelings and moods. Follow the guidelines for nonpunitive discipline listed in the book *Please Don't Sit on the Kids* by Clare Cherry (Fearon Teacher Aids).

   - Children who become angry, upset, or disruptive need your help. In fact, their actions may be the only way that they know how to reach you.
   - When children display unacceptable behavior, it is usually because they want something. It may be a toy, a turn, or a touch. They hope that their actions will help them get what they want. You can help them learn to ask for what they want in more acceptable ways.
   - Remember at all times that children are vulnerable. Another child, the adults in their lives, or the center as a whole may all or separately be just too overwhelming. Above all, children need your love, patience, and understanding.

7. **Director's Assistance**

   Let your director know in what ways she or he can help you. Don't hesitate to call the director into the child care area at any time. The children must always come first.

I3 Curriculum Plans

Curriculum plans fall into three categories:

1. **Overall long-range plans based on the philosophy and goals of the program, as stated in the operating policies of the center [Section A14] and restated for parents and caregivers in their handbook [Section E25].** The curriculum plan may be in the form of written statements for the center as a whole or for each individual child care room. It may be in the form of published programs to which you subscribe, programs described in child care provider's handbooks or curriculum guides, or programs that you have written yourself.
2. **Weekly lesson plans based on the long-range goals of your center.** You should give child care providers reminders of appropriate activities. In filling out these plans, not every area needs to be met every day—or even every week. But when a series of such plans are put together, all areas should be met in a balance deemed appropriate for the ages, needs, interests, and abilities of the children involved.

   At your center, probationary child care providers should be asked to review their weekly lesson plans with the director as part of their in-service training. Gradually, the "checking" of lesson plans can be decreased. Child care providers who demonstrate that they are meeting your expectations should be given the responsibility of carrying out their own lesson plans without being constantly checked. However, that doesn't mean you shouldn't remain aware of the ongoing program. You can do this by occasionally checking the lesson plans, frequently visiting the child care rooms, and communicating with the child care providers.

   Basically, the director's job is to hire competent persons who know how to plan and implement a curriculum appropriate for the developmental age of children in their groups, and then trust these persons to fulfill their responsibilities.
3. **Daily plans drawn up from the weekly plans by the child care providers, as a reminder for everyone involved in the child care room on a particular day.** This daily plan is especially helpful for assistant child care providers, volunteers, student teachers, and parents and caregivers who may be assisting for the day.

I4 Lesson Plan Evaluation

In evaluating the lesson plans prepared by your staff, it is important to remind them that a lesson plan is only as good as its flexibility. Sometimes a child care provider may prepare what adults view as an interesting activity—and then find that the children do not respond to it, no matter how it is presented. There are so many things for young children to be involved in that such an activity should be dropped—no matter what the preparations were—and another activity introduced.

Sometimes an activity needs to be modified in order to include children who have special needs or who require special help. Sometimes the activity needs to be expanded to meet the needs of children who have progressed beyond the majority and are capable of greater challenges.

Also, modifications may need to be made to adjust for such conditions as the weather, low attendance on a particular day, unexpected visitors, national events, substitute child care providers, unavailability of required materials, miscalculations as to the amount of time needed for an activity or the degree of difficulty, and related factors.

A checklist can be used to ask pertinent questions that will help to establish the validity of a particular plan:

1. Is it relevant to the ages, cultural backgrounds, and general development of the children? ___
2. Is it nonsexist? ___ Nonracist? ___ Multicultural? ___
3. Have safety factors been considered? ___
4. Have health factors been considered? ___
5. Are there opportunities to make choices? ___
6. Are there opportunities to be alone? ___
7. Are there opportunities for developing fine motor skills? ___
   Gross motor skills? ___ Eye-hand coordination? ___
   Body awareness? ___ Space awareness? ___
   Problem-solving skills? ___ Creative expression? ___
   The ability to follow directions? ___
   The ability to use and understand language? ___
8. Are there opportunities to promote physical growth and well-being? ___
   Emotional growth and well-being? ___ Social development? ___
   Understanding others? ___ Understanding self? ___
   The art of relaxation? ___
9. Are there built-in assurances of success? ___
10. Have personality differences been considered? ___
    Age differences? ___ Developmental levels? ___
    Individual special needs? ___ Individual talents? ___
    Special interests? ___ Current events? ___
11. Is there a rhythmic balance between indoor and outdoor activities, allowing for weather considerations? ___
12. Is there a rhythmic balance between active and sedentary activities? ___
13. Has consideration been given to activities in other rooms? ___
14. Have assistants been involved in the planning? ___

The following are samples of open-ended lesson planning. The items listed in the left-hand columns are only "reminder" items. On any particular day, child care providers may include as few or as many of those items as are appropriate or that fit into the program for that day.

Such advanced planning, not bound by strict time schedules, allows for enough flexibility to make changes as needed in accordance with the weather, unexpected school happenings, special events, the use of substitutes in case of illness, and similar reasons.

I5 Weekly Plan

WEEKLY PLAN

Child care provider: Week of to

Item	Monday	Tuesday	Wednesday	Thursday	Friday
Theme/Concept					
Dramatic Play					
Creative Art					
Science					
Creative Movement					
Songs/Music					
Story/Language					
Walk/Excursion					
Nutrition/ Cooking/Snack					
Math					
Sounds					
Relaxation					
Perceptual Motor					
Playground					
Conversation					
1-Wk Calendar					
Birthday/Holiday/ Special Event					
Visitor(s)					

I6 Daily Plan

DAILY PLAN

Child Care Provider: For Day of

Item	Theme/Concept	Materials	Duties of Assistant
Theme/Concept			
Dramatic Play			
Creative Art			
Science			
Creative Movement			
Songs/Music			
Story/Language			
Walk/Excursion			
Nutrition/ Cooking/Snack			
Math			
Sounds			
Relaxation			
Perceptual Motor			
Playground			
Conversation			
1-Wk Calendar			
Birthday/Holiday/ Special Event			
Visitor(s)			

I7 Schedules

The above plans are not time schedules. All scheduling is done in terms of large blocks of time. With an open education system, the basic schedule is also very flexible. Although it may vary from day to day according to special events, the time of the year, the weather, and special projects introduced from time to time on the lesson plans, the schedule for a typical day can be similar to the following example:

2–3-yr.-olds	4–6-yr.-olds	Appropriate Activity or Experience	Goals
A.M. 7:00–9:00	A.M. 7:00–9:00	Greet children, parents, and caregivers. Staff member gives health check in all-purpose room used for early morning care. Play.	Self-esteem; health awareness; personal relationships; comfort; and a good start for the day.
9:00–9:15	9:00–9:15	Arrival of all other children. Greeting and health check by director. All children, including those who arrived between 7 and 9, go to own rooms.	Same as above.
9:15–9:50	9:15–11:00	Free play. Exploration and use of all play centers and equipment in own room and others, indoors and out. Creative art, cooking, dramatic play, building, gross motor activities, table toys, and so on.	Vary according to individual experiences, ability, development, and skills. To learn to make choices, solve problems, develop social relationships, grow perceptually and cognitively.
	9:45–10:30	Snacks available (once) as wanted.	
9:50–10:00		Toilet and hand washing. (Repeated hourly for 2-year-olds.)	Healthful habits and learning to take responsibility for self.
10:00–10:20*		Snack and rest.	To meet physical needs; learning to relax.
10:20–10:50	11:00–11:45	Story. Singing. Creative movement. Followed by relaxation exercises.	Sensory-motor skills; auditory development; self-awareness and body control; self-expression; musical skills; group identification.
10:50–11:35		Playground (if weather permits). Otherwise, vigorous indoor games.	Gross motor skills; physical health.
11:35–12:00	11:45–12:00	Conversation, calendar, stories, finger games, plans, evaluation, getting ready to go home at noon or to have lunch.	Language development; listening skills; expression of feelings; relaxation; group identity.
P.M. all ages the same		Morning staff who work half-day leave at 1:00 or 1:30 P.M. Afternoon staff arrives at 12:00, 12:30, and 1:00 P.M.	
12:00–12:30		Lunch.	To meet physical needs; develop social skills.
12:30–1:00		Brisk walk, group games, or other group activity away from lunch area.	To aid digestion and to use up energy provided by meal.
1:00–3:00		Naps (resting for very oldest).	Healthful habits; relaxation.
3:15–3:30		Fruit or raw vegetables and juice; nuts.	Healthful nutrition.
3:30–4:45		Play in cross-aged groups.	Same as free play above.
4:45–6:00		Clay, puppets, stories, puzzles, drawing, and other quiet activities. Much staff-child conversation and holding. Going home at individual times. Greet parents and caregivers.	An "unwinding" time; relaxation; being wanted; close relationships at the end of a long, busy day. Reassuring parents and caregivers.

* Note: A rest period is not shown for the 4–6-year-olds. In a self-pacing open child care room, the children are able to move to their own body rhythms. Thus, they alternate their quiet and vigorous activities according to individual needs.

I8 Bulletin Boards

Strive for ways to make the child care areas child-oriented and child-sized by using small tables and chairs, low shelves, many floor and rug activities, miniature accessories, and so on. Bulletin boards should be placed at children's eye level. Be careful not to arrange them to impress parents, caregivers, or other visitors. Here are some guidelines to follow:

1. Keep most of the bulletin boards small, intimate, and low—where children can touch them and personally relate to them.
2. Keep the bulletin-board displays relevant to things with which children are familiar or are learning to become familiar. Use the wall displays primarily as background for the various interest centers you set up around the room [Section Cll].
3. Use harmonious colors in keeping with the time of the year, the general decor of the room, and the subject of the display.
4. Use variety in texture, materials, placement, and subject matter. For young children it is best not to decorate an entire room around one theme. They are usually interested in too many other things that are going on. Your displays should reflect those interests.
5. Change the displays frequently. Keep them simple enough so that when new interests come up, you have no qualms about taking a display down and replacing it with another. As with the interest centers, never change everything all at once. This enables children to retain a feeling of familiarity, which is important to their overall comfort and security. Change the displays often enough that faded and outdated materials don't detract from the challenges they may have once offered.
6. Use magazine pictures and illustrations from discarded picture books if you are unable to draw or if you don't have the time. Coloring books that have sample colored pictures are usually drawn better than pictures in other books. The colored pictures can be cut out and used for displays. (Discard the uncolored ones, so as not to give that kind of structured "art" idea to a child.)
7. Refer to your library of bulletin board reference materials and to your resource center for additional ideas.
8. Remember that bulletin boards are only one of the many interest centers in the room. They should be neither more nor less important than other centers.

I9 Toileting

Toilet facilities may not always be adjacent to each child care area. If this is the case, you must supervise children when they go. Give the staff at your center these guidelines:

1. Early in the year, two-year-olds are taken to the toilet almost every hour to assist in toilet training and establish regularity. As the year progresses, this interval is lengthened.
2. Don't look at toileting and washing routines as chores. They are an important part of the child's needs, and they provide all kinds of learning situations, such as waiting, self-awareness, courtesy, responsibility, independence, cleanliness, sensory awareness (washing hands with lots of soapsuds), physical satisfaction, helping others, following directions, sharing, and so on. It should be a pleasant, leisurely experience, rather than one in which the child is rushed and prodded.
3. Older children must be reminded not to turn off the lights in the restrooms, not to lock the doors and crawl under them, and not to use the restroom as a play area.

I10 Child Care Provider's Evaluation for Toileting Routines

1. When a group of children go to the lavatory, do you go with them yourself rather than send an assistant? Never ___ Sometimes ___ Usually ___

   You should always go with children during the first weeks of the program year. As the year progresses and you get to know the children well, then feel free to send your assistant.

2. Do you consider toileting and washing routines to be unpleasant chores? Usually ___ Sometimes ___ No ___
3. The rules we have established are as follows:
   a. No one is to crawl out under a locked door. It must be opened from the inside. (If a small child cannot unlock a door, push on it from the outside to loosen the sliding latch enough for the child to release it easily.)
   b. Hands are always washed thoroughly with soap after use of the toilet. Wash wrists, backs of hands, and between fingers.
   c. Use a paper towel to turn off the faucet.
   d. One paper towel will ordinarily dry hands well if it is unfolded before use. Before throwing the towel away, use it to wipe spilled soapsuds off the sinks to keep them looking neat and clean.
   e. Used towels are always thrown into the container provided.
   f. If a booth is out of toilet paper, an adult should be notified.
   g. The toilet should be flushed after each use. Flush handles should be cleaned several times a day.
   h. Paper towels, toilet paper rolls, or other objects are not to be put into the toilets.
   i. The light is not to be shut off during center hours.
   j. The outer door is not to be closed during center hours.
   k. The lavatories are not a place for playing games.
   l. When with a group, no one returns to the room until the adult gives instructions to do so.
   m. No one sits on the floor in the lavatory.
   n. Adults who accompany children to the lavatories are asked to keep toilets flushed and washbasins wiped clean, and to periodically clean faucets and flush handles. If everyone cooperates, the room always looks presentable and is always sanitary.
4. Do you take small children to the toilet at regular times? No ___ Yes ___

   Two-year-olds are taken to the toilet, five at a time, between 9:45 and 10:00 each morning, thus helping them to establish bladder control. They are taken again at 10:45, just before they go out to the playground.

5. Do you remember to take as many children as possible on each trip to the lavatory? No ___ Yes ___

If a two or three-year-old needs to go to the toilet while out in the playground, take three or four other children with you to reduce the number left to supervise.

6. Do you treat toilet accidents calmly and help the child into clean clothes in a matter-of-fact way? Usually ___ Always ___

   Children need to know that we, as understanding adults, know that toilet accidents are just that—accidents. Make as little fuss about them as possible. Help children into clean clothes in a calm and pleasant manner and casually wipe up the floor with a genuinely friendly expression. Reassure them that it's all right. Remember, you can't fool a small child. Don't fake it. Be sincere. Understand that toilet accidents are a natural part of growth in a child.

7. Do you take note of a child who seems to be having more "accidents" than usual, or who seems to need to urinate quite frequently?
   Haven't thought about it ___ Yes ___ No ___

   Frequent urination may indicate some hidden physical problem or even sexual abuse. It might indicate the beginning of a simple illness, such as a cold, or indicate a serious disease. In any case, the parent or caregiver should be notified of this change in the child's habits. Children who complain of having a stomachache and go to the toilet several times during a morning should be isolated from the other children, and their parents or caregivers should be called to pick them up. Be extra careful to wash faucets, flush handles, and toilet seats they have used. They may be developing some type of contagious stomach upset.

I11 Field Trips and Short Excursions

Excursions may be made either on or off the center property. They may be walking trips to visit people or places of interest, to become familiar with the center and neighborhood environment, or to make observations as a part of the curriculum. Ideas for walking trips include going to look at houses, trees, flowers, rocks, trucks, puddles, snow, people, animals, stores, traffic signals, birds, mailboxes—all kinds of things. Pebbles, leaves, sticks, and other nature items may be collected. Keep a record of field trips you feel are worth repeating.

I12 Staff Notice of Walks Around the Neighborhood

For walks to nearby places, the staff can use the simplified notification sheet on page 406 to inform the director that the group will temporarily be away from the center property.

NOTIFICATION OF WALK OFF THE SCHOOL GROUNDS

Group ________________ Date of walk: ________

Time leaving: __________ Time returning: ____________ No. of children: ________

No. of adults: __________ Destination (include purpose of excursion):

____

____

Children will/will not take their sweaters, jackets, coats.
They will/will not be taken to the toilet before they leave.
The route we plan to take is

____

____

I13 Field Trip Records and Suggestions

This form can be used to keep a record of field trips that were successful enough to be repeated and to record suggestions for future field trips.

Community Child Care Center

FIELD TRIP RECORD

Place	Contact Person	Phone	Address	Things to Know About This Trip
Airport				
Artist's studio				
Baker				
Bank				
Brick factory				
Bus trip				
Bus station				
Cafeteria				
Chicken farm				
Construction site				
Convalescent hospital				
Courthouse				
Creek				
Dairy				
Restaurant				
Farm				
Fast food kitchen				
Fire station				
Flower nursery				
Garage				
Gas station				
Grocery store				
Harbor				

FIELD TRIP RECORD, Page 2

Place	Contact Person	Phone	Address	Things to Know About This Trip
Hospital				
Lake				
Library				
Market				
Mountain				
Museum				
Nature preserve				
Open-air market				
Parent or caregiver work places				
Park				
Pet shop				
Police station				
Post office				
Rock-crushing plant				
Shopping center				
Train station				
Travel trailer plant				
Zoo				
Other				
Other				
Other				

What to see on Neighborhood Walks:

ants
flowers
lawns
rocks
cracks in sidewalk

doors
gardeners
chimneys
roofs
weeds

fences
bugs
leaves
trees

builders
houses
pets

I14 Field Trip Proposal Form (to be submitted in duplicate)

Approval for trip: ______________________ Date: __________
(director)

Group: ________ Ages of children: ________ Date of proposal: __________

Destination: ______________________ Date of trip: __________

Contact person: ________ Telephone: ________ Date contacted: __________

Arrangements made: ______________________

Permissions in file checked: ______________________

Parents and caregivers notified:

Date: ________ Transportation: ________ Appropriate clothing: ________

Whether or not all children can come, even if it's not their regular day: __________

Time leaving: ___ Time returning: ________ Sack lunch: __________

Charge, if any: ______________ Other: __________

Supervision planned: ______________________

Arrangements made: ______________________

Orientation of children for trip (list steps taken including safety reminders): __________

____

Other safety preparations including arrangements for emergency car: __________

____

Items to take along:

Cleansing tissue ________ First aid kit ________

Premoistened, disposable towelettes ________ Drinks ________ Snacks ________

Paper cups ________ Napkins ________

Sack lunches ________ Song sheets for volunteer assistants ________

Use of restroom before boarding bus: ________ Head count before boarding: ________

Marking roll books before leaving center grounds: ______________

Head recount before leaving: ________ Head count before returning: ________

Orderly return to rooms after trip: _____ Resting: _____ Use of toilets after trip: _____

Evaluation with children next day:

Discussion of things observed, learned, talked about, instructed, and so on.

Evaluation with staff:

Would you take this trip again? ______________________

List reasons: ______________________

Was supervision adequate? ______________________

List reasons: ______________________

Were any children difficult to supervise on the trip? ______________________

List reasons: ______________________

Was the timing appropriate? ______________________

List reasons: ______________________

I15 Field Trip Planning

Ages of Children

Two-year-olds will respond best to short neighborhood trips. A bus trip to a nearby park, ten minutes at the park, and then back to the center would be a maximum.

Three-year-olds will respond to simple trips up to 1 1/2 hours if plenty of time is allowed for resting, dawdling, walking slowly, and answering questions.

Four- and five-year-olds can do well on trips of up to two hours. Planning should allow for plenty of time to rest and to ask and answer questions.

Five- and six-year-olds can occasionally take a trip of three or four hours—again, if plenty of time is allowed for rest.

Destination

Be sure that the place you plan to go is appropriate for the age group you are taking. Simple, uncomplicated trips should be planned for younger children. Check ahead of time to make sure that the trip is appropriate for the particular time of the year it is being planned for.

Date of Trip

It is better to plan trips for midweek, because many children are more tired on Mondays from family weekend outings than on other days. By setting a midweek date, you allow for immediate planning with children before the trip and immediate follow-up afterward.

Contact Person

Be sure that you have made arrangements, where necessary, with the owner, officer in charge, or other person with whom you will check when you arrive at your destination (unless, of course, the trip is to a public place where no reservations are needed).

Transportation

Make bus or automobile arrangements far enough ahead of time so that parents and caregivers can be notified about the arrangements, and so that you can plan the needed supervision and other details. Remember to adhere to all transportation safety guidelines (Section H15).

Notifying Parents and Caregivers

Even if the trip has been announced on the center calendar or in a news bulletin, a special notice should be sent home for each separate trip. Some parents and caregivers worry a great deal when they know that their children are taking a field trip. They need your support, which you can give by notifying them in advance and by showing, through your communication with them, that you are making careful, thoughtful plans. Some insurance policies require a separate permission slip for each trip, even though you have a blanket permission that was signed at the time of enrollment. Check your insurance company's requirements carefully.

Orienting the Children

Discuss with children ahead of time where you are going, how you will get there, and what you might see when you arrive. Review your repertoire of "bus trip" songs.

Adults' Property

Ask any adults who accompany you to leave their belongings in a locked cupboard at the center so that they will have two free hands for the children. Naturally, if they drive, they will need to carry a driver's license. Another procedure is to put all of the belongings in a plastic bag, which is taken on the bus and of which one person is put in charge. Eight people with two free hands can provide better supervision than nine people with one free hand each.

Supervision

Plan for a ratio of one adult to two children for two-year-olds; one to four for three-year-olds; one to five for four-year-olds; one to six for five-year-olds; and one to eight for six-year-olds. Any group of 15 or more should have one extra person "in charge" who doesn't have any specific children assigned to him or her.

Safety Precautions

Review the safety rules with the children before the trip.

- No child may run ahead of the group.
- No child may cross a street, path, or roadway until instructed to do so by the group leader.
- All children and adults must hold hands and walk slowly while they are crossing.
- Adults must pay close attention to the children who they are supervising. They must not take advantage of the opportunity to converse with each other.
- Each child must wear a name tag so supervisors can call them by name.
- Each group leader should count the children in his or her group from time to time.
- Special friends should be placed in the same group so they won't be running back and forth to each other's groups to visit.
- If a particular child cannot respond to safety rules, that child should either not be taken on the trip, or one adult should be assigned to that child alone.

Emergency Car

An extra car should always be driven to the destination of the bus or automobile in case a child requires emergency medical treatment, or in case of engine trouble.

Songs

If you plan to do group singing, do so on the way to your destination. On return trips, children are usually very quiet, tired, or absorbed in thought.

Items to Take Along

Take cardboard boxes or plastic laundry baskets to carry things with you. Use a plastic wastebasket with a plastic liner for carrying heavy items, such as bottles of milk or juice. If you are going to eat lunch at your destination, each child should take a lunch in a paper sack (discourage the use of lunch pails, which have to be accounted for on the return trip). The child can take a sandwich, a cookie, and a piece of fruit or a vegetable for lunch. Always provide the beverage.

Use of Restrooms Before Boarding Bus

The importance of sending children to the toilet before the excursion can't be stressed enough. It simplifies the entire trip. If two- or three-year-olds are taken on a trip, be sure to take along some extra clothing in case of toilet accidents. Use of restrooms at the destination should be carefully supervised. Toilet seats can be washed off (by you) with paper towels and disinfectant soap. You might want to take along a can of spray disinfectant.

Orderly Return to Rooms

In the half-day program, parents and caregivers frequently come to the center purposely to be on hand to see their youngsters get off the bus. When children see their parents and caregivers, some of them may transfer their attention from the child care provider and rush off. This can disrupt the entire group. Therefore, we plan for and execute a very structured, orderly return to the room.

Discussing the Trip

This is best saved for the following days, after children have had time to make their own evaluations. Give children time to think about what they have experienced at their own paces, rather than immediately rushing them into follow-up activities. Listen to the children. They will help you make your own evaluation if you listen carefully to what they are saying.

Staff Evaluation

Be honest with your evaluation. Each succeeding trip will be more successful than the previous one if evaluations are taken seriously.

Final Note

Remember the importance of keeping trips simple. The preschool child is generally more excited about the "bouncing" bus than the elaborately planned "tour."

I16 Notifying Parents and Caregivers of Field Trips

Use letters like this to inform parents and caregivers in advance of any excursions that you are planning to take.

Community Child Care Center

111 THIRD STREET TELEPHONE 123-4579

Dear Parents and Caregivers,

Your child will be taken on a field trip to Bluelake Creek on Wednesday, April 16, at 9:30 A.M. All children in Groups I and II may go, whether it is their regular center day or not. Transportation will be by bus.

Please send $1.00, which is the admission fee to the Children's Zoo at Bluelake Creek. Please send a sack lunch, including one sandwich, one cookie, and a piece of fruit or a vegetable. We will supply milk.

Your child should wear old clothes and a warm sweater and should have long sleeves on underneath the sweater. It is very shady at the creek. You are requested to dress your child in long pants—no shorts or dresses, please.

The bus will return at 12 noon. Please call for your child at 12:30. Do not come to the center early. Your child will not be released until after a 15- or 20-minute rest. We ask your cooperation in this matter to help us in our planning.

Nine parents and caregivers have volunteered to accompany the child care providers. Your child will be well supervised.

Sincerely,

Director

------ Please sign this portion and return to us at your earliest convenience. ------

My child ________________________ has permission to go on a field trip to

_________________________________ on ____________________.

Signed ____________________________ Date: ____________________

(parent or caregiver)

I17 Transportation for Field Trips

This list is compiled from the questionnaire sent home to parents and caregivers requesting volunteer help [Section F25].

Name	Number of Children	Days Available	Phone

I18 Nutrition (Snacks)

Even a center that does not have a lunch program is concerned with children's nutrition, since it is so vital to health and growth. Thus, a midmorning or midafternoon snack should be viewed from the standpoint of nutritional benefits. The traditional snack of juice and crackers is satisfactory. However, the juice served should be 100% fruit juice and not a flavored drink. Expand your snack period into one in which many foods in addition to or in place of the juice and crackers are served. Following is a sample two-week plan for snacks. Other ideas may be found on the food lists in Part K.

I19 Sample Snack Schedule

Snack Schedule: Two Weeks

Whenever juice is not offered, water consumption is encouraged. Milk is always served.

10 A.M. Snack

Week 1:	Monday	Apple wedges, pretzels
	Tuesday	Carrot sticks, whole wheat bread spread with butter children made previous day
	Wednesday	Orange segments, soda crackers
	Thursday	Celery with peanut butter
	Friday	Pitted dates, slice of swiss cheese

Week 2:	Monday	Wheat crackers, apple juice
	Tuesday	20 raisins, string cheese
	Wednesday	Celery with cream cheese spread, oyster crackers
	Thursday	Peanuts, bananas
	Friday	Cheese cubes, pineapple juice

3:30 P.M. Snack

Week 1:	Monday	Celery sticks with peanut butter, pineapple juice
	Tuesday	Popcorn (made as group project), pear nectar
	Wednesday	Pear wedges, cheese cubes
	Thursday	Cauliflowerets, apple juice
	Friday	Frozen fruit juice popsicles, cheese cubes
Week 2:	Monday	Cheese crackers, olives, grape juice
	Tuesday	Sliced cucumbers, string cheese, milk
	Wednesday	Deviled eggs, cherry tomatoes, milk
	Thursday	Grapes, sliced swiss cheese
	Friday	Peanut butter balls (made by children previous afternoon as craft project), apple juice

I20 Computers in Your Center

Since computers are so much a part of our everyday lives, your Child Care Center should purchase inexpensive computers to be used by the children.

Computers are used primarily for playing perceptual recognition games. Not only are these games great fun for children, but they also familiarize children with computers so that they become eager to learn other computer skills.

When purchasing your computers and first introducing them to children, determine from the beginning that you do not expect computers to take over your teaching responsibilities, but rather to extend the already enriched curriculum you provide. Because of the sedentary nature of sitting before a computer, children should be limited to 15–20 minutes per session.

I21 Full-Day Care at Your Center

Many children now attending community child care centers stay for the entire day. Some come as early as 6:00 A.M. and go home as late as 7:00 P.M. Because this is a long, long time for little children, some aspects of entire preschool programs have had to be modified in consideration of the special needs of child care.

When a child stays all day, the most important single consideration is to ensure a homelike atmosphere. Even in brick, cement, and glass buildings, many things can be done to increase the comfort and security of children and lend "homeyness" to the environment. Some ideas to emphasize in your child care center include the following:

Love and Warmth

Although warmth is a prerequisite for all programs for young children, it becomes of even greater importance in a child care setting. All adults in the center community, including office staff, cooks, maintenance persons, and others should be nurturing toward children. The staff must constantly be aware that their primary objective is to give daily to each child the individual attention, love, and understanding he or she needs. Care must be taken to give this special attention even to those who outwardly appear to be self-sufficient, and to those children who by reasons of poor appearance, behavior problems, or physical or mental special needs often meet rejection from others.

Environment

The physical environment should be planned so that the furnishings and room arrangements have homelike areas. Pillows, small rugs, and informal furnishings offset the austerity and formality of the basic child care structure. Colors should be warm and comfortable, and not limited to the traditional red, blue, and yellow found in so many playthings.

Consistency

Consistency is important in the lives of all children. They like to know what to expect of adults and what the limits are. When children are in preschool for just half a day, they frequently run into problems of adjusting to one set of rules at the center and another set at home. Communication between staff members and parents and caregivers helps create common grounds of understanding and rules of behavior. In the child care setting, consistency becomes an even greater challenge.

Not only are there differences between what is expected at child care and at home, but during an eight-, nine-, ten-, or eleven-hour period, there may be differences in the way various members of the staff handle aspects of the center's program. It is extremely important that the staff work closely with one another to maintain consistency within the center, no matter who is on duty. Weekly staff meetings, daily interchange of information between staff members, recordings of high and low points in the handling of difficult situations, and other similar techniques should be employed to ensure ongoing communication and understanding.

The entire staff, too, needs to work closely with parents and caregivers to promote similarities between parents' and caregivers' actions toward a child and those of the staff to avoid one set of expectations in the child care program and another set of expectations at home. There must be consistency in the type of information going out from staff members to parents and caregivers. When in doubt, a wise child care provider should say to a parent or caregiver, "I'd like to have some time to think about that before giving you an answer," or "I think if you talk to the director, our procedure (or 'the reasons for our actions,' or 'some common causes of that type of behavior') can be clarified for you." To avoid confusion, all staff members should be trained in the same philosophy.

Peer Relationships

Children who play at home during the afternoon frequently have neighbors and family members of varying ages with whom to interact. In a child care center, being with a group of similar-aged children offers the child an excellent opportunity to test him or herself and interact with others without interference from older or younger children. You may choose to group children with other children of the same age in the morning hours. Then children from all age groups can be brought together for special events or for outdoor play in the afternoon. Both types of groupings offer good experiences for children and should be provided in a child care program.

Role Models

It is important that children have the opportunity to observe both male and female adults in their daily activities and behavior. Urge parents and caregivers to volunteer as often as possible to be child care assistants. Invite parents and caregivers to join you frequently on outings or just come in for visits. Since many children in a child care program are from one-parent families, it becomes even more important that they have the opportunity during the day to interact with both men and women.

Flexibility and Choice

In a home, even though children have a certain daily routine, they are not held to rigid time schedules as they often are in the child care center. Though some time scheduling is necessary, there are ways to retain scheduling and yet allow flexibility. Primarily, scheduling is done in fairly large blocks of time, allowing as much flexibility and rescheduling as needed within the basic time areas. As frequently as possible, opportunities are arranged so that children can choose to play indoors or out, alone or with others, quietly or noisily, sitting or running, or slow or fast. When this type of flexibility is introduced during large blocks of time, children readily adhere to very strict scheduling and group action when necessary, such as during routines, trips, meal, and nap times. In a flexible child care setting, child care providers are alert to the "teachable moment" for each particular child, rather than expecting groups of children to participate in staff-planned activities on a fixed schedule. Children are much happier and learning is more intense in this type of environment, which is closer to the home situation.

Freedom and Supervision

The child playing at home is frequently out of sight of adults, who are busy with their own activities. Thus, the child has opportunities for privacy and for deciding when to conform or to break rules. These opportunities to exercise initiative in deciding what to do and whether or not to live up to adult expectations are valuable to the child in developing a sense of personal identity. In a child care situation, responsibility for the safety of the child often causes staff members to restrict some of the child's freedom and privacy. It is, therefore, important to provide secret crannies and hiding places where children can be alone, but at the same time be close enough to an adult to ensure appropriate supervision.

I22 Nap Time

Nap time for children who stay all day at your center should be from 1:00 P.M. to 3:00 P.M. [Section C12]. The following considerations have proven to be conducive to making this period a pleasant experience for everyone involved:

1. Immediately following lunch, the children either go for a walk or play quietly, reading books, working puzzles, or playing with a limited number of manipulative toys. While they are involved, two staff members in the rooms where the children ate lunch should clean the tables and sweep the floor. Cots are then set up. Each child's blanket and sheet (brought from home) are placed on a cot, which is in the same location each day.
2. Children are sent into the nap area two or three at a time and are pleasantly helped to take off their shoes and socks and get into their cots. Preschoolers can

also use cots, and can be set up by themselves with a staff member assisting. Each child is covered and softly spoken to for comfort and reassurance according to individual needs and moods.

3. When all of children are lying down, play soft music for approximately fifteen minutes.
4. No coercion is used. Children who frequently have difficulty relaxing and are sometimes disturbing to the others are quietly removed to an adjacent room where they can be given the freedom for additional time to unwind. One staff member stays with them, which means a 1:2 or 1:3 ratio of adult to child, but it also means that these children, who possibly need to rest more than the others, are helped to achieve that rest according to their own needs.
5. Some children start waking up around 2:30. They are asked to lie quietly and look at books until "getting-up time." Thus, even though the length of time for sleeping varies from individual to individual, no child gets out of bed until almost 3:00 P.M.
6. While the children are asleep, minimal supervision is needed. There are always two staff persons with the sleepers, so if one child is taken to the restroom, or if there is any kind of emergency, the other children will not be left alone. Check with your local licensing agency for nap-time regulations.
7. At about 2:00 P.M., a few children who never nap are allowed to go into an "awake" playroom for quiet activities until the other children awaken.
8. As children get up, they are helped to put on their shoes and socks. They are urged to use the toilets. Then they go to an afternoon playroom set up with playthings that were not used during the morning. While playing quietly for 15 or 20 minutes, children have an opportunity to become fully awake.
9. A nutritious snack is served between 3:15 and 3:45 P.M., by which time the children are ready for afternoon play experiences.
10. Meanwhile, the cots are stacked and put into an out-of-the-way area until needed the next day.

I23 After-Nap Playtime

Following are listed some of the procedures useful for the late afternoon period, especially when some children have been at the center since 6:00 A.M.

1. Enough staff is kept between 3:00 P.M. and 5:00 P.M. so children can play in groups of seven or eight with one staff member.
2. Cross-age groups are mixed according to what time children usually go home. Thus, activities can be planned for without continued interruption. Also, this gives a nice change for children who spend so many long hours at the center.
3. As much time as possible between 3:30 and 5:00 P.M. is spent outdoors when weather permits. On days that are too cold, too hot, or too smoggy, activities are set up indoors to allow for an hour of very active play. Some afternoons are used for special art projects, dramatics, dancing, or special movies.

4. By 4:45 P.M., start quieting down the activities, so children who leave at 5:00 P.M. are not overstimulated when they go home. After 5:00 P.M., only quiet activities should be encouraged. These may include
   - *storytelling, with or without a book*
   - *blackboard stories*
   - *flannelboard stories*
   - *play acting*
   - *manipulation of plasticine (a very relaxing activity)*
   - *puppet shows*
   - *finger games and simple songs*
   - *word games, rhyming games*
   - *very large, difficult puzzles on which several persons work together*
5. At 5:15 P.M., those children still remaining can be given a small snack. This way, when parents and caregivers arrive, thoughts and conversation aren't overwhelmed by hunger.

When a Child Is Not Picked Up by 7:00 P.M.

Upon enrolling their children, parents and caregivers are told explicitly that there is no child care after 7:00 P.M. We recognize the fact, however, that emergency situations may arise. One staff member should be prepared to stay later, if necessary. If the parent or caregiver has called to report an emergency, there is no charge the first time. If it happens a second time, there is a substantial charge (see page 247). If it happens again, the child is subject to dismissal from the program.

I24 Evaluation of Children's Abilities and Needs

This evaluation is for the purpose of detecting any areas in which the child seems to be developmentally immature for his or her general age group. The purpose of this evaluation is not to compare one child with another, but rather to consider each child's stage of development in the unfolding of what should be that child's natural abilities.

Upon completion of all tasks, evaluate the child's strengths and weaknesses. Consider in which areas future growth will emerge naturally and in which areas the child may need to be given specialized developmental activities.

Name of child: __________________________ Date: ________________

Age (year and month): ____________ Administered by: ________________

Directions: Ask the child to perform the tasks listed under each division. Note especially the suggestions under column two. Sum up the child's performance in as short a statement as you can, such as "Excellent," "Confused," or "Rhythmic." Be specific, where necessary, especially in areas where the child may need help.

DIRECTIONS	WHAT TO WATCH FOR	EVALUATION
A. Gross Motor Development		
Say the following to the child:		
1. Crawl to me flat on your stomach.	Smooth and rhythmic use of arms and legs, alternate right-left movement (cross pattern)	
2. Creep to me on your hands and knees.	Ability to use alternate hands and legs (cross pattern) in rhythmic movement, opposite hand and knee touching ground simultaneously	
3. Lie down on the floor and roll sideways. Now roll the other way.	Did child roll to the left or right first? Easily or with difficulty?	
4. Walk to the door. Now walk backward to me.	Whether rhythmic or jerky. Do arms swing naturally and alternately forward and backward?	
5. Jump with your feet together, over this space (1 foot wide).	Ability to jump over flat area	
6. Now jump off this box (1 foot high). Now jump onto this box (6" high).	Ability to jump off or onto a space	
7. Go to the door, then run toward me and leap over this space (2 feet wide).	Ability to do a running leap	
8. Hop to the door on one foot. Now hop back on the other foot.	Which foot did child hop on first? Children often hop on nondominant foot.	
9. Spin like a top. Now spin the other way.	Which direction first?	
10. Gallop around the room.	Which foot leads? Combination movements often not achieved until elementary age.	
11. Skip around the room.	Rhythmic or not?	
12. Rock on your stomach. Hold on to your ankles. Now rock on your back. Hold on to your knees.	Flexibility	
13. Throw this beanbag into that box. Now throw it at that target.	Note control of arm movements. Overhand or underhand?	
B. Sensory-Motor Integration		
How well can the child		
1. walk forward on the balance beam (board 2" x 4", 10' long)? Walk to the middle of the beam and return? Walk sideways on the balance beam?	Ability to balance on board by stretching arms to each side	
2. control the balance board (2' x 2' plywood mounted on 2" square block)?	Ability to balance self	
3. walk up an inclined board (balancing with hands out)?	Ability to balance self	

DIRECTIONS	WHAT TO WATCH FOR	EVALUATION
4. stand on one foot with hands outstretched while you count to five? Stand on one foot with hands outstretched and eyes closed while you count to five?	Ability to stretch arms evenly while maintaining balance. Which foot does child lift? (This may be the dominant foot.)	
5. walk rhythmically to recorded music? (Alternate fast and slow music.)	Ability to keep time to the music	
6. walk through an obstacle course made from chairs tables, boxes, and such?	Ability to negotiate course by judging spaces and directions	
C. Laterality and Dominance		
Check which hand the child uses to		
1. pick up objects spaced widely apart on a table. Repeat many times.	Which hand is used most frequently, indicating dominant hand. Ability to use nondominant hand when necessary.	
2. pick up objects placed widely apart on the floor.	Same as above	
3. pick up objects spaced widely apart on the table.	Same as above	
4. use a crayon on paper.	Which hand is used?	
5. cut with scissors.	Which hand is used?	
6. sight with one eye through a tube. Have child hold tube with writing hand.	Crossing hand to opposite side of face when sighting may indicate crossed dominance. This means the dominant hand is controlled by the opposite side of the brain as the dominant eye.	
D. Tactile Discrimination		
How well can the child		
1. identify a variety of small objects inside a paper bag, by touch only, with one hand? With the other hand?	Ability to discriminate between shapes	
2. differentiate weights between several objects?	Ability to recognize differences in weights	
3. differentiate temperature of water? Cold ____ Cool ____ Warm ____ Hot ____	Ability to discriminate between temperatures	
4. differentiate textures? Soft ____ Hard ____ Sticky ____ Bumpy ____ Rough ____ Smooth ____	Ability to discriminate between textures	

E. Perceptual-Motor Skills

While administering these tasks, vary your voice enough so that you can determine the child's ability to distinguish sounds and respond to whispers.

1. Auditory Decoding

   How well does the child
   - understand questions?
   - follow directions?
   - repeat the alphabet?

DIRECTIONS	WHAT TO WATCH FOR	EVALUATION
2. Auditory Memory ***How well does the child*** • verbally recall information? • recall incidents? • recite nursery rhymes?		
3. Auditory Sequencing ***How well does the child*** • follow a sequence of directions? • follow the sequence backwards? • repeat random digits? • repeat random letters?	(Example: Place this chalk on the yellow book, bring the blue book to my desk, and then move this wastebasket to the corner of the room.) (Example: 2, 9, 5, 3, 1, 8 or 4, 7, 2, 9, 3, 5) (For example: t, v, j, m, or b, f, u, t, y)	
4. Visual Acuity ***Tell the child to*** • point to the nearest one (pencil, book, and so on). • point to the darkest one. • point to things that belong together. (Use things that write, fasten, are flat, are bumpy, and so on. Include an exception in each group.)		
5. Visual Coordination and Pursuit ***How well can the child*** follow the direction of an eraser at the end of a pencil?	Ability to do so smoothly	
6. Visual Memory Select eight small objects. Show them briefly to the child. Remove one and then ask the child to name the one removed. Add another object. Show them again, and ask which has been added. Briefly show a picture. Then ask the child to select the same picture from a group of pictures.	Ability to recall by memory	
7. Visual-Motor, Fine Motor Coordination Copy a square __ circle __ triangle __ rectangle with an *x* in the center __ Spatial Form Manipulation Copy arrangement of three blocks __ pegboard design __ copy a simple design __		
F. Conceptual Skills 1. Numerical Concepts ***How well does the child*** count? __ understand quantity? __ understand "more"? __ understand "less"? __		

DIRECTIONS	WHAT TO WATCH FOR	EVALUATION

2. Distance Concepts
   Does the child understand
   far? __ near? __ farther? __
   nearest? __ close? __ closest? __

3. Position Concepts
   Does the child understand
   above? __ below? __ over? __
   under? __ on? __ off? __
   in front of? __ in back of? __
   to the side of? __ higher? __
   lower? __ highest? __
   lowest? __

4. Size Concepts
   Does the child understand
   big, bigger, biggest? __
   small, smaller, smallest? __
   tiniest?__ largest? __
   longest? __ shortest? __
   thick? __ thin? __

G. Language

While you are conducting this assessment, encourage a conversational exchange with the child in order to assess needs and abilities in language. To evaluate the child's performance, compare three-year-olds with four-year-olds, four-year-olds with five- and three-year-olds, and so on. By comparison, you can judge whether a child is performing similarly to other children the same age. If the child is less able, developmental activities for that child need to be emphasized. Vision, hearing, and general physical well-being need to be evaluated by specialists, and physiological and psychological examinations may be called for.

I25 Extended Day Care

School-age children in kindergarten through sixth grade may need before- and after-school care while their parents or caregivers are working. Your center may want to provide this type of program, as well as the preschool program. School-age children need more outdoor play and autonomy. Encourage these children to work on craft projects, such as complex carpentry structures spread out over a two- or three-week period.

General Program Description

In the sample program outlined in the attached schedules, balance between indoor and outdoor activities and between sedentary and active play experiences has been taken into consideration. Staff persons observe carefully which children need more stimulation/participation and which need stress-reduction exercises.

The program is planned to provide separation in the general use of facilities between older and younger children. This is a legal requirement in many states. However, most of the equipment and materials used can be shared by all groups, but not at the same time.

Interaction between children of different ages is encouraged by use of a "big brother" or "big sister" and a "buddy" system. The goal is to develop understanding of family-type groupings, with younger children evoking sensitivity and responsibility in older children, and older children providing encouragement to younger children. Facilities can be arranged so that the oldest and the youngest, having special needs of their own, are given areas exclusively for their use.

Train your staff to be constantly aware of both individual and group needs and to re-adjust program components accordingly. Arrange for time to listen to children's problems and use the program to help children find balance in their own lives and with their own feelings.

Program Components

In the following schedules for various age groups, these components have been considered:

Indoor Activities—Free Play

- Manipulative games and toys (fine-motor experiences)
- Puzzles
- Books
- Language development games
- Use of arts and crafts materials, such as paints, crayons, scissors, paste, collage materials, and so on
- Blocks
- Puppets
- Housekeeping area
- Tape recorder; CD player
- Special science, nature, and creative art projects set up periodically by staff
- Gross-motor equipment: large ball, wedges, mats for tumbling, parachute

Outdoor Activities—Free Play

- Physical development equipment: playground equipment, boxes, tires
- Ball games
- Parachute
- Sand play (may include mud, water)
- Dramatic play with boxes, tires, planks, movable ladders

Organized/Group Activities—Indoors

In addition to items under free play, include the following:

- Dance, orchestra, music appreciation, creative movement, exercises
- Stress-reduction exercises
- Dramatic storytelling and play-acting
- Puppet show production
- Creative writing
- Science experiments
- Woodworking
- Sewing

Organized/Group Activities—Outdoors

In addition to items under free play, include the following:

- Team sports: volleyball, half-court basketball, kickball
- Gardening
- Short field trips: in neighborhood, including nature walks

Homework

- Assistance and time for homework assignments
- Encourage older children to assist younger children with school assignments

Snacks

See sample snack schedule for two-week period [Section I19].

Other

Release time should be arranged for Scout meetings, Camp Fire Girls, music lessons, and other personal activities, with permission from parents and caregivers.

Children with Special Needs

Careful consideration is given to planning programs that are inclusive of all children. Select materials and equipment that most children with special needs can use.

Purchase special equipment to be used for gross motor activities for those with special needs, although such equipment can also be used by physically able children. Provide your staff with training in techniques for adaptive physical education.

Buddy System

A "buddy" system is used so that each child with special needs has a buddy at all times to give support as needed. This responsibility is rotated between a number of the more dependable children.

Tutorial Program

An integral part of the program involves providing tutorial assistance for children needing help with their academic work. This component will consist of assistance with homework, tutoring in specific skills, and introduction to sensory-motor and perceptual-motor integrative exercises which have proven to be helpful for children lagging in their development.

Kindergarden Schedule, Morning and Afternoon Groups

7:00–9:00 A.M.	Arrival of children, according to parents' and caregivers' needs. Snack available for those who have not had breakfast.
7:00–8:00	Free play indoors: Dramatic play, table games, books, coloring, and related activities
8:00–8:30	Free play outdoors
8:30–9:00	Indoors; story; get ready for school *Morning kindergarten* children leave for school.
9:00–10:15	Art; craft projects; free-play activities indoors
10:15–10:30	Snack; story
10:30–11:15	Outdoor play
11:15–11:45	Rest
11:45–12:15	Lunch (brought by children from home) *Afternoon kindergarten* children leave for school. *Morning kindergarten* children arrive.
12:15–12:45 P.M.	Lunch (brought by children from home)
12:45–1:15	Outdoor play
1:15–2:00	Rest
2:00–2:15	First- and second-grade children arrive. Snack
2:15–3:00	Music, dancing, play-acting with first- and second-grade children
3:00–4:00	Free play indoors
4:00–5:00	Free play outdoors
5:00–6:00	Cleanup. Small group activities: stories, conversation, table games, circle games, finger plays

First and Second Grades

7:00–9:00 A.M.	Arrival of children, according to parents' and caregivers' needs. Snack available for those who have not had breakfast.
7:00–8:00	Free play indoors: Dramatic play, table games, books, coloring, and related activities
8:00–8:30	Free play outdoors
8:30–9:00	Indoors; story; get ready and leave for school
2:00–2:30 P.M.	Return from school Snack available upon arrival
2:15–3:00	Music, dancing, play-acting with other children
3:00–4:00	Free play indoors Homework, if any
4:00–5:00	Free play outdoors
5:00–6:00	Cleanup. Small group activities: stories, conversation, table games, circle games, finger plays

Third through Sixth Grades

7:00–9:00 A.M.	Arrival of children, according to parents' and caregivers' needs. Snack available for those who have not had breakfast.
7:00–8:00	Free play outdoors
8:00–8:40	Finish homework, if any. Assistance given as needed. If no homework, free play indoors
8:40–9:00	Cleanup, leave for school
3:00–3:15 P.M.	Return from school Snack upon arrival
3:15–4:00	Outdoor play
4:00–5:00	Homework, if any Free play indoors, enrichment activities
5:00–6:00	Cleanup. Small group activities: stories, conversation, games

I26 Care of Infants

The demands of infant and toddler care have grown in the area of child care. Because the adult-child ratio in some states are one adult to three children, many centers do not elect to provide this service. However, growing numbers of parents and caregivers with infants are now working, and the need for infant-toddler care centers is in demand.

With research reporting that children's early attachments have an influence on their brain development, programs that support quality care is essential. Everyone who cares for young children will want to provide a safe and healthy environment, with caregivers who are warm, loving, and responsive to children's cues.

Social and emotional growth may be planned for young children around the daily routine of feeding, toileting/diapering, and play times. The overall growth of the infant-toddler changes so rapidly that child care providers need to be alert to typical developmental stages and the corresponding ages in order to judge appropriateness of behavior and expectations. This enables them to provide suitable activities and play materials.

Individualizing care is ideally accomplished during diapering, bathing, feeding, and other routines in providing personal care. For example, opportunities for language may be initiated during diapering as a part of the social interaction that the adult and infant enjoy. Further individualization is accomplished by allowing each child the freedom to move according to personal needs and skills. They should crawl, creep, sit, and stand only when they are able to do so without artificial assistance. Therefore, equipment designed to encourage these movements is not necessary; rather, children need the space in which to practice individualized movements according to internal developmental timetables.

Equipment for infants should be safe and easy to clean. Their equipment should also incorporate into their designs qualities to stimulate eye-hand coordination, visual acuity, auditory discrimination, and tactile awareness.

The rooms for infants should be designed so that sleep areas, play areas, and toilet areas are clearly visible to supervising personnel.

Detailed record keeping of routines is of great value to parents and caregivers of infants and toddlers. Supply parents and caregivers with a quantity of forms similar to the following and have it sent to the center with the infant/toddler each day.

Community Child Care Center

111 THIRD STREET TELEPHONE 123-4579

Name of child: ____________________ Date: ____________________

Sleep — At what time: __________ Time awoke: ____________________

If disturbed, reason: ______________________________

Food — Items: ______________ Times: ____________________

Amount: ______________________________

Toileting — Bowel movement: No ______ Yes______ Times: __________

Normal ______ Loose ______ Tight ______

Mood upon awakening this morning: ______________________________

If child is upset, can you state why? ______________________________

Did anything unusual take place at home since child was last at center? ______________

Describe: ______________________________

____

In turn, the school sends home a note as follows:

Community Child Care Center

111 THIRD STREET TELEPHONE 123-4579

Name of child: ____________________ Date: ____________________

Time child slept: ______to______ ______to______ ______to______

Time child ate: ______ ______ ______ ______ ______ ______

Food child ate: ____________ ____________ ____________

(If formula, state amount): ______________________________

Bowel movements: Time __________ Condition ______________

Special activities, words, accomplishments today:

____

____

____

J

Community Relationships

1 Visitors
2 Student Observers and Other Participants
3 Guide for Student Teacher Evaluation
4 Guide for Student Teachers
5 Consultation Services
6 Professional Organizations
7 National Academy of Early Childhood Programs Accreditation Project
8 Other Obligations
9 Legislative Action
10 Sources of Information on Early Childhood Development and Education

As director, you are responsible for representing the center to the community [Section A1]. There are a number of ways to meet this responsibility. You can sponsor public events such as open houses and educational programs to which the public is invited. These events provide a service to the community and, at the same time, publicize your program to prospective future clients. Some community events you can sponsor might include the following:

- Junior art fair
- Dramatic productions on themes concerning family life
- Open house during the National Week of the Young Child and other times
- Panel discussions on children's health problems
- First aid courses
- Lecture series on child development issues

J1 Visitors

Welcoming visitors to your center is one of the best ways of building a good program of public relations. It is an indication of your confidence in the validity of your program. Visitors may be students, teachers, or administrators from other centers; representatives from the medical profession or from various social services; or interested persons from the general community. In fairness to your staff, and in order to give personal attention to visitors, the number of people invited for any one day should be limited. For a periodic evaluation of this program, it will help to keep a visitors' register similar to this one.

Community Child Care Center

111 THIRD STREET TELEPHONE 123-4579

Dear Visitor:

Thank you for coming to our center. You are always welcome. Please sign our guest book. This will help us tabulate information regarding the services we have given others in order that we may plan for ways to increase such services.

For Director's Use Only:

Date	Name	Address	Position	Reason for Visit	Time	Director's Time

J2 Student Observers and Other Participants

You can also serve the community by providing a training facility for local colleges and other educational institutions. Allow small groups or individuals from local institutions to observe and actually participate at the center. For example, student nurses who are specializing in pediatrics at a nearby college can spend one week as child care assistants. This opportunity enables them to acquire some practical experience with the well child before working with the sick. They are also able to learn curriculum techniques and activities that they can use with hospitalized children. A pediatrics instructor can sometimes accompany the group of nursing students and help supervise. The nursing students can spend one day observing and participating in an orientation program during which they become familiar with the Child Care Assistant's Manual [Section F16]. Assign them to various rooms for the rest of the week, giving each student an opportunity to work with two-, three-, four-, and five-year-olds.

High school students from community outreach classes can come to observe as well. You can train physically challenged people from time to time, either as child care assistants or office workers, depending on the individual's particular abilities. Child care providers, teachers, and administrators from other centers should have an open invitation to observe your program at any time.

Offer the use of your facilities to students who are majoring in child development. They can be assigned directly to the center for work experience training. Education majors working for teaching credentials and specializing in early childhood education can also use your facilities. These students may spend three to nine hours a week with you for either one quarter (thirteen weeks) or one semester (sixteen weeks). If you are asked to evaluate them, use the guide presented in Section J3, unless their school provides its own form.

J3 Guide for Student Teacher Evaluation

Name of student: ______________________ Supervisor: __________________

School: ______________________________ Instructor: __________________

1. What is the student's overall attitude at the center?
2. Has the student demonstrated an aptitude for caring for or teaching young children?
3. Has the student demonstrated an ability to use special skills and talents at the center?
4. Has the student demonstrated professional conduct and integrity?
5. Has the student demonstrated a willingness to follow directions and prescribed procedures, and to cooperate with your established practices?
6. Has the student demonstrated an ability to innovate ideas?

7. Has the student been successful in interpersonal relations with other members of the center community, including parents and caregivers?
8. Has the student's performance been such as to earn your future recommendation for possible employment as a preschool teacher or child care provider?

J4 Guide for Student Teachers

Community Child Care Center

111 THIRD STREET TELEPHONE 123-4579

To Participating Student Teachers:

We at the Community Child Care Center feel it is a privilege to have you in our center, and we hope that, in turn, you will feel privileged to be here. We want to make your experience as meaningful as possible to you, as well as productive for ourselves. Therefore, we intend to treat you as professionals. We expect professional behavior in return.

Please use the following guidelines:

1. Sign-in Sheet
   Please sign the ledger in the director's office when you arrive each morning. We need an accurate record of your participation to determine your dependability, reliability, and sense of responsibility, as well as the state of your health. (Frequent absences might indicate that you should choose a less strenuous occupation.)
2. Absences
   We expect you to notify the center of all cases of absence. Failure to do so is grounds for termination of placement with the Community Child Care Center.
3. Orientation
   During your first nine hours at the center, we will help you become familiar with handbooks, child care rooms, schedules, supplies, and equipment. We will also hold discussions on child care techniques and professional conduct and will give you a chance to observe each group.
4. Participation
   You will be assigned to a group for a period of four weeks. Your duties will include supervising small groups and planning for and supervising an entire day—including cleanup.
5. Curriculum
   You will have opportunities to develop your professional skills by working in a wide variety of curriculum areas with the children:
   - Storytelling and language experience
   - Art experiences
   - Music and rhythmic activities
   - Role playing
   - Science
   - Woodworking
   - Routines—personal care, clothing, food, rest, toileting
   - Motor activities
   - Block play
   - Dramatic play
   - Cooking
   - Manipulative activities
   - Field trips
   - Mathematical concepts
6. Staff Meetings
   You will be expected to participate in at least one staff business meeting and one staff in-service. These meetings are held at noon Mondays, alternate weeks. Please make an appointment with the director. Discussions at these meetings are privileged information. Professional integrity will be considered in our evaluation of your service to us.
7. Parent/Caregiver Conferences
   You will be given an opportunity to sit in on a parent/caregiver conference as an observer.
8. Other Duties
   You will be expected to attend at least one family-center function. You will also be asked to plan the bulletin board displays for a full week for one child care group.

J5 Consultation Services

Community services also include consulting with people who wish to enter the field of child care and early childhood education. If you can help other centers and the people involved in them enhance program quality, you can help to raise the level of education for everyone. You will therefore be called on from time to time to share your knowledge and experience with others. You may also be asked to speak to groups who are interested in this subject.

J6 Professional Organizations

The director is expected to become a member of professional organizations that are actively working for the improvement of early childhood education and the welfare of all children. The director is expected to play an active role in those organizations and to volunteer his or her personal services from time to time. Even though one cannot belong to every such organization, it is a director's responsibility to keep informed of the activities, or the available publications, of as many of them as possible. The following are two major organizations to which a director can belong:

NAEYC (National Association for the Education of Young Children)

This includes membership in both state and county affiliate groups. Consult the list of organizations presented in Section J10 for the address of this association. Write to find out if there is a local or regional affiliate in your area. For a slight difference in fee, your affiliate membership can carry with it membership in the national organization. NAEYC is primarily concerned with children from infancy through eight or nine years of age and is the nation's leading organization of early childhood educators.

ACEI (Association for Childhood Education International)

The address of this association may also be found in Section J10. ACEI is an international organization with headquarters in the United States. The organization is concerned with children from infancy through adolescence. Its membership includes many persons who are not teachers or educators, but who work with children in many other fields. When you join this group, your membership is channeled to the nearest branch.

Child care providers, too, should be affiliated with at least one local or regional educational group. Your child care can pay for membership in the local branch of the NAEYC for each of its staff members. Child care providers should respect that membership by participating in local or regional activities of the organization. Centers should allocate funds in its annual budget for this participation.

J7

National Academy of Early Childhood Programs Accreditation Project

In 1985, the National Association for the Education of Young Children introduced the National Academy of Early Childhood Programs. After three years of consultation and field testing with representative early childhood education facilities nationwide and in several foreign countries, the academy formulated a set of criteria for high quality early childhood programs. (Note: The program is sometimes referred to as CAP: Center Accreditation Program.)

The goal of the program is to "improve the quality of care and education provided for young children in group programs. . . ." (from *Guide to Accreditation,* National Association for the Education of Young Children). Accreditation is achieved through a self-study made by the center. The following issues are addressed:

A. Interactions among Staff and Children
B. Curriculum
C. Staff-Parent/Caregiver Interaction
D. Staff Qualifications and Development
E. Administration
F. Staffing
G. Physical Environment
H. Health and Safety
I. Nutrition and Food Service
J. Evaluation (of staff, program, individual children)

The self-study involves the staff, parents, caregivers, children, and administrators in evaluating the above criteria. The following general procedure is used:

1. The center applies for accreditation. The application and validation fee varies with the size of the center.
2. The center is sent the self-study materials. Consultation by phone is offered if help is needed in completing the self-study.
3. After completing the forms, if the center feels it is ready for accreditation, it pays a validation fee, which is based on the total number of children enrolled in the program.
4. A validator (person involved in early childhood education who was trained in verification methods) will come to the center to validate (verify) the information that has been written down for the self-study. Validators do not evaluate or consult—their job is purely to verify (or not verify) the information given them.
5. In cases of disagreement between the validator and the center, the center has an opportunity to justify its procedure.
6. The validator sends the center's self-study and the validator's study to the academy.
7. The academy assigns the papers to an accreditation commission, composed of a diverse group of three early childhood professionals. Members may be administrators, teachers, or researchers.

8. The commission may either grant accreditation or defer accreditation until improvements can be made. Decisions will not require complete compliance with all criteria. They will be decided on the degrees of compliance for each of the various components and the overall picture they present.
9. If accreditation is deferred, the center has the right to appeal. In such cases, a second commission will be asked for a decision. Only one such appeal may be made on an application.

All types of programs can apply for accreditation, including preschools, before- and after-school programs, infant/toddler programs, and child care centers. You can apply whether you operate full- or part-time, or if you are a nonprofit or profit organization. Contact the National Association for the Education of Young Children (NAEYC) for accreditation proceedings.

J8 Other Obligations

As you become established in the community and become acquainted with other community organizations and social groups, you should always be aware that you represent the center to the general public. Always speak of early childhood education in a positive and informative manner. You must keep yourself informed of current developments in fields of education and tell others about them. This is no small task.

J9 Legislative Action

Although your child care center may be nonpolitical, it should not be apolitical. Partisan politics are not the center's responsibility. But interest in and knowledge of educational legislation is. It is a director's responsibility to be as deeply involved in potential educational legislation as possible. Contact your local legislators and your senators and representatives, and let them know of your interest in such legislation. Establish a rapport with them and ask them to advise you of new bills. When you feel a proposed bill is urgent, help others write letters to the legislature.

Name of U.S. Representative: ______________________________

Address: ______________________________

Name of U.S. Senator: ______________________________

Address: ______________________________

Name of State Senator: ______________________________

Address: ______________________________

Name of State Legislator: ______________________________

Address: ______________________________

Name of Director of Department of Health, Education, and Welfare:

____

Address: ______________________________

It is important to acquaint yourself with members of the city government. Provide the officials responsible with valid statistics concerning the urgent need for continued growth in the field of early education. Read as much on the subject as you can so that you will be informed. Many local communities are not willing to provide financial support for preschools and child care centers. It is your task to join the urgent fight to convince legislators, lawmakers, and city officials that more money spent now on educating the very young means that less money will be required in the future for remediation programs.

J10 Sources of Information on Early Childhood Development and Education

Professional Organizations

American Academy of Pediatrics
141 Northwest Point Blvd.
Elk Grove Village, IL 60007-1098
(847) 228-5005
www.aap.org

American Montessori Society
281 Park Avenue South, Sixth Floor
New York, NY 10010-6102
(212) 358-1250
www.amshq.org

American Public Health Association
800 I Street NW
Washington, DC 20001-3710
(202) 777-2742
www.apha.org

Association for Childhood Education International (ACEI)
11904 Georgia Avenue, Suite 215
Olney, MD 20832-2277
(301) 570-2111
1-800-423-3513
www.udel.edu/bateman/acei
Journal: *Childhood Education*

Center for Parenting Studies
Wheelock College
200 the Riverway
Boston, MA 02215
(617) 734-5200, ext. 2183

Child Care Law Center
973 Market Street, Suite 550
San Francisco, CA 94103
(415) 495-5498
www.childcarelaw.org

Child Welfare League of America (CWLA)
440 First Street NW, Third Floor
Washington, DC 20001-2085
(202) 638-2952
1-800-407-6273
www.cwla.org

Children's Defense Fund
25 E Street NW
Washington, DC 20001
(202) 628-8787
www.childrensdefense.org

Children's Environmental Health Network
5900 Hollis Street, Suite R3
Emeryville, CA 94608
(510) 597-1393
www.cehn.org

Council for Exceptional Children (CEC)
1920 Association Drive
Reston, VA 20191-1589
(703) 620-3660
1-888-CEC-SPED
www.cec.sped.org
Journals: *Exceptional Children*
Teaching Exceptional Children Update

The Grantsmanship Center
1125 W. Sixth Street, Fifth Floor
P.O. Box 17220
Los Angeles, CA 90017
(213) 482-9860
www.tgci.com

National Association for the Education of Young Children (NAEYC)
1509 16th Street NW
Washington, DC 20036
(202) 232-8777
1-800-424-2460
www.naeyc.org
Journal: *Young Children*

National Black Child Development Institute (NBCDI)
1023 15th Street NW, Suite 600
Washington, DC 20005
(202) 387-1281
www.nbcdi.org
Journal: *Black Child Advocate*

National Child Care Information Center
243 Church Street NW, Second Floor
Vienna, VA 22180
(800) 616-2242
www.nccic.org

National Education Association (NEA)
1201 16th Street NW
Washington, DC 20036
(202) 833-4000
www.nea.org

National Mental Health Association
1021 Prince Street
Arlington, VA 22314-2971
(703) 684-7722
1-800-969-NMHA
www.nmha.org

National PTA
300 North Wabash Avenue
Chicago, IL 60611
(312) 670-6782
1-800-307-4PTA
www.pta.org

National Sudden Infant Death Syndrome Resource Center
2070 Chain Bridge Road, Suite 450
Vienna, VA 22182
(703) 821-8955
www.circsol.com/sids/index.htm

Prevent Child Abuse America
200 South Michigan Avenue, 17th Floor
Chicago, IL 60604-2404
(312) 663-3520
1-800-CHILDREN
www.preventchildabuse.org

Quality Care for Children
1447 Peachtree Street NE, Suite 700
Atlanta, GA 30309
(404) 885-1578
www.qualitycareforchildren.org

Society for Research in Child Development (SRCD)
505 E. Huron, Suite 301
Ann Arbor, MI 48104-1522
(734) 998-6578
www.srcd.org
Journal: *Child Development*

Sudden Infant Death Syndrome Alliance
1314 Bedford Avenue, Suite 210
Baltimore, MD 21208
(410) 653-8226
1-800-221-7437
www.sidsalliance.org

USA Toy Library Association
1213 Wilmette Avenue, Suite 201
Wilmette, IL 60091
(847) 920-9030
www.sjdccd.cc.ca.us/toylibrary/

U.S. Department of Education
400 Maryland Avenue SW
Washington, DC 20202
(202) 245-3192
1-800-USA-LEARN
www.ed.gov

U.S. Department of Health & Human Services
200 Independence Avenue SW
Washington, DC 20201
(202) 619-0257
1-877-696-6775
www.dhhs.gov

Zero to Three: National Center for Infants, Toddlers, and Families
734 15th Street NW, Suite 1000
Washington, DC 20005
(202) 638-1144
www.zerotothree.org
Journal: *Zero to Three*

Selected Periodicals

Child and Youth Care Quarterly (for staff)
Human Sciences Press
233 Spring Street
New York, NY 10013-1578
(212) 620-8000
1-800-221-9369

Childhood Education
Journal of the Association for Childhood Education International
17904 Georgia Avenue, Suite 215
Olney, MD 20832-2277
(301) 570-2111
1-800-423-3563
www.acei.org

Day Care and Early Education (for director)
Human Sciences Press
233 Spring St.
New York, NY 10013-1578
(212) 620-8000
1-800-221-9369

Early Childhood News (for staff)
The Journal of Professional Development
Peter Li, Inc.
330 Progress Rd.
Dayton, OH 45449
(937) 847-5900
www.earlychildhoodnews.com

Early Childhood Today (formerly *Pre-K Today*)
Scholastic Inc.
555 Broadway
New York, NY 10012
(212) 343-6140
1-800-544-2917
www.teacher.scholastic.com/products/ect.htm

High/Scope Resource: A Magazine for Educators
High/Scope Educational Research Foundation
600 North River Street
Ypsilanti, MI 48198-2898
(734) 485-2000
1-800-40-PRESS
www.highscope.org

Young Children, NAEYC
1509 16th Street NW
Washington, DC 20036
(202) 232-8777
1-800-424-2460
www.naeyc.org

Food Management and Nutrition

K1 Food Service and Nutrition Policies

When a child care program is involved in a preschool, or when the entire program is child care, food service becomes an important consideration. The center must meet state and local regulations regarding meal-preparation facilities. Requirements for institutional kitchens are very rigid in most areas, and compliance can prove to be very costly. A center may have to decide to start out with having children bring their own lunches from home. The regulations, however, must be respected. They generally have to do with health and safety and are for the protection of the center operator as well as the children.

Once the requirements for the facilities have been met and you begin the preparation of your own food, the serving of nutritious, well-balanced meals—in a manner that invites the indulgence of all the children—becomes an exciting challenge. Research is bringing to light new information on foods and nutrition all the time. It is important that you keep up with this research; discuss the findings with your staff, parents, and caregivers; and be bold enough to initiate steps toward change, where indicated.

Aside from the mechanics involved with the serving of food, such as how it is prepared, what is being served, how it is served, and what staff is involved with the service, it is important for the children that you keep the overall approach as natural, matter-of-fact, and casual as possible. Mealtimes should be periods of quiet, pleasant interchange of information between children and children, and between children and adults—times when they show consideration for one another and respect for individual needs and preferences.

While curriculum reinforcement should not be the primary goal of food service, children can be helped to become aware of colors, shapes, ethnic origins of foods, and other facts. Such awareness, however, is only of secondary importance to the satisfaction of the basic physical and emotional needs of everyone involved in the food program, both children and adults. It is the director's responsibility to develop nutritional policies. These policies will be important to your program and must be able to support the health and growth of children in your care. The policies should be written clearly and reflect the promotion of good health. Examples of nutritional policies may include, but not be limited to, menu planning guidelines, food preparation practices, nutritional guidelines, understanding basic nutrients, awareness of nutritional challenges, and food selection. Your staff should be familiar with basic knowledge of nutrition so that they can create proper snack menus and be able to teach the children, parents, and caregivers about good nutrition.

K2 Children's Nutritional Needs

Children need the same nutrients as adults. However, in planning meals for children, the following should be considered:

- Children need more protein, minerals, and vitamins for their size, because they are much more active than adults and their basal metabolic rate (the rate at which energy is used to keep the body processes operating) is higher. This doesn't mean children need large quantities of food, but food should be carefully selected so that it consists of good nutrients rather than fats and empty calories.

- Children need simple and easily digested foods, since their digestive ability is not as well developed as that of adults. Omit hard-to-digest foods, such as rich pastries and sweets, sauces, gravies, fried foods, pickles, and highly seasoned items.

Food Preparation

To minimize the loss of the nutritive value of foods, use the following guidelines in food preparation:

1. Follow tested recipes carefully.
2. Avoid bruising food. Handle fruits and vegetables carefully, using a sharp knife when trimming, cutting, or shredding.
3. Cook vegetables only until tender. Use just enough water to prevent scorching.
4. Cook vegetables in their skins whenever possible.
5. Use the liquid from canned fruits and vegetables.
6. Conserve the water in which cereals and grains have been cooked. Avoid rinsing.

K3 Equipping the Kitchen and Lunchroom

Use the following lists:

ITEM	COST
Equipment	
Dishwasher	
Garbage disposal	
Oven—gas, electric, and/or microwave	
Refrigerator	
Sink	
Stove	
Storage for appliances	
Storage for cookware and food containers	
Storage for staples	
Storage for tableware	
Table or counter for food preparation	
Utensils	
Apple corer	
Blender, mixer	
Bowls, mixing	
Can openers	
Chopping board	
Coffee pot	
Colander	
Containers, assorted	
Cookie sheets	
Dishpan	
Dish rack	
Dishcloths	
Double boiler	
Eggbeater, hand	
Egg custard cups	
Electric beater	
Food processor	
Garbage pail	
Grater	
Grinder, meat	
Juicer	
Knives, bread	
Knives, meat	
Knives, vegetable	
Ladle, soup, 1/4 cup	
Measuring cups	
Measuring spoons	
Muffin pan	
Pans, baking	
Pans, frying, large	
Pans, frying, small	
Pans, sauce (with lids)	
Pitcher, 16 oz., plastic	
Pots, soup, large	
Pressure cooker	
Roaster with rack	
Scoop, #16 (1/4 cup)	
Scrub brush	
Serving cart	
Serving spoons	
Spatulas, assorted	
Strainer, large	
Trays, large (12" x 18")	
Thermometer, refrigerator/freezer	
Vegetable brush	
Vegetable peeler	
Dinnerware	
Soup cups or bowls	
Luncheon plates	
Glasses, 4 oz.	
Dessert dishes	
Serving bowls	
Serving pitchers	
32 oz. (for adults)	
12 oz. (for children)*	
Flatware	
Soup spoons	
Teaspoons	
Forks, salad	
Knives, table (for adults)	
Consumable Supplies**	
Drinking cups, 4 oz.	
Dessert plates	
Divided luncheon plates	

* Small pitchers should be transparent so that children can determine the level of the liquid.

** Although a basic stock of dishes and glasses should be kept on hand, using disposable tableware will save time and money (in personnel hours). Divided paper plates are not only disposable, but also keep food items separate—the way most children prefer.

K4 Planning

Once you have equipped the kitchen (with the help of the nutritionist [cook, housekeeper]), compile a list of staples [Section K15]. Compare the costs of this list with the amount of money you have budgeted, and make adjustments accordingly. Based on a national average, 7 1/2 percent of your total child care budget will be allocated to food preparation, supplies, serving, and kitchen maintenance. Consult with a nutritionist, as well as with your cook, about ways to keep the food budget stable in spite of rising costs, while still meeting the nutritional needs of the child. If you find that costs have risen so that your budget is out of balance, do not resort to skimping on food. Consider instead a small increase in tuition. The increase will enable you to stay within the 7 1/2 percent allocation, which, with good management, can provide nutritious, interesting meals.

K5 Nutrition

The center's concern for children's health and development is reflected by the meals that are served. Meals should be as pleasant as possible, should meet the highest nutritional standards, and should be served in a hygienic manner. By concentrating on food choices commonly recommended by nutritionists, you can maintain high nutritional standards while battling the ever-rising costs of food products.

According to the Food Guide Pyramid, developed by the United States Department of Agriculture, the following daily requirements are recommended for children and adults. Preschool children need the same varieties of foods in their diets, but should eat smaller portions than adults. Your center may not be providing every meal per day per child, so a good balance in your nutritional plan is sufficient.

Bread, Cereal, Rice and Pasta—6 to 11 Servings per Day

Examples of one serving are one slice of bread; one ounce of cereal; three or four crackers; or 1/2 cup cooked cereal, rice, or pasta. Breads should be whole grain, homemade, or enriched. Read the labels and know what you're buying.

Vegetables—3 to 5 Servings per Day

Examples of one serving are one cup of raw leafy vegetables; 1/2 cup of vegetables, raw or cooked; one cup of vegetable soup, or 3/4 cup vegetable juice.

Fruits—2 to 4 Servings per Day

Examples of one serving are one medium apple, banana, or orange; 1/2 cup of cooked or canned fruit; or 3/4 cup fruit juice.

You can meet these needs by serving two or more vegetables and a fruit at one meal, plus a citrus fruit or juice once a day. Vegetables and fruit should be raw or lightly cooked.

Milk, Yogurt, and Cheese—2 to 3 Servings per Day

Examples of one serving are one cup milk or yogurt, 1 1/2 ounces of natural cheese, or two ounces of processed cheese.

Milk can be difficult for some children to tolerate, causing constipation, accumulation of mucus, or severe stomach pains. For such children, the nutritional balance may be accomplished by increasing other foods to make up for the protein and vitamins lost because of the elimination of milk from the diet.

Meat, Poultry, Fish, Dry Beans, Eggs, and Nuts—2 to 3 Servings per Day

Examples of one serving are two to three ounces of cooked lean meat, poultry, or fish; one egg; 1/2 cup cooked beans; two tablespoons peanut butter; or 1/3 cup nuts.

Children require more protein per kilogram of body weight than the average adult. To offer young children sufficient nutrients for their developing bodies, a good rule to remember is to serve protein with all carbohydrates. Bread or macaroni, essentially carbohydrates, even if they are made from whole grain, will contribute to a better nutritional balance when served with peanut butter or cheese. Apples and other fruits, which are also high in carbohydrates because of their sugar content, should be served with cheese, nuts, or eggs.

Fats, Oils, and Sweets—Use Sparingly

These are empty calories and have little nutritional value. Sugar and fat use should be limited.

For more information, contact the United States Department of Agriculture and ask them to send you a copy of the The Food Guide Pyramid.

United States Department of Agriculture
Center for Nutrition Policy and Promotion
1120 20th St. NW
Suite 200, North Lobby
Washington, DC 20036-3475
(202) 720-7327

You may also access nutritional materials from the CNPP web site at http://www.usda.gov/fcs/cnpp.htm.

Nutritional information should be included in newsletters to parents and caregivers and should be brought up for discussion at parent/caregiver meetings as well.

K6 Food Program for Infants

If you have infants in your center, you should follow the advice of a pediatrician in setting up their feeding program. Many infants in your care will have their own specific formulas provided by their own pediatricians. The preferences of the infant's parents or caregivers must be given primary consideration.

Prepared Formula

Prepared formulas available are usually supplemented so that no additional vitamins or minerals need to be administered. Commercially prepared formulas provide savings in time and cost of help, as well as consistency. The use of commercially prepared formulas also reduces the risk of infection, provided sterilization and dishwashing procedures meet the necessary standards.

Concerns in preparing formulas and feeding infants include, but are not limited to, the following:

a. Exacting sterilization equipment and procedures; adequate refrigeration facilities.
b. Keeping bottles and nipples sterile.
c. Accurate measurements. The formula should neither be diluted (to save money) nor made stronger than called for. The extra nutrients may do more harm than good.
d. Accurate doses of prescribed vitamins and oils. More does not mean better.
e. Monitoring the amount of formula that is taken in, thus being able to keep track of whether the infant is receiving adequate quantities, not enough, or too much.
f. Working out each infant's individualized schedule; feeding according to individual needs, not adult schedules.
g. Holding the infant during feeding. You might need extra help just for feeding tasks since this is such an important part of building infant–adult relationships. The infant should not be put in a sitting position for eating until old enough to sit naturally. This would be at about seven months of age, but may be as early as six months for some children.

When parents and caregivers bring the infant's food from home, make sure that they clearly label all bottles of formula or breast milk with the date and the child's name. Do not accept unlabeled bottles or give a child a bottle that has not been labeled. This will insure that you do not give a child someone else's bottle. Feed infants on demand unless the parent or caregiver gives you alternative instructions. Thaw frozen breast milk under cold running water, or leave it in the refrigerator. Never use a microwave to heat a child's bottle of formula or breast milk. Microwave ovens heat bottles unevenly, and may burn a child's mouth. You can warm a bottle in a bowl of hot water that has been heated in the microwave. Let it stand for five minutes, then shake and test the milk before feeding the child. To disinfect and clean, bottle caps, nipples and bottles can be washed in a dishwasher.

Food Program for Pretoddlers and Toddlers

Pretoddlers

Solid foods may be started at about the same time as the infant is ready to sit up. Finger foods can be introduced. Be careful not to cut the food into marble-like sizes. This size of food can be swallowed whole and cause a child to choke. Do not give cut round slices of hotdogs. Instead, cut them lengthwise and into quarters and cut across into pieces. Whole grapes, marshmallows, melon balls, and pretzels must be cut in half.

Pretoddlers should be given water and only 100 percent juice on a regular basis.

Children that can walk should never be allowed to carry their bottles. They can be introduced to the use of a cup.

Toddlers

Their foods can be similar to what you prepare for older children, but modified both in ease of chewing and in size of servings, according to their ages. Do not feed them sticky, high-sugar foods such as raisins. When foods stick to the teeth, they can promote tooth decay. Serve toddlers small portions but offer more food when needed. Never use food as a reward or punishment with any age child. Mealtimes should be times when children can develop social and motor skills as well as introducing new tastes. The use of small utensils and child-sized dishes will assist toddlers in feeding themselves. In serving their food, think in terms of self-help, but always be available to give help when it is needed or asked for.

K8 Food Program for Extended-Day Children

If you have extended-day children coming to your center after public school, they should be provided with a nutritious midafternoon snack, just as you provide for your all-day children. They can be given snacks, such as milk and graham crackers, fruit, peanut butter sandwiches, and other items similar to those given to preschool children, but in larger quantities. This is a considerable added expense. You could charge an extra fee in order to serve milk (along with one other snack) every afternoon. Another alternative is to have all your extended-day children bring an extra midafternoon snack from home along with their regular school lunches. Whatever plan you use, give children a small snack just before they go home to take the edge off their appetites, so that they have an opportunity to talk with their families about things other than "When do we eat?" as soon as they come home.

K9 The Vegetarian Diet

In planning food service, consideration must be given to children whose families are vegetarians. It is not necessary to serve meat in order for children to have a nutritionally balanced diet. Meals for vegetarians can be centered on a lacto-ovo vegetarian diet, which includes eggs, milk, and other dairy products. (Be aware that some vegetarian diets do not include dairy products.)

Include legumes, grains, nuts, oil seeds, and fortified soy milk in order to provide the needed protein, iron, B vitamins, carbohydrates, fats, and other vitamins, along with trace minerals that are usually found in meat. It is unlikely that a young child will develop protein deficiency if given adequate calories from various sources, with at least 596 of the protein calories from milk, eggs, or other equivalent protein foods.

There are many good vegetarian cookbooks available. Talk to your librarian or the public library for vegetarian alternatives that can be used with the children. You may also want to look on-line at vegetarian Web sites for information as well as tasty recipes. Check with the parents and caregivers about the children's diets. They will be able to help you choose the right foods for their children.

K10 Nutritional Sense and Cents

Here are some suggestions on how to save money without sacrificing nutrition:

1. Follow seasonal food-buying guides. Foods are less expensive when readily available.
2. Buying in bulk is less expensive than buying small packages. Compare costs per serving.
3. In considering prices and comparing the differences between various cuts of meat or forms of packaging (fresh, canned, frozen), compare the amount of waste that might be expected from each. Sometimes the "expensive" food costs less per serving than the "cheap" food because there is less waste. Seek ways to eliminate waste: a good soup stock can be made from the normally discarded ends of fresh vegetables.
4. Practice comparison shopping. Don't depend on one supplier. Look for new sources that can provide comparable foods at lower prices.
5. Keep records. For example, compare the amounts served to the amounts eaten.
6. If you have served an item that children do not like, serve it two or three more times. Then, if you determine that they really don't like it, don't continue to serve it just because "it's good for them." Spend your money on foods that children will eat. Sometimes the rejected food can be prepared a different way or combined with foods that children like.
7. Processed foods, such as luncheon meats and delicatessen products, cost considerably more per serving than foods you prepare yourself and may be of less nutritional value. Check the additives, preservatives, and fat content of processed foods, especially common products such as hot dogs and bologna. If you buy these, look for brands marked "kosher," which are processed under highly supervised conditions. "Kosher style" is not authentic.
8. Foods containing refined sugar and starches waste the food dollar. Cut down on such foods to save money for proteins, dairy products, and fresh fruits and vegetables. For example, serve real fruit juices instead of powdered mixes.
9. Powdered milk is the least expensive form of milk, but just as nutritious, with a higher protein content and lower fat content. Some states regulate its use as a beverage but allow it in cooking. Use powdered milk, for example, to thicken gravies and cream sauces.
10. Ask the local Agriculture Extension Service how to get a milk subsidy. (Your program may be eligible, even if it is not government funded.)
11. Consider centralized purchasing. By joining together and working out a basic menu plan, a group of preschools can save money by buying in large quantities from one of the larger food service companies. Also consider enlisting volunteer parents and caregivers in a food-buying cooperative enterprise.
12. Notice the order in which the ingredients of any processed food or beverage are listed on the label. Under U.S. government labeling regulations, ingredients are listed in descending order according to the amount of each used in the product. If a beverage, for example, contains a high proportion of pure juice, the juice will be listed first on the label. Avoid, as much as possible, foods with high amounts of sugar, artificial colors and flavorings, and other additives [Section K14].

13. Serve small helpings but make allowances for additional servings for children who seem to require more. All children in the same age group do not require the same amount of food. Small helpings will eliminate waste.
14. Serve simple, easily recognizable foods, lightly seasoned. Children prefer simple finger foods to complicated casseroles.

K11 Menu Planning and Sample Menu

Menus will, of course, be influenced by your food budget as well as how carefully you have selected your cook, arranged and equipped your kitchen, and the varying ethnic backgrounds of the children you enroll.

Although there are several methods of nutritious menu planning, the easiest way is to use foods from the Food Guide Pyramid [Section K5]. When planning your menus, the cook, with your approval, can use the following recommended food list based on that plan:

MEAL PATTERNS

FOOD ITEMS	APPROXIMATE SERVING FOR A 4-YEAR-OLD
BREAKFAST	
For children who eat breakfast at your center, we recommend the following menu:	
Milk	3/4 cup
Egg	1 medium
Citrus juice or fruit	1/2 cup (Juice can be served as a snack if other fruit is served for breakfast.)
Cereal, cooked, whole grain	1/3 cup
Enriched or whole grain bread	1/2 slice (includes muffins, biscuits, rolls, pancakes, and so forth)
Use peanut butter on bread and pancakes for extra protein. Try not to use pancake syrup; substitute jam.	
LUNCH	
Milk	3/4 cup
Lean meat, fish, poultry, or cheese	1/2 oz.
or egg (if not given for breakfast)	1 each
or cooked dry beans	1/4 cup
or peanut butter	2–3 tablespoons
Vegetable or fruit (or serve two vegetables instead)	1/4 cup
Bread (with butter)	1/2 slice (or 1 slice, thin)

Sample Menu

COMMUNITY CHILD CARE CENTER SAMPLE MENU PLAN

	BREAKFAST	LUNCH	SNACK
Meal Pattern	Juice or fruit or vegetable Grains/bread Milk	Meat or meat alternate Vegetable and/or fruit (two or more) Grains/breads Milk	Select two of the following: Meat or meat alternate Vegetable or fruit or juice Grains/breads Milk
Monday	Banana slices Cold cereal Milk	Spaghetti and meat sauce Green salad Cubed pineapple Milk	Apple juice Cheese cubes Crackers Water
Tuesday	Whole wheat English muffin Strawberries Milk	Baked breaded fish Green peas Cheesy mashed potatoes Peach slices Milk	Oatmeal cookies Milk Water
Wednesday	Applesauce French toast Milk	Baked turkey Cornbread stuffing Baby carrots Pear and orange salad Roll Milk	Fruit kabobs Wheat crackers Water
Thursday	Orange slices Bran cereal Milk	Macaroni and cheese Beef patty Whole-wheat buns Lettuce and tomato Baby carrots	Carrot sticks Wheat crackers Water Milk
Friday	Peaches Oatmeal Milk	Tuna salad with low-fat mayonnaise Lettuce/tomato salad Roll Milk	Mini banana muffin Grape juice

K12

Serving Meals

Atmosphere

The tables should be aesthetically arranged for both convenience of serving and social interaction. If the dining area is also used as a play area, all toys should be put away and the room put in order. Such factors help children remain calm and relaxed during a meal.

An Attractive Table

Colorful placemats, sufficient tableware, and an interesting centerpiece help children to approach each meal as something special. The centerpiece may be flowers, a plant, an interesting ceramic figure, objects collected by children on a nature walk, a new toy, or a collage created by a child. Such centerpieces stimulate meaningful conversation and anticipation, especially in the four- to five-year-old groups, for whom eating has become an important social event.

Seating

Space chairs to avoid overcrowding, and seat quiet children between the noisier ones. Overcrowding leads to increased tension, more spills, disorder, and waste.

Food-Serving Styles

Select one style and use it most of the time, but vary it on special occasions for different learning opportunities.

Family style, in which children serve themselves, creates a homelike atmosphere, an important consideration for the child who is in child care all day. An adult sits at the table with the children to give assistance as needed. It allows for small portions and seconds and prevents children from being overwhelmed by too much food on their plates. Children should be allowed to pour their own beverages, if appropriate. Upon finishing the main course, children may be allowed to clear their own dishes from the table and bring back a fruit dessert.

Cafeteria style allows each child to decide what to eat. Making choices helps to develop important feelings of independence and responsibility.

Buffet style gives children opportunities to learn to take care of their own needs, to judge quantities (even though an adult helps dish out the food), and to develop self-esteem (because the menus include such items as finger foods and sandwiches that the child can manage without difficulty). Help children select their own finger foods by making little diagrams showing how many of each item they may take.

Picnic style, eating outdoors from paper sacks, extends children's knowledge of food-serving styles. The pleasant anticipation that accompanies going on a picnic helps children accept a change in routine comfortably. In preparing for a picnic, the older children may make their own sandwiches and pack their own bags. Two- and three-year-olds may select items from trays (one item from each) and place them in their own bags themselves. An added delight can be having children decorate their bags in advance with crayons, markers, or other art media.

Helping Self

Allowing children to help themselves as much as possible develops their self-esteem and self-awareness. However, children should have the security of knowing at all times that an adult is there to help them when they indicate the need. A child may need help because of emotional stress or as a result of losing control of a step in the process (spilling food, dropping a utensil, difficulty in manipulating a fork, and so on).

Discipline

Well-meaning adults sometimes unintentionally heap emotional abuse on children during meals for the sake of the child's "well-being." Mealtime is not the time for punitive attitudes and overly structured procedures. Foods must not be withheld as a punishment or offered as a reward. A child who becomes emotional should be gently led to another area for a short time and then returned to the table, or should be allowed to finish the meal elsewhere. An attitude of firm but gentle understanding shows that you are not punishing, but helping the child express his or her emotions.

Staff Members and Guests

Staff members and other adults who are in the center building at mealtime are always invited to join children at the tables. Adults provide "instant supervision," in addition to the important aspect of camaraderie. They lead the way in establishing an atmosphere of pleasant conversation, helping the child to socialize, while keeping voices in a low key. Parents and caregivers are invited at various times during the year to have lunch with their children.

Timing

Timing is planned so that meals are unhurried and unharried. Distinction must be carefully made between dawdling and naturally slow eating. Recognition must be given to the eating plateaus that children reach at various stages of development. At one period of time, the child may seem to need twice as much time as usual in order to complete a meal. At other times, the child wolfs food down in a series of big bites and gulps. Usually it is during periods of more rapid growth that appetites increase. When growth is stabilized, appetites decrease.

Fads and Jags

Give recognition to a child's right to food fads and jags. Sometimes a child has an inner sense (call it *intuition*) of what he or she biologically or physiologically requires to satisfy certain nutritional needs. Food jags and food cravings are natural and temporary. Avoid making a fuss. Treat them casually and matter-of-factly. Enjoy them as a part of growth in the developing child.

K13 Table Setting

Children can be assigned table-setting tasks on a rotating basis. Each day, children can check a chart, similar to the one shown here, to watch for their turns. Stretch a rubber band from the child's name to the picture of the assigned job. Give three or four children jobs to do each day.

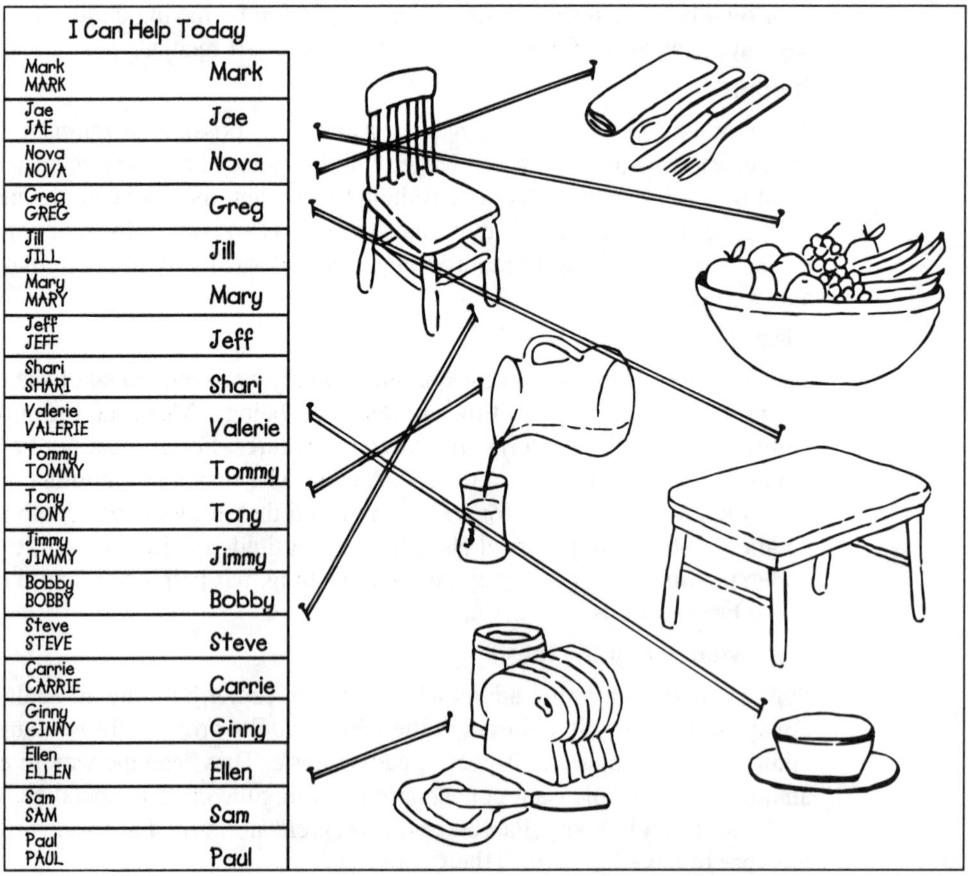

I Can Help Today	
Mark MARK	Mark
Jae JAE	Jae
Nova NOVA	Nova
Greg GREG	Greg
Jill JILL	Jill
Mary MARY	Mary
Jeff JEFF	Jeff
Shari SHARI	Shari
Valerie VALERIE	Valerie
Tommy TOMMY	Tommy
Tony TONY	Tony
Jimmy JIMMY	Jimmy
Bobby BOBBY	Bobby
Steve STEVE	Steve
Carrie CARRIE	Carrie
Ginny GINNY	Ginny
Ellen ELLEN	Ellen
Sam SAM	Sam
Paul PAUL	Paul

K14

Food Poisoning and Poisons in Food

Food poisoning and poisons in food can be very serious for small children. Preventive measures are of utmost importance when large amounts of food are being prepared and served. The following precautions should be taken:

1. Refrigeration should be in good working condition, temperatures below 45°F (7.2°C) and appropriate foods stored under refrigeration, even in cold weather.
2. Utensils should be cleaned under hygienic conditions, disinfected, and used only in a sanitary manner.
3. Food handlers should practice good health habits, must always wash hands with soap after use of lavatory, and must be free of disease or infection. Some states require an annual health and TB clearance for food handlers and helpers.
4. Food must be protected from contact with flies and rodents.
5. Do not risk home-canned foods with children in your charge. Botulism spores are not always killed in the canning process; botulism can cause death in a majority of cases. Be cautious of any possibly improperly processed or canned foods, or of damaged or dented commercially canned foods.
6. Use only approved water and milk supplies. Keep plumbing in sanitary condition.
7. Avoid use of shellfish that may have come from contaminated waters. Be aware of any allergies to fish or shellfish among children and staff.
8. Do not use wild mushrooms. They can be deadly. Use only commercially cultivated mushrooms.
9. Cook all meat and meat products until well done. Buy only those processed products that you know were properly prepared.
10. Be cautious by refrigerating until used all meat and fish salads, salads with mayonnaise and eggs, custards, cream pies and sauces, gravies, hash, all chopped food, soups, and similar dishes.
11. Refrigerate leftover foods immediately if they are to be used again. If they have been out for any length of time, they should be disposed of. It is not worth the risk to use them.
12. Perishable food should be placed in a covered container and refrigerated at 45°F (7.2°C).
13. Much has been published recently regarding research findings on food additives and preservatives, as well as information concerning some of the processed and highly refined foods to avoid. New information is being brought to light daily, leading to gradual changes in this nation's eating patterns. Because of its utmost importance in the wholesome development of young children, food additives might be the subject for a study group for your parents and caregivers—or at least for a special meeting and for newsletter information [Sections F10, F36].
14. All fruits and vegetables should be washed and scrubbed as thoroughly as possible to remove every bit of residue from insecticides used in their production. Never allow children to eat unpeeled foods that have not been very carefully cleaned. It is safer to remove the peels. Insecticides contain a great deal of

arsenic, which can be damaging to the system. Apples should be scrubbed thoroughly, peeled, and made into applesauce for children to consume the greatest possible amount. Do not purchase commercially prepared applesauce. It may not have had the chemicals thoroughly cleaned from the fruit.

15. Pesticides and chemicals should not be stored in food preparation or food storage areas.

When in doubt at any time, or if you have any questions concerning possible food contamination or poisoning, telephone the County or City Health Department at once. In an emergency, call the nearest poison center. (If you call an ambulance, the ambulance service will contact the nearest poison control center and have the needed information for you by the time it arrives.)

K15

Food Selection Lists

1. Compile a list of all possible entrees you may wish to consider serving. Enter each item on one line of a chart similar to this form:

MENU MINDER: ENTREES

Food Item (select one)	Dates selected for this item									
1. Beef, braised	1/12									
2. Beef, roast										
3. Beef, ground, patties										
4. Cottage cheese	1/9									

2. Prepare similar charts for vegetables, salads, breads, cereals, and other items you will be serving, considering how the taste will combine with the entree. Consider, too, color combinations and textural variety.
3. Starting with the entree and date, for example, January 9, select the item for January 9 and note it on the chart.
4. Go to each of the other charts and put the date, January 9, after those items you will serve with the already selected entree. Consider seasonal foods.
5. Continue selecting entrees and accompanying foods for approximately a 20-day period, to assist in planning for bulk purchases.
6. Send advance menus home so family planning can take into account what meals the child has had at child care or preschool.
7. Star those items that children liked especially well.
8. Draw a line through those items that the majority did not like. There are plenty of foods available to substitute for a disliked food, so you need not serve it again.
9. Make adjustments to the menu, as needed, to take advantage of special sale items and seasonal fruits and vegetables.
10. Complete your own charts by selecting those items from the following lists that are compatible with your own philosophy.

Entrees (select one)

Beans, baked with meat cubes
Beans, lima with cheddar cheese
Beef, braised
- chipped
- corned
- ground, loaf
- ground, patties
- ground, noodle casserole
- ground, mini meatballs
- roast
- steak, Swiss
- stew

Cheese cubes
Chicken, creamed on toast
- fried
- oven fried
- roast
- stew

Cold bean salad
Cottage cheese
Cottage cheese with fruit
Egg, foo young
- noodles and cottage cheese
- noodles and hamburger
- noodles and tuna
- noodles and turkey

English muffin pizza (with cheese hamburger, broiled)
Fish, baked
- fried
- salmon loaf
- pattie
- shrimp, fried
- sticks
- tuna salad
- turbot (very inexpensive)

Lamb, braised
- chops
- ground, loaf
- noodle casserole patties
- roast
- stew

Macaroni and cheese
- and hamburger

Omelet, bacon
- cheese
- diced ham
- plain

Pork, and beans
- fresh, ground
- roast
- cured, ham
- cooked and sliced
- cooked and chopped
- smoked

Pork, shoulder roast
Rice, fried with meat and vegetables
- Spanish with hamburger or bacon

Sandwiches, cheese, cream cheese and jelly, cream cheese and pineapple, dates, or raisins
- chicken salad
- chopped liver
- egg salad
- fish, loaf or salad
- ham salad
- hamburger
- hot dogs (all-beef only) (kosher has fewer additives but is more expensive)
- hot dogs with chili
- meat, loaf or salad
- melted cheese
- peanut butter
- peanut butter with raisins/ shredded carrot
- salmon salad
- sloppy joes (two-year-olds don't usually like these)
- tuna salad
- turkey salad

Shish kebab (meat cubes with vegetables)
Spaghetti, with cheese and meat sauce and meatballs
Spaghetti-O's™ with meat cubes
Soup, barley, bean, and/or beef
- bean and bacon (thick)
- split pea
- vegetable beef (thick)
- other hearty soups served with a sandwich

Soybeans, baked
Tacos with hamburger and cheese
Turkey, roast

Vegetables (select one)

Artichokes
Asparagus
Beans, green
  lima
  soy
Broccoli
Cabbage
Carrot, buttered rings and peas
Cauliflower
Celery
Corn, creamed/whole kernel
  on-the-cob
Cucumbers
Eggplant
Garbanzos
Hominy
Lettuce
Okra
Olives
Parsnips
Boiled Peas, black-eyed
  green
Potatoes, baked
  fried
  mashed
  sweet
Rice
Rutabaga
Spinach
Squash, acorn, summer yellow
Zucchini
Turnip greens
(Vegetables can be served fresh and uncooked for variety.)

Salads (select one)

Ambrosia—grated carrot and shredded coconut
Cabbage—shredded cabbage with diced apples, diced celery, grapes, mayonnaise
Carrot—peas, green beans
  raisin/pineapple
Chop Suey—fresh bean sprouts, thin-sliced celery, thin-sliced carrots, sliced olives, mayonnaise
Cole Slaw (simple), vary with carrots
  cooked, chilled vegetables with mayonnaise
Cucumbers and tomatoes
Finger vegetables, olives
  (See vegetable list for ideas. Refer also to snack list section.)
Fruit cup
Green peas with dry noodles, hard-cooked eggs, mayonnaise
Jell-O™, with bananas/carrots
  with fruit cocktail
  lime, with cottage cheese and pineapple
Lettuce and tomato
Potato salad with lots of eggs
Tossed lettuce with diced celery
Vegetable, tossed
Waldorf—apples, celery, walnuts, banana chips, mayonnaise

Occasional Desserts (select one for fruit serving)

Applesauce
Bread pudding with fruit
Brown Betty (apple crisp)
Cake (for birthdays only)
Cookies (for special events only—made with honey and whole grain flour)
Egg custard (put honey and diced dates or other fruit in bottom of cup)
Ice cream (for birthdays—homemade is more wholesome)
Jell-O™ with fruit
Pie, fruit
Puddings
Rice pudding with raisins/apricots/pineapple/currants
(Avoid concept development of "A treat must be a sweet"; i.e., can a party be an Easter party of "rabbit food"?)
Yogurt

Bread

Bagel
Boston brown
Cheese
Corn
Egg
English muffins with raisins
Whole-grain wheat
Enriched white bread sticks
French
Italian
Pumpernickel
Raisin
Rye
Blackberry muffins
Blueberry muffins
Whole wheat biscuits
- banana bread
- date bread
- nut bread

(These can be spread with cream cheese for desserts.)

(Note: There is some current emphasis on the undesirability of preservatives in bread. Try to obtain breads with high fiber content. Homemade bread is wholesome.)

Snacks and Finger Foods

Dried fruits
- apples
- apricots
- dates
- figs
- peaches
- pears
- prunes
- raisins

Fresh Fruits (to use in place of dessert, too)

Apples
Apricots
Bananas
Berries
Cantaloupe
Cherries
Grapes
Grapefruit
Honeydew
Nectarines
Oranges
Papaya
Peaches
Persimmons
Pineapple
Plums
Pomegranates
Tangerines
Watermelon
(Imported fruits can be offered with other multicultural foods.)

High Protein and Dairy Foods

Cheddar cheese spread on celery stalks
Cheddar cheese spread on crackers or fruit
Cheese cubes
Cheese slices
Cheese sticks
Cream cheese on apples
Cream cheese spread on celery stalks
Cream cheese on whole-wheat crackers
Deviled eggs
Hard-cooked eggs (can be diced)
Peanut butter on celery stalks
Peanut butter on crackers
Peanut butter on apples or other fruit

K16 Common Food Substitutes

INGREDIENT	QUANTITY	SUBSTITUTE
Buttermilk	1 cup	Add 2 Tbsp. vinegar or lemon juice to enough sweet milk to make 1 cup
Butter or margarine	1 cup	1 cup hydrogenated fat less 2 Tbsp. ± 1/2 tsp. salt.
Baking powder, double acting	1 tsp.	2 tsp. quick-acting; or 1/4 tsp. baking soda with 1/2 cup sour milk or buttermilk
Cornstarch	1 Tbsp.	2 Tbsp. flour
Cream, coffee or table	1 cup	1 cup milk less 2 Tbsp. ± 3 Tbsp. fat
Cream, heavy	1 cup	3/4 cup milk + 1/3 cup fat
Eggs	1 whole	2 egg yolks; or 2 1/2 Tbsp. sifted dry egg (yolk + 1 1/2 Tbsp. warm water)
	1 yolk	2 Tbsp. dry egg yolk + 2 Tbsp. warm water
	1 white	2 tsp. dry egg powder + 2 Tbsp. warm water
Flour, for thickening	1 Tbsp.	1/2 Tbsp. cornstarch; 2 tsp. quick-cooking tapioca
Flour, all-purpose	1 cup	1 cup regular + 2 Tbsp. cake flour
Flour, cake	1 cup	2 Tbsp. cornstarch plus 1 cup of flour less 2 Tbsp.
Honey	1 cup	1 1/2 cups sugar + 1/4 cup water or juice
Milk	1 cup whole	1 cup reconstituted nonfat dry milk + 2 1/2 tsp. fat; or 1/2 cup evaporated milk + 1/2 cup water
	1 cup nonfat	3 1/2 Tbsp. dry nonfat milk powder + 1 cup water
Sugar	1 cup	3/4 cup honey + 1/4 cup liquid or 1 cup corn syrup with 1/3 cup liquid
Tomatoes, canned	1 cup	1 1/3 cups fresh tomatoes, peeled, cut up, simmered for 10 min.
Chocolate, unsweetened	1 oz.	3 Tbsp. cocoa + 1 Tbsp. fat
Water for Jell-O™	1 cup	1 cup liquid from canned fruit

K17 Can Sizes and Number of Servings

SIZES OF CANS	YIELD	USED FOR	NO. OF CHILDREN SERVED BY 1 CAN
300 (15 1/2 oz. or 13 1/2 fluid oz.)	1 3/4 cups	Baked beans, cranberry sauce, spaghetti, macaroni, date nut bread	7
303 (1 lb. or 15 fl. oz.)	2 cups	Vegetables, fruits, soups	8
2 1/2 (20 oz. or 18 fl. oz.)	2 1/2 cups	Vegetables, fruits, juice	10
46 oz. (1 qt. 14 fl. oz.)	5 3/4 cups	Fruit and veg. juices; some institutional-sized soups, vegetables	22
10	3 qts. fl. or 12–13 cups	Institutional size for most foods	50

K18 Measurement Equivalents

ITEM	MEASUREMENT	EQUIVALENT
Dry, fat, or liquid	3 tsp.	1 Tbsp.
	2 Tbsp.	1/8 cup
	1/4 cup	4 Tbsp.
	1/3 cup	5 Tbsp. + 1 tsp.
	1/2 cup	8 Tbsp.
Fat or liquid	1 oz.	2 Tbsp.
	4 oz.	1/2 cup
	16 oz.	1 lb. or 1 pt.
	2 cups	1 lb. or 1 pt.
	5/8 cup	1/2 cup + 2 Tbsp.
	7/8 cup	3/4 cup + 2 Tbsp.
Flour, sifted	4 cups	1 lb.
Sugar, confectioners	1 lb.	2 2/3 cups
Sugar, brown, packed	1 lb.	2 1/4 cups
Butter	1 lb.	4 sticks or 2 cups
Liquids	2 pts.	1 qt.
	1 qt.	4 cups
	4 qts.	1 gallon

K19 Metric Conversions

1 teaspoon	1 tsp.	5 milliliters	5 mL	1 mL	0.03 fl. oz.
1 tablespoon	1 Tbsp.	15 milliliters	15 mL	1 L	2.1 pt.
1 fluid ounce	1 fl. oz.	30 milliliters	30 mL	1 L	0.26 gal.
1 cup	1 c.	0.24 liter	0.24 L	1 g	0.0315 oz.
1 pint	1 pt.	0.47 liter	0.47 L	1 kg	2.2 lbs.
1 quart	1 qt.	0.95 liter	0.95 L		
1 gallon	1 gal.	3.8 liters	3.8 L		
1 ounce (weight)	1 oz.	28 grams	28 g		
1 pound	1 lb.	0.45 kilogram	0.45 kg		

Temperature Conversions

Boiling point of water: 212°F = 100°C

To convert Fahrenheit to Celsius, subtract 32 from F temperature, then multiply by 5/9.

To convert Celsius to Fahrenheit, multiply C temperature by 9/5, then add 32.

K20 Child Care Food Program

The Child Care Food Program sponsored by the U.S. Department of Agriculture is designed to provide funding and assistance in planning and implementing both meals and nutrition education programs for young children. There are income eligibility guidelines for families to determine whether or not they are entitled to these services. Write to the U.S. Department of Agriculture, CCFP, for this information [Section K22].

NET (Nutrition Education Training) courses are also sponsored by the U.S. Department of Agriculture. These courses are often available in local areas at school or colleges for training personnel involved in food services.

K21 Pilfering and Waste

No one likes to bring up the subject of pilfering and waste. Yet these are common complaints by many persons in the field of child care, especially by those who are new to the business of serving food. Aside from the very careful consideration given to the selection of people you hire, it is wise to outline a plan that may include some of the following points:

- One of the best methods of preventing pilfering is to speak of the possibility openly, letting your staff know about the importance of trust, honesty, and nonwasteful habits.
- Make it clear, upon hiring an employee, that pilfering will result in immediate dismissal.
- Establish a method of inventory control, checking foods that are purchased against foods that are used. Such a control system is valid only if kept up daily.
- Determine in advance what will happen to leftover foods. They certainly should not be wasted by being discarded.
- Small amounts of leftover foods should be kept separated from other foods and made accessible to the staff.
- Frequently discuss principles of economy with the cook. Post equivalency charts. Keep records of how much food is generally used for a particular item on the menu. Make comparisons when that item is served again.

K22

References

To assist you in keeping your food management program up-to-date, helpful pamphlets and information are available from the following institutions:

Department of Health and
Human Services
200 Independence Avenue NW
Washington, DC 20201
(202) 619-0257
1-877-696-6775 (toll free)
www.dhhs.gov

Food and Drug Administration (FDA)
HFI-40
Rockville, MD 20857
1-888-INFO-FDA
www.fda.gov

National Center for Nutrition and
Dietetics
American Dietetics Association
216 West Jackson Boulevard,
Suite 800
Chicago, IL 60606-6995
(312) 899-0040 ext. 4750
1-800-877-1600 ext. 4821
www.eatright.org/ncnd.html

National Dairy Council
Nutrition Education Division
10255 W. Higgins Road, Suite 900
Rosemont Road, IL 60018-5616
(847) 803-2000
www.nationaldairycouncil.org

National Food Service
Management Institute
University of Mississippi
Post Office Drawer 188
University, MS 38677-0188
(601) 232-7658
1-800-321-3054
www.olemiss.edu/depts/nfsmi

U.S. Department of Agriculture
Food and Nutrition Service
14th Street & Independence
Avenue SW
Washington, DC 20250
(202) 720-2791
www.fns.usda.gov/fns

U.S. Office of Education
400 Maryland Avenue SW
Washington, DC 20202
1-800-USA-LEARN
www.ed.gov

Write frequently for new pamphlets and updates. Revisions in nutritional patterns and foods for children are written frequently to reflect changes. Keep in touch with your County Agriculture Extension Service for current publications and information.

Index

INDEX

INDEX